A NATION OF CITIES

THE URBAN LIFE IN AMERICA SERIES

RICHARD C. WADE, GENERAL EDITOR

A
NATION
OF
CITIES
The Federal Government and Urban America, 1933-1965

MARK I. GELFAND

New York
OXFORD UNIVERSITY PRESS
1975

To My Mother and Father

Foreword

The central facts about twentieth-century America can easily be stated. In 1920 the Federal census demonstrated that over half of the people lived in cities; by 1970 that figure had reached three-quarters. This development was the culmination of forces that had gathered strength throughout the nineteenth century and reached their climax in the modern era. In one of the most rapid demographic alterations in history, the United States moved from a rural society to an urban one. Yet the magnitude of this change was only slowly appreciated and even less understood. Municipal authorities first felt the consequences and each municipality grappled with its problems alone. Only later was it clear that urbanization was a national as well as a local phenomenon. The Federal Government, however, had no experience in the field; indeed, the word "city" does not appear anywhere in the Constitution. Yet Washington was nonetheless caught in the urban undertow, and falteringly and hesitatingly began to enter city affairs.

This volume traces the discovery of the "urban crisis" by the Federal Government and the gradual institutionalization of its concern, beginning with the calculated neglect of the nineteenth and the early twentieth century to the deepening involvement that originated in the Depression. The relationship is seen from both sides; if the Federal Government felt no obligation to cities, municipal leaders asked for none. Indeed the argument for "Home Rule" applied equally to state and federal interference. The gradual drift to a new alignment stemmed from the crisis in the cities, not as the consequence of an imperial bureaucracy in Washington seeking greater power.

The shift began with the financial crisis of municipalities after the collapse of 1929. Faced with mounting want and distress and witnessing the contraction of their tax base, the cities looked to Washington for help. A reluctant New Deal and a rural-oriented President hesitated. It was not until bankruptcy threatened to engulf the nation's largest metropolises that the Federal Government moved. Mr. Gelfand is especially skillful in describing both the magnitude of the problem and the confusion and disarray in the nation's capital. Washington finally acted in a piecemeal fashion, public works here, relief there, hoping always that economic recovery would arrive and restore viability to local authorities. Though many of the lasting New Deal reforms ultimately shored up urban economies and provided some security for city dwellers, the Roosevelt administration never developed a coherent policy, or even strategy, toward metropolitan America.

Worse still, the Eisenhower administration even recoiled at the uncertain arrangements it inherited from the Democrats, feeling that public authority was already too centralized in Washington. A temporary recovery of fiscal soundness and a new generation of activist mayors concealed the attrition of the cities. And the consequences of the massive flight to the suburbs and the large influx of blacks were apparent to only a few. The author points out clearly the costs of the years of "marking time."

Yet one of the more significant contributions of this volume is its attention to the intellectual preparation for a more coherent national policy. The author finds the sources in the three decades leading up to 1960. It began in the academy with scholars who described and analyzed the rise of the modern city and the social dislocations that this process occasioned. Another group of reformers active in city affairs, both in elective and appointive offices, began to see that neither "Home Rule" nor more sympathetic state governments would provide the resources needed to meet the impending crisis. Rather they began to develop a rationale for federal intervention and assistance. The author handles compellingly the slow accumulation of urban data and the growing consensus among "experts" on appropriate public policies. In the process the cities discovered the possibilities in Washington; and the Federal Government began to understand the dimensions of the problem. By the 1960's the scene was set both for trouble and for a new relationship between city halls and Capitol Hill.

Two areas were central in this new relationship: housing and cabinet status for the cities. The two were ultimately joined with the creation of the Department of Housing and Urban Development. Federal intervention in housing began on a large scale in the thirties. Public housing was devised for low income city dwellers, and Federal Housing Administration mortgages for those buying homes. Presumably one would serve the center city and the other the urban periphery and suburbs. Mr. Gelfand details the failures of both. The dual policy ultimately segregated the metropolis by both class and race, aggravating the very problems that other programs tried vainly to solve.

But cabinet status held out the promise of more coordination in the future. Before its establishment, urban affairs were scattered throughout several departments and agencies, many of them in the hands of rural or suburban interests. To be sure, H.U.D. lacked adequate jurisdiction and was badly underfinanced, but its appearance signalled the recognition of an historic change. The nation was permanently urban, and the voice of the majority could be expressed in the highest circles. The country is still seeking a coherent policy that takes into account its inevitable metropolitan future. But at least the administrative agency is available when some broader consensus develops.

One of the most striking features of this volume is the way in which Mr. Gelfand places administrative history in its political and intellectual context. This is no dry narrative of the accumulation of agencies, programs, and widening jurisdictions. It is a full account of the way a country discovered its cities, analyzed their problems, and groped for a way to handle them. The author, even while explaining Washington's growing involvement in municipal affairs, never underestimates the power of private economic forces and the tenacity of local authorities. Moreover, he gauges the varying impact of election returns, both national and local, on the intensity of official urban concerns.

Equally impressive is the range of the author's sources. The literature before the Depression is, of course, modest and not difficult to handle. But with the crisis of the thirties, the sheer bulk becomes staggering. Every level of government studied and restudied the urban malaise; universities created institutes; and journalists, the natural historians of cities, probed the human consequences of the "urban explosion." The author picks his way through this endless thicket with great skill and judgment. And he does so without losing his central themes or letting the narrative lag.

A Nation of Cities will be of special interest, of course, to historians who have long felt the need for a study of this topic but hesitated to take it on. But its audience will be much larger. Other academics interested in cities, infelicitously described as "urbanologists," will find it more than a "background study." And it ought to be a manual for municipal policy makers of all levels where information is essential for effective action. In this sense, it has an even greater immediacy than other volumes in the *Urban Life in America* series, which attempts to illuminate persistent contemporary problems by placing them in historical perspective.

Richard C. Wade
GENERAL EDITOR
URBAN LIFE IN AMERICA SERIES

New York
June 1975

Preface

On the evening of August 11, 1965, a California highway patrolman stopped a Negro youth for a speeding violation. This everyday occurrence set into motion a chain of events that would lead to large-scale rioting in the Watts district of Los Angeles; similar law enforcement efforts would spark civil disorders in scores of cities over the next three years. The United States had entered into the ordeal of the long, hot summers, and during both cold and warm months Americans were continually bombarded with descriptions of and warnings about the nation's urban crisis. Newspapers and magazines ran feature articles on the subject, network television specials were produced, mayors appeared before congressional committees to appeal for billions in federal aid, and the President set up expert commissions to study urban problems. Both major party platforms in 1968 contained planks on urban matters, and the successful Presidential candidate, as one of the initial acts of his new administration, appointed an urban affairs adviser. Clearly, cities had become an important political issue.

Yet if the term "urban crisis" did not become part of the popular vocabulary until the late 1960s, the rise of federal involvement in urban affairs can be traced back to an earlier decade. Indeed, on the very afternoon of the August day that violence rocked Watts, the

Senate completed its consideration of a measure, already passed in slightly different form by the House, that had been in the congressional bill hopper since the mid-1950s. When signed by the President this act would establish a cabinet Department of Housing and Urban Development. The first real piece of federal urban legislation had been enacted in 1949, but the seeds of what Congress did in 1965 and what the American people expected the Federal Government to do after 1965 were actually planted in 1933. The Great Society consummated the federal-city partnership that the New Deal inaugurated in 1933.

In 1920, when the Bureau of the Census reported that for the first time in the American experience more people resided in urban communities than in rural areas, not a single dollar of federal expenditures was budgeted for the operation of municipal administration, nor did federal aid programs have any special urban characteristics. Neither was there a concerted demand from urban areas for federal assistance. Congress, if it thought of urban problems at all, thought in terms of how population concentrations affected Volstead Act enforcement and immigration patterns.

By 1965 hundreds of millions of dollars of federal monies were being funneled directly to city governments and many hundreds of millions more were getting there by way of the states. In addition, powerful—although often divided—lobbies had lined up to urge even greater aid to urban centers. National debate regarding the squalid central cities had passed beyond the subjects of temperance and ethnic purity to include the new concerns of housing, urban renewal, transportation, pollution control, and all the other social problems peculiar to urban society. This study seeks to examine how these great changes came to pass.

Although this book discusses the significant social and economic trends in big cities it should not be read as a history of urban America from 1933 to 1965. It is an inquiry into how urban affairs came to be established on the agenda of liberal reform in this period, not how the city was transformed over these years. Essentially, this work asks and tries to answer the question: What happened between the 1920s and 1965 to bring about a federal commitment to the American city?

The focus of this study is not the urban America as defined by the Bureau of the Census (any community over 2500 people), but metropolitan America, especially its large central cities (population of 250,000 and over). Up until the 1960s, the links between federal and municipal governments were of prime importance mainly to the big cities, and it was the leaders and residents of these big cities who worked hardest to expand these ties. There was a widening of vision in the 1960s at both the local and national levels; the metropolitan region, not just the central city, it was realized, should be the area of federal interest. But as will be shown, the big cities remained the chief source of support for the federal-urban alliance.

In the pages to follow there may seem to be more discussion of speeches, conferences, and reports than of actions. But in this period words *were* more prevalent than deeds. Talk often serves as no more than a substitute for performance, but in the area of urban-federal affairs this extended discourse proved to have been a necessary prelude. The cities were a new field for federal activity and before problems could be solved there had to be intelligibility in the posing of questions and in the consideration of prospective solutions. If there are some who will say that we are today still finding more new questions than answers and producing more promises than results let me be included among them. Americans have not yet decided what kind of urban society they want and what role they wish the Federal Government to play in creating it. But without the development of an urban-federal interaction what is now long overdue would have been impossible.

Mark I. Gelfand

Chestnut Hill, Massachusetts
May 1975

Acknowledgments

Many people contributed in a variety of ways to the making of this study. I am indebted to the numerous librarians and archivists who made my examination of their collections such a pleasant experience. Special thanks are due to a group which more commonly comes in for criticism: federal bureaucrats; in this instance, the conscientious civil servants who staff the National Archives and the Presidential Libraries. Their keen knowledge of the available records and their eagerness to be of assistance restored the human scale to these often forbidding national monuments. A further personal element was provided by several participants in the developments described herein who gave generously of time and thought by sharing their recollections with me. I hope they will recognize themselves in the pages that follow. At Oxford University Press, Ann Lindsay, Sheldon Meyer, and Susan Rabiner saw the manuscript through to publication. They have my sincere appreciation (and apologies) for their fierce struggle with my prose.

Two long-time friends, Bruce Lindner and Martin Rosenfeld, helped remind me that there was a world outside the library, especially that unique urban space called Central Park. The project might have been completed sooner if it had not been for those softball games in the middle of Manhattan. Lawrence Bruser,

Richard Calhoun, and Bonnie Fox Schwartz, fellow graduate students at Columbia, were a constant source of encouragement and sound advice. Steven Lawson, who preceded me down Amsterdam Avenue from St. Nicholas Terrace to Morningside Heights, was an excellent companion on research trips, a good friend in need and an indispensable morale booster. At extended lunch hours dominated by discussions on the third-base problems of the Mets, we shared our encounters with the recent American past and sharpened our perspectives.

Professor Stuart Bruchey helped me through some of the procedural obstacles of my graduate career with unfailing kindness and wise counsel. I benefited greatly from Professor Kenneth T. Jackson's encyclopedic knowledge of urban history and from his astute criticism of early drafts.

His students and colleagues have virtually exhausted the supply of superlatives in describing the contributions of William E. Leuchtenburg. I feel somewhat sheepish in adding my own poor voice to that distinguished chorus of praise, but only those who have experienced the sensation of getting back a chapter with Professor Leuchtenburg's comments on it can truly appreciate his selflessness and devotion to the historical craft. As a teacher he opened up broad new vistas; as a person he set an example I would hope to follow.

Although raised and educated in the nation's greatest metropolis, I have been reared in an extended family environment more usually associated with simpler societies and simpler times. Most things in my life have truly been collaborative efforts and this excursion into history has been no different. Brothers, sisters-in-law, nephew and niece, aunts, uncles, and cousins have all taken part; with their company it has been an enjoyable voyage. They cannot, of course, be held responsible for the trip's inadequacies.

Inadequate is my command of the English language to express my gratitude to my parents. They created an atmosphere of love and devotion around their four sons and encouraged us to develop as individuals. Yet they are always there when we need them.

Contents

A NATION OF CITIES

1

Cities in the
Federal System Before 1933

The true view of cities is to regard them as places where the activities of the whole nation come to a head. . . . There is no way to separate the cities from the nation. Upon the cities are concentrated the extreme consequences, the concrete results, of that revolution in the manners of men's life which modern science is working.

Walter Lippmann (1931)

On the whole, the American environment has proved friendly to the development of cities. All three factors credited by sociologists with promoting urban growth have been present to a high degree in this country. An abundance of natural resources plus excellent geographical locations furnished the foundations upon which cities could be built. The invention and rapid application of advanced technology enabled cities to expand. Last, but not least, the absence of rigid class structures and commitment to the work ethic created a climate conducive to commerce and industry. Associating social advancement and material wealth with the myriad opportunities available in cities, millions of Americans, native-born as well as those of foreign parentage, migrated to urban centers. Hence, despite some philosophical misgivings about urban life,[1] the United States, in 1930, ranked as one of the great urbanized nations of the world.

I

American city-building is to a large extent the story of "privatism," [2] but government has played a role too. From the start, the concepts of individual gain and commonweal were intertwined. Although British colonization of North America was financed almost entirely out of private funds, the Crown attempted to shape the form of settlement. The imperial rulers placed a premium on the organization of towns as a means of facilitating their control of colonial economic life. By drawing tradesmen into a limited number of locations, and by fostering the farmers' dependence upon towns, the English authorities hoped to make regulation of the overseas plantations more complete. Thus, while many of the colonists had come independently to the conclusion that cities were culturally and economically essential to the success of their ventures, the government in London, through its instructions to royal officials on this side of the Atlantic, reinforced the trend toward urbanization.

Urban dissatisfaction with tightening imperial administration helped precipitate the Revolution and led to a new legal relationship between municipalities and the other levels of government. City merchants and politicians supplied much of the leadership for the Patriot cause, and it was the British effort to chastise Boston with the Coercive Acts of 1774 that set the stage for the resort to arms. Significantly, the final product of the Revolutionary period—the Constitution—failed to mention cities at all. During colonial times the ultimate power to incorporate towns resided with the officials in England; cities, then, were creatures of the central body.[3] But in the general reaction against concentrated authority, this arrangement was not retained in the Federal Constitution. Except for the provision for federal jurisdiction over the national capital, the Constitution said nothing about local government. Under the concept of retained powers, the Constitution's silence on this matter left to the states full responsibility over municipalities. "From a constitutional point of view cities do not exist." [4]

The Revolution also brought important changes in the cities' legal position vis-à-vis the former colonies. Before 1776, cities were incorporated under royal charters, which were regarded as contracts between the executive part of colonial government and the community. Viewed as contracts, these charters were not believed to be capable of unilateral amendment. Furthermore, since municipal incorporation was held to be an executive prerogative, cities enjoyed almost complete freedom from legislative interference. Ironically, national independence led to a decline in municipal autonomy. As part of the widespread revulsion against a too-powerful executive, all of the new state constitutions, implicitly or explicitly, vested the incorporating authority with the legislature, transforming the character of the municipal charter. Gone was the notion of the charter as a contract; instead the charter became just another ordinary act of legislation, which, like all statutes, could be amended by the action of the legislature.

Although the plenary power of the state legislatures over city government was unmistakably established in the Revolutionary era, it was not until nearly a century later that the principle of absolute state supremacy was expressed with any vigor. In 1868, an Iowa judge, John F. Dillon, handed down an opinion that became the famous Dillon Rule:[5]

Municipal corporations owe their origin to, and derive their powers and rights wholly from, the [state] legislature. It breathes into them the breath of life, and without which they cannot exist. As it creates, so it may destroy. . . . [Municipal corporations] are the mere tenants at the will of the legislature.

Forty years later, in *Hunter v. Pittsburgh*, the Supreme Court adopted the Dillon Rule as its own:[6]

The number, nature and duration of the powers conferred upon these corporations and the territory over which they shall be exercised rests in the absolute discretion of the States. . . . The State, therefore, at its pleasure, may modify or withdraw all such powers . . . expand or contract the territorial area, unite the whole or a part with another municipality, repeal the charter and destroy the corporation. All this may be done . . . with or without the consent of the citizens, or even against their protest.

The Court, in a case decided in 1923, also held that municipalities were not entitled to the protection of the Constitution granted other corporations. State sovereignty over cities was final.[7]

This authority had been exercised with a very light hand in the seventy-five years following independence. Custom and circumstances help explain the states' failure to use this power. The tradition of local self-government, a strong political force since the earliest colonial days, gained added potency from the movement toward greater popular democracy after 1800. Most Americans agreed with the observations of the French traveler, Alexis de Tocqueville: "Municipal institutions constitute the strength of free nations. . . . A nation may establish a free government, but without municipal institutions it cannot have the spirit of liberty." Nor was there much impetus for the states to break with the pre-Revolutionary practice of non-interference in the internal concerns of municipal corporations. Legislators found little of interest in the "petty housekeeping of a few small communities which in the aggregate composed but an insignificant part of the entire population." [8] New York City, for example, which in 1810 contained 100,000 people, expended only $100,000. There were but thirteen towns in the United States with populations over 8,000 in 1820, and their combined population was less than 5 per cent of the national total. In only one area of municipal concern—the granting of charters— did the states act with any decisiveness: in the span 1779–1800, fifty charters were issued. Only one new effective incorporation had been granted by the royal officials during the three decades preceding the Revolution.[9]

State supremacy became a fact of urban life in the mid-nineteenth century. The mushrooming urban populations and the development of political parties created the excuse and the incentive for state control of municipal affairs. Urban populations grew three times faster than that of the nation as a whole between 1810 and 1860; in

1820, only twelve cities had 10,000 people or more; by 1860, the number was 101. Both Eastern and Midwestern cities experienced tremendous population expansion in the fifty years before the Civil War: New York's population went from slightly under 100,000 in 1810 to slightly over 800,000 in 1860; Chicago, which did not even get its charter until 1833, had more than 110,000 people in 1860. With this population explosion came a greatly increased demand for municipal services: police and fire protection, water supply, public health, and others. Since municipal governments, in almost every instance, operated under charters conveying only very specific and restricted powers, localities found it necessary to petition state legislatures for amendments expanding their authority. The legislatures usually acceded to these requests but after a while assumed the role of initiator as well, introducing and enacting special legislation not asked for and sometimes strongly opposed by the municipality. Inefficiency and dishonesty in municipal government were often cited as the reasons for these restrictions on local autonomy, but partisan advantage commonly lay at the root of the legislatures' new interest in the cities. As the scope of municipal activities widened, so too did the opportunities for political patronage and spoils. The proliferation of city jobs and contracts presented politicians with an opportunity to use the municipal budget to strengthen their own power bases in the struggle for domination of the national government. State rule was substituted for local determination in the cause of party gain.

In many states the legislatures all but took the place of municipal government in the decades after 1850. New York, Maryland, Illinois, Michigan, and Missouri abolished the local police departments of their largest cities and established state boards in their stead. The tenure of the members of the state board of police for Chicago was changed three times between 1861 and 1865 as Republicans and Democrats alternated in control of the Illinois legislature in Springfield. Other city agencies were also brought under state supervision. Legislatures created new city positions, ordered salary raises, and mandated pension hikes; they passed bills relating to the smallest

minutiae of city life, such as naming streets and closing alleys.
Massachusetts enacted 400 special laws dealing solely with the city
of Boston from 1885 to 1908. It took the New York legislature only
ten years—1880 to 1889—to pass 390 acts for New York City. The
laws concerning local government passed by the Illinois legislature
in 1869 filled 1,850 pages; the general statutes enacted that same
year occupied but 290 pages.[10] A classic case of state meddling in
city affairs was the Pennsylvania legislature's decision in 1870 to
erect a new civic center in Philadelphia. The legislature set up a
commission with tax-levying powers to build the complex, named
the body's members, and allowed them to choose their successors.
"The public buildings at Broad and Market Streets" were, a judge
later commented, "projected upon a scale of magnificence better
suited for the capital of an empire than the municipal buildings of a
debt-burdened city." [11] A political scientist at the beginning of the
twentieth century bemoaned that state legislatures had turned municipalities into "the playthings of state and national party politics."[12]

States assumed greater control of the internal business of municipalities at about the time that cities found themselves less able to
influence those very state policies that so affected them. Few states
had ever subscribed fully to the representation theory of "one man,
one vote." Allotment schemes that favored some sections over others
had been endemic in the colonial legislatures, and while there was a
trend toward more equitable apportionment in the post-Revolution-
ary era various forms of discrimination still existed at the advent of
Jacksonian Democracy. At first, the more established cities and
towns benefited from these disparities since in many states the longer
settled areas held power at the expense of frontier regions. The wave
of constitution redrafting spurred by the Transportation Revolution
afforded these burgeoning fringe territories an opportunity to redress
the balance. Delegates to Maine's 1819 Constitutional Convention,
for example, remembering the hardships caused wilderness areas by
Boston's preponderant influence in Massachusetts politics, slapped a
limit on the number of representatives any one town could have in
the state legislature. New Orleans was stripped of its paramount role

in the operation of the Louisiana legislature by a provision of the 1845 Constitution that restricted the city, which contained 20 per cent of the state's population, to 12.5 per cent of the state senators and 10 per cent of the state assemblymen.[13]

State action to curtail the political power of urban centers became even more prevalent in the decades following 1890. The emergence of giant urban agglomerations after the Civil War threatened to upset the delicate equilibrium between political parties and to put rural dwellers at the mercy of city voters. Unless something was done to curb the numerical supremacy of cities, the careers of politicians and the survival of those parties whose main appeal lay in country districts would be seriously endangered. The motives of frightened political leaders were usually skillfully hidden by appeals to the traditional American mistrust of cities. It had been the agrarian democrat Thomas Jefferson who wrote in his *Notes on the State of Virginia*, "The mobs of great cities add just so much to the support of pure government as sores do to the strength of the human body," but it was conservatives—both rural and urban—who used his arguments to thwart the will of the majority.

New York's decision in 1894 to deny its premier city representation in proportion to its population was the product of this marriage of partisan interests and anti-urban sentiment. The question of New York City's role in state politics had arisen at least as early as 1820 during the Constitutional Convention's debates on universal suffrage. Spearheading the drive against the extension of the franchise was the state's distinguished chancellor, James Kent. Like so many others, Kent had been drawn to the great port city to make his fortune, but this Federalist jurist had his misgivings about the consequences of the trend toward urban concentration:

The growth of the city of New York [he declared] is enough to startle and awaken those who are pursuing the *ignis fatuus* of universal suffrage.

In 1773 it had 21,000 souls.

    1801 " "   60,000 do.

    1806 " "   76,000 do.

    1820 " " 123,000 do.

It is rapidly swelling into the unwieldy population, and with the burdensome
pauperism, of an European metropolis. New York is destined to become the
future London of America; and in less than a century, that city, with the
operation of universal suffrage, will govern the state.

Agriculture, Kent proclaimed, "is the great leading and governing
interest of the state; and what madness would it be to commit that
interest to the winds." As long as the electorate was confined to "the
owners and actual cultivators of the soil," he explained, the state was
assured of a government of "moderation, frugality, order, honesty,
and a due sense of independence, liberty, and justice." There would
be no security against "fraud and violence," Kent warned, if the vote
was given to "men of no property, together with crowds of
dependents connected with great manufacturing and commercial
establishments, and the motley and undefinable population of
crowded ports." [14]

Kent's impassioned pleas were no match for the rising tide of
egalitarianism, but seventy-five years later—with many of Kent's
prophecies apparently having proved true—the chancellor's political
descendants met with greater success. New York City and its
environs had a population (1890) of 2.5 million, about 45 per cent of
the state's population. Many of these people were desperately poor
and voted for the entrenched Democratic machine. Corruption was
rampant; all city offices were available for a price. The growing
strength of the Democratic party greatly disturbed Republican
chieftains; the G.O.P.'s strongholds in rural upstate areas were in
peril of being overwhelmed by the multitude of voters in Gotham. "I
cannot look with complacency upon the fact that a little territory in
the southern part of the state is likely to have in the near future a
preponderance in the legislature of the state," a Republican delegate
from Franklin County in the Adirondack region told the 1894
Constitutional Convention.[15] The G.O.P. response to this threat was
a complex mathematical formula giving rural areas perpetual control
of both houses of the legislature. Defending the Republican plan

against charges that it would have the effect of disfranchising urban residents, a delegate from agricultural Oneida County claimed: "The average citizen in the rural district is superior in intelligence, superior in morality, superior in self-government, to the average citizen of the great cities . . . and your government will be safer in his hands than the hands of the average citizen of the great cities." [16] Elihu Root, the top Republican strategist at the convention, who, like Kent, had achieved a legal eminence in his adopted city of New York, urged his colleagues to accept the following principle governing relations between large urban centers and the rest of the state:

The small and widely-scattered agricultural communities, with their feeble power comparatively, because of their divisions, shall, by the distribution of representation, be put upon an even footing, so far as may be, with the concentrated power of the great cities.

Otherwise, Root contended, "we never can have a truly representative and truly republican government." [17] The Republican-controlled convention ratified the Root prescription, thus making the state legislature, in the words of Alfred E. Smith, "constitutionally Republican." [18] During the next seven decades, Democrats gained majorities in Albany for just six years; for the rest of the time, the affairs of the nation's largest city lay under the reins of rural legislators generally unsympathetic to the municipality's problems.

By 1920, when the census reported that for the first time more Americans lived in urban than in rural areas, practically every big city was being shortchanged on representation. Various methods were used to deprive municipalities of an equitable voice in the legislature. Some states, such as New York, applied different population ratios to urban and rural counties in determining representation. Others, such as Ohio, favored the agricultural districts by guaranteeing a seat to every county no matter how small. Still others imposed arbitrary limits on how many representatives any single city or county could have; Pennsylvania, for example, restricted Philadelphia to one-sixth of the state's senators at a time when it held one-fifth of the state's population and was destined to hold still more. Another frequently utilized technique was to stop reapportioning. Many state constitutions called for a reallocation of seats every decade to reflect population changes; rather than give cities their due, a number of states simply ignored these provisions. But whatever the system followed, the results were uniformly the same: America's cities were mistreated by their states.

II

The cities' growing subservience to the states during the last half of the nineteenth century was accompanied by a change in the cities' relations to the national government. Despite the Federal Constitution's silence on the subject of local government, cities in the young nation dared not forget that they operated within a federal system. Their municipal charters may have come from the states, but city dwellers in the hundred years following independence were aware that decisions made in Washington could be crucial to their prosperity or even survival. Without any goals and often unconscious of what it was doing, the national government nevertheless played an important role in shaping American urban development before the 1880s.

Federal politics influenced the patterns of urban settlement in a variety of ways. The matter of postal service, for example, bulked large in every new locality's hopes for the future. Extension of this federal activity was not universal. With it a community had a means of communication with the outside world that made commerce possible at a time when travel was difficult and expensive; without it a community remained isolated and often became a ghost town.[19] Similarly, many municipalities were dependent upon federal contributions to their economic base. The struggling town of Kansas City was kept alive in the 1850s by federal contracts and payrolls.[20] Foreign policy made by national officials also affected the way cities grew. Jefferson's imposition of the Embargo and the War of 1812 hurt commercially oriented cities like Boston and New York, and spurred the rise of factory towns at the falls of rivers. Some of the lesser seaports such as Newburyport in Massachusetts and New Haven never recovered their earlier affluence.[21] Federally prescribed tariff schedules were still another fact of urban life, helping some cities and hurting others. New York's merchants were so disturbed by the high Morrill Tariff of 1861 that some toyed with the idea of setting New York up as a Free City independent of all the states and released from any federal control of its commercial intercourse.

In no other field, perhaps, was federal action as significant as in that of internal improvements. During the early years of the republic, there was an urgent need for a network of transportation routes to bind the union tighter. Cities were particularly eager to see this construction undertaken since commerce was the source of most urban prosperity in ante-bellum America; access to the rich hinterland was necessary for a city's material advancement. Older cities like New York, Philadelphia, and Baltimore possessed sufficient internal resources to raise the funds for these transportation projects or were powerful enough to gain state assistance, but the growing number of communities along the Western frontier lacked assets. To expand and move ahead of their competitors, these towns required federal aid.

Constitutional arguments prevented the national government from responding to these requests for the first three decades, but in the 1820s strict interpretations loosened somewhat and Washington began entering into agreements with states and localities for internal improvements. Federal technicians from the Army Corps of Engineers were lent out to municipalities to make surveys of proposed port and canal construction projects. In 1826 Congress passed an Omnibus Rivers and Harbors Act making federal tax monies available for the enhancement of the country's waterways and this type of legislation soon became a regular component of Capitol Hill's output. By 1860 nearly $6 million had been appropriated for this program.[22] The Federal Government also subscribed funds to canal-building companies and gave gifts of land to states and towns to pay for local canal projects.

All these programs, however, were small compared with the huge federal investment in railroad construction. Between 1850 and 1871, more than 130 million acres of the public domain were donated to the states or directly to the railroad corporations.[23] Although municipalities were not a partner in this gigantic cooperative venture,[24] the endeavor provided great bonanzas for certain cities and helped mold the contours of urban settlement on the prairies and the plains.[25]

With such vast amounts of assistance accessible and so much at stake, communities did not hesitate to press Washington for local projects. The citizens of Milwaukee, for example, eleven years before the town received a charter from the territorial authorities, drafted a resolution at a public meeting in 1835 asking Congress for a grant of land to pay for the building of a canal to the interior. Congress agreed to their appeal in 1838, but by then the Milwaukeeans were already campaigning for appropriations for harbor improvements. Residents of Minneapolis were banging at the doors of Congress less than a year after that community was incorporated in 1867. They wanted federal aid to save the waterfalls that supplied the city's mills with power. Most of the time lobbying by localities was restricted to resolutions by city councils and chambers of commerce, but on occasion delegations would be dispatched to make the request in person. City congressmen could also be counted upon to watch out for their communities' interests in the nation's capital.[26]

Urban rivalries were rampant throughout most of the nineteenth century and the distribution of federal largesse sometimes figured in the outcome of these inter-city competitions. Federal bounties may have tipped the scales in the bitter struggle between St. Louis and Chicago for commercial hegemony in the Middle West. The city on the Mississippi had a headstart on its Great Lakes foe, but St. Louis's merchants proved to be complacent and timid. They neglected to push aggressively for federal programs to improve navigation on the Mississippi and failed to exert themselves in opposition to the bill authorizing federal land grants for a railroad from Chicago to the Gulf of Mexico. Other forms of national assistance—mail subsidies, federal installations—also flowed into Chicago at a faster rate, strengthening its economic foundations and making it more attractive to new business. At the outbreak of the Civil War, St. Louis still had more people than the Windy City, but primary control of the economy of the West was shifting toward Chicago.[27]

"Municipal mercantilism" [28] could also influence national politics and did so as far back as pre-Revolutionary days. Colonial Boston's inability to match the economic growth of Philadelphia and New York after 1740 helped make that city the center of independence activity. "Boston's primacy as the 'Cradle of Liberty,' " Arthur Schlesinger, Sr., has noted, "may well have sprung from her lagging progress in relation to other ports, inciting her at any cost to remove the obstacles that Parliament was thrusting in her way." Eighty years later, Chicago's determined drive to overtake St. Louis as the entrepôt of the Middle West contributed to the heightening of sectional animosities. Eager to establish Chicago as the eastern terminus of a federally sponsored transcontinental railroad, Senator Stephen A. Douglas of Illinois introduced a bill in 1853 providing for the organization of the Nebraska Territory.[29] By the time his measure was signed into law, it had disrupted the party system and intensified North-South distrust. With this bill the nation took its "greatest single step in its blind march toward the abyss of secession and civil war." [30]

The post-Civil War era witnessed a decline in the importance of federal action for cities. The national government, an active if not very visible participant in the town-building that was a feature of the ante-bellum period, stood passively on the sidelines as the modern metropolis began to emerge toward the end of the nineteenth century. Developments in Washington, the state capitals, and, most significantly, in the cities themselves, were responsible for this change.

Washington's diminished role in urban affairs reflected its smaller part in the economic life of the country. The "Era of National Subsidy," with its policy of liberal land grants, came to an end in

1871. Except for its tariff laws, the Federal Government adopted a hands-off attitude toward the economy. From Congress to the White House to the Supreme Court, national leaders before 1900 almost unanimously championed private decision-making free from governmental interference, be it financial aid or regulation. The Federal Government did re-enter the transportation field with the creation of the Interstate Commerce Commission (1887), but that agency's ability to influence trade patterns was extremely limited. Similarly, privately controlled telegraph and telephone facilities eclipsed the postal service as a quick means of communication. Nor did the bigger and more economically diversified urban centers in the East and Midwest continue to depend very heavily on federal contracts and installations. Only in Western areas, where the national government remained the greatest land owner, did cities have to keep a watchful eye on Washington. San Francisco, for example, waged a tough thirteen-year fight in the early 1900s to gain federal approval for a plan to use the Hetch Hetchy Valley in Yosemite National Park as a reservoir for the water-hungry city.

State assertiveness in exercising legal powers over cities during the second half of the nineteenth century also reduced federal-local contacts. Prior to 1850, with states maintaining a low profile in the internal affairs of municipalities, municipal petitions directly to the generous Federal Government for transportation aid were not considered extraordinary. But as the states moved in to take control of municipal administration, city leaders found it advisable to put aside their nascent ties to the far-away and now less openhanded national government and to concentrate their attention on events at the state capital. With legislatures able, by simple statutory act, to withdraw charters (the Tennessee legislature did so abolish the city of Memphis in 1879), to replace elected local officials with state appointees (the Pennsylvania legislature authorized the governor to do this in 1901), or to deny municipalities the right to operate public utilities (the New York legislature rejected New York City's request for permission to operate an electric generating plant), municipalities focused their political resources on the active defense and advance of city interests at the statehouse. Washington could be of no help in the municipalities' fight to preserve self-rule; court decisions left cities at the mercy of their states.

Most importantly, perhaps, changes taking place within the cities altered the urban attitude toward the national government. Urban population multiplied at a faster rate in the forty years before the Civil War than it did in the forty years following the war, but the later period saw a more profound transformation of city life. American urbanization before 1860 involved the founding of individual cities and their organization into an inter-urban network; post-war urbanization brought about dramatic alterations in the nature of the city itself.[31] "New York in 1850," Richard Wade has observed, "was more as it had been in 1800 than it would be in 1900." [32] Large-scale industrialization and innovations in mass transit led to cities of unprecedented dimensions. In 1840, only one city had as many as 250,000 people; by 1890 eleven did, and three of these were over the million mark. This immense concentration of humanity in urban centers revolutionized the daily life styles of cities and gave rise to a new set of problems. Having prospered and become big, cities now faced the task of making themselves fit places for so many to live. Packing such large numbers of people into relatively small areas placed severe strains on the municipalities' ability to supply essential needs: good water and sanitation, fire protection, efficient local transportation. But whereas few municipal leaders in the first half of the nineteenth century had hesitated in calling upon outside aid to help their cities through their developmental stage, urban politicians perceived no reason for requesting federal or state assistance in making the adjustment to maturity. Fat profits could be made from the provision of many municipal services; the opportunities for graft were endless. Bringing in the Federal Government would only mean a further division of the spoils. Aside from intervening to preserve law and order during labor strife in cities in 1877 and 1894, national authorities kept aloof from municipal affairs, with no protest from local leaders.

III

Although never mentioned in national political contests, urban problems were increasingly discussed as the twentieth century approached. The precarious balance of power existing between the two major parties made government officials wary of spelling out clear positions on socio-economic issues created by the new metropolitan environment, but non-partisan critics of the emerging industrial society were under no such restraint. The problems of urbanization were examined from two naturally antagonistic perspectives: that of the Jeffersonian agrarian and that of the businessman reformer. These conflicting vantage points combined to widen the political gulf separating the cities from their Federal Government.

Rural areas, with their long-standing and curious love-hate relationships with urban centers, believed that urban growth was at their expense. Agricultural income rose during the period 1870–90, but the farmers' share of national wealth dropped from 20.5 per cent to 16.7 per cent in the two decades, and profits earned from the land often went to city bankers to pay off loans. Besides being overwhelmed economically, rural districts saw their cultural values being eroded by the ever more dominant urban way of life. By the thousands, the sons and daughters of farmers left home to seek their fate under the bright lights of the cities. Disturbed by these developments, people in the countryside became convinced that the city represented "a serious menace to American civilization." In the best-selling book *Our Country: Its Possible Future and Its Present Crisis* (1885), by village-born Congregationalist minister Josiah Strong, every danger to American democracy—poverty and crime, socialism and corruption, immigration and Catholicism—was traced to the city. While generally proposing moralistic solutions to the "urban problem," the Strong critique and the many others like it lent encouragement to the use of a political device to curb the allegedly baneful effects of urbanization: depriving cities of equitable representation in state legislatures. The triumph of the hostile rural ethic would plague the cities in the decades to come.

Big-city businessmen were less interested in a code of values than in power, less concerned about safeguarding virtues than in making cities a good place to make money. To most municipal reformers at the turn of the century, the "urban problem" was essentially one of government and administration. Their enemy was the inefficient, incompetent, and scandal-ridden political machine. Rationalization and bureaucratization were bringing stability and profits to the business world, but this world could not be secure as long as municipal services remained uncertain and inadequate, and taxes were levied by politicians more directly tied to immigrant blocs than to those who paid the assessments. The reformers wanted municipal government to be run as just one more business, with control of funds remaining with those contributing most to its operation.

To administer a municipality as one would a business required that the city be released from the tutelage of the state government. Laissez-faire was the policy that worked best in the economic sphere; similarly, reformers argued, municipal corporations were entitled to complete freedom in the conduct of their affairs. "Home rule"—by which the city would be responsible to itself alone—became the rallying cry. Pressing hard under the banner of local self-determination, the St. Louis delegation to the 1875 Missouri Constitutional Convention succeeded in winning an amendment allowing the city to frame its own charter. California followed suit four years later with a constitutional provision allotting a wide area of exclusive authority to its cities. By 1925, fourteen states, including New York, Ohio, and Michigan, had enacted home rule plans. But while these measures released municipalities from the most virulent types of special state legislation, most states maintained administrative supervision over city functions and held tight reins over local taxing and borrowing powers. Cities were not yet masters of their own houses.

With the new powers they did have, municipal reformers strove to remove what they considered one of the basic causes of city misgovernment: the introduction of state and national politics into municipal affairs. Electoral contests for city offices were fought along national party lines; differences over the tariff and money questions often overshadowed local issues. Once elected, the reformers charged, these partisan leaders subordinated the interests of the city to those of their parties by filling government posts with spoilsmen and robbing the municipal treasury to fill the party coffers. American city government would remain "the worst in Christendom," the foes of the machine warned, until the national political parties were prevented from feasting upon the municipal exchequer.[33] Party divisions on the national and state levels were inevitable and proper, reformers argued, since general principles were involved, but no such issues were raised by the conduct of municipal affairs: "Good men," declared a New York State commission appointed in 1876 to devise a plan for the government of cities,

cannot and do not differ as to whether municipal debt ought to be restricted, extravagance checked, and municipal affairs lodged in the hands of competent and faithful officers. There is no more just reason why the control of the public works of a great city should be lodged in the hands of a democrat or a republican, than there is why an adherent of one or the other of the great parties should be made the superintendent of a business corporation.[34]

The goal was to secure the services of "the best men," and the only way this could be achieved was by taking partisanship out of municipal government. The reformers' favorite remedies were to conduct balloting for municipal positions at separate times from state and national contests, and to prohibit local candidates from identifying themselves with party labels. Some cities, although none of the really big ones, moved even closer to the business ideal by putting professional administrators—called city managers—in charge of municipal operations. While not altogether successful in cleaning up city government, the reform impulse of the late nineteenth and early twentieth century did materially redirect the consuming passions and effective action of municipal politicians and influential citizens away from Washington.

Not every element of the amorphous Progressive movement

accepted the "good government" contingent's description of the "urban problem." Those concerned more about the welfare of city residents than about the cost-conscious efficiency of city administration rejected the idea of cutting the municipalities' ties to other strata of government. Settlement house workers, consumer advocates, and others who labored strenuously to increase city services to the poor were not prepared to rule out the possibility of federal assistance. Just what Washington might do to help had not yet been defined, but they wanted to keep this option open. Charles Beard spoke for this brand of municipal reform in 1917 when he observed:[35]

It is true that there seems to be no connection between ship subsidies, tariffs, labor legislation, farm loans, and kindred matters and the problems that arise in our great urban centers. Superficially, there is none. But I cannot be too emphatic when I say that not a single one of our really serious municipal questions—poverty, high cost of living, overcrowding, unemployment, low standards of life, physical degeneracy—can be solved, can be even approached by municipalities without the cooperation of the state and national government, and the solution of these problems calls for state and national parties.

But the Beard position was a minority one. A 1904 textbook on municipal government had declared that "the city has no relations with the national government." [36] In 1920, after nearly two decades of Progressive administration of the national government and more than a generation of municipal ferment, that statement still accurately described the state of federal-municipal kinship.[37]

Nothing happened in the 1920s to alter that relationship. Although more Americans now lived in urban than in rural areas, neither the cities nor the Federal Government saw any reason to drop their half-century-old attitude of mutual indifference. The tide of municipal reform slackened and the stories of government corruption were gone from the pages of the nation's magazines. The problems Beard had written about were still there, but they were easily overlooked in an era of metropolitan expansion (the proportion of Americans residing in big urban centers approached one-

third) and prosperity. Cities had few financial worries: private
construction was booming and the market for municipal bonds to
pay for large public works projects was excellent. Who cared about
the millions of city dwellers earning low wages and occupying
squalid tenements? Surely not the rural-dominated state legislatures.
Urban-rural antagonisms were at a fever pitch for most of the
decade as country districts fought a rearguard action against
metropolitan cultural and economic domination. Nor was there
anyone in power in Washington seriously interested—beyond ban-
ning liquor and keeping foreigners out—about the condition of life
within cities. President Coolidge's December 1925 State of the
Union Message, in which he declared that "the greatest solicitude
should be exercised to prevent any encroachment upon the states or
their various political subdivisions," reflected popular contemporary
thinking about the federal system:

Local self-government is one of our most precious possessions. It is the
greatest contributing factor to the stability, strength, liberty, and progress of
the nation. It ought not to be infringed by assault or undermined by
purchase. It ought not to abdicate its power through weakness or resign its
authority through favor. It does not at all follow that because abuses exist it
is the concern of the Federal Government to attempt their reform.

In effect, Coolidge claimed, "society is in much more danger from
encumbering the National Government beyond its wisdom to
comprehend, or its ability to administer, than from leaving the local
communities to bear their own burdens and remedy their own
evils." [38]
     The American approach to the management of urban areas was
unique. At the International Congress of Cities in 1932, the United
States delegation was the only one to report that no direct central
government–local ties existed.[39] The great economic cataclysm then
engulfing the world would soon end that distinction.

2

A New Deal
for the Cities: 1933–39

Whether we like it or not, the national economy of the future will be controlled from urban centers and by urban conditions. Urbanism will dominate the future. Since we cannot recapture the pre-machine age, our obligation is to make the machine age safe for the future city.

C. A. Dykstra (1934)

The strong tremors set off by the Great Depression left few American institutions safe from challenge. Badly shaken by the collapse of so much in which it had placed its faith, the nation engaged in a sweeping self-examination. The city, both as one of the most conspicuous symbols of the now discredited 1920s and as the object of great suspicion since the early days of the republic, came under particularly rigorous scrutiny. "At this moment," declared one student of urbanism in 1934,

the city trembles in the balance. Its citizens are in large numbers unemployed, its finances are in chaos, its services and its structures deteriorating, and both public and private hopes are sagging. We begin to realize that somewhere we missed the mark or took the wrong turn. . . . The industrial city to date has not proved its place in the sun.[1]

Much popular thinking and some political discussion on the cities'
plight focused on the advantages of breaking up the large urban
centers. But in the end, the Depression decade was to witness not the
demise of big cities, but the beginning of a new federal-city
relationship.

I

The man who assumed the burdens of the Presidency as the
economic crash reached its nadir shared with the nation its
traditional distrust of large cities. Franklin D. Roosevelt, whom
Rexford G. Tugwell has characterized as "a child of the country,"
profoundly believed that rural life bred better qualities in a man;
thus, he never viewed the cities as "other than a perhaps necessary
nuisance." Completely at home in open countryside, Roosevelt
considered himself in alien territory walking the narrow streets of
congested cities. His term as governor of New York reflected this
bias: aside from his efforts to deal with the Depression, Roosevelt
devoted his energies to assisting the state's country districts.[2] In
addition, his own inescapable embroilment in the sordid affairs of
the state's great metropolis did little to mitigate this prejudice. The
Jimmy Walker episode severely tarnished his reform image. Conveniently, Roosevelt's disposition to look to the countryside for suste-
nance coincided with the political direction in which he would have
to move in the 1932 Presidential contest. Agriculture held the key to
his nomination and election, and campaign strategy dictated that he
sow his political seeds among his philosophical kinfolk.[3] Although
President Hoover's failure to halt the nation's economic decline
assured Roosevelt a receptive audience in the big cities, Roosevelt
was, admittedly, not comfortable addressing this part of his constituency. "Al Smith knows these city people better," Roosevelt told
Raymond Moley. "He can move them. I can't." [4]

Roosevelt's rural bias colored his first months in the White House.
At his insistence, a $3.3 billion public works bill enacted in June
1933 allocated $25 million for a subsistence homesteads program to

finance the movement of city workers back to the land. The extent and effect of the depression-linked mass unemployment in the great industrial centers buttressed his anti-urban orientation.[5] Citing the hard times as proof that "our urban industrial economy is fraught with tremendous perils," Roosevelt argued that while farmers were experiencing dire distress the cities were the scenes of still greater suffering and posed a greater threat to orderly society. To avert this danger and to provide the people with some sense of security, a way had to be found to exchange "speculative living in the city for one of stabilized living in a real home in the country." Contending that technological advances now made it possible to enjoy all the attractions of urban life in a bucolic setting, Roosevelt suggested that the government foster the development of rural-industrial communities uniting subsistence farming with part-time factory employment.[6] He was advocating nothing less than an officially sponsored exodus from the cities.

"Balance," a repeating term in early New Deal philosophy, influenced much of Roosevelt's thinking on this subject. Convinced that "the pendulum has swung too far in the direction of the cities and that a readjustment must take place to restore the economic and sociological balance," he urged a national program of population redistribution to relieve "the overbalance of population in our industrial centers." Should the economy return to 1929 levels, he maintained, "there would still be a million people on relief in New York City." By reversing the flow of people to the cities, by draining off the urban centers' excess population, Roosevelt hoped to reduce the cost of relief, attack part of the unemployment problem, and redirect the development of American society.[7] It was an ambitious plan and one that quite clearly rejected an urban future.

Carried away by popular accounts of a sizable back-to-the-land movement, Roosevelt assumed he would have little difficulty finding people willing to seize the opportunity "to secure through the good earth the permanent jobs they have lost in the overcrowded, industrial cities and towns." But contrary to the imputed widespread dissatisfaction with urban life, the drift of population out of agricultural areas continued, except for one year, throughout the Depression decade. Despite its drawbacks, the city still remained a beacon of hope for a brighter tomorrow while, in contrast, the retreat to the land threatened, as critics of the homesteads idea pointed out, to create "a new American peasantry with a standard of living and an outlook for the future probably about equal to that obtainable in the Balkan regions." [8]

Further, the subsistence homesteads endeavor suffered from a basic misconception held by its sponsors. Advocates of rural settlements recognized that the movement's success depended upon the migration of industry to the new communities. They did not expect this to be much of a problem since most contemporary observers agreed that flight from the central cities by manufacturing concerns was a prominent feature of the 1920s. But what proponents of population redistribution had hopefully interpreted as dispersion over the length of the land was actually diffusion within the major industrial areas; reconcentration, rather than decentralization, more accurately described the new arrangement. This crucial misreading stripped the experiment of any firm economic base and practically guaranteed its failure.[9]

At any rate, the subsistence homesteads project failed to build the same popular support it had initially aroused in legislative circles and, stigmatized by mismanagement and bad publicity, did not receive even a fraction of the funds it required. The nation would accept a solution to the problems of the Depression only within an urban context. As one advocate of "the country as a way of life" admitted in 1934, "We cannot look to the disappearance of the city as a way of escape from city problems. Despite its discomforts and its few amenities, the city declines to be removed from the scene." [10]

However disappointed Roosevelt may have been, he could not afford to ignore the people's verdict. If the country were to come out of the Depression, it would have to provide relief for the cities as well as the farms. Alleviating immediate want would take precedence over instituting fundamental structural changes in American society. In the process, the nature of American federalism would be transformed.

II

Until the Depression struck, few urban political and civic leaders expressed dismay at the national government's lack of concern for the conditions of city life. Only the thin ranks of social workers and city planners had made any attempt even to articulate the problems of poverty, poor housing, and inadequate transportation. And not even all these reformers were prepared to see the federal authorities move into fields traditionally reserved for local action. Furthermore, as subordinates of the states, city corporations had long felt the sting of state control. The wisdom of inviting another master into one's house appeared suspect.

But the crisis of the early 1930s forced those concerned with the problems of the cities to re-examine and reweigh the disadvantages of federal entry into municipal affairs. Harassed by the twin problems of rising relief expenditures and growing tax delinquencies, urban leaders were exposed earlier than the nation's governors to the need for massive action to reverse the deflationary trend. City Halls around the country became the targets of protests by armies of the unemployed. Frightened out of their complacency by these sometimes violent demonstrations, city officials first sent urgent pleas to state capitals, but rural-dominated legislatures and budget-minded governors opposed loosening the purse strings to assist "profligate" cities. In addition, the chief executives of most of the states were committed philosophically as well as politically to letting the natural laws of economics run their course. Not surprisingly, therefore, the 1931 and 1932 Governors' Conferences both avoided any frank discussion of the Depression. Rebuffed at the state level, municipal politicians began turning to Washington for help.

Besieged in their own cities, the mayors sent their first appeals to the Federal Government individually or through private organizations. United action by the nation's cities to induce the Federal

Government to assist cities was still unknown in 1932; indeed, rivalry, not cooperation, marked most inter-city relations. But the Crash bound the cities, as New York Mayor Fiorello H. La Guardia told a House committee in 1934, in "a common misery and misfortune" that threatened "to put every municipality in the country right to the wall." The time for a new national organization of cities had come.

In response to the Progressive movement's emphasis on administrative reform, several groups devoted to the improvement of municipal government had been established prior to 1932. None of these associations, however, could effectively present the cities' case in Washington. The National Municipal League, founded shortly before the turn of the century by civic-minded laymen committed to the cause of honest, efficient local government, concentrated its energies on publicizing the benefits of proportional representation and the city manager system. As a group that had developed to foster local efforts to divorce municipal politics from national issues and to enlarge the scope of municipal home rule, it naturally turned a generally unsympathetic ear to suggestions that the Federal Government aid the cities during the economic emergency. Writing in 1933, one league official would describe the New Deal's relief policies as "a very serious blow to home rule" and an obstacle to sound, economical municipal government. He argued that "it is better to let the local governments muddle along and work out their own salvation and opportunities for improvement. Federal intervention should not relieve communities from the consequences of their own folly." [11]

Another existing organization, the International City Managers Association (ICMA), although heavily indebted to the National Municipal League for its very creation, held a vastly different view of the city's responsibilities to its citizens and offered a possible vehicle for national action. With a membership composed almost entirely of professional city managers, the ICMA had come face-to-face with the practical difficulties of governing localities in the midst of economic depression. The association's October 1931 convention served as the forum for the "first serious discussion by municipal officials on the possibility of federal activities affecting municipalities." [12] But talk on such momentous issues as federal aid for the unemployed was all the ICMA could do. Conceived as an agency for the exchange of information among city managers (most of whom directed cities with populations under twenty thousand), the ICMA did not include lobbying as one of its functions. Furthermore, while many of its members were held in high esteem in administrative circles, none had a reputation adequate to carry weight in the national political arena. The ICMA, content to serve as a clearing-house of technical information for its specialized clientele, would not suffice as a pressure group in Washington for urban interests.

But another organization, similar in purpose to the ICMA but much more broadly based, began taking shape just as the Depression started. Since the early years of the century municipalities had been getting together on the state level to compare experiences and to protect their common interests in the state legislature. In 1924, these state leagues established a loose federation, the American Municipal Association (AMA), to act "as a national bureau for the interchange of ideas and techniques on the various phases of municipal government." Although the AMA's primary mission was to "raise the standard of city government," the Depression-caused crisis in the cities forced Paul V. Betters, its executive secretary, to direct his attention to the Federal Government.[13] Initially, the AMA restricted itself to assisting municipalities in the preparation of their applications for Reconstruction Finance Corporation (RFC) loans for public works projects, but the cities' unhappy experience with the self-liquidating provisions of the Emergency Relief and Construction Act of 1932 led Betters to assume an advocacy role. Appearing before a Senate committee in early 1933, he demanded a thorough overhaul of the Federal Government's relief and public works program, which he characterized as "a complete and dismal failure." While individual mayors had previously testified before congressional committees, for the first time Congress now heard a witness who claimed to speak for nearly seven thousand of the nation's municipalities.

The AMA's structural setup, however, frustrated Betters's attempts to make the group an effective champion of urban interests in national councils. Leadership and control were vested with the non-partisan secretaries of the state leagues, rather than with the elected political officials who actually governed the cities. Moreover, nowhere did the AMA's constitution provide for the adoption of policy declarations binding upon the autonomous leagues; the association could only submit resolutions to them for their consideration. As it worked out, the state leagues differed sharply on many issues, preventing the AMA from speaking with one voice. By 1936, the association decided formally to withdraw from pressure-group activity and devote itself solely to its original function of supplying information.[14] Clearly, a new alliance built around a different constituency had to be created.

As the chief spokesmen for their respective cities and as successful politicians, the big-city mayors understood the virtues of organization. As elected officials they commanded attention if not always respect. The Depression both muted old jealousies and provided a rallying cause. All that was needed was a leader, someone to settle on a program and align the other mayors behind it. Detroit's Mayor Frank Murphy filled this crucial role.

It is somehow fitting that the chief executive of Detroit, the symbol of the business-minded 1920s, should lead the struggle to expand the social welfare activities of the national government. Detroit's vast factories had produced the automobiles upon which so much of the prosperity of the 1920s rested. Its high wage scales had won the admiration of the nation and attracted thousands of unskilled laborers to its booming industries. The ninth biggest city in the country in 1910, with a population of less than half a million, it ranked fourth by 1930, with over three times as many people. Imbued with the optimistic spirit of the age, it had gone on a spree of annexations of adjoining communities, and its public works construction was matched only by the speculation-crazy cities of Florida.[15]

Without question, the automobile was at the center of Detroit's economic life; fully two-thirds of its work force found jobs in the auto or an auto-related industry. When car production started slipping in 1927, it generated widespread hardship. As one of the few urban communities in the country that had steadfastly adhered to the principle of publicly administered relief, Detroit accepted the responsibility of caring for its unemployed. But like most of America, Detroit expected prosperity to return at any moment, and municipal officials did not prepare for an extended period of economic hardship. Its relief program was limited and loosely run. Before the Crash, four thousand families represented the normal welfare load. By June 1930 fourteen thousand families were receiving assistance from the city, with no economic upturn in sight. "I have never confronted such misery as on the zero day of my arrival in Detroit," one social worker reported. "The only worst [sic] thing I've seen was the look in the faces of a company of French poilus who had been in the trenches four years; all hope seemed to have been wiped out and an intense weariness had taken its place." [16]

A special mayoralty election in the fall of 1930 forced the first public recognition of the city's temper. By directing his campaign solely to the issue of unemployment relief, Frank Murphy scored an upset victory, riding into City Hall on the votes of the municipality's working class. Citing the papal encyclical *Rerum Novarum*, Murphy promised to mobilize the resources of the municipal government in behalf of those out of work.[17] Although the new mayor described the problem as "obviously a national one," he strongly believed that "we can attack it locally." [18] While he urged federal programs for old-age pensions and unemployment insurance to help relieve the municipality of some of its burdens, Murphy committed his administration to a full-scale battle against the Depression.

Murphy's efforts to ease the relief situation attracted national attention but were doomed to failure. His Unemployment Committee won widespread praise for its pioneering activities in registering the jobless, operating an employment bureau, spurring public works, cooperating with private firms in devising plans to "spread the work," and raising voluntary contributions. The only mayor invited to the Progressive Conference in March 1931 Murphy received acclaim for Detroit's unmatched concern for its needy residents. But demonstrating compassion for the unfortunate proved to be a very costly enterprise for the Motor City. With nearly one-third of its industrial work force unemployed and over forty thousand families on its relief rolls, Detroit was spending an average of $2 million a month for the dole. Its per capita rate of expenditure for the first quarter of 1931 for outdoor relief was $3.37, 60¢ more than that of the second large city, Boston.[19] By the spring of 1931 Murphy realized that Detroit could not continue to spend these large sums of money much longer. "This load of relief," he declared, "is one that cannot be shouldered indefinitely by any city, without bringing in its wake financial ruin. It is necessary to find some means of transferring part of the weight to the county, state and federal governments." [20]

For a variety of reasons Detroit reached the brink of financial collapse first among the big cities. Completely dependent upon the automobile industry, which acted as the bellwether for the national economy, Detroit felt the effects of the Crash sooner and more severely than any other metropolitan area. In most other large cities private charities carried the relief load during the beginning stages of the turndown.[21] In Detroit, the government took care of the unemployed out of its own funds. Some states, such as New York and Pennsylvania, appropriated emergency funds to help their municipalities, but the Republican and rural-dominated Michigan government had little sympathy for Detroit's Democratic mayor. Thus, while it had less than one-fourth of New York City's population, Detroit spent twice as much on relief in 1930–31. No less than 20 per cent of Detroit's relief monies went to Ford employees, even though the company did not contribute one penny in taxes. In fact, most of the factories employing Detroit's workers were located outside of the city limits and consequently paid no city levies. Faced with a decline in assessed valuation of 40.4 per cent and a tax delinquency rate of 25 per cent, the city of Detroit, even had it been financially prudent before the Depression, would have had serious financial problems. But with the large bonded debt it had incurred during the reckless spending spree of the 1920s eating up a quarter of its budget in 1930–31, Detroit teetered on the edge of bankruptcy.[22]

Murphy responded by cutting back on a wide range of city functions. Finding work relief too expensive, he halted all public works projects and restricted municipal assistance to the dole. He practically eliminated funds for the City Planning Commission, ordered a sharp curtailment of health, recreational, and cultural services, and pared the manpower of the police and fire departments. Yet even with these slashes, only an emergency loan permitted the city to meet its payroll in June 1931; the rising tide of tax delinquency was playing havoc with Murphy's budget-balancing efforts. Finally under heavy pressure from the New York banks that held Detroit's bonds, he agreed to limit relief appropriations for 1931–32 to $7 million, a reduction of 50 per cent. Thousands of needy families were dropped from relief rolls, and already unsatisfactory standards were lowered even more. Political expediency, as well as his deep-rooted beliefs in justice and benevolence, now led Murphy to concentrate his energies on getting federal aid. In June 1931, endorsing a plea of his Unemployment Committee to President Hoover requesting a special session of Congress to deal with the Depression, Murphy expressed the hope that it would "stimulate other cities to take similar steps and urge our Federal Government to adopt an unemployment relief program for the entire nation." Detroit, he said, "has reached its limit." [23]

Concerted action by cities still lay in the distant future as Detroit headed into the harsh winter of 1931–32. Up for re-election in November, Murphy won the overwhelming endorsement of the voters, despite opposition from the city's financial leaders, who felt "his idealism and his desire to help the man in hard luck led him astray" in the welfare field.[24] Murphy appeared before a Senate committee in January to repeat his contention that the cities could no longer provide adequate assistance to their jobless and that federal intervention was essential. February saw the mayor in New York beseeching his city's creditors to give Detroit additional loans. Their price: further budget cuts. Murphy had to slash city payrolls 50 per cent in April and May after he found it impossible to float the city's short-term paper in a tight money market. Faced with a similar crisis with the relief funds for June, Murphy decided he had to do something dramatic to draw attention to Detroit's desperate predicament. To accomplish this he had to demonstrate that Detroit's problems were New York's problems, and Chicago's problems, and therefore the nation's problems.

Coordinated demands by the nation's largest cities, he felt, would carry more influence in Washington. As a preliminary step in uniting the mayors of the country, in May 1932 Murphy invited the chief executives of Michigan's other municipalities, which, like Detroit, suffered at the hands of a conservative state administration, to a meeting. "The Federal Government has recognized the need for Federal relief," Murphy told them, "but thus far only for the corporate interests. It is time they help out on the human side." Following his lead, the mayors addressed a petition to the President and Congress pleading for national aid as "the one remaining source to which we can turn in this emergency." Asking for federal appropriations for direct relief and a $5 billion "Prosperity Loan," they warned that failure to act would place "the very foundations of our social order in jeopardy." Before adjourning, the Michigan mayors instructed Murphy to call a national conference of mayors as soon as possible.[25]

The idea was not entirely new; almost a year before, Milwaukee's Socialist Mayor Daniel W. Hoan had suggested just such a parley. In contrast to Murphy, who reluctantly came to request federal intervention only after local monies ran out, Hoan argued from the very start of the Depression the need for a national program.[26] Writing in July 1931 to the mayors of the one hundred largest cities, Hoan had denounced the Hoover administration for its "do-nothing policy" and asked his colleagues to consider holding a conference for the purpose of petitioning Congress "to adopt some relief commensurate with what we have done in the past for the starving peoples of Europe." [27] Most of those who took the trouble to reply backed the plan, citing their inability to handle the growing welfare load, and the President's failure to act upon their individual appeals.[28] Some mayors, however, severely criticized the proposal, reminding Hoan again that any sort of federal action in this area would be "an invasion of community rights."[29] Although Hoan interpreted the over-all response as an endorsement of his scheme, he decided against calling the meeting because he had not heard from any of the major cities: New York, Chicago, Philadelphia, or Detroit. Without their participation, any conference would be meaningless. Furthermore, Hoover's appointment of a President's Committee on Unemployment Relief and his announcement of an expanded public works program offered the prospect that the national government might, after all, be changing its position on relief.[30]

When Hoan wrote his hundred letters in the summer of 1931 the relief problem had not yet reached a crisis; by the time Murphy extended his invitation in the spring of 1932 that crisis had arrived. Even with belated infusions of state funds, New York and Chicago discovered what Detroit had learned months before: nothing short of federal assistance would enable them to clothe and feed their destitute, or, in Chicago's case, permit it to pay its teachers. With Hoover plodding along on his generally unresponsive course, Murphy's plans went ahead smoothly. While two-thirds of those invited did not come, the majority of the absentees expressed support for the conference's aims. Delayed a week to permit New York's Mayor James J. Walker to complete testimony before a legislative committee investigating his administration, the June 1 meeting attracted representatives from twenty-nine cities, including the mayors of New York, Boston, Cleveland, Milwaukee, Minneapolis, Denver, Richmond, and New Orleans. Democrats predominated, but this was to be expected in an election year where criticism of a Republican President was sure to be voiced.[31]

Murphy's welcoming remarks set a serious, businesslike tone for the meeting. "Every man in this room knows best the needs of his own city," he explained. "It is not necessary for us to deliberate at length. We have but one objective—help to our people, which only the Federal Government can give adequately. Let us memorialize Congress to that effect in words that cannot be mistaken and then adjourn." Before turning the floor over to Walker, whose presence guaranteed extensive press coverage of the event, Murphy summed up his position: "We have done everything humanly possible to do, and it has not been enough. The hour is at hand for the Federal Government to cooperate."

Casting aside his playboy attitude for a moment, Walker moved his audience with his description of the cities' plight:[32]

The municipal government is the maternal, the intimate side of government; the side with a heart. The Federal Government doesn't have to look into suffering faces; it doesn't have to wander through darkened hallways of our hospitals, to witness the pain and suffering there. It doesn't have to stand on the bread lines, but the time has come when it must face the facts and its responsibility.

We of the cities have diagnosed and thus far met the problem; but we have come to the end of our resources. It is now up to the Federal Government to assume its share. We can't cure conditions by ourselves. Let us make it known just whose responsibility this now becomes.

Only three mayors dissented from this viewpoint. Denver's Republican mayor denied that his city could no longer carry on alone and advised his colleagues not to "further complicate our national financial crisis by another demand on federal resources that do not exist." The Democratic mayor of Richmond told the meeting that if municipalities would simply learn to live within their incomes, all their problems would disappear. Syracuse's chief executive, a Republican, raised the old fear of federal dictatorship in expressing his opposition to national relief assistance. But these were distinctly minority opinions.

Rushing to complete its work in one day, the conference

overwhelmingly endorsed resolutions, prepared in advance by Murphy's staff, requesting $5 billion in federal works expenditures, a national relief program big enough to "satisfy all needs," and federal loans to municipalities to enable them to refund their maturing obligations. Asking Congress to "declare war not figuratively but literally against unemployment and depression," the mayors appointed a delegation, headed by Murphy, to fight for their demands in Washington.

This decision of municipal officials to look to the national government marked a turning point in American urban history. Louis Brownlow, a former city manager, and director of the Public Administration Clearing House, was to observe in 1934 that, "it has been said that the Federal Government has discovered the cities, it is equally true that the cities have discovered the Federal Government." [33] Formerly ignored in plans for improving the conditions of urban life, Washington now became the arena for city lobbying activities. Abandoning their fruitless efforts to move the rural-oriented state governments, urban advocates joined the ranks of interest groups who looked to the Federal Government for their salvation.

The mayors' initial contact with national leaders, however, proved disappointing, as they wound up on the losing side in a classic confrontation between the executive and legislative branches. House Speaker John Nance Garner welcomed the Murphy delegation warmly and had its petition printed in the *Congressional Record* as evidence in support of his huge spending bill. With the mayors looking on approvingly from the galleries, the House passed the $2.1 billion public works, lending, and relief measure. [34] But at the other end of Pennsylvania Avenue the mayors received a frosty reception. The President considered their request inimical to the spirit of the Constitution. Committed to the principle of local responsibility, Hoover vetoed a revised version of the Garner bill and urged congressional endorsement of a much smaller lending bill. Although the mayors had achieved some national recognition, they had barely raised the lid of federal coffers. The Emergency Relief and Construction Act of 1932 in its final form fell far short of what they were after. Instead of $5 billion for public works the Act authorized $1.5 billion and included a debilitating proviso that these projects be self-liquidating. It failed to take care of the municipal debt problem. According to Murphy, the $300 million in loans the Act set aside for emergency relief was, "inadequate and superficial." Rebuffed in their first appearance on the national scene, the mayors returned home to prepare for another bad winter and to participate in the upcoming Presidential election campaign.

It was clear by the end of 1932 that the Emergency Relief and Construction Act could not solve Detroit's monetary woes. Although Detroit had been totally relieved of the burden of its relief program by the Emergency Relief Act loans,[35] the city's financial structure continued to deteriorate. Debt service was absorbing two-thirds of the municipality's budget, and 40 per cent of Detroit's taxes remained unpaid as the city entered the new year. The only way out seemed to be refunding through the Reconstruction Finance Corporation. As many other cities faced similar crises, Murphy decided to call another mayors' meeting, this time in Washington. Forty-nine cities sent representatives to the February 1933 conference; all joined in the appeal for RFC help, but the lame-duck Congress adjourned without taking action on the required legislation.[36]

The mayors assembled at the February session also reached agreement on a step of more lasting consequence: they decided to create a permanent organization, to be called the United States Conference of Mayors (USCM). Such a move had been discussed at the Detroit meeting in June 1932 and had subsequently found a strong sponsor in Paul Betters, the American Municipal Association's executive secretary. Keeping in touch with Murphy during the second half of 1932, Betters advised the Detroit chief executive on the virtues of a mayoral coalition:[37]

The crying need in America today is for the public to realize that essentially our national problems are *municipal* or urban problems, and the mayors could materially focus public attention on this fact. . . . Congress now has the benefit of no real spokesman for the cities. . . . Collectively, the mayors would have great influence and prestige.

At Murphy's invitation Betters helped to arrange the February 1933 meeting, and he wrote the constitution for the new group.

Betters shaped the USCM to make it an effective lobbying instrument. With the frustrations created by the AMA's old federated structure vivid in his mind, Betters provided for direct membership by cities in the conference. Policy statements were to be issued at the annual meeting and, significantly, might also be promulgated in emergencies by the USCM's Executive Board. Composition of the board further set the USCM apart from the AMA. Instead of the non-partisan administrative technicians who held the reins at the AMA, municipal political leaders would be in charge at the USCM. These elected officials spoke the same language as the politicians in Washington, and Betters expected this would facilitate federal-city communication.[38] One additional feature of the USCM constitution sharply differentiated the USCM from the AMA. Whereas the AMA, through its state leagues, served localities of all sizes, the USCM restricted its membership to cities of 50,000 people and over. The mayors of big cities believed that their communities had special needs and, unlike most of the leaders of smaller towns, felt that federal action was needed to cope with their problems. Entering the national arena as the champion of the interests of the nation's large urban centers,[39] the USCM attacked the old dogmas of home rule and states' rights and espoused expanded cooperative federalism.

III

The forging of a new federal-city partnership in the field of unemployment relief took first priority. In 1930–32, while governors, business and labor leaders, and social workers received White House invitations to Hoover-sponsored conferences on housing, health, the jobless, and other pressing issues, mayors were conspicuously absent. "It is entirely possible," observed a prominent city manager in the fall of 1931,[40]

> that what is passing for Federal action in the unemployment crisis is making the city's job still harder—and this with the best will in the world on the part of national authorities. If after eighteen months' consideration and study the latest news out of Washington is that cities can best handle their own industrial crisis problems, we certainly had little Federal suggestion or action. . . . What the cities need just now from Washington is correlated information on unemployment, and a national program of employment agencies and employment distribution. What they get is the cheerful news that distress is a local and municipal problem.

The Emergency Relief and Construction Act of 1932 reflected the state and federal bias against national government intervention in municipal affairs and the gaps in federal knowledge of urban conditions. Legal impediments resulting from the nature of municipal charters negated the value of the act's public works title, and political obstacles weakened the effectiveness of the relief provisions. By linking relief loans to state highway allotments and requiring gubernatorial approval of all local requests for aid, the act ensured that big-city pleas for help would encounter stiff resistance. Since all federal highway grants were used for the construction of rural roads, country areas naturally opposed any diversion of these funds to the cities. Few governors were disposed to incur rural displeasure and many gave their consent only after having obtained from the cities strict promises to repay the money. Some state chief executives, such as Roosevelt of New York, objected to the legal requirement that a pauper's oath be taken by the state before aid could be extended. Out of desperation, a number of municipalities sought and received direct RFC loans, but this only moved some, such as Detroit, closer to bankruptcy.[41]

When Roosevelt moved into the White House in March 1933 he did not contemplate any immediate change in policy on the relief front; by his calculations the RFC had enough funds to last until May, and hence no real emergency existed. But the climate of "the hundred days" and the rapidly deteriorating situation in Chicago combined to produce an entirely new picture. Chicago's crucial role in the relief drama is somewhat ironic. Murphy's valiant efforts in behalf of Detroit's unemployed had driven his city to the brink of disaster, but he had still not been able to get the Federal Government deeply interested in his problem. Chicago's financial troubles, on the other hand, were not so much the result of its relief program, which one analyst has described as "haphazard and unimaginative," but of a decade of fiscal mismanagement and outright corruption. Nonetheless, it was Chicago's wretched condition that broke the back of conservative opposition to federal aid in the summer of 1932. With his teachers unpaid for five months and the rest of his municipal employees not having seen a paycheck in three months, Mayor Anton Cermak intimated to a House committee in June that violence in the streets of Chicago could be expected after August 1, when state grants would be exhausted. "It would be cheaper for Congress," he advised, "to provide a loan of $152 million to the City of Chicago, than to pay for the services of Federal troops at a future date." [42] Within a week of the enactment of the Emergency Relief and Construction bill, Chicago had received its first RFC loan. By March 1933, however, it had reached the maximum statutory allotment of $45 million; if civil disorder was to be averted in Chicago, and elsewhere, another way of getting money to the cities would have to be found. Upon the recommendation of his aides, Roosevelt requested, and Congress appropriated, $500 million for federal relief grants.

Although the mayors were overjoyed by the prospect of grants instead of loans, they objected to those provisions that again delegated extensive administrative responsibilities to the states. The Federal Emergency Relief Administration (FERA) made block grants to the states, which then disbursed the funds as they saw fit to their political subdivisions. The states' anti-urban handling of the federal aid funds under the 1932 Act was still very fresh in the mayors' memories. They feared that the cities would never see the FERA monies, or, at least, not an equitable share. To some extent, events justified the mayors' anxiety. Over the two-and-a-half-year life span of FERA, local contributions in large urban areas were relatively greater than those in rural regions; similarly, state funds accounted for a smaller part of the total costs in the big cities than they did in lesser-sized communities.[43] Much of this disparity can be attributed to politics and the rural outlook of most state governments, but other elements also played a role. In spite of all their difficulties, the large cities still commanded greater resources than rural units and, as one economist pointed out, have "traditionally borne the relief burden with less reluctance and parsimony than small cities, towns, and counties." [44]

The mayors were also disturbed by the vast discretionary power vested in the administrator to apportion the funds among the states. Provided with few guidelines on which to base his decisions, Harry Hopkins often had to rely on unmeasurable and intangible factors in distributing the money. This produced what one mayor described as "a 'poker-playing' program—with the Federal Government engaged in a game with forty-eight individual governors." "The sad part of it is," he continued, "that the position of any state or community largely depended on what kind of contestant the governor happened to be." [45] But on the whole Hopkins did a good job, getting aid to where it was needed most. Some injustices may have resulted, but there is no evidence that Hopkins consciously favored one state or region over another.[46] The mayors stood on firmer ground when they chided the New Deal for its delay in putting the relief program on a more permanent footing so that each locality could plan its budget for the year ahead with greater assurance of what it could expect from the national government.[47]

Although the large urban areas had the greatest number unemployed and received the bulk of the federal funds appropriated through FERA, on balance, FERA probably returned greater dividends to rural sections.[48] After the infusion of federal money, relief expenditures in country districts grew at a faster rate than in cities; likewise, while the percentage of relief costs in the cities financed by the Federal Government matched the average for the nation as a whole, Washington assumed the greatest share in the predominantly rural states of the South and the Rocky Mountain area.[49] What began as an attempt to meet basically urban needs wound up directly benefitting rural sections as much, if not more.[50] Political and practical considerations required that the rural interest be satisfied; indeed, blurring of urban-rural differences aided the prospects of a program. Later, when the works program took on more of a city complexion, relief became a divisive issue in Congress.

On the basis of its actual performance and the limits within which it operated, FERA offered little cause for criticism by the mayors. Although it did not provide recipients with anything more than subsistence allowance, FERA relieved the cities of a tremendous burden and permitted them to start putting their financial houses in order. But as much as they appreciated what FERA had done, the mayors found considerable room for improvement. Concerned about the morale of their constituents, they wished to substitute work relief for the dole. It was an occasion for rejoicing, therefore, when Hopkins announced plans, in the fall of 1933, for the establishment of the Civil Works Administration (CWA). The USCM happily agreed to his request that Betters be lent to the new agency as a consultant. In the four months of CWA's existence the gloom in the cities began to lift for the first time since the Depression had struck; essentially urban-oriented, the CWA restored a sense of vitality to city life.[51] When the time came to wind up its activities, a step New York's Mayor Fiorello La Guardia called "disastrous for cities," Hopkins exercised special care to see that quotas for Northern industrial and metropolitan areas remained at full strength through the winter.[52] While its short tenure prevented CWA from making any significant physical impression upon the cities, it provided a helpful precedent for future federal action.

In September 1934 a delegation from the USCM headed by La Guardia journeyed to Hyde Park to present the mayors' work relief proposals to the President. Resigned to the fact that private enterprise could not supply jobs to all those seeking employment, the mayors called upon the Federal Government to fill the gap by creating jobs on its own. Roosevelt's endorsement of this plan in a message to Congress in early 1935 represented a tremendous victory for the mayors, and they quickly became the Works Progress Administration's (WPA) staunchest champions. Indeed, since cities sponsored the vast majority of WPA projects, the USCM vigorously defended the program against all detractors. Over the course of the next five years, the USCM prepared a number of surveys based on mayors' reports of local projects. These surveys uniformly praised the work being done under WPA auspices and stressed the need for its continued operation. Usually released through the White House for maximum exposure, the reports also applied pressure on Roosevelt to increase the scope of the works program.

The most persistent complaint of the mayors concerned WPA's failure to furnish jobs to all who could work. Even at its peak, WPA provided for only about one-third of the ten million idle; the remainder continued to burden local economies. The USCM kept up a constant campaign for larger, more adequate appropriations, but both the President, anxious to balance his budget, and Congress, becoming more and more conservative every day after 1936, turned a deaf ear to the mayors.[53] Only the mobilization for war would end unemployment as a municipal problem.

Compared with this inherent limitation in WPA's performance, the USCM's other reservations about WPA's set-up were relatively mild. The USCM sought separate administrative districts for each of the twenty-five largest cities, but except for New York, where sheer size and La Guardia's close ties to Roosevelt worked for its approval, these were not created. Generally, however, despite the traditional pleas for greater local autonomy, the mayors considered the national character of WPA a vast improvement over FERA's reliance upon the states.[54] In an important reversal of its previous stand, the USCM opposed congressional efforts to earmark relief funds and devise an allocation formula. The mayors now had faith in Hopkins, and felt that the rural-dominated federal legislature had shown a bias in its apportionment of federal monies as large sums were being set aside for rural electrification, soil erosion control, and farm-to-market highways.[55] Alerted by the mayors to this problem, Roosevelt used his discretionary powers to direct the remaining general relief funds into the cities. WPA spent half of its grants in the fifty largest cities containing 25 per cent of the nation's population.[56] But the President ignored the USCM's recommendation that the works program be made a permanent feature of the Federal Government. Just as under FERA, the cities did not know the size of their next year's WPA grants.

Beginning in 1937, the USCM marshalled its strength to save WPA from its growing band of enemies. Backed by Roosevelt, the mayors successfully repulsed Senator James Byrnes's attempt to require local contributions of at least 40 per cent on WPA projects. Such a step, the conference argued, would mean the collapse of the entire works program since municipal finances were still in very precarious condition. Byrnes's fiscal conservatism explains his opposition to huge federal spending, but the South Carolinian's frequent charges that New York City was not paying its fair share of relief costs also gave evidence of increasing rural dissatisfaction with WPA's urban outlook. It was a clear warning that the cities were to face trouble from their country neighbors in the months ahead.

The USCM also triumphed when congressional Republicans launched a partisan attack on WPA and tried to turn the administration of relief over to the states. Uniting behind Cleveland's Republican chief executive, Harold H. Burton, the mayors defended federal control as more equitable and efficient. These victories, along with Roosevelt's request for more WPA appropriations in the spring of 1938, represented the apogee of the USCM's success in lobbying activities.

But as the President's control of Congress weakened, the mayors found themselves also weakened. In 1939, for the first time since Roosevelt's inauguration, Congress slashed a Presidential request for relief funds and imposed, again against Roosevelt's wishes, a minimum local contribution of 25 per cent.[57] The works program, despite good support from urban congressmen, continued to operate only in skeletal form,[58] while farm-subsidy spending went on at levels higher than Roosevelt wanted. Big-city legislators were simply outnumbered in Congress, where over half of the districts contained no municipality with a population as large as fifty thousand, and half the representatives resided in communities of fewer than twenty-five thousand people.[59] Providentially for the mayors, national mobilization for another type of emergency considerably eased the relief crisis.

The phasing out and eventual demise of WPA during the war did not go unmourned in the cities. Although at no time large enough to empty the soup kitchens, WPA had carried the cities back from the edge of civil and financial chaos. "If it were not for the Federal aid," La Guardia told the 1935 USCM meeting, "I don't know what any of us could have done." Federal appreciation of the cities' plight had come a long way since the bleak, early days of the Depression. The mayors had begun to be heard.

IV

Next to relief the mayors' combined voices were pitched highest in support of a federal program of public works. Since 1930, cities had found it increasingly difficult to borrow for municipal improvements. The tight money market and their weakened credit standings had forced most cities to cut back drastically on their construction schedules. By the spring of 1932 local public works had practically ground to a halt. At their meeting in June the mayors requested a $5 billion federal loan program to finance municipal projects. The Emergency Relief and Construction Act of 1932 authorized less than a third of that amount, and to prevent federal money from being wasted on useless schemes, Congress had added the requirement that all projects be self-liquidating. As few municipal enterprises could meet that obligation, the mayors were lobbying for revisions when the New Deal came to power.[60]

The public works title of the National Industrial Recovery Act of 1933 dropped the self-liquidating provision. The statute also substituted a combination of loans and grants for the previous policy of loans only and reduced the rate of interest on the loans made. A new day in federal-municipal ties had dawned. Public Works Administrator Harold L. Ickes appointed Betters to serve as his unofficial liaison with cities and to help localities prepare their applications for federal assistance. When the cities experienced delays in receiving PWA approval of these proposals, charges were generated that "red tape" and the "semi-colon boys" within PWA were sabotaging the President's program. Responding to these criticisms in a speech to the October 1933 convention of the USCM, Ickes made the mayors "a sporting proposition"; he asked the conference to prepare a list of concrete suggestions on how to speed up PWA's processing procedures. Delighted by the Ickes offer, the USCM quickly put together its recommendations. Almost as rapidly, Ickes placed the bulk of them in operation: increased personnel to review requests, simplified forms, more and better instructions.[61] But he ignored their most crucial piece of advice: to decentralize his office and place more confidence in municipal officials. "Honest Harold," a lifelong foe of corruption in Chicago government, was unwilling to let even a hint of scandal attach itself to his agency; thus, the bottleneck in the administrator's office continued, and so did the complaints.[62]

Although their consultations with Ickes accomplished little of a substantive nature, the USCM was able to set a precedent in the cities' nascent relations with the Federal Government. Almost completely overlooked in the administration of relief under both RFC and FERA, the mayors finally received recognition from Washington. Official confirmation of the cities' qualifications to participate in federal programs came in April 1935, when Roosevelt gave representation to the USCM, along with business, finance, labor, and agriculture, on the Advisory Committee on Allotments (ACA), the policy-making body for the vast works program about to get under way. Anxious to capitalize on their debut in the federal councils, the mayors chose La Guardia as their agent.[63] He alone, of the twenty-three governmental and non-governmental members of the committee, attended every one of its sixteen sessions. Although the ACA acted as little more than a rubber stamp for the President, the fiery New York mayor ably defended every urban interest.[64]

From the cities' perspective, the most urgent issue facing the ACA concerned the terms by which new PWA funds were to be made available to municipalities. Naturally, La Guardia wanted the grants to be large and the interest rate low. Under the 1933 law, PWA matched a 30 per cent grant with a 70 per cent loan at an interest rate of 4 per cent. The interest rate aroused the greatest dissatisfaction; localities objected to paying the going market rate to finance public improvements that, they argued, returned wide social benefits. At their 1934 meeting, the mayors demanded that the Federal Government supply money at no charge or at most, at the rate of $\frac{1}{8}$ per cent. "Unless the matter of interest is eliminated, which is today crushing municipal operations," Betters wrote in a memo to La Guardia, "very little public works will, and (in our opinion) ought to be undertaken by cities." But Roosevelt's advisers, especially Secretary of the Treasury Henry Morgenthau, vigorously opposed this proposition; eager to balance the budget, they wanted an interest rate that would cover the Treasury's borrowing costs. When La Guardia forced discussion of the matter at ACA's early meetings, Roosevelt indicated support for a policy of 45 per cent grant, 55 per cent loan at 3 per cent interest. Convinced that the cities had scored a major triumph, La Guardia later called this period, "the happiest days of my life." Praising the President's stand, he noted that it represented "the first time that the conditions of cities have been considered by the Federal Government in any general plan for the whole country." [65] La Guardia's ecstasy was short-lived. After hearing Morgenthau argue that this new rate would be prohibitive, Roosevelt retained the 4 per cent charge. The more favorable 45:55, grant:loan ratio for cities was instituted, however.

Although PWA performed disappointingly as a pump-priming device, it was indispensable in retarding the pace of physical deterioration in the central cities. During the 1930s schools were built, water and sewage plants constructed, and transportation facilities improved; none of this would have been possible without the infusion of federal funds. But PWA could not reverse the trend of decay; the job was too big and the appropriations too small. It had laid the foundations, however, for later more ambitious federal efforts in urban reconstruction.

V

Federal relief and public works programs reduced much of the pressure on municipal finances, but other Depression-related problems still demanded attention. The sharp break in economic activity cut heavily into local tax resources; tax delinquencies rose as unemployed city residents exhausted their savings. Detroit's woes were unusually severe, but not unique. Assessed valuations of real property in the largest cities, the most important source of local revenues, fell by 1933 an average of 17.8 per cent from their 1929 peak. In Los Angeles the drop was 45.2 per cent, in Cleveland, 42.2 per cent. At the same time, the proportion of unpaid taxes jumped from less than 10 per cent to nearly 30 per cent. Expenditures were slashed and city services curtailed, but one item could not be trimmed from city budgets even in the midst of the deflationary spiral: interest payments on bonded debt. Caught up in the expansive mood of the 1920s, the thirteen largest cities had increased their debt an average of 50 per cent; now they found it increasingly difficult to meet their obligations.[66] Unlike the Federal Government, which possessed virtually unlimited powers to raise funds, the cities were confronted with state-imposed debt limits and a credit market that considered municipal bonds a bad risk. Confronted by the threat of default, the cities turned to Washington for help.

The crisis in Detroit's exchequer came to a head just as Roosevelt took office. With debt service charges eating up 70 per cent of his budget in early 1933, Murphy asked for a federal loan to permit him to refund his bonds, lower his interest costs, and pass along some measure of tax relief to his beleaguered constituents.[67] The lame-duck Congress showed little enthusiasm for the idea, however, and

Detroit barely continued to function while the nation awaited the new President's leadership. But time ran out for Detroit. The city's banks closed in February, the municipality technically defaulted on its bonds, and scrip replaced currency as the medium of exchange. Describing the city as "at the end of her financial rope," Murphy rushed to Washington with a plan. The federal courts, he told Congress, should be empowered to declare a moratorium on interest payments for up to ten years whenever they found that municipalities were unable to fulfill their duties to both their creditors and their residents.[68] Stirred by Murphy's depiction of Detroit's predicament, the Judiciary Committees of both houses cleared his bill for floor action, but Congress adjourned on March 3 without any debate.

Although the national bank holiday and subsequent reopening of the banks helped ease Detroit's difficulties, Murphy pushed on with his fight for the moratorium bill. Unable to reach an accommodation with his bondholders, he returned to Washington to impress upon Roosevelt that the cities' plight was "every bit as desperate as the farmers'." The only alternative to his plan, Murphy claimed, was "the suspension of government in the large cities." [69] But large lending institutions, put on notice by his previous abortive efforts in the lame-duck session, were now mobilized to defeat the measure, which they felt offered no protection for the creditor. In its place, they supported a bill that would permit municipalities and their bondholders, under judicial supervision, to negotiate adjustments in the terms of the debt. Their counterproposal had been thought out as a solution to the problem of the numerous small Florida cities that had borrowed heavily during the 1920s and could not meet their liabilities when the land bubble burst.

Murphy denounced this substitute plan. His objection was basic: while the creditors were given no role in his moratorium bill, they would have to agree to any new arrangement devised under the adjustment bill. With over two years of bitter disputes with Detroit's creditors over relief cuts behind him, Murphy did not look forward to bargaining with them once again. Attacking the adjustment measure as an attempt to "hand the reins of government over to the large financial interests," Murphy pleaded with national officials to adopt his proposal.[70] But Murphy had lost even the support of his own mayors' group. Most of the chief executives enjoyed good relations with their local banking communities and were unwilling to jeopardize further an already demoralized municipal bond market. The USCM Executive Board endorsed the lending institutions' proposal. As Murphy left the country in June to take up his post as governor-general of the Philippines, the House of Representatives passed the Debt Adjustment bill, although final congressional approval would not come for another year.

It is ironic that the one act passed during the 1930s containing the word "municipal" in its title returned practically no benefits to the large cities. No city with more than thirty thousand people ever used the Municipal Debt Adjustment Act;[71] the big cities' problem was not with the small obstinate bondowner who resisted any accommodation, but with the hard bargaining giants of the financial fraternity. None of the big urban centers actually experienced extended defaults; they all reached some sort of settlement with their creditors, but only at a terrific cost. After Murphy's departure, the banks holding Detroit's bonds consented to a two-year suspension of principal payments; to get this period of grace, however, the city would have to pay out an additional $125 million in interest charges.[72] Similar pacts were made in numerous other cities where "financial dictators replaced political bosses"; New York's Bankers' Agreement, observed one expert on municipal bonds, put the great metropolis in "virtual receivership." [73] By 1936, with a general upturn in economic conditions, the local budget picture showed some signs of improvement; new revenues, better collection of taxes, federal aid, and lower interest rates all combined to produce the brighter outlook.[74] In that year also, in a case involving a Texas irrigation district, the Supreme Court struck down the Municipal Debt Adjustment Act as an unconstitutional infringement upon state responsibilities.[75]

Although the USCM supported the bankruptcy legislation, it concentrated its energies during the 1932–34 period on gaining more positive federal action in the financial area. The mayors wanted the national government to supply them with loans at interest rates below those charged in the private money markets. Borrowing had become prohibitively expensive. Cities encountered great difficulty in placing short-term notes to cover their operational expenses. Several methods of bypassing the usual credit channels were suggested. One plan would give the cities the right to deposit their bonds with the Controller of the Currency in exchange for which they would receive an equal amount in bank notes; another would allow the cities to present their securities to the Federal Reserve Banks for rediscounting.[76] The most popular proposal would authorize the RFC to lend money directly to cities. "If the RFC can assist the corporate banks, railroads, and insurance companies," Murphy was to write in late 1932, "it ought to be available to aid the corporate cities—the oldest and most important of all corporations and the ones that will be here after all the others have disappeared." [77]

The proposal reached Congress in January 1932, during its examination of the bill establishing the RFC. Claiming that the banks were "squeezing" New York City, Mayor Walker asked that the measure be amended to permit loans to cities with good financial records. Supported by big-city and inflationist Democrats and insurgent Republicans, the amendment fell before a coalition of conservatives from both parties who were respecting Hoover's wishes to limit the RFC's lending powers to a restricted group of private institutions. Helping to send the proposal down to defeat was a statement from Murphy opposing "any bill which would relieve municipalities from recourse to uncompromising economy in order to bring expenditures within income such as we have done in Detroit." This declaration accurately reflected Murphy's initial feelings; he passionately believed that he could not request state or federal help until every alternative on the local level had been exhausted.[78]

By the time of the mayors' meeting in June 1932 Murphy had swung over to Walker's position. "Debt services are way out of line with all other obligations of government," Murphy explained later. After setting aside funds to meet Detroit's maturing debts, the city would have only enough money left to operate for three months in the next fiscal year. "The problem can no longer be solved by governmental economies," he continued.[79]

That job has been completed in Detroit and is now behind us. We have reduced the operating costs of government almost $30 million in a little over two years. There is no way out I can see for American municipalities . . . but to arrive at some financial plan that will preserve governmental credit and its economic integrity and, at the same time, refund the principal requirements in the annual debt charges.

The mayors, at Murphy's urging, adopted a resolution requesting RFC loans.

Prospects for federal assistance along these lines brightened momentarily in July 1932 with congressional approval of the $2.1 billion Wagner-Garner bill, which added $1.5 billion to the RFC's lending authority for loans to states, municipalities, private enterprises, and individuals. But, as expected, Hoover vetoed the bill and in a stinging message to the Congress denounced this measure as opening the way for states and localities "to dump their financial liabilities and problems upon the Federal Government." [80] The final version of the bill, which received the President's signature, did not contain this amendment.

Confronted with another debt crisis at the start of 1933, Murphy resumed his campaign and called another mayors' meeting in February. In a strongly worded statement, the conference warned that the continued failure of Congress and the President "to do for municipal corporations what they have done for private corporations" would bring "chaos in most cities." Murphy received a mixed reception during his appearance before a Senate committee holding hearings on the relief program. New York's Robert F. Wagner spoke favorably of the mayors' proposal but added that the "Senate is not quite ready for it." If any confirmation of this was needed, James

Couzens of Michigan, an ex-mayor of Detroit and a staunch ally of
Murphy in his relief battles, supplied it. Arguing that the debt mess
was the states' responsibility, Couzens advised his friend that "you
can't come running to the United States Government for help for
everything." With legislative initiative unlikely, the mayors' only
hope resided with the incoming administration.[81]

Eager to establish a good working relationship with the New Deal,
the USCM modified its demands. Whereas Murphy was interested in
refunding his city's bonded debt, most of the other mayors were
more concerned about the paucity of short-term credit; sixty of the
ninety-three largest cities reported that their local banks could not
supply the financing they needed to maintain essential services.
After Murphy resigned as USCM president to assume his post in the
Philippines, the conference dropped its request for refunding loans,
acknowledging that federal assumption of their billions of capital
debt might be an "unbearable burden." The conference asked that
the RFC be permitted to purchase the tax delinquency and tax
anticipation warrants of municipalities. According to the mayors,
$300 million would meet their needs. Hopeful of enlisting Roose-
velt's support for this more limited program, they visited the White
House in May 1933 to present their case, stressing that the
"continued existence of American municipalities is at stake."

To the mayors' dismay, Roosevelt proved an unsympathetic host.
He had already committed the Federal Government to tasks of
staggering and unprecedented proportions. He did not feel he could
take on the cities' debts as well. Familiar with municipal corruption,
he also tended to blame the mayors' own mismanagement, and not
the general contraction of credit, for the cities' predicament. The
possible costs of the project disturbed Roosevelt; like Hoover, he
was wary of the real value of the notes the government would be
buying. He expected hundreds of municipalities and counties to
default on their bonds in 1933 and 1934. "If the Federal Government attempts to finance them," he remarked soon after taking
office, "it will run into billions." Roosevelt's analysis of the situation
had not changed when he saw the mayors in May. Doing

some simple arithmetic, [Roosevelt] showed them that if you did it for the cities and counties and townships and did it for the electric light districts and the water districts and the sidewalk districts and the school districts and so on, that it might cost the Federal Government, just in advance to take care of their current obligations, as high as $10 billion, and therefore it was a perfectly absurd thing to talk about.[82]

Clearly, Roosevelt had misunderstood what the mayors wanted; he was thinking of refunding. The USCM was interested in short-term credit for the big cities exclusively. But pressures for congressional adjournment did not give the mayors time to rectify the error, and thus the "hundred days" passed without any broadening of the RFC's authority.

Other considerations also influenced Roosevelt's decision to reject the USCM proposal. Although he espoused the expansion of national powers to combat the Depression, Roosevelt remained attached to some of the traditional principles of states' rights. He examined the subject of federal aid to cities from the angle of constitutional theory, and came to the verdict that since "municipalities are the creatures of State Legislatures, primary duty is on the state to see to their solvency." Sharing the Progressives' faith in greater home rule, Roosevelt maintained that "the less the Federal Government has to do with running a municipality in this country the better off we are going to be in the days to come." [83] If the Federal Government started to finance cities, he told the mayors, "it would give us some kind of obligation to see that they were run right. It would throw the Federal Government immediately into municipal politics and we would have to say that City A was beautifully run and that City B was terribly run and needed a new mayor." Unwilling to take on this responsibility, Roosevelt advised the mayors to seek help from their states.[84]

Disappointed but undeterred, the mayors renewed their lobbying efforts in Washington in the winter of 1934. They had a friend in FERA Administrator Hopkins. Looking for a way to enlarge the cities' capacity to handle the relief load, he urged the USCM to

prepare a study on the unification of all government credit. The
conference acted quickly, engaging the services of Simeon E. Leland,
a professor of political economy at the University of Chicago and a
well-known expert on public finance. Leland, an advocate of the
complete overhaul of the nation's revenue system, fashioned a
memorandum sharply critical of the existing public credit structure.
Federal and state-local fiscal policies were working at cross purposes
in the recovery drive: the national government was expanding its
expenditures while the other units were cutting back due to high
interest rates. A way had to be found "to integrate and coordinate
governmental fiscal policies." The already operating RFC could
assist in this job, but a new federal municipal finance corporation
would help even more. Organized to handle the short-term needs of
cities, the corporation could harmonize their borrowing with that of
the Federal Government; by assuming some supervisory functions it
would provide "an excellent opportunity to bring about desired
reforms in the financial administration and fiscal practices of
municipalities." Here was a good way "to eliminate the rather costly
and unorganized system used to market state and municipal
paper." [85] The Leland memorandum set off a flurry of discussions
between the USCM and Washington officials. "For the first time,"
Betters reported in February to his Executive Committee, "it
definitely appears that the Federal Government is giving real
consideration to the problems of municipal credit."

Using the Leland report as its model, a small *ad hoc* group headed
by Hopkins drafted a new memorandum in support of federal loans.
It observed that "had credit been available in any volume, the cities
could have played a much more responsible part financially in the
Civil Works program. This is true with regard to relief and to a lesser
extent with public works." On the basis of this experience, the
Federal Government could continue to ignore this matter only at its
own peril:

Failure to provide credit under conditions substantially similar to the credit
provided to all types of private enterprises will undoubtedly retard the

recovery program; if the municipal credit situation becomes more acute, it could well cause irreparable damage to the recovery program.

A National Municipal Bank, declared the group, might be the best setup for supplying the loans. Attempting to appease the economizers in the administration, they assured the President that the project would be self-liquidating.[86]

Although Hopkins's endorsement furnished the mayors with a sympathetic voice in government councils, Roosevelt relied more heavily on Treasury Secretary Morgenthau and RFC chairman Jesse H. Jones for advice on financial matters. Morgenthau, a balanced budget advocate who did not wish to set the government in competition with private capital, was generally hostile to the USCM proposal. He felt that with the expected pickup in the economy, the cities would soon find their normal credit channels open again.[87] Jones, usually eager to expand RFC's domain, also backed away. Entangled in his own fight for the authority to make direct loans to business and industry, he did not want to spread his resources over too wide an area. "The printing presses would have to roll" if the RFC had to service both business and localities, he warned. As concerned as any private banker about the safety of his loans, Jones also considered municipal paper a very poor investment. The RFC would be subjected "to all the pressures in the world," he predicted. "They get the loans first and repudiate them afterwards." [88] Like Morgenthau, Jones thought that "with recovery well under way, it should not be necessary for the United States Government to help municipalities in this manner." [89]

To appease the mayors, however, Morgenthau and Jones agreed to Leland's appointment as a special consultant to the Treasury. His assignment: to conduct a survey of municipal credit to determine if a crisis in the short-term market really existed. Leland sent out his questionnaires in early March 1934; by April he had accumulated enough data to file a preliminary opinion with Jones. "The need for federal assistance in this field is demonstrated by the facts already assembled," he wrote. "The banks are able to provide only 39 per

cent of county credit requirements and 53 per cent of the cities'."
But Jones, his mind made up, rejected this conclusion and announced that the cities would have to depend upon their regular
sources for credit.[90]

In one last hopeless gamble, the USCM decided to bring the
scheme directly to the floor of the Senate that May to force "a clear
test of whether the government was discriminating against municipalities in favor of private enterprise." Couzens attacked the measure
as a serious threat to the welfare of the Treasury and an unwise
intrusion into local affairs: "We will never educate communities or
make them rely upon themselves so long as the Government
unnecessarily comes to their support." Contending that the Federal
Government "cannot finance everybody," Majority Leader Joseph
Robinson (Ark.), whose state's numerous irrigation, drainage, and
levee districts had received assistance under the Emergency Farm
Mortgage Act of 1933, argued that the proposal would impose "an
appalling and impossible obligation on the Federal Government."
The amendment to the RFC bill, opposed by both the administration and the banking community, was buried under an avalanche of
conservative and loyal Democratic votes. Conceding defeat, the
USCM dropped the idea.

Over-all, the New Deal's permanent impression upon municipal
finances was only slight. While its spending helped tide the cities
over the Depression, it did not inflate the urban purse. The
Municipal Debt Adjustment Act had a very limited application;
rejection of the credit bank proposal left the cities, from La
Guardia's perspective, "at the mercy of the money lenders." Some
administration policies actually aggravated local fiscal problems.
Searching for new revenues to pay for a vastly enlarged federal
budget, the national government pre-empted certain areas of taxation, such as liquor levies, which municipalities wished to exploit.
Roosevelt also depressed the municipal bond market for a time by
launching a campaign to end the tax-exempt status of state and
municipal bonds; here, however, the cities, joined by the states,
successfully held their ground. Most observers agreed that if

municipalities continued to rely upon property taxes as their main source of funds, they faced eventual bankruptcy, even if prosperity returned. With their central areas decaying, the migration of affluent families to the suburbs growing, and assessment rates nearing their limits, the cities could anticipate an unhappy future. Only a redistribution of revenues and functions among the three levels of government appeared to offer a long-term solution.[91] Federal officials, including the President, knew of the problem, but their priorities were set by the immediate crises caused by the Depression.[92] The cities survived the 1930s but were not supplied with sufficient financial resources to cope successfully with the future.

VI

While the mayors in the 1930s focused their sights on federal aid to deal with emergency problems, other city groups used the economic crisis to secure a lasting national commitment to the improvement of the urban environment. Housing, which covered nearly 60 per cent of developed urban land and was one of the three basic requirements of life, provided the rallying point.

The problems of housing had both economic and social components. A sick industry for much of the 1920s, the home construction business came to a virtual standstill in the early 1930s. With nearly 30 per cent of the nation's jobless in the building trades, Roosevelt placed special importance upon reviving the housing sector. The establishment of the Federal Housing Administration (FHA) in 1934 reflected the New Deal's faith in private enterprise, as well as Roosevelt's belief that home ownership was one of the fundamental canons of the American way of life. Multifamily dwellings held little attraction for him; his ideal was the individual home surrounded by a small plot of ground. Finding a way to translate this dream into reality for the bottom third of the population became the main activity of the Central Housing Committee (CHC), a coordinating body Roosevelt created to formulate housing policy. But difficulties in perfecting prefabrication methods and devising a uniform na-

tional building code stymied the committee's work; these troubles
had yet to be solved when the approach of war gave defense housing
top priority. Neither home construction nor privately built low-cost
housing made much progress during the decade; yet if one-third of
the nation was not to remain ill-housed, the government would have
to play a new role.

America's slum districts had been a national disgrace for over a
century before the Federal Government began showing interest. The
urban housing supply had rarely kept up with the demand, high land
prices turned overcrowding into an economic necessity, and the
absence of local regulations allowed landlords to charge exorbitant
rents in substandard dwellings. The reformers of the Progressive era
struck some blows against the last two evils through exercise of the
municipal police power, but their regulatory legislation could not put
up the new houses that were so badly needed. Municipal and state
attempts to stimulate the construction of low-priced housing in the
1920s through tax abatements to limited-dividend corporations
barely got off the ground; with so many avenues for profitable
investment available, private capital found these publicly regulated
ventures most unattractive. Nor would investors be interested when
the Federal Government inaugurated a similar program in 1932 to
revive the dormant building industry. The Emergency Relief and
Construction Act authorized RFC loans to limited-dividend companies for low-cost housing, but the timidity of developers and legal
obstacles restricted aid to just two projects.[93]

Just as in the Hoover administration, low-cost housing found its
way onto the New Deal agenda by its inclusion in an omnibus piece
of legislation. The public works title of the National Industrial
Recovery Act of 1933 (NIRA) sanctioned the use of federal money
for an attack on slums. Under Ickes's close supervision, the PWA's
Housing Division, first, through loans to limited-divided corporations, and then, through direct government construction, started
pecking away at America's estimated six million substandard urban
dwellings. But pecking was all the Division could do. In five years, it
built fewer than 25,000 units. It was just a demonstration program,

not the long-range undertaking its sponsors had envisioned.[94] Several factors accounted for the Division's disappointing perform- ance. Administrative red tape and unfavorable court decisions hindered the pace of construction; as a result, its allotments suffered exceptionally deep cuts when Roosevelt transferred PWA funds to Hopkins's relief agencies. Compounding these operational complica- tions was Roosevelt's refusal to endorse public housing as an important part of his recovery drive. When he spoke of PWA "rebuilding the face of the country," he had "the face of nature" uppermost in his mind.[95] Even Ickes, who considered housing "one of the most worthwhile things that we are doing," confessed that "low cost housing activities constitute but one item in a broad, comprehensive program. It is an item that incidentally followed rather than preceded the other activities (for example, highways, bridges, dams) of the program." [96] More at ease visiting subsistence homesteads or the Resettlement Administration's suburban com- munities than the PWA's apartment house complexes, Roosevelt failed to defend the Housing Division from its enemies in the private sector. Having entered through the back door, public housing had, by the end of 1935, exhausted the New Deal's lukewarm hospitality.

But the friends of public housing did not give up. Provision for slum clearance in the NIRA had been the handiwork of Senator Robert F. Wagner and a small band of New York social workers and architects. The pacesetter for housing reform since the early days of Progressivism, New York had more run-down tenements than most cities had people. Indeed, the very size of the New York slum problem posed an obstacle to federal action; practically all the literature on the subject of dilapidated housing dealt with the mess in New York. Thus, while everyone knew about the horrors of the Lower East Side, there was scant public awareness that scores of other cities had their own pockets of shame. As long as New York dominated the housing movement to the exclusion of all other cities, the prospects for federal legislation remained slim. Here the PWA's Housing Division performed the indispensable service of creating a broader-based alliance. Through its publications and building activities, it threw a spotlight on the nationwide character of slums. Reaching down into communities of 10,000 people, the Division demonstrated that the shortage of decent housing was not restricted solely to the big cities. By 1937, thirty-one states, stirred into action by PWA's activities, passed legislation enabling their localities to cooperate with the federal housing program; this in turn put pressure on Washington to act.[97] State and local housing administrators joined forces to form the National Association of Housing Officials (NAHO), which, while not primarily a lobbying group, also drummed up support for a continuing federal commitment. Additional help came from organized labor. In its dual role of producer and consumer, the labor movement saw public housing as a way of providing both jobs and pleasant homes for its members. Backed by this coalition, Wagner, beginning in 1935, besieged Roosevelt for two years with requests for an endorsement of his plan for a permanent housing agency. Unsympathetic toward the PWA's rental policies, unwilling to expend the vast sums Wagner requested, and uneasy about invading an area reserved heretofore for private initiative, the President hesitated to place the legislation on his "must list." But Wagner's persistence finally paid off in 1937 when Roosevelt threw his support behind the proposal.[98]

Even with the White House's stamp of approval, the housing bill experienced some rough treatment in the Congress. Most of the controversy centered on the program's potential impact on private enterprise; echoing the views of real estate and home-building interests, some congressmen predicted that government construction would eventually drive private firms out of the housing field. The financial details of the measure also attracted attention as fiscal conservatives, at both ends of Pennsylvania Avenue, tried to reduce the cost to the Federal Government. They succeeded in cutting the money authorization in half, clamping a limit on building expenses, and requiring local contributions as a condition for federal aid.[99] The bill ran into further trouble from still another quarter—rural congressmen who feared that only large cities would profit from its enactment. At the very start of the Senate debate Wagner was asked to explain if "this bill isn't largely for the benefit of the big cities rather than for the general benefit of people throughout the United States." Time and time again, public housing's friends had to respond to charges that the program would "not be of the slightest service to the rural areas or towns or small cities," that it "would not apply to more than six, eight, or ten cities in the country." Wagner argued that the bill fully recognized rural housing problems and promised his colleagues that the new United States Housing Authority (USHA) would "attack poor housing wherever it existed." Holding Wagner to his pledge, critics pushed through an amendment preventing the expenditure of more than 10 per cent of USHA funds in any one state, a restriction specifically aimed at forestalling a "monopolization of grants" by New York City. With these modifications, the United States Housing Act of 1937 passed Congress by comfortable 4-1 (Senate) and 3-1 (House) margins.

Although rural reservations about the Wagner bill did not seriously threaten its approval by Congress, the New Deal could not afford to disregard these doubts in administering the new law. The measure's pump-priming features had been an important point in its favor; but if Congress ever tired of this activity public housing would be judged on its own merits as a piece of social legislation. To be ready for that day, the USHA had to develop a national constituency. Recognizing the problem, Roosevelt was cautious in choosing an administrator; most of the leading candidates came from New York, the spearhead of the drive for the bill. But the President felt, as he told Ickes, that "it would be bad if the country got the idea that a little group in New York was running housing." [100] In the end, however, Roosevelt chose a New Yorker, Nathan Straus, an old friend, to head the USHA. Straus fully understood the nature of his assignment and with Roosevelt's blessing tried to interest small cities in his agency's operations. Since the big cities were initially better prepared to submit the detailed applications required by USHA, they obtained most of the early grants; but within a short time, smaller communities, with USHA help, began applying for and receiving substantial allotments. While the large urban areas secured the bulk of the Authority's outlays, communities with populations under 25,000 accounted for over 25 per cent of the projects. Appearing before a House committee in 1938 to ask for additional funds, Straus proudly announced that "this is not a program that is working only in large cities—it is working out everywhere."

But as the New Deal sailed into a stormier political climate, buffeted by blasts from a growing conservative opposition, the USHA suffered particularly hard blows. In early 1939, seeing the dark clouds on the horizon, Straus attempted to move into farm housing. He drafted legislation that would increase USHA's spending authority by $800 million and set aside 25 per cent of this amount for single-unit farm dwellings. "We certainly do not subscribe to the principle," Straus declared before a House committee,

that slum conditions and the ill-housed poor are phenomena existing only in large metropolitan areas. Our assistance in attacking the low-rent housing problem is based not on the population or the urban or rural character of the applicant, but rather on the demonstrated need for assistance.

Soliciting votes for Straus's proposal, Roosevelt noted that the USHA's "first projects dealt with the most important and crying needs of the larger cities"; now, he went on, "we are ready to deal with the smaller cities in nearly every state." Despite these efforts to disassociate public housing from its big-city origins, the USHA measure did not survive the economizers' general counterattack against the New Deal's social welfare agencies. A minority of rural Democrats joined the nearly solid Republican bloc in the House to defeat the bill.[101] It would be another decade before Congress appropriated more money for public housing.[102]

As the war approached, all hope that the USHA's work could continue to make an important contribution to the fight on urban blight rapidly faded. Straus's scattergun strategy, a practical political maneuver, meant that the Authority's already scanty resources, $800 million for a task that could easily absorb billions, would not go very far in the big cities. Prospects for getting more remained bleak as long as banking, real estate, and construction groups continued to denounce the program as "socialistic." Limited in concept and strenuously resisted by powerful segments of the urban community, public housing could not serve as the vehicle for a significant federal drive to enhance the quality of city life. Nevertheless, the PWA-USHA program helped establish the principle of federal action in cities.

VII

The New Deal marked a new epoch in American urban history. Overlooked by the Constitution and ignored in a century-and-a-half of national legislation, the cities finally gained some recognition from Washington.[103] Federal authorities, having taken on vast unprecedented responsibility for the urban-centered economic crisis, came to the cities' aid as part of the national fight against the Great Depression. Each successive relief and recovery measure opened up new lines of communications between two levels of government that had not previously acknowledged the other's existence. The Federal Emergency Relief Administration, hastily put together in order to dampen the fires of civil disorders, adhered to custom and relied upon the states to distribute its largesse. But the later agencies—PWA, CWA, and especially WPA—worked directly with city governments in assisting the unemployed. As never before, municipal officials influenced the writing of federal laws and regulations and participated in the national decision-making process. With the passage of the Housing Act of 1937, federal-municipal ties were placed on a permanent, though not very secure or broad, foundation; there would be no turning back. "Municipalities in this country," Louis Brownlow observed, "are no longer mere political subdivisions of the several states. We are now entering upon a recognized new relation of the urban citizenry with the citizenry of the nation itself." [104]

Urban political leaders actively promoted this overhaul of American federalism. After months, and in some cases years, of fruitless appeals to their states for assistance, many mayors had reached the conclusion that state governments were nothing but "instruments of social stagnation insofar as the urban areas within their boundaries are concerned." [105] The rural domination and administrative stupor so characteristic of state capitals left the cities no choice but to seek help from another source: the Federal Government. Unsure at first how to respond to these extraordinary requests, the New Deal administration proved to be a comparatively generous benefactor. Praising Washington for its "sympathetic and informed approach to our problems," one mayor declared that "almost without exception, the cities have fared better, have been listened to more attentively, and have received more prompt action from the central government than they have from their own individual states." Mayoral pilgrimages to the city on the Potomac became as common as the old trip to the statehouse. A Southern mayor in 1934 aptly described the new arrangements: "Mayors are a familiar sight in Washington these days. Whether we like it or not, the destinies of our cities are clearly tied in with national politics."

The mayors' identification with national politics represented a dramatic reversal in municipal attitudes. Progressive reform had tried to divorce local issues from state and federal politics. In rejecting the Progressives' faith in expanded home rule, the mayors also released municipal governments from quarantine. Cities, along with farmers, businessmen, and workers, would now have a big stake in what happened in Washington. But success in the national political arena would necessarily depend upon a group's ability to apply continuous pressure on the executive and legislative branches, an ability subject to fragmentation and dissipation unless organized. Numerous civic associations and public official leagues had developed prior to 1932. All, however, eschewed lobbying on the national level. Not until a new breed of reformers, men like Murphy and La Guardia, came into office, did urban areas acquire an effective voice at the nation's capital. From the perspective of political scientist Leonard D. White, 1933 ranked as "the most eventful [year] for municipal affairs in the twentieth century" and its most significant product was "the rapid growth of the corporate consciousness and corporate organization of the cities themselves." With the creation of the United States Conference of Mayors, White wrote, "American cities, for the first time, put themselves in a position to act collectively, and to act decisively." [106]

The harsh realities of economic and political life in the 1930s aided the mayors' efforts to nurture an urban consciousness in national circles. As much as Roosevelt would have preferred to believe otherwise, he learned that the Depression could not be beaten solely, or even primarily, by remedial farm legislation. America would not be prosperous again until its factories were returned to full use, its lines of commerce revived, and its city people restored to productive labor; the cries of the urban unemployed for food, clothing, and shelter would be dismissed only at grave peril to domestic tranquility and Roosevelt's lease on the White House. Ever since the Bryan debacle of 1896, the Democrats had been the minority party; to a large extent, they enjoyed this unenviable station because their Southern, agrarian image held little attraction for the urban voter. Al Smith had made momentous inroads in the cities in 1928 and Roosevelt did even better in 1932, but Smith was an atypical Democratic candidate, and 1932 was not a normal election year. Roosevelt might dream of moving the masses of urbanites back to the land, but he was too much of a politician to allow himself to be crucified upon a cross of corn. Only deeds, not mere words, would permit the gentleman farmer from Dutchess County, New York, to maintain his urban following. And it was deeds that he gave them: relief monies poured into the cities, accompanied by important patronage posts for the various urban ethnic groups. The city electorate repaid Roosevelt handsomely. Attempting to explain the wildly enthusiastic welcome Roosevelt received in Chicago during the 1936 campaign, journalist Arthur Krock noted that his administration "was coeval with the city's

comeback from the deepest gulf in which the depression plunged any community, with the exception of Detroit. . . . Under Roosevelt, Washing-

ton began to relieve cities in Chicago's general condition which had
discovered the difficulties of self-sustenance in such times. Chicago still has
relief problems, slums, poverty and great groups of the unemployed. But the
difference between present conditions and those in 1932 is the difference
between black and white.

The President, Krock predicted, "will sweep the city." [107] Sweep it he
did, along with every other big metropolis in the country.[108]

Roosevelt's pursuit of the urban vote may have turned national
politics upside down, but it left the physical contours of the urban
environment much the same. The President achieved his electoral
success not by showing concern for city life, per se, but by catering
to the demands of the numerous interest groups that comprised the
urban population. His program was urban only in the sense that it
assisted people who lived in cities: guarantees of collective bargaining for the organized; work relief for the jobless; public housing
for the slum resident; judgeships for the immigrant blocs. None of
these programs represented a deliberate attempt to remake the cities
as the Rural Electrification Administration, the Resettlement Administration, and the Tennessee Valley Authority changed the face
of the countryside. The demands of the fight against the Depression
and the dictates of good politics set the boundaries of executive
leadership in the urban field; when fundamental reforms, such as a
municipal credit bank were suggested, Roosevelt had them pigeon-
holed. He was interested in the city dweller, not the city.[109]

But if Roosevelt did not look beyond the latest unemployment
figures in determining the Federal Government's commitment to
help the cities, few urbanites did either. Except for some social
scientists who comprehended the nation's stake in balanced, well-
planned metropolitan development,[110] little thought was given in the
1930s to the federal role in urban affairs in the post-Depression era.
Only the mayors claimed to speak for the cities and they viewed the
future through narrow-lensed glasses. Their prime concern was
finding enough money to keep municipal governments running; like

so many other groups in this period, they lobbied for federal subsidies and credit so they could hold on to their jobs. Constantly scurrying around trying to gain more federal relief funds to close gaps in budgets, the mayors had little time left to consider the non-Depression problems—traffic-choked streets, spreading blight, polluted air, and so forth—that plagued their cities or how the national authorities might aid in solving them. Social workers, backed up by the labor movement, had successfully pinpointed slum clearance as a legitimate area for federal action, but by 1940 the public housing program was virtually dead. Rural opposition contributed conspicuously to its demise, but just as important was the heavy barrage of criticism laid down by urban-based groups. Powerful real estate, banking, and construction lobbies, worried about rising federal expenditures and taxes and further infringements upon private enterprise, were not at all happy with the new federal-city partnership. Chanting the slogans of home rule, states' rights, and individual initiative, they used their influence in Washington to clamp down on the New Deal after 1937. Until these groups could be co-opted, or their strength neutralized, federal involvement in the cities would remain marginal.

The New Deal rescued local government from financial ruin and revolutionized federal-municipal relations but never came to grips with the city as an economic and social entity. In 1931, one city manager had observed: "Search the traditional administrative organization at the National Capital, and you will not find that coordinating national agency which recognizes or deals with the problems of urban dwellers, two-thirds of our population." Six years later, with the New Deal at high tide, little had changed. "Where," asked this same city manager in 1937, "is the department, or bureau, or even division or section, in the Federal Government which systematically or even casually undertakes to study the daily problems which face the cities and the people who live in them? Where is there being developed a policy or program which thinks in terms of cities on a national scale?" [111] The Roosevelt Presidency, if not intentionally then at least by necessity, transformed the urban political universe, but American ideology and federal bureaucratic structure lagged far behind. It would be decades before they would catch up.

3

Preparing for an
Urban Future: 1933–43

[The city] has not been adequately recognized by Government, nor has the citizenry become fully aware that the urbanization of the Nation calls for explicit consideration of the city as an entity. Compared to the attention that has been devoted to agriculture and the rural phases of American life, that part of America which is symbolized by the city has been almost completely neglected and has never fully emerged into our national consciousness.

Our Cities (1937)

"In a liberal democracy," the historian Robert Bremner has observed, "it is literally true that the first step toward the achievement of reform is the exploration of and diffusion of knowledge about the realities of the prevailing situation." The New Deal had rushed to the cities' rescue because the manifestations of their distress—long bread lines, payless paydays, mortgage foreclosures—were too prominent to be ignored. But since economic crisis, and not any particularly keen understanding of the urban condition, had galvanized the Federal Government into action, Washington's response was circumscribed. Federal-municipal contacts were the product of the relief and recovery stages of the New Deal. Significant changes in federal perception of urban needs would have to await the accumulation of extensive information about city life. Beginning steps in that compilation were taken in the 1930s.

I

Federal data-collecting on the cities can be traced back to the formative days of the Republic, but these early efforts failed to employ explicit definitions differentiating between urban and rural areas. While each decennial census conducted during the ninety years after the ratification of the Constitution counted the people living within cities, there was no provision for the uniform reporting of this information. Summarizing the results of the Seventh Census (1850) for Congress in 1854, the well-known magazine editor, J. D. B. De Bow, wrote:[1]

The Census does not furnish material for separating the urban and rural population of the United States so as to admit of a statement showing the extent of either. . . . So imperfect is the Census of 1850 in this respect that hundreds of important towns and cities in all parts of the country, and especially in the South and West, are not even distinguished in the returns from the body of the counties in which they are situated, and therefore their population cannot be ascertained at all. . . . But what is of more importance and the greatest cause of embarrassment is the fact that in New England and the Northern States, what are returned as cities and towns often include whole rural districts.

These "imperfections" and "embarrassments" reappeared in the 1860 and 1870 enumerations.

As the Tenth Census (1880) approached, demands for reform of the decennial count were strong. The American society was being transformed by the Industrial Revolution, and entrepreneurs moving into new fields of economic activity needed more information on which to make their investments. Politicians and social leaders found themselves in the market for more concrete data to help evaluate the changes in their constituencies and society as a whole. In addition, the burst of patriotism generated by the centennial celebration of the signing of the Declaration of Independence spurred interest in a comprehensive self-portrait of the nation. Generally regarded as "the first modern census of the United States," the 1880 enumeration was a landmark both in the range of subjects covered and the sophistication of administrative machinery used to carry it out.[2]

This modernization of the census proved to be a boon to the collection of urban statistics. During the period 1860–80 cities had a population growth rate twice that of the nation as a whole and had started to solidify their dominance of the economic and social life of the country. These developments dismayed many observers of the American scene, but few could deny the necessity of studying the urbanization phenomenon. The men in charge of the 1880 Census rose to the challenge:[3]

The fact [the Superintendent declared] that such vast numbers are brought within limited areas not only offers an opportunity for pursuing statistical inquiries which it would be difficult if not impossible to extend over the whole country, but it also creates a legitimate demand for additional information respecting such communities, inasmuch as they are, by the nature of city life, made subject to vital conditions widely different from those of the population generally.

For the first time, the census attempted to define a "city" and differentiate between urban and rural regions. All incorporated communities with more than 8,000 people were placed in the urban category; by this standard, 22.5 per cent of the 1880 population was classified as urban.[4] In addition, the census published a two-volume, 1758-page work called *Social Statistics of Cities*, which presented running descriptions and some detailed data on the topography, history, physical layout, cultural facilities, transportation facilities, manufacturing facilities and governmental services of the 222 cities with over 10,000 people.

The last decade of the nineteenth century saw further expansion by the Federal Government into the area of information-gathering on urban areas. In 1892, Congress, reacting to organized labor's complaints about the influx of low-paid immigrants and the increasing national recognition of the extent of inadequate housing, authorized the commissioner of Labor to conduct a special investigation into slum areas in cities of 200,000 people or more. Unfortunately, the sum appropriated for this task, $20,000, proved sufficient to cover only four of the sixteen cities meeting the population criteria. The careful house-to-house survey unveiled little in the way of startling new facts; moreover, compared to the popular journalistic accounts of decrepit working-class neighborhoods, *The Slums of Baltimore, Chicago, New York, and Philadelphia* (1894) made for extremely dull reading. Nor did Congress take action upon the commissioner's finding of a positive correlation between slums and high rates of crime and illiteracy. But if the slum study joined scores of other congressionally financed reports consigned to the legislative waste bin, Congress was willing to compile data for the use of others. In 1898 the legislature instructed the Department of Labor to publish annually the official statistics of cities in such areas as public utilities, schools and libraries, police and fire, and government finances. This step was in response to the pleas of the municipal reform movement, which had gained strength in the cities in the 1890s. Led by businessmen, these "good government" groups emphasized the need for reliable, up-to-date information on their own cities and on others as well; the exchange of data among municipalities was viewed as crucial to the operation of efficient local government.[5] With the establishment of a permanent Bureau of the Census in 1902, that agency assumed responsibility for providing this service.

Additional refinements in federal handling of urban statistics came with the Thirteenth Census (1910). Back in 1880 the editor of the census volumes on *Social Statistics*, in analyzing the City of New York, had called attention to the regional ramifications of the existence of a metropolis, indicating that it seemed

proper, in treating of the vast population occupying the cities of New York, Brooklyn, Jersey City, Newark, and Hoboken, to consider them not only as constituting five different municipalities, but as one great metropolitan community. This population has grown from one nucleus . . . and its separation into different civil divisions is by physical and political lines, which have had little influence on the character of the people, their industries, or their modes of life.

For these reasons he decided to consolidate the data on the various cities under "the one head of 'The Metropolis' which they constitute." [6] But the census did not fully come to grips with this developing nationwide phenomenon until 1910, when it created the new urban categories of "suburb" and "metropolitan district" to account for the extension of influence of the large cities over their hinterland regions. Twenty-five "metropolitan districts" were identified, ranging from New York, with a total area of 616,927 acres and a population of 6,474,568 to Portland, Oregon, with 43,538 acres and 215,048 residents. [7]

The 1910 enumeration, with the introduction of the census tract, began turning a microscope on the city. First used in a population study of New York City sponsored by the Federation of Churches in 1906, the census tract was "a small, permanently established, geographical area with about 4,000 people laid out with attention to achieving some uniformity of population characteristics, economic status, and living conditions." Municipal governments, which were required to pay some of the costs of compiling census-tract data, could now get a better picture of life within the different neighborhoods of the city and could trace the improvement or deterioration of these areas over time. Eight cities participated in the program in 1910; by 1930, eighteen cities with 17 per cent of the nation's population were census tracted. [8]

The Thirteenth Census also marked the initial employment of separate urban and rural tables for the presentation of significant data. Previously, the census just listed all urban places, indicated their total populations, and noted the rising proportion of people living in cities. With the 1910 count the Bureau of the Census broke down its gross figures in such fields as vital statistics, nativity, and education, in order to make comparisons between urban and rural regions, and among urban areas. "Fundamental differences in industrial and social life between cities and rural districts," the bureau explained,[9]

result in marked differences in the composition and characteristics of the population. In many cases it is impossible to understand the differences between States or sections of the country with respect to population statistics except by taking account of this distinction between urban and rural communities.

These observations took on added significance in 1920 when the Fourteenth Census announced that 51.4 per cent of the nation's population was now classified as urban.

Yet as the data of the decennial census provided increasing recognition of the city, the other urban services of the Census Bureau declined. In 1906 the director of the bureau, taking note of the growing concentration of people in urban centers, wrote that "the problem of self-government is therefore becoming one of city government, and no class of statistics is of such vital importance as that relating to cities." But budget cuts and a preoccupation with municipal financial data led to the demise in 1917 of the bureau's series on the "general statistics of cities," which had been inaugurated by the Department of Labor in 1898. No longer did municipalities have ready access to information on what other cities were doing about such problems as street lighting, sewage, food and milk inspection, or water supply. Official figures on suburban transportation, which had been collected as early as 1890, were not available in 1920 even though this type of intrametropolitan travel had jumped tremendously during the intervening thirty years. The bureau's compilation of municipal financial statistics greatly encouraged the adoption by the various cities of uniform accounting procedures. But even in this field the range of federal coverage dropped from 544 cities in 1903 to 94 cities in 1932. At the very time that urbanites achieved numerical supremacy in American society, special federal studies of city life were actually decreasing.[10]

The failure of federally collected statistics to convey a complete picture of urban civilization was particularly disturbing to the city planning movement that emerged in the first two decades of the twentieth century. Important civic leaders had been converted to the view that conscious, rational control of the urban environment was necessary both for a beautiful city and a healthy city. But well-conceived, comprehensive city plans, they argued, had to rest upon a bedrock of extensive, accurate, and current information on all facets of the urban condition. Since most cities lacked the resources or experience to compile the required data, a number of people interested in municipal improvement looked to the Federal Government for help. The first meeting of the National Conference on City Planning, held in 1909, heard repeated appeals for a federally conducted civic census that would provide the framework for local planning studies.

The National Conference served as the center of agitation for greater federal scrutiny of the urban scene for the next ten years. Addressing the 1911 session, Philip Kates, a Tulsa, Oklahoma attorney, expounded a theme that would have even greater relevance in the 1930s. The problems of the city, he declared, were due to the inability "to coordinate properly the industrial system with the city itself." Municipal fiscal and social troubles could be directly attributed to the malfunctioning of the economy; taking issue with most of the "good government" reformers, Kates claimed that the city "is essentially an industrial, not a political problem." Therefore, he continued, "the city problem is a national problem, in the same sense that agriculture is a national problem." Amelioration of urban ills required an exhaustive investigation of the industrial system and its effects on cities, which only the Federal Government was capable of undertaking. The following year, in a magazine article, Kates urged the establishment of a federal department of municipalities to gather information on municipal conditions throughout the world. Reflecting the Progressives' faith that with knowledge came advance, Kates felt that this new agency would provide the facts to help municipalities adjust themselves to the new industrial society.

Thus, while each city would retain primary responsibility for its own destiny, federal assistance, through the use of its data-collecting facilities, was seen as essential to urban redemption.[11]

Similar views from a different perspective came at the 1916 conference from George E. Hooker, secretary of the Chicago City Club. Citing the costs of congestion and poor transportation as evidence of the harmful effects of uncontrolled urban development on the nation's social and economic life, Hooker contended that good city planning was of "such national scope and importance" as to demand "national legislation, administrative machinery, and educational effort." Pointing to the encouragement offered local planning in Great Britain by the Town Planning Act of 1909, he announced that "the time has come for the Federal Government—through the Interior Department or some other branch—to consider city planning a national matter" and to begin an expert inquiry into the procedures and goals of city planning. "City planning problems raise national issues which demand national attention," he concluded.[12]

The Kates and Hooker proposals demonstrated the limits of Progressive reform. Neither scheme contemplated national action beyond research and data-collection. The idea of enlisting federal financial aid for a direct attack on city slums, inadequate community facilities, or pollution never came up for discussion at meetings of the National Municipal League and the National Conference on City Planning. Not even the relatively successful, albeit small, town-building program of the United States Housing Corporation during World War I could shake the Progressives' strong feeling that, aside from providing technical services, the Federal Government had no useful function to perform in urban areas. Leading architects and social reformers, such as Frederick Law Olmsted, Jr. and Robert W. De Forest, did protest the sale of USHC projects before their innovative features—curvilinear street patterns, the row house, and balanced residential neighborhoods—could be completed and evaluated, but they did not ask that any new ventures be started. Their plans, made public in 1919, for a federal agency to deal with "housing, town planning, and other municipal affairs" restricted the Federal Government to a service role: encouraging research and disseminating information.[13]

These requests for expanded federal technical assistance received a sympathetic response from the Republican secretary of Commerce (1921–28), Herbert Hoover. Eager to widen the sphere of his agency's operations, Hoover gladly increased the department's aids to municipal government. The Bureau of Standards worked with local officials in setting up purchasing criteria; the Coast and Geodetic Survey supplied municipal engineers with some of the basic data required for their public improvements projects; the Advisory Committee on Building Codes and the National Conference on Street and Highway Safety helped draft uniform municipal ordinances in these two important areas of local administration. "Taken as a whole," one student of federal-municipal relations observed in 1931, "the services rendered by the Department of Commerce to cities are greater in number and more varied in scope than of any other department." [14]

Indicative of Hoover's attentiveness to urban affairs was his appointment, in 1921, of an Advisory Committee on City Planning and Zoning. The techniques of zoning had first been applied in German cities as early as 1900, but it was not until New York's adoption of a zoning law for the entire city in 1916 that the idea really caught on in this country. By 1921, 48 cities with nearly eleven million people had passed zoning statutes, and many more municipalities were preparing to follow suit. Recognizing the need to give direction to this burgeoning movement, Hoover created his Advisory Committee to write a model state enabling act under which cities could adopt zoning regulations.[15]

Secretary Hoover's attempts to make his department of greater use to municipal government raised the hopes of those seeking a more systematic federal approach to urban needs. By his very success in making the Commerce Department an important aid to local administration, Hoover inspired demands for a single federal bureau to handle all municipal contacts in Washington. Dozens of existing agencies scattered throughout the federal organizational charts, from the Food and Drug Administration to the Bureau of Investigation to the Office of Education, operated in urban areas, but none acknowledged the city as a distinct entity or dealt with urban society on its own terms. Even the Department of Commerce, which the *American City* described, in 1927, as "now performing many functions of a Federal Bureau of Municipalities," had primary interests far removed from the promotion of a healthy urban environment. Establishment of just such a bureau, which would "perform for cities services somewhat analogous to those performed for rural sections by the Department of Agriculture," had long been the goal of that magazine's influential publisher, Harold S. Buttenheim. Working with Louis Brownlow, then chairman of the board of commissioners of the District of Columbia, Buttenheim had tried to win President Wilson's approval for a plan to have the Commerce Department set up a clearinghouse for federal information on urban life. Nothing came of this effort or of subsequent attempts to interest Presidents Coolidge and Hoover in the proposal.[16]

Although President Hoover declined to grant the urban economy the same governmental recognition accorded the rural economy, he did sponsor a wide-ranging study of American society that picked out the metropolis for some special consideration. Perceiving the "sprawl of great cities" as one of the significant developments of the first third of the twentieth century, the President's Research Committee on Social Trends, in 1930, commissioned an investigation of "the metropolitan community." This project, assigned to University of Michigan sociologist Roderick D. McKenzie, sought to show "some of the basic changes that have taken place in American cities since the advent of motor transportation."

The designation of McKenzie marked the coming of age of the new academic discipline of urban sociology. Before 1915, the examination of the city had been the almost exclusive domain of the newspaper reporter in search of sensational headlines, the housing reformer uncovering the horrors of the tenement, the settlement worker seeking to understand the poor, and the rural-minded moral crusader who associated urbanization with the decline of civilization. But that year saw the publication of Robert E. Park's seminal article "The City: Suggestions for the Investigation of Human Behavior in the City Environment." A member of the small, but vibrant, sociology department at the University of Chicago, Park viewed the city as an ideal "laboratory in which human nature and social processes may be conveniently and profitably studied." Interested in constructing a theory of urban life, he sent his graduate students out to discover the character and origins of slums, ethnic colonies, suburban dormitories, and other types of neighborhoods: Park's only admonition to them was that they approach their subject with "the same objectivity and detachment with which the zoologist dissects a potato bug." [17] Using Chicago as their workroom, his students explored such topics as the gang, the ghetto, the hobo, and the "gold coast." The first fruits of Park's endeavors appeared in 1925 when the American Sociological Society, of which he was president, devoted its annual meeting to "The Urban Community." One of Park's early protégés, McKenzie contributed a paper to that conference and joined in the writing of the Chicago School's influential introduction to urban sociology, *The City* (1925).

McKenzie's volume on *The Metropolitan Community* (1933) for the President's Research Committee on Social Trends reflected his professional training. Applying the concept of human ecology he had developed under Park, McKenzie reported that it was the "disturbing" introduction of the automobile that had exerted "the most potent force" since 1900 in causing the redistribution of America's population and the social disorganization of America's cities. The centrifugal drift of people away from central city areas, he wrote, had given rise to a whole host of problems: blight, overloaded public facilities, insufficient tax resources, haphazard suburban building, to name but a few. But having identified the nature and sources of the urban problem, McKenzie stopped short of suggesting remedies. His task, as laid down by Park and the Research Committee itself, was to describe and explain, not to prescribe cures. A valuable addition to the growing literature on urban America,

McKenzie's work found few readers outside the community of scholars.

The Research Committee's own short review of the metropolis added nothing to the public's appreciation of the urban complex as an issue of national concern. Instead of focusing attention on the city as a center of significant social change and a breeding ground of social problems, the committee restricted itself to the popular question of "whether the larger cities are becoming too crowded to be comfortable or economical." Drawing upon McKenzie's work, the committee concluded that the future size of our cities would be determined not so much by conscious planning as by "powerful economic factors and business policies." [18] From this perspective, the city would always be a tail to the economic kite; the formulation of an urban policy appeared to be out of the question.

III

Ironically, it was the malfunctioning of the economy in the 1930s that led to greater federal understanding of the cities' role in the life of the nation. In the course of mobilizing the country's resources to combat the Great Depression, the New Deal opened up several new types of federal fact-gathering enterprises. Both as a job-creating venture and as a helpful guide in setting policy and allocating funds, the proliferating alphabetical agencies in Washington found it extremely useful to collect information concerning cities. FERA and WPA established research and statistical divisions to study the unemployment situation; FHA launched broad surveys of the housing market and local economic conditions; RA examined population, industrial, and commercial trends in one hundred of the largest urban areas to determine the best sites for its suburban resettlement projects. Sometimes the new data created demands for federal legislation to ameliorate a previously unexposed problem. The CWA-conducted Real Property Inventory provided the nation with its first good look at the deplorable state of housing in the big

cities and helped consolidate support behind public housing proposals. But the most important investigation of urban society emerged
from the activities of the National Resources Board.

An outgrowth of Roosevelt's passion for planning, the NRB could
trace its ancestry directly back to the pump-priming phase of the
New Deal. Seeking advice on the operation of the new Public Works
Administration, Administrator Harold L. Ickes appointed a three-
member National Planning Board in July 1933 to promote and
coordinate public works planning. Before passing out of existence
ten years later, after three reorganizations and name changes, the
board ranked as the federal agency most interested in urban affairs.
As so often happens, the board's extensive knowledge of city
conditions was more the product of circumstance than of design.
Since city planning afforded the nation's only extended experience in
conscious public control of development, Ickes turned to those
familiar with these efforts for assistance with his more ambitious
endeavors.

Few could match the planning credentials of the man Ickes
selected for chairman, Frederic A. Delano. Uncle of the President,
Delano had helped "change the face of three great American cities."
He first became interested in urban design in the early 1900s when as
president of the Wabash Railroad he tried unsuccessfully to
consolidate the widely scattered railway terminals in Chicago. This
failure led him to promote actively Daniel Burnham's "Plan for
Chicago," a grand scheme to reshape the Windy City. After seeing
this project through its formative stages, Delano moved to New
York, where, beginning in 1921, he guided the work of the
pathsetting Committee on the Regional Plan of New York and Its
Environs. Later in the decade, as president of the American Civic
Association, a citizens' group devoted to conservation, Delano won
congressional approval for a National Capital Parks and Planning
Commission for the Federal City. His chairmanship of the commis-
sion in 1933 made him a logical choice to head the new National
Planning Board. Delano brought along Charles W. Eliot, 2nd, the

NCPPC's director, to serve as the board's executive officer. A professional landscape architect, Eliot complemented the amateur Delano's concern for an improved environment.[19]

Charles E. Merriam, another member of the board, contributed a different kind of urban expertise. Professor of political science at the University of Chicago and a leading authority on public administration, Merriam was also a scarred veteran of Chicago's political wars. Perhaps even more than Woodrow Wilson, Merriam managed to get "political science off the dusty shelves of the chroniclers and the analysts and out of the closets of the theorists by bringing about a synthesis of history, theory and experimental application which justifies the otherwise presumptuous name political 'science.' " [20] In contrast to Wilson, however, he experienced great frustration at the ballot box. Merriam represented the Hyde Park ward on the City Council for six years, but in 1911, and again in 1919, he lost hotly contested races for mayor; after the second defeat he gave up his political career. Merriam would gain prominence through his writings, his organizational activities, and by appointments to public positions. A founder of both the Social Science Research Council and the Public Administration Clearing House, Merriam also served as vice-chairman of Hoover's Research Committee on Social Trends.[21]

Brought up in rural Iowa, Merriam established himself as one of the foremost champions of the urban way of life. Indeed, the very intellectual-cultural deprivations of his childhood helped develop within him an "emphatic sense of the color and sophistication" of the great metropolis.[22] While some observers interpreted the long breadlines of the early 1930s as a sign that the day of the city had passed, Merriam's faith in the future of urban communities never faltered. "The trouble with Lot's wife," he told the United States Conference of Mayors in 1934, "was that she looked backward and saw Sodom and Gomorrah. If she had looked forward, she would have seen that heaven is also pictured as a city." Merriam also refused to let personal political disappointments deter him from defending municipal government against constant, and often unfair, charges of corruption and inefficiency. Claiming that cities had made greater advances than states or rural areas in improving the conduct of government, he urged that each of the nation's largest cities be given independent statehood, and thus be freed from the negative influence of state-rural control.[23]

Merriam's espousal of the city-state plan also fit in with his plea that the Federal Government pay more attention to urban problems. Sooner than most, he recognized that the ills besetting urban America transcended municipal boundaries. Statehood for cities, Merriam believed, would facilitate direct federal-city relations and hasten federal appreciation of urban requirements. For similar reasons he encouraged the formation of the American Municipal Association and the Conference of Mayors as urban lobbying groups. They were needed because the cities were "lagging behind agriculture and commerce in asking the national government for assistance." It would not be long, Merriam predicted somewhat overoptimistically to the AMA in 1931, before the cities became the "dominant political force in the country." According to Merriam, no matter whether it be the economy, government, or social trends, "as the cities go, so goes the nation." With Charles Merriam in its councils, the Resources Board could scarcely ignore the cities.[24]

The cities would, however, have to wait their turn. The board's first task was to provide guidelines for the vast public works program. Its *Final Report* issued in June 1934, emphasized physical design, although in a section entitled "A Plan for Planning," the board acknowledged the need for social and economic research as an essential tool for intelligent planning. But any ideas the board might have entertained about initiating such a project were shelved when it received a new mandate from the President that summer. Reconstituting the NPB as an interdepartmental unit, the National Resources Board (NRB), Roosevelt instructed the board to prepare an inventory of the nation's land, water, and mineral assets. Completion of this assignment in late 1934 freed the board to consider the human element in the term "national resources," and thus, under Merriam's constant prodding, the board began to examine the more elusive social, economic, and political aspects of central planning. Areas of investigation included the structure of American industry, personal consumption patterns, technological advances, population changes, research as a national resource, and regionalism. As part of this sweeping look at American life, the board inaugurated a study of "the role of the urban community in the national economy."

The suggestion that the board study urban communities seems to have originated with Merriam.[25] Long an advocate of projecting urban problems onto the national scene, he seized upon the unemployment crisis in the cities—and its implications for national planning—as a vehicle for an NRB-conducted analysis of urban life. The focus of the inquiry would be economic: how did the concentration of population in urban centers affect the operation of the economy? How did the economy influence city development? Merriam hoped there would emerge from this investigation "a sound national policy regarding the place of the urban community in the American national economy." Picking up endorsements from the AMA and USCM for his study of "the national aspects of city planning," Merriam presented the proposal to the NRB in January 1935 and won its preliminary approval.[26]

Organizational problems, a constant nuisance over the two-year lifespan of the project, hampered work from the very start. Following the board's usual practice, Merriam attempted to find someone from outside the NRB staff to draw up a detailed program of research. A month of fruitless hunting left Merriam on the brink of dropping the whole scheme. "Our study of urbanism droops and lags," he wrote dejectedly. "After trying three or four people . . . and after repeated consultations with various groups I found no one willing to take the laboring oar." [27] Rather than give it up, however, Merriam assumed the job himself. By June he had completed the outline and recruited a distinguished Research Committee on Urbanism to direct the enterprise and make a report to the NRB.

Merriam's prospectus marked out five major lines of inquiry. The first involved an inventory of urban physical, social, and economic conditions, comparable to that already put together by the NRB for the nation's natural resources. Next, Merriam proposed an examination of emerging trends in urbanization; what kind of shape would the urban future take? From these studies, he expected to identify outstanding problems and to ferret out the underlying causes of urban distress. Lastly, Merriam wanted to develop proposals for remedying these deficiencies. Upon this foundation, he believed, the Federal Government could then go ahead and formulate an urban policy.[28]

The composition of the Urbanism Committee showed Merriam's preference for expert technicians. None of the members carried any weight in the political arena; their fame, usually restricted to professional circles, rested upon administrative or scholarly accomplishments. The chairman, C. A. Dykstra, city manager of Cincinnati, was ranked at the top of his craft, having won great acclaim for his excellent job of steering the "Queen City" through the darkest days of the Depression. He was also among the first municipal leaders to urge federal relief aid for cities. Louis Brownlow, a former city manager and presently director of the Public Administration Clearing House, would soon take charge of Roosevelt's committee to realign the federal bureaucracy. Still another administrator, Harold D. Smith, director of the Michigan Municipal League and president of the American Municipal Association, was also invited to join the urbanism group. The city planners were represented by Professor Arthur C. Comey of Harvard and Charles W. Eliot, 2nd, of the NRB. Interestingly, despite the economic focus of the report, only one economist, Carter Goodrich, then concluding a study of industrial migration, was included on the committee.[29] From the field of sociology, Merriam recruited the highly respected University of Chicago urbanist, Louis Wirth. So that rural problems and interests might receive appropriate attention during the committee's work, the NRB invited M. L. Wilson, the undersecretary of Agriculture and a strong supporter of subsistence homesteads, to participate.[30] To handle its day-to-day operations, the committee appointed city planner Ladislas Segoe as director.

The committee assembled a small staff, based in Cincinnati, to coordinate the research, most of which was assigned to outside contributors. These special studies closely followed the list of topics suggested by Merriam and covered a broad spectrum of urban life. In the economic sphere, monographs were prepared on the relation of industrial location and transportation to urbanization, the business structure of urban communities, and the influence of municipal land policies on urban development. Two investigations were authorized in the field of city planning: one to examine the experiences of 144 planned communities, the other to deal with the methods to be employed in drafting comprehensive plans. Reports on municipal administration included analyses of trends in urban government, associations of cities, and federal-municipal relations. Wirth set his doctoral candidates to work on drawing a composite picture of urban social conditions; they amassed data on jobs, incomes, standards of living, education, public safety, recreation, communications, religious life, and many other features of the cityscape. Together, these studies would "offer strategic approaches to the understanding and . . . correction of defects and prevention of breakdown in the urban world." [31]

External criticism and internal bickering hampered the Urbanism Committee's work. As in most Resources Board endeavors, the old, established agencies, in this case the Central Statistical Board (CSB) and the Bureau of the Census, resented the intrusion of the NRB into their areas and tried to restrict its activities. The CSB and the bureau objected to the detailed questionnaires the Urbanism Committee sent to city governments around the country, claiming that these duplicated their own efforts and would endanger future local cooperation with the permanent agencies of the national government. Contention also marked the committee's own business. Complaints of bureaucratic red tape and boondoggling were freely exchanged between the committee's staff in Cincinnati and Chicago and the board's headquarters in Washington. [32] Functioning only intermittently, the Urbanism Committee could not maintain firm control over the project; consequently, it did not meet its original goal of a summer 1936 report. Only Merriam's steadying and dominating presence allowed the committee to finish its task.[33]

Anxious to demonstrate some signs of progress, the Resources Board, in April 1936, instructed the Urbanism Committee to prepare an interim report. Within a month the staff drafted a paper on the subject it knew best: the failure of the Federal Government to collect the basic facts about urban society. Indeed, the very lack of information severely hampered the committee in its own researches. To remedy this deficiency, the staff report offered a detailed 116-page description of the material that should be gathered in an expanded system of urban inquiry. This job would best be carried out, the authors advised, by a new Federal Bureau of Urban Affairs. Besides fact-collecting, this bureau "might also appraise and evaluate the conditions and progress of urban life and the success or failure of policies designed to deal with urban problems." [34] The staff knew this recommendation was controversial, as there was a movement underway in Washington to consolidate government agencies and to curb the creation of new ones.[35] They were not surprised, therefore, when the Resources Board, while accepting their indictment of past federal efforts in this field, ordered the deletion of any reference to the new urban bureau. Wishing to avoid any further confrontations with the Central Statistical Board, the Resources Board took the "sting" out of the discussion of the CSB's activities and stressed that the CSB should be given the coordinating mission envisioned for the Bureau of Urban Affairs.[36]

Distributed in mimeograph form to a limited audience, the "Interim Report" helped lead to the establishment, in late 1936, of a Municipal Reference Library and Information Service in the Census Bureau. This service, set up at the Resources Board's instigation and funded through the WPA writers project, simply gathered important municipal statistics and documents from all cities with populations over 50,000 and made the data available to interested parties; it did not attempt to, as some of its sponsors desired, evaluate any of this raw material. Nor did the Census Bureau adopt the elaborate questionnaire schedules that the Urbanism Committee had drawn up.

The Urbanism Committee's final report was not published until the fall of 1937. Contributing to the delay was the Resources Board's insistence upon some stylistic changes in the Urbanism Committee's draft and an important excision from its list of recommendations. Although casting a generally approving eye over the manuscript, Merriam and the other board members feared that the urbanism group's often petulant charges that rural areas had received more political attention and financial aid from the Federal Government would stir up old antagonisms in the countryside and would foreclose any action on the report's proposals. They agreed that a pattern of discrimination did exist but wanted the committee's comments on this point softened. Similarly, the board ordered deleted the Urbanism Committee's suggestion that "the Federal Government should consider the possibility of substituting direct relations with at least the larger urban communities in place of the prevailing system which almost invariably requires clearance through the state." Here again, the board was afraid that the recommendation—as equivocal as it was and as much as it represented Merriam's own feelings—would supply ammunition to conservatives who were claiming that the New Deal wanted to abolish state government. The administration had enough fights on its hands in 1937; it surely did not need any more.[37] At last, on September 20, 1937, the White House announced the issuance of *Our Cities: Their Role in the National Economy.*

Roosevelt's accompanying statement, drafted by the NRB, emphasized the pioneering nature of the study. "For the first time in our history," he declared,

the attention of the United States Government has been officially directed to the role of the city in our national economy. This report examines urban life in a manner comparable to that given the problems of rural areas in a period extending over many years.

The President explained the significance of this investigatory time lag:

It may be questioned whether the National Government has given the same careful attention to some of the specific and common problems of urban dwellers as it has to the problems of farmers through the Department of Agriculture, and it is the purpose of this report to indicate some of the emerging city problems in which the nation as a whole has an interest and in which the National Government may be helpful.

As if anticipating criticism from those opposed to any extension of federal authority, Roosevelt stated flatly that "it is not the business of the United States Government to assume responsibility for the solution of purely local problems." Nevertheless, he concluded, the Federal Government cannot "remain indifferent to the common life of American citizens simply because they happen to be found in what we call 'cities.' "

The authors of the 85-page urbanism report hoped, above all, to draw the attention of policy-makers to the fact that America was an urban nation. By an impressive marshalling of facts and figures, by descriptive summaries, and by analyses and recommendations for future action, they gave substantive meaning to the bare finding of the 1920 Census that more than half of America's people lived in urban areas. In practically every facet of national life—economic, social, political—urbanism was a predominant element, they asserted. "If urbanization is a measure of the maturity of a country," the committee pointed out, "then the United States may be said to have come of age." But this shift from a rural to an urban nation had not been accompanied by a general recognition, by either the government or the citizenry-at-large, of "the importance of the city in conditioning the welfare of the country." The Resources Board had appointed the Urbanism Committee to remedy this defect in the nation's perspective:[38]

As long as the United States was principally a rural and agricultural country, as long as our economy was relatively primitive, local, self-sufficient, as long as our rich natural resources were scarcely known or exploited, and as long as a relatively secure and expanding life was within reach of even a rapidly increasing population, it was to be expected that our outlook and policies should have been largely rural. But since the city has come to play such a preponderant role in our national existence, it becomes imperative that it acquire a central position in the formulation of national policy.

Each of the report's three main sections reiterated this theme. The committee's discourse on "the urban way of life" demonstrated how the cities had changed traditional social patterns. Established institutions, such as the family, the church, and the government, underwent far-reaching transitions as a consequence of the movement of individuals from rural areas to the big cities. Urban-based organizations controlled much of the nation's communications media, thus setting the trends for vast areas of national life. Reviewing the factors behind the urbanization process, the committee noted that the future of our civilization may "in large measure depend not upon man's ability to escape from the city but upon his ability to master and use the forces that move and control it." The cities were here to stay; making "cities livable for human beings in a machine age," not returning to some rural fantasyland, was "the central problem of national life in regard to cities." In its detailed listing of the "maladjustments militating against the attainment of a satisfactory urban life," the committee amply showed the dangers of continued disregard of urban problems. The poverty, insecurity, vulnerability, disorganization, pollution, crime, congestion, slums, and myriad other discomforts so common in city living were the price the nation had to pay for failing to plan urban development. For this failure the report blamed the nation's inability to treat the city as a "unified economic problem." This, the committee concluded, was the product of urban political disunity: "the disfranchisement or underrepresentation of the city in the political and administrative councils of the nation," and the "widespread neglect of cities as a major segment of national existence."

Little in the committee's recounting of the facts about urban

America contained anything surprising or unfamiliar. As one board member commented after reading the report: "Lots of words, lots of stuff everyone knows. . . . Editing could bring it down to ⅕ at least." A board staffer observed that "a great deal of this is nothing new." Most readers, especially those from urban backgrounds, he noted, would find many parts obvious and repetitious.[39]

Yet if the report left the impression of going over much that had been known previously, it also made valuable contributions. For the first time, the nation had a handy reference work, bearing an official government imprint, charting past experiences and developing trends in urban society. Besides gathering scattered data, the committee's report also provided a great impetus for further urban scholarship. The research carried out under Wirth's direction served as the basis for his classic paper "Urbanism as a Way of Life," whose persuasive and penetrating insights would guide the study of the city for the next generation. Urban political science also received a big boost from *Our Cities*. It became the textbook for a budding flock of students of city government. The urbanism report was, in addition, directly responsible for the establishment of a Bureau of Urban Research at Princeton University in the summer of 1941. Responding to the committee's plea that academic institutions continue its work, the Princeton trustees set up the bureau to "contribute to the development of greater knowledge of the relationships between the different activities which together form the city." [40] The Princeton unit would serve as a model for later urban study centers.

The Urbanism Committee's "statements of general policy and recommendations" ranged all over the urban landscape. They called for action at each of the three levels of government, as well as by the private sector. Some of the suggestions dated back to the Progressive era, but others were of more recent vintage, reflecting the 1930s' engrossment with economic issues; this latter type predominated. According to the committee,

some of the most fundamental problems of contemporary urban life flow from the economic insecurity of the urban worker. Many of the gravest urban problems do not appear possible of solution, nor can an acceptable standard of stable community life be attained, unless high incomes and greater security are assured for the great masses of urban dwellers.

Consequently, the bulk of the recommendations dealt with ways of restoring and maintaining the health of the national economy. The committee urged an intensified attack on the Depression, continuation of public assistance under the Social Security Act, and a permanent federal public works program to offset fluctuations in business enterprise. In addition, it backed national industrial and transportation planning as leading to "more efficient and socially more desirable distribution of economic activity and urbanization." For chronically depressed areas, the committee requested special federal relief.

Once outside the economic sector, the report emphasized the role of the states and cities in solving urban problems. It advocated wider home rule powers, state encouragement of metropolitan government, increased application of the merit system, more liberal municipal land acquisition policies as part of comprehensive local planning, and greater cooperation among municipalities. Going beyond the Progressives' concern for good government, the committee also backed an aggressive local campaign to eradicate slums.

Most of the committee's non-economic recommendations concerning the Federal Government dealt with a restructuring of its organization to promote greater recognition of urban needs. Although the report urged the adoption of a national leisure policy and more federal aid for crime prevention and control, the committee believed that, in general, "direct federal expenditures in cities should be reduced to a minimum." On the administrative side, the committee called for a Bureau of the Budget study on ways to coordinate federal activities in urban communities and to facilitate federal-city collaboration. Similarly, it urged the creation of a division of urban information within the Census Bureau to carry out the suggestions of the "Interim Report." To complement this work, the committee suggested the establishment of an urban research section within a permanent National Planning Board "to perform for urban communities functions comparable to those now performed for rural communities by the Bureau of Agricultural Economics and the Bureau of Agricultural Engineering."

In its conclusion, the committee rejected once again the idea of wholesale population dispersal as a solution to the problems of the nation's cities. Such a step, it warned, would be impractical and wasteful. Rather, the city should be recognized as a basically healthy organism that needed only some "judicious reshaping" to provide a desirable environment. But achievement of this goal would require "much better appreciation and understanding of the city and its distinctive problems, greatly improved governmental organization and wider powers, and far more fundamental and much more effective planning on all levels of government."

The Resources Board's foreward, written by Merriam, skillfully condensed the Urbanism Committee's 85-page report into nine tightly packed pages. Even more than the report, the foreward stressed the economic basis of urban dilemmas. This, undoubtedly, resulted from Merriam's political calculation that the great popular concern over the economy might provide the entering wedge for federal involvement in city affairs: "Scanning the troubled horizons of the past few years for those symptoms of national strength and national strain, we find first of all that the city has become not only one of the fundamental supports but also one of the primary problems of the Nation's economy." To solve its economic difficulties, the nation would have to come to grips with "the condition of urban life." So as to allay rural fears that this new awareness of the city would lead to a slackening of interest in the needs of the countryside, Merriam emphasized the interdependence of rural and urban areas:

It is the function of the Government to consider maladjustments, whether rural or urban, in the light of the national goals and to aid where possible in the solution of these problems, but not primarily as rural or urban problems, but first and foremost as American problems, as limitations on the attainment of American ideals.

Endorsing the Urbanism Committee's recommendations, Merriam reiterated one of his favorite themes: "The prosperity and happiness of the teeming millions who dwell there [i.e., cities] are closely bound up with that of America, for if the city fails, America fails."

IV

Everyone associated with *Our Cities* considered it a beginning, a stimulant to further discussion of and research into the role of the urban community in contemporary society. Limited by time and available data, the committee was only able to make "an initial exploration of the field with restricted penetration." [41] Its real value would be determined by the extent and level of the political debate it set off and the amount of legislation it generated. By these standards the report was not successful.

A combination of factors circumscribed the report's impact. Topping the list was Presidential indifference. The White House may have put out a press release on *Our Cities*, but Roosevelt almost certainly never read the Urbanism Committee's findings or even the board's foreword. The subject held little interest for him, either personally or politically; the recommendations of the President's Committee on Administrative Management and the President's Special Committee on Farm Tenancy, both of which appeared in 1937, were much closer to his heart. Barely a week after the publication of *Our Cities*, Roosevelt, in a speech dedicating the Bonneville Dam, called for a study of methods to achieve a better urban-rural balance: "Today many people are beginning to realize that there is inherent weakness in cities which become too large for their times and inherent strength in a wider geographical distribution of population." The gentleman-farmer from Dutchess County was hardly the man to push for quick implementation of the Urbanism Committee's program. Nor is there any evidence that anyone on Capitol Hill looked at the report; the *Congressional Record* contains no mention of its existence. Since none of the standing congressional committees had obvious jurisdiction in the urban field, there was no place to refer the copies of *Our Cities* that the Resources Board sent up to the Hill.[42]

It is not unusual for official government reports to go unnoticed, but *Our Cities* received less attention than most. The overall problem was that *Our Cities* lacked a strong constituency. No one particular urban crisis had inspired the project; no one particular urban crisis greeted its findings. The study had been the brainchild of an academician, and it remained in the hands of scholars through every stage of its development; the dull sound of the finished product reflected its authorship and sponsorship. The committee directly responsible for the research and writing did not include any people with political influence; Dykstra, Wirth, Comey, Smith, and the rest may have been highly respected by their professional colleagues, but they were little known in Washington. Kept alive only by Roosevelt's fascination for planning, the Resources Board possessed few friends in the executive or legislative branches. Outside the government, there was no organization willing and able to fight for implementation of the committee's recommendations. As the report itself had explained, there were few general urban interest groups, just a lot of narrow-based, often squabbling, special interests that happened to be located in cities. The mayors, through the USCM, claimed to speak for the city as a whole, but they were too busy trying to keep WPA alive to give the Urbanism Committee any assistance. Immediate issues—the new housing act, labor disputes, and the relief question—dominated the proceedings of the November 1937 annual meeting of the USCM; not a word was said about *Our Cities*. Other organizations, such as the International City Managers Association and the National Municipal League lauded the report but could not follow up their rhetoric with any positive action.[43] Beyond these scattered signs of concern, the Urbanism Committee's work was met by silence.

Press coverage of *Our Cities* both mirrored and contributed to the lethargic response to the report. Skipping over its major themes, wire service dispatches emphasized the specific economic recommendations of the committee. The United Press described the proposals as "a program to put underprivileged city residents on an economic parity with the farm and small town population"; the Associated Press stressed the idea that "economically 'decadent' cities were to be reorganized and their inhabitants resettled." [44] A few big-city papers ran feature articles on the report, but many neglected it altogether.[45] Editorial reaction to *Our Cities* was mixed. The handful of newspapers that bothered to comment typically commended the committee for putting together "an illuminating textbook on the American city and its problems" but then criticized its recommendations, mild as they were, for encouraging increased federal encroachment on local prerogatives.[46]

The political climate by the fall of 1937 also ruled out implementation of the Urbanism Committee's suggestions. Conservative and rural opposition to the New Deal had been rising since Roosevelt's introduction of the "court packing" plan in February; it took all of the President's renowned powers of persuasion to free the public housing bill from the hostile clutches of the House Banking and Currency Committee that August. Even if he had wanted to, Roosevelt probably could not have steered the *Our Cities* proposals through Congress.[47] The legislature's pigeonholing of Roosevelt's reorganization bill also killed the Budget Bureau management review urged in the report and delayed the establishment of a research section in the Resources Board for almost four years. Prospects for gaining more federal recognition of cities sunk to a new low in the summer of 1939 when the conservative-rural coalition in the House stopped the flow of funds to the fledgling public housing program.

V

By 1939 the New Deal had all but lost its ability to aid cities through substantive programs, but it still retained enough vigor to inaugurate additional studies of urban life. The impetus for these new data-collection services came from new federal agencies and, even more significantly, from business groups. And Charles Merriam was still around hoping to bring Washington and the cities into a closer partnership.

Government and industry demands for more data led to the first housing census in 1940. The decennial census had started counting residential dwellings in 1850; later enumerations gathered statistics on home-ownership, types of structures, and values. This sort of material proved sufficient as long as the home construction field remained very localized and dominated by small companies, but as federal authorities moved into this crucial sector of the economy in the 1930s and national trade associations emerged, administrators— public and private—found themselves groping in the dark for guidelines. Before the Federal Home Loan Bank Board could intelligently charter new savings and loan associations, before the Federal Housing Administration could prudently guarantee mortgages, before the United States Housing Authority could fairly allot grants for slum clearance, each had to have some idea of the market for housing, vacancy rates, availability of credit, and the condition of the housing supply in different communities. The profits of real estate brokers and large-tract builders also depended upon access to this information. At the request of the various federal housing agencies and industry groups, Senator Wagner introduced a bill, in the spring of 1939, providing for a complete housing survey as part of the regular decennial census. With this broad backing, the measure passed the Senate without any difficulty. Ironically, it came up for debate in the lower chamber the day after the House had defeated additional appropriations for public housing. Republican opponents of the low-rent program charged that the census proposal was an administration attempt to "assemble propaganda and spur agitation for further paternalistic and socialistic housing legislation." One congressman from Ohio claimed that the findings would be "classified, charted, and statistically arranged into a political sob story to exploit the taxpayers in the name of charity." Advocates of the bill retorted that the Congress needed more data to legislate intelligently in the housing field; it was this very lack of hard facts, many felt, that had led to the USHA defeat the previous afternoon.

"We are spending the Government's money in total blindness," declared a Texas representative. Enough members changed their anti-housing votes overnight to send the census bill on to the White House for Roosevelt's signature. For the cities, the 1940 Census marked the first comprehensive inventory of the structures covering about 60 per cent of their developed land.

Business also inspired another national urban research effort. Concerned with the extent of deterioration in central cities as neighborhoods became older and their residents poorer, the National Association of Real Estate Boards (NAREB) had begun, in the late 1930s, exploring schemes for urban redevelopment. The association soon interested the Home Owners' Loan Corporation and the Federal Housing Administration, both of which held large investments in urban areas, in the problem, but neither felt qualified to lead the attack. They suggested that NAREB bring the matter to the attention of the newly reorganized National Resources Planning Board (NRPB).[48] Merriam welcomed the realtors' overtures, and in a March 1941 letter to prominent urban spokesmen proposed that the Resources Board act as "a central agency [for the drafting of] effective programs for the prevention and cure of this disease [i.e., blight] in the body politic."[49] Heartened by the enthusiastic response to the idea, Merriam moved to resurrect a key recommendation of the Urbanism Committee.[50]

At Merriam's urging, the Resources Board established an Urban Section to study "the major aspects of the urban problem." The rationale for the section was that there existed "no recognized agency in the Federal Government specifically concerned with the problems of urban areas and urban peoples, and that in the absence of such an agency some of the outstanding problems of American life go unrecognized, unanalyzed, and untreated."[51] To head the unit Merriam looked for someone outside the housing and city planning fields, which he considered too parochial for the wide-ranging research he envisioned. Finally, in June 1941, the board offered the post to Charles S. Ascher, a veteran of the Radburn "garden city" experiment and a former assistant to Louis Brownlow at the Public Administration Clearing House.

Ascher focused his section's limited resources on an examination of the suggested programs for post-war urban development. Concentrating on administrative problems, he investigated ways of increasing social control of land use, improving local finances, and funneling federal aid effectively into the cities. Seeking outside help, he prodded other government agencies and private organizations to compile the data necessary for making intelligent estimates of post-war requirements in housing, water supplies, transportation, health, welfare, and other crucial areas of city life so that sound city planning could proceed. Ascher also devised a Progressive Urban Planning Project to test new approaches to community planning.

Drawing upon some of this work, Ascher prepared a policy statement on "urban conservation and development" for the Resources Board's annual report for 1942. In it, he put the board firmly behind proposals for federal aid for urban redevelopment: "The welfare of more than half the population of the country and indeed the entire national economy are at stake in freeing the [blighted] land for city rebuilding." Ascher was not yet ready to specify the terms and conditions on which this aid should be given, but he did call for a governmental reorganization to consolidate federal leadership on those urban dilemmas with national implications. Going beyond the proposals of the Urbanism Committee, he recommended the establishment of a "Federal urban affairs agency" to assist in "the formulation of objectives, in the advancement of knowledge and understanding of urban forces, and to help provide unity in the attack of the many federal units now dealing with the problems of city dwellers." This new agency would take in its fold the bureaus presently responsible for the administration of federal aid for housing, highways, recreation, public works, and all other services designed predominantly with city residents in mind. Unlike all other previous suggestions for an urban agency, Ascher's plan called for the establishment of an agency with operational and research duties.[52]

The exigencies of war presented Ascher with an opportunity to popularize his ideas within the government. Growing dissatisfaction with the management of the defense housing program in the fall of 1941 prompted Roosevelt to ask his close aide Samuel I. Rosenman to examine the entire federal housing setup. While most of the people Rosenman consulted gave him organization charts for a new super-housing agency, a few took a broader perspective. Those two veterans of the fight for greater federal assistance to cities, Harold Buttenheim and Louis Brownlow, proposed an "Urban Planning and Housing Agency" and a "Department of Urbanism." Throwing his support behind an urban department, Ascher argued that "it is cities, not houses, that are big enough to sit at the cabinet table." But aware that rural congressmen would block cabinet-level recognition of the cities, Ascher, in the end, merely urged Rosenman to create a unified housing body that "has the skeleton to permit it to become a department of urban affairs." [53] A big step along these lines was taken in February 1942 when Roosevelt established the National Housing Agency (NHA) by executive order.

The years 1942–43 witnessed an important shift in the bureaucratic agencies of the Federal Government given financial support in their urban programs. Beset by constant sniping from congressional conservatives who felt that its plans for the post-war world were tainted with socialism, the NRPB suffered deep cuts in its budget for fiscal 1943. The board's ambitious urban research program was all but scuttled. In June 1943, Congress shut down the NRPB for good. Ascher was not present for the closing. He had left the board the previous year, for personal reasons, to join the new National Housing Agency. Although not the urban department he would have desired, Ascher found the NHA an appropriate place for his talents. "The organizations comprising the NHA," he wrote the agency's director, "constitute the greatest single influence upon the future patterns of our cities: they can affect that pattern for good or evil for the next generation." [54] Urbanism was to become synonymous with

housing; the cities had found a new home, but one that would prove
to be very confining.

VI

As America prepared for the post-war world the country possessed a
great deal more data about its cities than it had fifteen years earlier.
The proliferation of federal activities within the domestic sphere had
created an almost insatiable demand for information about all
aspects of American life, including the makeup of the cities. In the
compilation of statistics on employment, welfare, business, transportation, and dozens of other categories notable advances were made,
but the most important breakthrough, as far as urban areas were
concerned, came with the inauguration of the decennial census of
housing in 1940. With this material in hand, municipalities could
now begin the long, arduous planning process.

Urbanists looked upon these federal data-collecting enterprises as
double-edged programs. Not only would the gathering of urban facts
help localities help themselves, but it might also result, "as it did in
agriculture, in the formulation of policy and promotion at the
national level." [55] Collection would lead to analysis, and analysis to
action. The national government would become a positive force in
shaping a better urban environment.

The saga of *Our Cities* demonstrated, however, that the road to
federal action would not be a smooth one, gutted by potholes of
rural hostility, conservative intransigence and, above all, by plain
indifference—executive, legislative, and public. There existed no firm
foundation of a strong, united urban constituency that knew what it
wanted and could fight for the required repair work. When the
interests of program technicians and business coincided, such as on
the housing census, some progress was made, but the blind curves
and narrow roadbed remained. And as the mushrooming federal
bureaucracy began to turn out reports by the score, traffic jams
started to develop; there was no policeman to direct the information

to where it could do the most good. The facts about urban America were now becoming available; whether and how they would be used was still a question mark.

NHA's displacement of the National Resources Planning Board as the center of urban study in Washington would influence the outcome. The NRPB had ranged far and wide in its examinations of American life and the cities; practically everything that goes into the making of a city—water resources, transportation, population movements, industrial location, and so forth—fell within the board's purview. It saw the urban community as a composite of all of these elements and tried to make provision for each in planning the city of tomorrow. The NHA had a much more limited perspective. Its job was to build houses, as many houses as it could. While the NRPB attempted to place the city in a national context, the NHA tended to see the city simply as a place to construct—or not to construct— homes. The difference was crucial, the consequences momentous.

4

The Road to
Urban Redevelopment: 1933–49

American cities are now challenged as never before. . . . It is my conclusion that we are on the verge of a new era in city development which might bring about the broad improvements in urban life for which some of us have dreamed and fought for so many years—a period of vibrant, dynamic development. All this would demand a new focusing of city interest far broader than the older city planning, reconsideration and reorganization of urban experience and problems, new programs for sounder urban living, a new mustering of citizen interest in their common affairs.

Charles E. Merriam
"Make No Small Plans" (1943)

The New Deal forged unprecedented links between the Federal Government and the cities, but it did not legislate new programs specifically directed toward the solution of problems uniquely urban. In the process of administering this new federal aid, however, national authorities accumulated important, fresh stores of information on the ills plaguing urban America. With old theories of the constitutional division of powers under serious challenge in the 1930s and 1940s, the opportunities for translating this factual material into action programs increased. Before the New Deal-Fair

Deal epoch of reform had run its course in 1949, the Federal Government had committed itself to relieving a flagrant sign of municipal distress.

I

"The slum," proclaimed the Urbanism Committee in 1937, "is the most glaring symptom of urban disintegration." Defined in the legal terminology of the United States Housing Act of 1937 as "any area where dwellings predominate which, by reason of dilapidation, overcrowding, faulty arrangement and design, lack of ventilation, light or sanitation facilities, or any combination of these factors, are detrimental to safety, health or morals," slums presented unmistakable evidence of the country's failure in city building. Jacob Riis's graphic description of New York's Lower East Side in 1890 might well have been written half-a-century later about scores of neighborhoods in municipalities all over the United States:[1]

Leaving the Elevated Railroad where it dives under the Brooklyn Bridge at Franklin Square, scarce a dozen steps will take us where we wish to go. With its rush and roar echoing yet in our ears, we have turned the corner from prosperity to poverty. We stand upon the domain of the tenement. . . . Suppose we look into one. No. —— Cherry Street. Be a little careful, please! The hall is dark and you might stumble over the children pitching pennies back there. Not that it would hurt them; kicks and cuffs are their daily diet. They have little else. Here where the hall turns and dives into utter darkness is a step, and another, another. A flight of steps. You can feel your way, if you cannot see it. . . . All the fresh air that ever enters these stairs comes from the hall door that is forever slamming, and from the windows of dark bedrooms that in turn receive from the stairs their sole supply of the elements God meant to be free, but man deals out with such niggardly hand. That was a woman filling her pail by the hydrant you just bumped against. The sinks are in the hallway, that all the tenants may have access—and all be poisoned alike by their summer stenches. Hear the pump squeak! It is the lullaby of tenement-house babes. . . . Here is a door. Listen! That short hacking cough, that tiny helpless wail—what do they mean? They mean that the soiled bow of white you saw on the door downstairs will have another story to tell—Oh! a sadly familiar story—before the day is at an end. The child is dying with measles. With half a chance it might have lived; but it had none. That dark bedroom killed it.

Known by different names in different cities—the Basin Section in Cincinnati, the Hill District in Pittsburgh, South End in Boston—the slum was "the cut-over areas and the eroding lands of the city, the places of material decay and human corrosion." [2]

Closely related to the slum was the phenomenon of blight. The product of changing urban land uses (for example, commercial encroachment into adjacent residential quarters), the failure of business sections to expand in accordance with the expectations of landowners, the exodus of affluent elements of the population to outlying areas, and above all, the ravages of old age, blight characterized those city neighborhoods that were no longer profitable to maintain or improve. Cities began generating decadent neighborhoods practically the day they were founded; by the mid-1930s large sections of municipalities fell into that category. Blighted districts covered almost one-third of the built-up parts of Brooklyn; nearly one-fourth of Birmingham's dwelling units were located in declining areas; more than a quarter of Cleveland's population lived in run-down neighborhoods; Chicago's Loop was surrounded by a three-mile-wide band of obsolete, wretched buildings.[3]

The root causes of slums and blight were deeply imbedded in the nation's political, economic, and social systems. Land owned in fee simple was exploited for the owner's, rather than the public's benefit. A citizen had little recourse in law to prevent a property holder from shutting out his neighbor's sunshine, making light rooms gloomy, filling the air with dust and soot, and crowding the streets with noisy trucks. Profit-making took priority over the amenities of life. Retail firms and residents of fashionable districts that felt threatened by the movement of factories into their areas fought successfully for the adoption of zoning ordinances to halt this infiltration, but all too often these same regulations promoted blight in other sections of the city by setting aside too much land for commercial uses. Municipal tax policies also contributed to the spread of blight. Since localities were dependent upon property levies for most of their revenues, they naturally were hesitant about reducing assessments. By helping support fictitious land values, city governments forestalled the deflationary price spiral that was necessary for the reclamation of deteriorated sections. The absence of adequate planning legislation permitted the premature opening of subdivisions on municipal peripheries and suburbs that only speeded up the decline of inner city neighborhoods.

Besides being eyesores, slums and blighted areas also threatened the well-being of the cities. These districts were a breeding ground for disease and crime. In Detroit, for example, deaths from pneumonia in slum neighborhoods were 3 times the rate for good residential sections, infant mortality 6 times, and fatalities from tuberculosis 10.5 times. A Cleveland slum with but 2.4 per cent of the city's population accounted for 5.7 per cent of the municipality's robberies, 7.8 per cent of its juvenile delinquencies, 10.4 per cent of its illegitimate births, and 21.3 per cent of its murders. Tackling these problems cost the cities money, lots of money. Boston spent more than twice as much on each slum resident than it collected in taxes from him. The blighted sections of Atlanta provided 5.5 per cent of the city's real property tax revenues, but consumed 53 per cent of its police, fire, sanitary, and other service expenditures.[4]

As long as the cities continued to grow they could close their eyes to this imbalance; during the 1920s and 1930s, however, their margin of safety narrowed dangerously. The trek of people from core-city areas to the outskirts had been a predominant feature of American urban development from the start; mass production of the automobile in the relatively prosperous 1920s merely accelerated the trend. But while cities had previously kept up with this population dispersion by annexing their rural-suburban neighbors, by 1910 the territorial aggrandizement of most large Eastern and Midwestern municipalities had ceased for a variety of political reasons. Millions of well-to-do families now lived outside the central cities' limits, beyond the reach of their taxing powers. The Depression cut further into municipal revenues. Falling rents and a rise in vacancies forced many landlords of blighted properties to become delinquent in paying their taxes; slums were contributing less to city treasuries at the very time they were placing heavier burdens upon them. "If nothing is done to check the expansion of slum and blighted areas," wrote one student of the problem in 1935, "our cities are facing death from dry rot at the center and bankruptcy because of increased taxation, within a comparatively few years." [5]

Although often used interchangeably in popular literature, the terms "slums" and "blight" came to have distinctly different meanings for the professional groups concerned with the urban environment. Slums connoted poor housing conditions and all the attendant social evils; blight, on the other hand, had economic significance. To say that a district was blighted meant that the area was unprofitable, both to private investors and the municipal government. Housing in such sections could be in reasonably good shape or there might not be any housing at all; commercial and industrial districts could be blighted, too. Thus, while slums, with their overcrowding and low upkeep, usually returned handsome dividends to property owners, blighted areas were, by definition, a drain on individual and official pocketbooks. Viewed from these divergent social and economic perspectives, slums and blight attracted the attention of dissimilar interests. The campaign against the slum became the preserve of liberal and philanthropic organizations that found rat-infested tenements detrimental to family welfare. They concentrated their efforts on increasing the supply of decent housing for the bottom third of the population; their crowning achievement was the 1937 Housing Act, which joined a program of slum clearance with public construction. In contrast, the anti-blight crusade was led by large landowners and downtown businessmen worried about falling property values and rising taxes. These people wished to gain government aid to protect their investments in real estate and buildings; for the most part, they opposed public housing as unfair competition with private enterprise. Reconciling the differences would be difficult and would delay action on both fronts. Great confusion also marked the ultimate legislative product.

II

While there has probably never been a time in the history of American cities when slums and blight were wholly absent from cities, slum- and blight-consciousness reached new heights in the 1930s. This awareness did not arise because life in a cold-water flat of the fourth decade of the twentieth century was demonstrably worse than that in the last decade of the nineteenth—it wasn't. Rather, this appreciation was the result of a transformation in the nation's outlook. After years of seemingly boundless growth, the country was rudely awakened to the harsh reality that expansion was not divinely ordained; depression could be just as normal a condition as prosperity. Particularly hard hit by the economic contraction, cities began taking stock of themselves. Some of the big metropolises, due to the decline in birthrates and rural out-migration, actually experienced a decrease in population between the 1930 and 1940 Censuses. For the first time since New York City crossed the quarter-million mark in 1840, the large urban communities saw their percentage of the national population drop. Municipal politicians and local chambers of commerce, which previously had been interested only in increasing their cities' size, now started turning their attention to the quality of life in urban society; the "boom-town" psychology of the past had no place in the apparently stagnant economy of 1930s' America. City planning commissions, a prime target for municipal budget slashers in the immediate aftermath of the Great Crash, made a remarkable recovery toward the end of the 1930s as localities strove to improve their appearance and efficiency. The Depression also rekindled the nation's social consciousness. Neither war nor a soaring securities market had completely extinguished the flames of Progressive reform; the hard times replenished the fire's fuel supply and broadened its sources.

By enlarging the role of the Federal Government in domestic

affairs, the New Deal contributed greatly to the public's awareness of slums and blight. From a purely informational standpoint, the Civil Works Administration-conducted Real Property Survey (1934) performed the signal service of giving the nation its first accurate picture of how extensive the deteriorated housing problem was— about 30 per cent of urban dwellings were found to be substandard. On the operational side, the Public Works Administration inaugurated a program of slum clearance and construction of low-rent apartments. Municipalities had won the right during the Progressive era to close down tenements as health or fire hazards, but few cities ever exercised these police powers because of the costs involved and the problems posed in having to find accommodations for the displaced residents. Federal subsidies for demolition and new building, disbursed initially by PWA and after 1937 by the U.S. Housing Authority, eased these difficulties. Furthermore, since PWA-USHA regulations required cities to provide evidence of their need for federal aid, Washington forced localities to face their slum problems squarely. Similarly, the federal authorities' insistence upon municipal government approval for any application for assistance thrust the issue of bad housing into local politics.

The Federal Government's drive against the slum aroused mixed emotions. Social welfare and labor groups worked diligently to convert the temporary pump-priming venture into a permanent federal activity. They seemed to have achieved their goal with the passage of the 1937 Housing Act. Others had more ambitious dreams. Dissatisfied with the slow pace of PWA's endeavors, one White House aide, for example, suggested that the Federal Government "clear out the slums and poor housing, and build a city the way it ought to be built, instead of doing patchwork here and patchwork there." [6] Roosevelt, not keen about public housing in the first place, rejected such schemes out of hand, but important segments of the business community were willing to listen—up to a point. They had no complaints about the clearance phase of the federal program; the sight of decrepit rookeries crumbling beneath the wrecker's ball was enough to warm the heart of even the most ardent conservative. On the other hand, the businessmen intensely disliked the second half of the operation: the use of tax funds to house low-income families. Coming around to the position that federal subsidies were essential for the eradication of blight, these private interests wanted priority to be given to entrepreneurial opportunity and profits.

III

The National Association of Real Estate Boards (NAREB) spearheaded the crusade on blight. As managers and brokers for huge chunks of urban land, realtors had a tremendous stake in the maintenance of residential and commercial property values. City real estate prices, which had kept pace with the upward slope of the economy through the 1920s, collapsed just as swiftly after 1929.[7] The sudden break in the land market sped up the decaying process; short of cash, hard pressed to meet taxes on over-assessed properties, owners fell behind on necessary repairs.[8] Besides the old blighted areas, most cities in the 1930s were also pockmarked with unwanted reminders of the "New Era." Residential developments in outlying districts, built to meet the post-World War I housing shortage, shoddily constructed and laid out in inappropriate gridiron street patterns, were abandoned by their occupants who could not make interest payments to the banks. The Depression, by slowing down the exodus to the suburbs, gave downtown shopping centers a reprieve, but only a reprieve. These core areas became more obsolete and less attractive each year; few landlords had enough faith in their cities' future to reinvest profits in older structures. Local governments' own financial stringencies added to the realty industry's problems. Caught in a squeeze between higher relief costs and higher tax delinquencies, municipalities raised property levies. Thus, the landowner's equity faced erosion from two sides: the encroachment of blight and confiscation through taxes. Cities were caught in a dilemma; the realtors were headed toward ruin.

Under the leadership of its executive vice-president, Herbert U. Nelson, NAREB committed itself to saving the city and the realtor.

Nelson, who dominated the association for three decades before his retirement in the mid-1950s, was the self-proclaimed champion of the free enterprise system. But, as his critics never failed to point out, this role was somewhat incongruous with his avid support of the Federal Housing Administration's mortgage insurance program, which practically guaranteed a builder his profit. A highly emotional man, Nelson was apt to lose self-control whenever the discussion turned to public housing; during the heat of the battle over the extension of the program in the 1940s, he caused a furor by linking Robert Taft to Communism. Nelson claimed that public housing destroyed the American way of life and predicted that it would lead to a regimented society controlled by a totalitarian big brother. Yet Nelson, himself, was hardly a friend of popular rule. In a 1949 letter to NAREB's president, he wrote:[9]

I do not believe in democracy. I think it stinks. I believe in a republic operated by elected representatives who are permitted to do the job, as the board of directors should. I don't think anybody except direct taxpayers should be allowed to vote.

Not surprisingly, proposals carrying the NAREB imprint were more likely to enhance property rather than human values.

The association's proposal for "Neighborhood Protection and Improvement Districts," announced in October 1935, operated on the traditional American ideal of group cooperation at the lowest possible level. At the same time it tried to overcome one of the main obstacles to the successful treatment of blight: the problem of land assembly. Diffused title to property within a neighborhood made extensive reclamation practically impossible. Earlier in the decade the New York Building Congress had attempted to rehabilitate parts of Manhattan's Lower East Side through a voluntary pooling of interests by local landlords, but this project collapsed when the congress discovered that it could not get all the owners on even one block to accept mutually agreeable terms.[10] To prevent a recalcitrant minority from choking off action in the future, NAREB suggested the employment of the government's coercive legal authority. Once 75 per cent of the property owners in a suitably defined neighborhood came together to form a Protection and Improvement District, they would be authorized to draw up a plan for their area. After approval by the municipal government, the district could execute the plan through its powers of condemnation and taxation. Thoughtfully applied, Nelson argued, this device would protect the nation's huge investment in municipal utilities, restore confidence in urban real estate, and end the senseless flight to the suburbs.[11]

An extensive NAREB publicity campaign on behalf of the association's proposal generated considerable discussion, but little positive state action. Although leading members of the city planning profession agreed with the association's goals, they questioned the wisdom of its approach. Allowing neighborhoods to decide for themselves how they wished to develop, critics warned, would promote piecemeal planning and spot zoning. Comprehensive plans for the entire urban area had to be prepared before any program for neighborhood improvement could get underway; otherwise, the welfare of the city might be subordinated to the parochial concerns of small groups. Some commentators also pointed out that by restricting membership in the district to property owners, the scheme would deprive tenants of a role in determining the future of the areas where they lived and/or worked. This denial of democratic rights would not be serious in neighborhoods where most people possessed their own homes, but in many run-down sections, where almost all families rented apartments, the realtors' plan would clothe profit-motivated outsiders with official authority to do what they pleased. Opponents of the NAREB idea also expressed doubts about its financial feasibility. While good sections might be able to raise enough tax monies to prevent their decline, neighborhoods already deteriorated surely did not have the resources to pay the costs of a complete face-lifting—some form of subsidy would be needed here. These defects, as well as rural indifference to urban matters, kept the NAREB model state statute off most state legislative calendars.[12]

Passage of the Housing Act of 1937 shifted NAREB's attention from the statehouses to Washington. With the federal Treasury now opened up for the battle on the slums, realtors saw an opportunity to go beyond the slow-moving process of rehabilitation into the much more challenging but also potentially more lucrative field of clearance and rebuilding. First, however, a way would have to be found to channel federal funds away from the "socialistic" public housing program and into subsidies for private enterprise. NAREB felt it could not back any scheme for city rebuilding as long as there remained some possibility that even a part of the reconstruction task might be handled by public housing agencies. Fearful that low-income, non-taxpaying projects would monopolize the best sites, realtors saw destruction of the USHA as an essential prerequisite to the successful prosecution of their battle to preserve the "private city." The primary target of the association's anti-blight propaganda barrage during the late 1930s, therefore, was not substandard housing, but the one instrument committed to the improvement of the urban environment. Joining forces with other conservative groups seeking to undo the New Deal's welfare reforms, NAREB succeeded in convincing the House of Representatives to kill USHA's request for additional authorizations in 1939. When further appeals for more public housing funds were similarly denied in 1940, the association, at last reasonably secure that USHA could not offer any effective competition, began preparing a detailed proposal.[13] The product of NAREB's labors appeared in the summer of 1941 as the Report of the Association's Committee on Housing and Blighted Areas.

Written by Nelson and a few leading big-city realtors, the report presented a reasonable argument for federal aid to cities with still another assault on public housing. States and municipalities simply lacked the tax resources to raise the astronomical sums—$40 billion according to a previous NAREB estimate—required to buy the vast tracts of blighted land that had to be procured as a prelude to urban reconstruction. Federal funds were now being used to ease the transition of the farm economy into the machine age; it was only fair that the Federal Government help the urban economy adjust to the automotive era, especially since the latter problem involved the welfare of more than 50 per cent of the nation's population. From NAREB's perspective, renewal of past federal programs for slum clearance and low-rent housing held no promise of striking at the roots of the cities' predicament and might even make things worse. "Any piecemeal attack on the housing question which ignores the basic need of planning," the report declared, "can have only partial success, and may aggravate the disease of blight which first must be cured." According to the committee, a federal-municipal-private enterprise partnership was the cities' sole hope for a brighter tomorrow.[14]

Drawing upon some of the criticisms levelled at its earlier and relatively modest proposal for Neighborhood Protection and Improvement Districts, NAREB concocted a bold design for reconstructing the cities. Two formidable barriers, the difficulties of land assembly and astronomical land costs, blocked the path to sound urban redevelopment.[15] Given the premise that large-scale operations were the only way to stop blight, it then became necessary to amass huge parcels of land under single ownership. Hence, uncooperative landlords, by holding out for ridiculously high prices for their property, could wreck rebuilding plans before they left the architects' drafting boards. To overcome this obstacle, the committee urged the creation of metropolitan land commissions possessing broad condemnation powers. Unlike their Improvement District counterparts, these commissions would be representative of the community as a whole and directly responsible to local governments. Even with this expansion of their legal authority, however, municipalities still faced another steep hurdle to rebuilding: land assessments far in excess of their actual redevelopment value. Blight had persisted because no one could pay the inflated prices attached to the land and develop it profitably for suitable uses. This difference between price and reuse value determined the "write-down" that would have to be absorbed by society if any new building on these sites were to occur. Under the NAREB scheme, the Federal

Government and localities would share these "write-down" expenses: using funds supplied through a program of long-term, low-interest loans, to be administered by a "Federal Urban Land Commission" set up within the Federal Loan Agency, municipalities would be able to purchase blighted properties and resell them to private developers at below-market prices. Builders would get the profits and cities would get valuable additions to their tax rolls. The realtors suggested imposing two conditions for federal assistance: 1) that the local plan for redevelopment of a specific blighted area conform to the comprehensive master plan for the entire metropolitan region; and 2) that the rebuilding be handled completely by private enterprise.

NAREB's daring proposition to involve the Federal Government in local affairs stirred mixed reactions in housing and planning circles. Some took the Committee Report as a positive sign of a new civic awareness among realtors. Frederic A. Delano, chairman of the National Resources Planning Board, for example, considered it "a matter of importance to find the real estate men taking an active interest in trying to solve the problems to which they have been somewhat indifferent and which, it seems to me, they have largely created." Without looking into the details of the NAREB scheme, Delano felt more confident about the cities' future now that the realtors had realized that "their business depends on the maintenance of fair and livable city conditions." The Cincinnati city planner and former director of research for the Urbanism Committee, Ladislas Segoe, did examine the specifics of the NAREB plan, and he did not like what he saw. Most of the funds appeared to be headed for the pockets of slumlords instead of into programs to build better homes for slum dwellers. From Segoe's vantage point, the NAREB proposal promised to be "a great boon to private investors," while not offering any hope that "slum families or municipal treasuries will benefit commensurate with the public subsidy involved." Since NAREB had vehemently denounced the principle of subsidies when such federal largesse was being handled by the USHA, critics charged the association with duplicity in advocating this aid for redevelopment corporations. "Let us condemn it [i.e., government subsidies] universally," challenged Dorothy Rosenman, a friend of public housing, "or find its value with openmindedness." [16] Battle lines along the urban redevelopment front were beginning to form.

IV

The NAREB approach encountered its first serious competition in December 1941 with the publication of a booklet *Urban Redevelopment and Housing—A Plan for Post-War*, prepared by two economists. Since no one could accuse Alvin H. Hansen or Guy Greer of having a personal stake in preserving urban property values, their pamphlet also supplied the redevelopment idea with greater respectability. A professor of economics at Harvard University, Hansen had become the leading American apostle of Keynesian doctrines. Urban redevelopment appealed to Hansen as an excellent device for compensatory public spending in behalf of the general welfare. Guy Greer, a consultant on housing to the Federal Reserve Board, was particularly eager to bring some order to the chaotic home construction industry. He hoped that a large-scale city rebuilding program financed with federal funds would give Washington sufficient leverage to force needed reforms in this vital sector of the economy.

Despite many similarities between the NAREB and Hansen-Greer analyses, there were notable differences in outlook. Both might agree that there was "no alternative to having the Federal Government shoulder the cost of cleaning up the social and fiscal mess left by past generations," but whereas NAREB sketched a plan for city rebuilding, Hansen and Greer outlined a comprehensive national urban policy. According to the Hansen-Greer proposal, all urban redevelopment should be undertaken from a "national point of view." Not until the National Resources Planning Board had determined "the proper and desirable role of each urban community in the State, region, and nation" would cities be authorized to commence reconstruction. Following the recommendations of the

Urbanism Committee, Hansen and Greer urged creation of a new federal agency to handle all federal-municipal contacts and the establishment of federally funded "institutes of urbanism" in a dozen universities scattered across the country to reduce the shortage of trained city planners. It was an audacious program, aimed at making cities "not only tolerable places to live and work in but wholesome and beautiful as well."

Hansen and Greer's specific recommendations for city rebuilding closely paralleled those of the realtors with one important exception: financing. In its report, NAREB asked merely for long-term federal loans at low interest. The association considered federal aid absolutely necessary, but it disliked direct appropriations from federal tax funds because this method would entail higher levies. Selling bonds seemed to be a painless way of raising money; furthermore, since new construction was a long-term investment, it appeared perfectly sound to pay for these costs over an extended period of time. The two economists had no arguments with the deferred financing technique; rather, they questioned whether the cities should be obliged to amortize the loans at all. Tying redevelopment to the redemption of bonds meant that the projects would have to show a profit; if this became the main criterion, Hansen and Greer believed, it was very likely that new blight and slums would replace the old as builders overcrowded their sites in order to maximize their income. To allow the development of cleared land for its most appropriate social uses, Hansen and Greer proposed that the Federal Government "advance" money to municipalities. Such profits as rebuilding projects did generate would be applied to repaying these "advances," but any portion not recovered at the end of fifty years would "simply be written off as the price to be paid for the errors of past generations." While Hansen and Greer hesitated to put a price tag on their plan for fear of frightening their readers, they insisted that the economy could stand the burden and would even benefit from the exertion: healthy cities and a healthy economy were inseparable.[17]

The NAREB and Hansen-Greer studies provided the framework

for the emerging debate over urban redevelopment. Practically everyone interested in city rebuilding accepted four points as axiomatic: 1) federal subsidies were essential; 2) reconstruction must be on a large scale; 3) all new building must be done in accordance with comprehensive master plans for both the metropolitan area and the neighborhood; 4) government-business cooperation. Details about financing and administration still had to be worked out, but these items were negotiable. Other tricky questions, however, might not be so easily answered. What safeguards were needed to insure that the benefits of the subsidies accrued primarily to the community rather than to private groups? What would be the role of public housing in urban redevelopment? The program also required a clearer statement of purpose: was it to be directed principally to the improvement of the nation's housing supply or to the fundamental reshaping of the cities? And finally, should the Federal Government formulate a national urban policy?

V

This expanding probe into the causes and cures of blight did not go unnoticed in government circles. Vastly enlarged by the New Deal, the sprawling, yet still youthful, federal bureaucracy reacted much more quickly than it had in previous administrations to developments on the local level. Agencies involved in selected physical improvement projects within urban regions, such as the Bureau of Public Roads and the Public Buildings Branch, recognized the potential threat to their projects posed by the spread of decay. Since residential areas accounted for the largest percentage of urban land use, housing agencies took a special interest in the problem. Housing officials assumed the lead in preparing the case for federal intervention, although the other concerned parties would later contest their primacy.

Initial discussions in Washington on the cities' physical deterioration focused on slums. Demands by the social reform and labor elements of the New Deal coalition for a federal program to rehouse poor families in decent accommodations brought forth a spate of proposals from individuals, pressure groups, and government agencies. One of the more noteworthy was written by Frederic A. Delano, chairman of the Central Housing Committee. Delano's December 1936 memorandum, entitled "A Tentative Program for Federal Cooperation with Local Governments and Private Enterprise," characterized aid to city planning as "a proper field of federal activity":

The Federal Government gave our railways land in exchange for their services in spreading our population over the continent, and granted homesteads to any who would undertake to develop them. It would only be reasonable for the Federal Government to assist local governments to purchase land [to promote sound community rebuilding].

These properties would be made available to private firms and developed for their best use; under this scheme, cleared slum land in central areas could become the sites for shopping and office complexes, while the former slum residents would be supplied with new housing in outlying sections of the city.[18] Lacking many specifics, Delano's plan was particularly deficient when it came to assigning priorities: which should come first—meeting the housing needs of low-income families or making downtown districts profitable again for municipal government and business groups. As events were to show, Delano was not alone in his confusion.

The framers of the Housing Act of 1937, however, had no doubts as to their prime objective: better housing for the poor. Some of the people supporting federal subsidies for slum clearance wished to see this money devoted to "a gigantic program of urban reconstruction and community planning," [19] but the stated aims of Congress in passing the measure were merely "to remedy the unsafe and insanitary housing conditions and the acute shortage of decent, safe, and sanitary dwellings for families of low-income that are injurious to the health, safety, and morals of the citizens of the Nation." If, as the Delano memorandum implied, the salvation of the city depended upon spurring private investment in all types of urban building and adding to the municipal tax rolls, then USHA's operations were, in fact, harmful to the cities' welfare. Only public funds were involved, leading to charges from private homebuilders that they were being driven out of business; furthermore, USHA projects paid no local property levies. For these reasons, and others, public housing was a very controversial program; indeed, Congress refused to vote any additional appropriations for USHA from 1939 to 1948. On the eve of American entrance into World War II, fewer than 100,000 dwellings had been built by USHA, and fewer than 70,000 of the estimated 6,000,000 substandard urban housing units destroyed.[20]

While the USHA nibbled away at the slums, another agency, the Federal Home Loan Bank Board (FHLBB), searched for ways to prevent their growth. Neighborhood decline presented a serious menace to the billions of dollars invested in residential mortgages by the savings and loan associations under the board's supervision. Hence, in 1938, with the cooperation of local authorities, the FHLBB launched a pilot project in the Waverly section of Baltimore to discover how the deterioration of older areas might be halted. Conservation of urban neighborhoods, the board soon learned, "is not only a matter of repairing groups of properties, but touches upon the broader aspects of city planning and includes rezoning, street adjustments, parks and playgrounds, and modifications of traffic." The board's experiment demonstrated that rehabilitation and "organized community housekeeping" could save areas not yet completely blighted, but translating this into an effective, widespread program was more than the FHLBB could manage. Neighborhood conservation involved a slow upgrading process devoid of any dramatic qualities, making it very difficult to sustain popular interest. The FHLBB's close supervision of the Waverly trial run led to its success, but the board lacked the manpower to extend similar assistance to other communities on a regular basis.[21] Rehabilitation would always remain in the shadow of the more spectacular schemes for massive clearance and rebuilding.[22]

Urban blight problems also came under scrutiny from an unexpected quarter: the Federal Housing Administration. Ever since its inception in 1934, the FHA had been a target for criticism from central-city interests who felt its policies stimulated new construction on the suburban fringes at the expense of the inner city.[23] While official data on the geographical distribution of FHA financing is scanty, such material that is available tends to substantiate these charges.[24] Operated to run at a profit just like any private business, the FHA refused to insure mortgages in built-up, old urban areas because they were considered poor economic risks; consequently, half of Detroit's districts and one-third of Chicago's were ruled ineligible for this type of federal aid. One survey found that of 374 FHA guaranteed mortgages in the Chicago metropolitan region, only three were in the central part of the city.[25] The agency defended its conduct as actuarially sound and in step with the fancies of the huge majority of prospective home buyers. As one FHA official told the 1939 American Institute of Planners Convention: "Decentralization is not a policy, it is a reality—and it is as impossible for us to change this trend as it is to change the desire of birds to migrate to a more suitable location." This explanation, of course, conveniently passed over the fact that FHA rules made it extremely difficult to get a mortgage on a house within central city limits. But at the prodding of NAREB, the FHA agreed to reconsider its position. In 1940, it announced plans for a study "to determine how fully the new home building in the outskirts of cities rests on a sound economic foundation from the point of view of the entire metropolitan community." The agency also issued revised regulations that year to permit the granting of mortgage insurance on rehabilitated rental housing in blighted neighborhoods.[26] Although neither the study nor the new regulations truly altered the direction of FHA policies—the vast proportion of new housing construction continued to be in the suburbs, and the dollar amounts involved in the rehabilitation program were just a fraction of those applied to the regular home-building program—they were significant, nevertheless, as signs of greater official cognizance of the cities' troubles.

Ironically, FHA was the first government agency to use the term "urban redevelopment" in the title of one of its publications. Responding to pleas from NAREB and others, the FHA, in 1940, began an examination into "the possible redevelopment on an economic basis of substandard blighted areas." Such districts, the FHA pointed out, usually occupied choice locations that, if restored to productive uses, would return excellent dividends to private investors and the community at large. Prepared by a housing and planning specialist, the agency's *Handbook on Urban Redevelopment of Cities in the United States* appreared in November 1941. Step-by-step, the *Handbook* mapped out the course to be followed by municipalities in acquiring, holding, and disposing of real property for rebuilding. The stress was on what localities had to do to help themselves, but the *Handbook* did not neglect the possibility of federal aid. Until there was a thoroughgoing reform of the nation's taxation system, it explained, cities could not supply the necessary funds for sound redevelopment. Given "the importance of urban economic health and stability to the economic health of the nation," federal assistance for replanning and reconstruction would be justified. The only alternative might be to let the cities "go out of business."

This burst of activity at the scattered housing agencies aroused old passions at the National Resources Planning Board. During the three years following publication of *Our Cities* (1937), urbanism practically disappeared from the NRPB's agenda, its place taken by more pressing matters of the day; no one on the board's staff had any special responsibilities in the urban field. The general indifference that greeted the recommendations contained in *Our Cities* made further explorations into urban society appear senseless,[27] but as discussion about urban redevelopment, an expression not yet coined in 1937, became more widespread in the late 1930s, the NRPB was ready for a second look. Writing to his friend and colleague, Louis Wirth, in the spring of 1941, Charles Merriam observed: "The country is ripe for a bold and determined attack on urban blight." [28] Not surprisingly, Merriam wished to lead the assault.

With the blessing of the FHLBB and FHA, the Planning Board established itself as the center of federal thinking about city rebuilding. The board's assumption of command seemed appropriate for, as Frederic Delano explained, "only the NRPB has the comprehensive approach that is essential to orderly development." At Merriam's urging the board created a division in June 1941 to study "urban conservation and development." [29] Before the year was out, division chief Charles S. Ascher had placed urban reconstruction high on the NRPB's list of post-war priorities. In his section of the board's *National Resources Development Report for 1942*, Ascher declared:

The international crisis has given a new intensity to our thinking about the future of cities: the determination that the communities of the future must be nobler embodiments of the democratic respect for the worth of the individual, if our war effort is to be justified.

After reviewing the previous literature on the subject, where he found general agreement on the main points, especially the need for federal aid, Ascher struck the now familiar refrain: "The welfare of more than half the population of the country, and indeed the entire national economy, are at stake in freeing the land for city rebuilding." All that remained to be settled were the "terms and conditions" of federal assistance.

Working with a small staff, Ascher began investigating various aspects of urban redevelopment. "The air is full of schemes for the large-scale rebuilding of cities," Ascher noted in early 1942; some sort of consensus had to be reached on objectives and techniques before outlandish proposals gave the whole concept a bad name and frightened off possible friends.[30] An administrator by profession, Ascher focused on the governmental management problems raised by the program. Memoranda were prepared on the role of the three levels of government in the land acquisition process, the scope of federal aid, reorganization of local and federal agencies to facilitate metropolitan planning, and the relationship between planning and rebuilding. Ascher also commissioned reports surveying the legal obstacles to greater social control of land use across the nation and the availability of funds through local taxes. Calling upon outside help, he persuaded the FHA to make an analysis of "write-down" costs and the impact of deflated land values upon municipal revenues; USHA economists agreed to frame estimates of the magnitude of the reconstruction task before the country. Armed with this information, Ascher expected to draw up specific recommendations for post-war national legislation.[31]

But the board's early demise in 1943 ruined Ascher's timetable and drastically changed the Federal Government's perspective on urban redevelopment. Official sponsorship of the proposal passed to the newly established National Housing Agency, whose administrator, John B. Blandford, Jr., had told the National Conference on Planning the year before that "the rebuilding of our urban communities stands alongside full employment as one of our primary post-war goals." Acting through its Urban Studies Division, the consolidated housing agency continued many of the NRPB's research projects. However, this shift from the NRPB to the NHA also brought about a shift in official perspectives on urban development. NAREB, Hansen and Greer, and Ascher all believed comprehensive replanning to be the foundation of sound urban redevelopment—decay would be attacked wherever it appeared and the areas rebuilt to provide the cities with the widest and firmest economic base.[32] NHA executives, on the other hand, had a more limited goal. Their paramount mission was to increase the nation's supply of decent housing in good neighborhoods and to destroy slums. The agency wanted a national housing policy, not a national urban policy. In NHA's hands, urban redevelopment would become a device "to make cities out of housing programs." [33]

VI

The winter of 1943 saw urban redevelopment move beyond discussion into the bill-drafting phase. Heartened by the growing interest in business, planning, and government circles, NAREB (through its research affiliate, the Urban Land Institute [ULI]) and Hansen and Greer had continued to refine their ideas and started putting them into legislative form. The two economists reached the congressional bill hopper first. With the assistance of Alfred Bettman, the nation's foremost expert on planning and zoning law,[34] they composed the "Federal Urban Redevelopment Act," which Senator Elbert Thomas (D.-Utah) introduced in April 1943.[35] Two months later, at the request of the Urban Land Institute, Senator Robert F. Wagner (D.-N.Y.) presented the "Neighborhood Development Act." [36] Neither measure ever emerged from committee, but each helped sharpen the issues involved in city rebuilding.

Although in accord on the great importance of federal assistance and government-business cooperation, the two bills adopted different approaches to urban redevelopment. While paying homage to local initiative, the Bettman bill clearly contemplated a vastly enlarged role for the Federal Government in urban planning and rebuilding. Administration of the program would be lodged with a new Urban Redevelopment Authority which its sponsors hoped would mature into a cabinet-level Department of Urban Affairs. All subsequent federal grants-in-aid to municipalities, including those for public works and roads as well as for land acquisition, would be contingent upon URA approval of a locally prepared comprehensive master plan for the entire metropolitan region. These stiff requirements reflected Bettman's belief that the problems of the cities were national in origin (for example, transportation patterns, industrial location, fiscal policies) and that they could be solved only through strong national leadership. In contrast, the ULI measure—which Wagner subtitled "an encouragement to enterprise bill"—proposed an absolute minimum of direct federal supervision. Uncle Sam would simply act as a benevolent banker taking a few precautionary steps to insure the safety of his investment.[37] The Bettman bill established strict standards to be followed in replanning; the ULI bill left almost all the decisions to the individual locality. From the realtors' viewpoint, the extension of federal credit for the purchase of blighted neighborhoods did not represent "anything really new"; hence, the experienced National Housing Agency could handle the job. Overall, the ULI bill indicated keener interest in remaking the cities as profitable sites for private capital than in remaking the national economy. Planners and businessmen were beginning to go their separate ways.

With the publication of the Bettman and ULI measures, another group actively joined the urban redevelopment debate: the public housers. Actually, of course, the housing reformers who fought for the Housing Act of 1937 had been a party to the controversy over city rebuilding from the start. Their success in gaining federal aid for low-rent dwellings had supplied some of the impetus for NAREB's schemes; NAREB never attempted to hide its desire to substitute private enterprise programs for the USHA. Since the most vocal of urban redevelopment's supporters [that is, the realtors] were also public housing's most fervent enemies, many liberals tended to reject the anti-blight crusade out of hand. The attitude of Nathan Straus was typical. The first administrator of USHA and a favorite target for opponents of public housing, Straus labeled the NAREB-ULI proposals "a self-seeking effort by reactionary" cliques to divert government subsidies from disadvantaged families into the pockets of slumlords and greedy speculators.[38] Urban redevelopment, whether of the NAREB or Hansen-Greer variety, appeared destined, many reformers felt, to "bail out" the real estate interests at the expense of poor tenants.[39] But as the political stock of USHA continued to fall after 1939 and that of urban redevelopment rose, the public housers reappraised their stand. Instead of categorically denouncing plans for a government-business partnership to recon-struct blighted districts, they started offering a quid pro quo: the realtors could have their "urban land Triple-A" if the low-income segment of the population received public housing.[40]

Neither the Bettman bill nor the ULI bill offered this kind of deal. Rather, each tried to avoid the controversial public housing question entirely; both were deliberately vague on just how the shortage of decent dwellings would be overcome. The public housers found this silence unacceptable. Urban redevelopment, warned Leon Keyserling, NHA general counsel and author of the 1937 Housing Act, could be "most dangerous unless something solid is done on the housing front first, or at least simultaneously." Without an accompanying comprehensive housing program, he explained, "a large-scale urban redevelopment program would be predominantly a benefit to property owners and insurance companies, and might even work to the detriment of the present occupants of the sites." Unless steps were taken to increase the general supply of better housing, urban redevelopment would simply move slums around, not destroy them.[41]

Housing reformers were also greatly distressed by the Bettman and ULI bills' failure to safeguard adequately the welfare of displaced tenants. The sad experience of Stuyvesant Town, the nation's first publicly assisted redevelopment venture, underscored their concern. On the very day in April 1943 that the Bettman measure had been introduced, the Metropolitan Life Insurance Company released plans for a huge housing complex on Manhattan's Lower East Side, to be built with aid supplied through the New York State Urban Redevelopment Act. Yet even with substantial tax relief from the city, Stuyvesant Town would only serve families in the middle-income range. At most, 3 per cent of the area's residents could afford the project's rents, and the law did not force the company to assume any responsibility for rehousing the remainder. Surveys indicated that most of the families uprooted in the name of municipal improvement would have to find shelter in one or another of New York's many slums, thus aggravating an already bad overcrowding problem.[42] Determined to prevent a repetition of such hardships in the future, liberals demanded that federal urban redevelopment legislation contain firm rules guaranteeing decent accommodations for all those displaced by government-financed projects. According to the reformers' calculations, this requirement would make an expanded USHA program unavoidable, since private builders could not profitably construct low-rent dwellings. Throughout the legislative battle to follow, the liberals steadfastly refused to accept any separation of urban redevelopment and public housing.[43]

On one point the public housers and realtors did agree: urban redevelopment should be administered by the NHA. As the reformers envisioned city rebuilding, it would be primarily a task of constructing good housing for families of all income levels; thus, the NHA seemed the natural agency to direct the program. Also, the public housers contended that creation of an additional agency would only complicate federal-local ties and deprive municipalities of the NHA's expertise in community building. Given USHA's special knowledge of the intricacies of slum clearance and housing finance, many liberals felt that a good cause could be made for putting urban redevelopment under the control of the public housing branch of NHA; this arrangement would insure that both programs operated in unison.[44]

The public housers' designs for urban redevelopment ran diametrically counter to those of Bettman and his associates in the American Institute of Planners and the American Society of Planning Officials. When the welfare organizations and labor unions that supported public housing looked at urban society, they saw the slums; when site planners and landscape architects looked at this same urban society, they saw the inappropriate street patterns, poor transportation facilities, obsolete business districts, and aging factories. One group focused on the social well-being of the family, the other on the economic health of the metropolitan community. Whereas the housing reformers viewed urban redevelopment as just another tool for improving the housing picture, the planners dreamed of using the program to reshape American cities in a new image. In this latter view, adapting the city to the automobile would necessitate extensive realignment of urban land uses, such as converting a decaying residential neighborhood into a shopping center with acres of parking space. Therefore, it would be a tragic mistake, Bettman argued, "to conceive of urban redevelopment as a subject identical with housing or housing with little variations— housing the theme, urban redevelopment the variations." Bettman agreed that housing would surely form the larger part of all rebuilding, but insisted that it be considered as only one of many possible uses for cleared blighted land, not the sole one. Thus, he went on, direction of urban redevelopment should not be given to an agency with a vested interest in a single type of construction; NHA would merely perpetuate the same narrowness of vision that had made the cities old before their time. A new department, charged with the whole range of urban affairs, was required to guarantee socially and economically sound results.[45] The fight was on for the program's very soul.

VII

Although the public housers fought to change the course of urban redevelopment, they did not challenge the program's underlying premises. Proponents of city rebuilding in the business world, the planning fraternity, and the housing and social service fields all acted upon the basic assumption that the cities were worth saving, that with a reasonable expenditure of public funds and private capital they could be redeemed. Too many people had invested their fortunes in urban land, too much government money had already been spent on making the cities habitable, and too large a segment of the people had to live within city limits, to allow the cities to deteriorate any further. Replanning and reconstruction would undeniably not be easy, but the cities appeared to possess "enough permanent value to demand their preservation and to offer a foundation for a new concept of usefulness and modernization." [46] Social critic Lewis Mumford, however, unequivocally renounced all these notions.

Mumford's monumental work of the depression decade, *The Culture of Cities*, published in 1938, pictured megalopolis in its death throes. "With language itself," he wrote, the city "remains man's greatest work of art"; it had been "the seat of the temple, the market, the hall of justice, the academy of learning." But the swollen urban conglomerations of today, "far removed from the sources of life, expanding without purpose," had turned "living forms into frozen metal." The metropolis destroyed the individual's identity and self-esteem; only by dispersing the inhabitants into regional clusters would people find communion with their surroundings and each other. Mumford believed that the giant city was just a temporary phenomenon, a product of the nineteenth century's great population explosion and unprecedented industrial expansion. As long as this growth continued, America and the rest of the world had been able to absorb the social consequences of the "parasitic and predatory" methods of a pecuniary economy. Now, however, as the country approached the midpoint of the twentieth century in a state of equilibrium, the accumulated disadvantages of the big cities promised to make them "cemeteries for the dead."

Contraction of the metropolitan economy, not its rejuvenation, offered the only cure for the dehumanizing processes of modern city life. "Under the best of conditions," Mumford admitted,[47]

this will be a painful procedure. But it would be much more sensible to let this existing decay eat further into our cities—than to attempt a replacement of structures without also providing for a pattern of building and living that will be closer to the needs of a balanced economy.

Pointing to the achievements of the nation's best-known executor of public works, Mumford predicted that "even if Robert Moses rebuilt New York from end to end in the fashion he has already followed, it would still be a doomed city. Indeed, its rebuilding would probably hasten its doom." Mumford believed that current urban redevelopment proposals "will give a new lease on life to the very forces that have led to the congestion and blight"; in particular, to the bankers and real estate promoters whose huge stake in overcapitalized downtown properties had previously blocked real reform.[48]

Mumford's aloofness from politics, befitting that of an Olympian philosopher, kept him from playing an active role in the redevelopment debate, but his ideas—in modified form—did reach numerous public forums. Many professional planners shared Mumford's gloomy appraisal of the chances for drastically overhauling the physical structure of existing cities. The drag of inertia seemed insurmountable; even when natural disasters swept away practically all of the buildings and utilities in such cities as San Francisco, Galveston, and Dayton, they had been rebuilt on exactly the same lines as before. Redevelopment promised to do no better: it would be "at best a makeshift, temporizing with essentials, complicated by land values, tied hand and foot by ancient street patterns, and economic Gordian knots." Instead of repairing old, out of date urban communities "to help them run badly a little longer," the nation might more wisely spend its money "to start all over and build modern cities." [49]

In 1935, these sentiments had received a sympathetic hearing from the chief of the just created Resettlement Administration (RA), Rexford G. Tugwell. The leading New Deal advocate of planning, Tugwell became convinced that the building of new towns offered "the best chance we have ever had in this country of affecting our living and working environment favorably." Slum clearance, he explained, "has to fight a good many entrenched interests; the land costs are too high even to protect the rights of children, or even to provide recreation for adults." Tugwell's solution to the slum mess was remarkably simple:[50]

My idea [he wrote in his Diary] is to go just outside centers of population, pick up cheap land, build a whole community, and entice people into it. Then go back into the cities and tear down whole slums and make parks of them.

Under his leadership, the RA constructed "Greenbelt" towns in three large metropolitan regions to demonstrate the advantages of community planning.

Tugwell's "Greenbelts" provided their residents with good housing and pleasant surroundings, but the towns were not without their flaws or their critics. The tremendously expensive job of starting a city from scratch, especially the cost of installing public utilities, pushed the rents RA charged for apartments out of the low-income range into the middle-income bracket. There was no place for poor people in "Tugwelltown"; just like most of their suburban neighbors, the "Greenbelts" became single-class communities. Another characteristic that the "garden cities" had in common with privately developed suburbs was the total dependence of their residents on the central city for employment. Except for a few stores, the "Greenbelts" had no businesses that could supply jobs; they were merely bedroom communities, not true cities. Thus, the "Greenbelts" did not fit Mumford's description of a socially balanced, self-sufficient regional center. What Tugwell accomplished was enough, however, to arouse the opposition of core-city officials and private builders. The friends of the central city perceived any federal encouragement of middle-class migration to the suburbs as the ruination of the downtown areas; home construction firms disliked intensely the prospect of federal competition in developing suburban subdivisions.[51] Hurt by unfavorable court decisions and charges of gross inefficiency, the RA program ceased with the completion of the initial three projects.

Defenders of "Greenbelt" always insisted that decentralization of the urban complex represented the wave of the future. The impulse for the "garden cities," Tugwell claimed, came less from the widely publicized English experiments with new towns than from "studies of United States population movements that showed steady growth on the periphery of cities." Suburban resettlement "accepted a trend instead of trying to reverse it." [52] Figures from the 1940 Census confirmed the accelerating flow of people to the fringes; preparations for defense and war further added to the human tide.[53] To many observers, the facts behind the statistics seemed to cast doubt on the wisdom of trying to salvage the central city. "The fundamental desire for light, air, and spaciousness lies at the root of the peaceful explosion of our cities toward their peripheries," Delano wrote. "The day of the larger cities has passed." [54] Others were even more emphatic. "The forces of dispersion are technological," declared a leading architect, "and cannot be resisted. We must try to work along with them instead of against them." According to this view, common sense dictated that primary attention be given to the sound development of outlying areas: they would determine the fate of urban America.

The outstanding champion of this position was Catherine Bauer. A disciple of Mumford's, she combined, as the master could not, the detachment of a social critic with the passion of a social reformer. Mumford was adept at picking out the faults of society and proposing solutions, but aside from the use of his pen, refrained from any direct contact with the political process. By contrast, Bauer worked actively to translate her research findings into practical programs for change. Just out of college in the 1920s, she found a job with the City Housing Corporation, which was then building the garden community of Radburn, "a town for the motor age." Designed as a test for the planning theories of Ebenezer Howard, Patrick Geddes, and other new town enthusiasts, Radburn, located seventeen miles from New York City, never lived up to expectations because of its failure to attract industry; with the coming of the Depression, it also proved to be an economic disaster.[55] Bauer spent the early part of the 1930s in Europe on a foundation grant studying how various European countries handled their housing problems. She returned convinced that public housing was the only answer to the shortage of decent accommodations in the United States, and after the publication of her book, *Modern Housing*, in 1934, she became organized labor's top lobbyist for a low-rent housing program. An aggressive and persistent woman, Bauer was considered something of a nuisance by Roosevelt and his housing advisers, but her determination paid off in 1937 with the passage of the public housing measure she had partially drafted. Employed as a consultant by the USHA, Bauer helped frame the Housing Authority's policy which favored construction of projects on vacant land over those on slum sites. "Exclusive emphasis on slum clearance," she had written in *Modern Housing*, "is as illogical as if the early automobile manufacturers had directed all their efforts to buying out the still prosperous carriage makers and razing their factories instead of building automobiles." Rather than try "vainly to salvage the past," she advised, "we must first safeguard the future."

From Bauer's perspective, urban redevelopment failed to satisfy this standard. Having battled the realtors in the 1930s over public housing, she was instinctively suspicious of their interest in city rebuilding in the 1940s. Like most liberals, she felt the NAREB-ULI plan invited too much speculation and neglected the urgent matter of rehousing.[56] Her major criticism, however, struck at the very essence of the urban redevelopment principle. Bauer had "no objection to bailing the boys out" provided "we get more workable cities" in return, but concentration on central reconstruction would make this impossible. The building of war plants in the suburbs, plus the anticipated post-war housing deficit, guaranteed "an enormous further wave of decentralization" at home once the hostilities overseas had ceased; thus, it was "too late, if indeed it ever was possible, to think of 'saving' the old city centers in their congested nineteenth century form." Precedence had to be given to "the protection of outlying areas." "The whole shape and quality and efficiency of the urban environment for a generation to come is about to be set," she declared. "The location and design of the new suburban subdivisions will make, or finally break, our metropolitan regions." [57] The big building boom presented the nation with a terrific opportunity and a terrible peril:[58]

It can give us well-integrated satellite communities, with protected open spaces between them and some sensible relation to work places . . . or it can engulf us in a final circle of chaos and potential blight.

VIII

Despite the nation's preoccupation with the fighting across the oceans, public discussion of urban problems increased during World War II. Even as the country mobilized its resources to defeat the Axis Powers, government, business, and other private groups looked ahead to the society the soldiers would be coming home to. The cities—the centers of population, industry, commerce, culture, and transportation—bulked large in these ruminations: "the life and fate of Americans are entangled with the destiny of our cities," proclaimed one popular magazine in 1944. "The better world we are fighting for can only be realized if our cities are transformed into better places to live and work." [59] Seeking to explain the growing interest in civic affairs that marked the war years, a financial periodical noted:[60] "The strain of war has apparently worked with a suppressed, explosive force among urban populations so that there is now talk of 'rebuilding' our cities just as if they had been bombed." The next step was translating this talk into concrete action.

As in most matters, the cities knocked at the statehouses first. The states possessed the legal authority and financial resources the cities needed for reconstruction. New York, upholding its traditional pace-setting role in the housing field, led the way. At the urging of the Merchants Association of New York City and other business organizations, the state legislature passed an Urban Redevelopment Act in 1941, which allowed localities to grant tax exemptions and the power of eminent domain to private corporations engaged in slum clearance and rebuilding. All projects had to be approved by the City Planning Commission, and the developers were limited to a 5 per cent profit. Over the next four years, thirteen additional states enacted basically similar laws. But little work actually resulted from this legislation. The financial inducements were not attractive enough for investors who continued to find outlying districts more lucrative and less encumbered by regulations. Three years after the end of the war, with twenty-five state laws on the statute books, only New York City had any projects past the site clearance stage. The fatal defect of the laws was their failure, except in two instances, to provide any state subsidies for "write-downs." As usual, the rural-dominated state governments were unwilling to spend their funds to assist the cities. With state treasuries closed off to urban redevelopment, the program's supporters descended upon Washington in 1944–45 to request federal aid.[61]

Significantly, the case for urban redevelopment received its initial hearing in Congress within the context of an investigation of housing. Although Roosevelt had reformed the Executive Branch's poorly coordinated housing activities by establishing the NHA in early 1942, many legislators still felt that an in-depth review of the government's entire relationship to this vital sector of American life was required. When Congress convened in 1943, Senators Robert A. Taft (R.-Ohio), Allen J. Ellender (D.-La.), and Robert F. Wagner introduced a resolution calling for a comprehensive study of housing. Among the topics to be covered was an analysis of methods for "eliminating slums and other deteriorated areas." Under pressure from this bipartisan group, the conservative leaders of the Special Senate Committee on Post-War Economic Policy and Planning agreed to form a Subcommittee on Housing and Urban Redevelopment. The subcommittee was to be chaired by Taft, a champion of a free economy and local responsibility. After considerable preparation, hearings began in earnest in January 1945.

The sometimes heated debate over public housing dominated the proceedings, but the subcommittee heard revealing testimony about urban redevelopment. The lead-off witness, NHA Administrator John Blandford, firmly endorsed federal subsidies for blighted land acquisition with subsequent redevelopment by private enterprise. While Blandford was not yet prepared to present all the details of such a program, those matters he discussed made it quite clear that he was adopting the public housers' approach to city rebuilding. Specifically, Blandford insisted that any urban redevelopment legislation must guarantee adequate housing at reasonable rents for families displaced by slum clearance; in addition, he recommended that the USHA program be resumed.[62]

USHA's friends turned out in force for the Taft hearings. Most in the public housing lobby were truly enthusiastic about urban redevelopment, provided that the low-rent program was expanded, but some wondered if the reformers were not making a bad bargain. As the executive director of the National Association of Housing Officials told the subcommittee:[63]

There is no magic formula whereby the vast cost of rebuilding cities can automatically be translated into profits and surpluses. Besides, the terribly complicated problems attendant upon extensive urban rebuilding—even assuming complete willingness to proceed and the availability of huge sums to do the job—will mean that there is no waving of a post-war wand that will get the job done quickly. . . . I am concerned with the families—the men, the women, the children, the babies—who are living by the hundreds of thousands and the multiplied millions in the slums and dilapidated neighborhoods of American cities and towns and rural communities, and I don't want them to have to wait for decent housing until we have developed brand new techniques and formulas, and have found great reservoirs of money to rebuild the cities of America wholesale. Some day our pictures of alabaster cities gleaming undimmed by human tears may find reality—but on the long march to that day I want to see some of the actual misery and degradation and indignity and the terrible cost of our slums cleared up.

Herbert Nelson's testimony on behalf of NAREB revealed that the public housers would have trouble making any bargain at all. Back in 1943, when the ULI bill was introduced, NAREB had pledged its "full support," observing that the measure "represented the product of seven years of active conferences within the real estate field." This was followed by the publication of a NAREB booklet, *Post-War Cities*, in September 1944, which called for the creation of a Federal Community Development Authority to assist in urban rebuilding. "Government aid in such a program," the booklet pointed out, "is not government interference with business— it will be government cooperation and help for business." But in February 1945, Nelson disclaimed any association with the ULI bill and made no mention of the NAREB pamphlet. Drawn into discussing urban redevelopment only by Taft's questions, Nelson indicated that realtors preferred state and local action in this area to federal. He stopped short of completely rejecting federal subsidies, but made it plain that he hoped such intervention could be avoided.

NAREB's sudden coolness toward federal urban redevelopment legislation exposed the realtors' growing doubts as to their ability to determine the shape of the ultimate program. In particular, the real estate industry was disturbed by the public housing movement's

increasing strength. The war emergency had given the reformers new
opportunities to push for government construction; although USHA
was not directly engaged in low-rent home building under the 1937
Act, it was still very much alive and active, in 1945, despite the
realtors' best efforts. Blandford's recommendation to the Taft Subcommittee that public housing be started up again further heightened
NAREB's fears; NHA, it appeared, was overrun by advocates of
"socialistic" programs—urban redevelopment would not be safe in
that agency's hands. Greatly upset by the possibility that city rebuilding might be tainted with public housing, many conservatives renounced the whole idea of federal aid: "If I have to choose between
seeing every old city in the country as an ash heap and seeing the
government become landlord to its own citizens," declared a Philadelphia realtor who had helped write NAREB's 1941 report, "I should
prefer to see the ash heaps."[64] Since only New York State had shown
any interest in subsidizing low-income housing, important segments
of the real estate industry began promoting state urban redevelopment programs as the free enterprise alternative to federal assistance.

The sharp differences of opinion among urban redevelopment's
supporters were further revealed by the remarks of Alfred Bettman.
Appearing on behalf of the American Institute of Planners, Bettman
urged national action on city rebuilding, because "urban blight is a
blight on the national economy." Old, poorly designed cities cost the
country dearly in traffic deaths and delays, industrial inefficiency,
health hazards, crime, and other social disorders. Whereas most
advocates of urban redevelopment usually envisioned a program to
restore specific deteriorated districts to profitable (for example,
high-rent apartments or office buildings) or worthwhile (for example,
public housing) uses, Bettman set larger goals for the "urban
redevelopment treatment": "the patient is not only the obsolescent
areas; it is the whole urban community." He proposed to restructure
the physical layout of American cities—moving factories and
railroad yards, improving transportation systems, protecting residential neighborhoods with open green spaces—in order "to prevent a
new era of blight and guarantee a quality of urban living fit for

American citizens." Repudiating the public housers' position, Bettman declared that "a terrible mistake will be made if urban redevelopment be conceived of as the replanning and rebuilding of slum areas only or the replacing or rebuilding for housing only." [65]

For the most part, Taft remained silent during the testimony on urban redevelopment, but Bettman's presentation elicited some salient comments by the subcommittee chairman. Although just starting his second term in the Senate, Taft was already recognized as the chief Republican spokesman in the upper chamber on domestic issues. The Ohioan's rhetoric often made him seem like a diehard opponent of New Deal reform, but, as one liberal writer observed, when it came to helping society's disadvantaged, he was "no archreactionary." Believing that good housing was a prerequisite to good citizenship and convinced that "you don't get decent low-cost housing from the free-enterprise system," Taft saw no substitute for public housing.[66] But Taft was not prepared to engage the Federal Government in the other areas Bettman had in mind. Disagreeing with the lawyer's contention that the blight covering 25 per cent of urban land (Bettman's estimate) acted as a severe drag upon the country's economy, Taft replied that "as a whole, the city is still sound." Values in certain sections might have declined, but the municipality could "more than make up for it in some other part of the city." Cincinnati, the city both he and Bettman called home, was "just as good a city as it ever was, and it is going to get better constantly." Since obsolescence and blight were essentially local problems, Taft failed to perceive any "national interest" in replanning. It was of no concern to the Federal Government "what a city looks like, or whether it has a lot of tumbled-down structures around a railroad yard." Federal responsibility properly extended only to residential slums, where on "social-welfare grounds," the national authorities had a stake in the "elimination of extreme poverty and hardship." While Bettman wished to keep urban redevelopment entirely apart from housing, Taft grasped no "federal interest beyond housing and beyond the elimination of slums." [67]

During its four weeks of hearings, the Taft Subcommittee heard a broad variety of proposals on how to solve the nation's urban housing problems, but there were some glaring gaps. The most noticeable was the Mumford-Bauer alternative of new town development, which received no discussion at all. Nowhere in the over 1,000 pages of printed record did the subcommittee explore the possibilities of using the post-war housing boom to make fundamental changes in the framework of urban society. Tugwell's "Greenbelts" were mentioned, but only in connection with ways of disposing of federally owned housing. Although some professional organizations spoke of the need for metropolitan and regional planning, these recommendations were lost in the torrent of demands that the Federal Government assist in the building of as many homes and the clearance of as many slums as soon as possible.[68] The FHA, the agency most directly involved in the suburbs, significantly had nothing to say about either urban development or redevelopment.

On August 1, Taft submitted his subcommittee's findings to the Senate. The twenty-three-page report examined practically every proposal for a federal housing policy—from those requesting organization of federal agencies to those seeking aid for home-mortgage financing to those proposing housing research, public housing, or urban redevelopment. On this last point, the subcommittee advised that "revealing testimony has been presented on the tremendous task that our cities face in eliminating slums and blighted areas and in restoring the land in these districts to appropriate uses." While many "unknowns" (for example, the costs involved, the amount of "write-downs") still had to be determined, the subcommittee felt the problem was serious enough to require a provisional system of federal assistance.

The report's outline for such a program clearly reflected Taft's thinking on urban redevelopment. In language reminiscent of the senator's exchange with Bettman, the report declared: "The Subcommittee is not convinced that the Federal Government should embark upon a general program of aid to cities looking to their rebuilding in more attractive and economical patterns." The only "accepted national interest" was in improving housing conditions.

Yet, because he recognized that "the task of redevelopment involves much more than a program of rehousing," Taft was willing to meet the planners halfway. Federal aid would be provided where

the area in question is to be redeveloped primarily for residential use or where the area is now predominantly residential in character and the clearance of the area would in itself serve a useful purpose through the removal of unsafe and unsanitary dwelling structures.

Either by constructing new housing or by tearing down slums, or both, urban redevelopment was expected "to rid cities of unhealthy housing conditions and restore blighted areas to productive use by private enterprise." [69]

This "predominantly residential" requirement represented a stunning defeat for the planners. Their objective had been to redo the cities wholesale, knocking down and putting up buildings wherever it might benefit the entire urban community the most. They saw urban redevelopment as directly tied to the day-to-day life of people at home, at work, at leisure, and in transit within the city. The Taft approach was much narrower. Instead of focusing on the city, it focused on the housing project. Rather than insisting upon the comprehensive master plan demanded by the old Bettman bill, the Taft proposal would simply ask for "a general guiding plan for the clearance of all slums in the city." Just as Bettman had feared, housing was to be the theme and urban redevelopment the variations.

On the subject of financing, the report recommended an aid system very much like that utilized by the USHA. The federal subsidy would be supplied in the form of annual contributions, over a forty-five-year period, to help defray the costs of "write-downs." By this method a large amount of reconstruction could be achieved with a small yearly drain on the federal budget; Taft estimated that an authorization of $20 million for annual contributions would produce $750 million worth of urban redevelopment in five years. To guarantee that federal losses be kept to a minimum and to promote local responsibility the report urged that municipalities be forced to assume one-third of the "write-down expenses." Administratively, Taft tried to appease the public housers and the realtors. In order to keep urban redevelopment free of the controversies surrounding USHA he rejected the liberals' plea that USHA be put in charge of the program; but wishing to stress urban redevelopment's close ties to housing, Taft urged that control be lodged with the NHA.

IX

The same day that Taft presented his report, urban redevelopment received another shot-in-the-arm from a more expected source: Robert Wagner. The Senate's dean of housing, Wagner had been distressed by the Ohioan's dilatory direction of the subcommittee's activities and had put his own staff to work drafting an omnibus housing bill. After consultations with trade associations and reform groups, Wagner's aides put together a package that included additional federal incentives to private construction and an expansion of public housing expenditures. Introduced on August 1 with Ellender as co-sponsor, the measure (S. 1342) contained a title on "Participation by Private Enterprise in Redevelopment of Slum and Blighted Areas." Since Wagner had relied most heavily on the advice of public housers in writing this section, it bore a striking resemblance to Taft's proposals, particularly in regard to the "predominantly residential" requirement and financing. As Wagner told the Senate, on the "new subject of urban redevelopment the [Taft] report and the bill are entirely and completely in accord." The only major innovation in Wagner's bill was the Democrats' insistence that redevelopment plans include "a feasible method for relocating displaced families." Given their fundamental agreement on housing policy, the three men had little difficulty uniting behind a single, new General Housing Bill (S. 1592) that reproduced virtually untouched the redevelopment section of the earlier version. With President Truman already on record in support of the program,[70] urban redevelopment entered the legislative arena in late 1945 with very impressive backing; the proposal would need every bit of it.

The urban redevelopment title of the Wagner-Ellender-Taft bill was a composite of ideas that had been discussed for years. The Bettman bill had suggested the necessity for direct federal appropriations to subsidize sound local land purchases. In addition, the newer bill adopted the ULI measure's philosophy that such aid be furnished "with the minimum of federal interference with local redevelopment." But in deference to the planners, it implicitly required preparation of plans as a prerequisite for assistance. Over-all, the public housers seemed to have won the most. S. 1592 placed urban redevelopment squarely in the context of housing: projects could be undertaken only when directly related to the improvement of housing conditions; accommodations had to be found for those displaced by slum clearance operations; and new funds were authorized for public housing. The last provision cost the bill dearly in political support.

By linking urban redevelopment so closely to public housing, S. 1592 aroused the opposition of nearly the entire business community.[71] Some parts of the business world were, of course, against the bill before it was even drafted. Nothing Wagner, Ellender, and Taft would do in the housing field (except, perhaps, repealing all previous housing legislation) could please such rigidly doctrinaire organizations as the Chamber of Commerce of the United States, the National Association of Manufacturers, and the Commerce and Industry Association of New York. At congressional hearing after congressional hearing, they denounced federal aid for city rebuilding just as they denounced practically every other New Deal-Fair Deal proposal. Urban redevelopment, these groups claimed, was a local responsibility; raiding the federal treasury to assist the cities would lead to further centralization of power in Washington, political abuses, widespread extravagance and waste, and, worst of all, higher taxes.

Realtors and downtown bankers, on the other hand, repeated the familiar warnings about federal domination and inflation, but indicated that they would be agreeable to help from Washington if it was on their own terms. First and foremost, public housing had to be scrapped. Private enterprise was not going to accept any competition from the public sector. Second, they demanded iron-clad guarantees of local—not federal—control of redevelopment projects from start to finish. This meant that the "vicious" USHA annual contributions formula, which permitted federal supervision for up to forty-five years, would have to be replaced by a system of one-time, lump-sum capital grants. Another benefit of the single grant arrangement, from the realtors-bankers' perspective, was that it facilitated calculation of the exact cost of the program. To further protect the federal budget, they also demanded that the ratio for sharing of losses between the federal and local governments be changed from 2:1 to 1:1. Finally, the realtors and bankers urged that administration of urban redevelopment be transferred from the National Housing Agency to the Federal Works Agency or the Reconstruction Finance Corporation. Compared to the public housing-infested NHA, FWA and RFC seemed much more friendly to private business and non-residential construction.[72]

The public housers were willing to make only slight concessions. Keeping NHA in charge, they felt, was essential if the program's housing objectives were to be achieved. Low-income families could not be accommodated on urban redevelopment sites unless the "write-downs" were very substantial; thus, the federal share had to be retained at two-thirds. On the matter of annual contributions versus capital grants, however, the public housers did demonstrate some flexibility. Taft, who heartily went along with the realtor-banker desire for as little federal oversight as possible, became convinced that the capital grant method was a "much more straightforward proposition"; he had little trouble persuading his two Democratic colleagues to make the switch.[73] But absolutely no such spirit of compromise was evident when the question of public housing's survival was under review. Wagner, Ellender, Taft, the housing reformers, the NHA, and the White House were all firm on this issue: there would be no federal subsidies for private enterprise through urban redevelopment unless and until public housing received a new lease on life.

The result was a stalemate. Urban redevelopment floundered around the halls of Congress for four years as the legislature tried to make up its mind about public housing. S. 1592 and its successors in the next two congresses were under the constant scrutiny of the Banking and Currency Committees on either side of Capitol Hill and a special Joint Committee on Housing. Thousands upon thousands of pages of testimony were taken on every facet of housing; yet, the only real unresolved problem was what to do with the USHA. Lined up on one side were NAREB, the United States Savings and Loan League, the American Bankers Association, and other business groups, each of which would have liked to get urban redevelopment started, but not at the price of more public housing. Although these organizations did not possess enough strength to enact their own program, they were, until 1949, sufficiently powerful to block passage of the omnibus bill. Ranged against them were the liberal-welfare groups, many veterans organizations, the big-city mayors,[74] and the Executive Branch. This bloc was able to prevent the detachment of urban redevelopment from public housing; it could not, however, gain approval for both. In the Congress, itself, urban redevelopment was rarely mentioned and was at no point tested by a roll-call vote. Public housing may have been only one element of urban redevelopment, but the tail was wagging the dog.

X

As the public housers and private builders fought each other to a standstill (1945–48), leading members of the planning fraternity launched their own counterattack against the basic principles of the Wagner-Ellender-Taft design for urban redevelopment. The planners' target was not so much the "predominantly residential" requirement, although they still felt this was a big mistake, as it was S. 1592's failure to give adequate attention to suburban development. While the bill authorized the acquisition of "open suburban land essential to the locality for sound community growth," S. 1592's authors made it clear that this provision had been inserted to permit the construction of public housing on the outskirts where people displaced by slum clearance could be absorbed. There would be no attempt to regulate peripheral development or to build brand-new communities. According to the planners, it was just these two tasks that required the most urgent consideration.

Planners were attracted to the need for guiding suburban growth and establishing new towns in the mid- and late-1940s because of a variety of circumstances. Exactly as Catherine Bauer and others had predicted, the nation suffered through a severe post-war housing shortage—3.2 million units was the estimated deficit.[75] With millions of families forced to double-up even in substandard dwellings, there appeared to be little prospect for a large-scale slum clearance program in the foreseeable future. Instead of tearing down deteriorated structures, the country's primary job was to put up new homes; and since the suburbs offered the largest area of vacant land, that was where most of the construction would take place. If nothing was done to control suburban sprawl, the planners warned, then the nation would behold "every already insolvable urban problem multiplied." [76] The dropping of the A-Bomb on Hiroshima and Nagasaki also spurred interest in outlying areas. A number of planners, though by no means all, reached the conclusion that urban dispersal was mandatory for national survival in the atomic age.[77] Passage of the New Towns Act of 1946 by England's Labour government helped Americans rediscover their own experiments with "Greenbelts" in the 1930s. When the president of the prestigious Regional Plan Association of New York advocated new towns as the answer to that metropolitan district's growing pains in 1948, the entire planning profession took notice.[78]

But few outside the tight circle of planners were ready to adopt this action program. Private builders, who saw a house-hungry populace willing and able to buy whatever they could produce, naturally opposed any proposals that would slow the pace of construction and lower profits. Since planning, in their view, meant nothing but red-tape, annoying regulations, and higher costs, the private developers wanted no part of it. Neither did the "people." Those millions of returning war veterans and their families who lacked a place to call their own cared little about protecting the future; they wanted homes now. The symbol of the era was Robert Moses, the public works czar of New York. Moses had nothing but disdain for "long-haired planners," those perfectionists like Mumford and Tugwell who wished to abandon the flawed metropolis and start entirely anew. "In municipal planning," Moses announced, "we must decide between revolution and common sense—between the subsidized lamas in their remote mountain temples and those who work in the marketplace." Limited objectives—a new park, an improved highway, better street lighting—were what Moses strove for and what the public desired.[79] New towns also ran into criticism from many housing reformers. Obsessed with the idea of slum clearance, they denounced any scheme that would divert energies from the attack on poor housing. Given the shortage of decent dwellings, the liberals were willing to accept some federally aided building on open land sites, but only if it was directly tied to a program of tenement elimination.

The abortive attempt of the Federal Works Agency to wrest control of urban redevelopment from the NHA[80] demonstrated the weakness of the planners' position. Successor to the old Public Works Administration, the FWA distributed federal grants to states and localities for higway construction and community facilities; in addition, through its Public Buildings Administration, the FWA was responsible for the erection of federal offices. These diverse activities gave the agency a certain familiarity with the problems of urban traffic congestion, land usage, decentralization, and decay. Appearing before a House committee conducting hearings on post-war planning in March 1944, the commissioner of the PBA testified that "urban blight and slums, next to the war, constitute the greatest social and economic problem which confronts the American people." But, he went on, "planning for the redevelopment of blighted areas is only one element of the much broader problem of the comprehensive planning of the whole urban region. Urban expansion into new areas must be planned and controlled in the public interest." Although the FWA implied that it would like to assist in this field, the agency neglected to press its case before the Taft Subcommittee. When the Wagner-Ellender-Taft bill named the NHA to direct urban redevelopment and set down the "predominantly residential" rule, FWA raised only mild objections, arguing that "the problem [i.e., city rebuilding] should be handled as one embracing all of urban life and not only housing." FWA did not seriously contest NHA's primacy in 1945–46, but as the deadlock in Congress on public housing deepened, the agency went on the offensive. It began popularizing Bettman's position that urban redevelopment's goal should be the "complete redesigning and rebuilding of the urban community" and lauding the merits of new towns.[81] After President Truman indicated some interest in FWA's "broad program" in December 1948, the agency drew up its alternative to the Wagner-Ellender-Taft measure. The FWA legislation emphasized comprehensive planning for the metropolitan region and shifted the focus from housing construction to the improvement of transportation and community facilities. As might be expected, it also provided for administration by FWA.[82]

Truman's legislative advisers wanted no part of the scheme. Despite their troubles with Congress over the proposed extension of public housing, the White House aides believed that housing was the only approach that could carry urban redevelopment past Capitol Hill. They were not eager to open discussion, as the FWA bill seemed likely to do, on the economics and sociology of urban life. So long as the urban redevelopment program remained tied to housing and slum clearance, it connoted no new federal involvement in local affairs. The FWA measure, in contrast, would inaugurate "federal intervention in all phases of municipal existence, not pegged to any social purpose already recognized as national." This country, they concluded, "is not prepared for such wholesale intervention."[83] Getting a national housing policy proved difficult enough for the

Truman administration; it did not wish to enter the unchartered territory of a national urban policy.

XI

FWA's attempt to reshape urban redevelopment collapsed just as the legislative traffic jam eased. Truman's come-from-behind victory in the 1948 Presidential contest, combined with renewed Democratic control of both chambers of the 81st Congress, supplied the public housers with a slim, but working majority. Showing the same kind of aggressiveness that marked his successful election campaign against the "do-nothing 80th Congress," Truman, for the first time, committed the full resources of his office to the enactment of the Wagner-Ellender-Taft (W-E-T) bill. Such presidential action was not really necessary in the Senate. The upper chamber had been voting regularly for public housing since 1946; 1949 was to be no different. With the freshman contingent of liberal senators lining up solidly behind the low-rent program, W-E-T passed by a comfortable 57–13 margin. Pressures from the Executive Branch proved to be decisive in the lower body, however. The conservative Republican-Southern Democrat coalition that had prevented the public housing bill from emerging from committee for four years tried their delaying tactics once again, but persistent White House lobbying and firm Democratic leadership in the House broke through this blockade. During the six long days of debate on the House floor, marred by a fistfight and bitter charges and countercharges about public housing, Title I, the urban redevelopment section, was hardly discussed at all. Some rural congressmen complained that their constituents were being taxed to save the big cities from their own errors,[84] but no one organized a serious challenge to Title I. When public housing squeaked through by five votes on its crucial roll call, the road to urban redevelopment appeared to be open.

Title I of the Housing Act of 1949 showed only slight differences, after three redraftings and five rounds of hearings, from the original urban redevelopment provisions of the W-E-T bill. The sole significant change was in the form of the federal subsidy. To appease the realtors, Taft and his co-sponsors switched from annual contributions to lump-sum capital grants; the measure authorized $500 million in aid over five years. The "predominantly residential" requirement and 2:1 cost sharing ratio remained intact. Two additions demonstrated a growing appreciation of the complicated job facing the cities. In order not to compound the already bad housing shortage, the bill imposed a year's delay on all slum clearance projects. Similarly, to spur local programs for the prevention of slums and blight, the act instructed the NHA administrator to encourage the modernization of municipal building and health codes. None of these modifications, however, altered the basic goal of the measure: housing betterment. A direct commitment to urban revitalization would have to wait.

XII

Compared to most other items on the Fair Deal agenda, such as federal aid to education and national health insurance, urban redevelopment practically raced through Congress. Barely eight years elapsed between the nearly simultaneous publication of the NAREB, Hansen-Greer, and FHA proposals, and the passage of the Housing Act of 1949. Title I owed its good fortune to at least two factors. Its inclusion in the omnibus housing bill gave the program momentum that alone it probably could not have sustained. Just as the White House staff had pointed out, so long as urban redevelopment remained connected to housing it was really nothing new. While it is true that the public housing title held up approval of W-E-T, this controversy over the low-rent section also deflected criticism that might otherwise have been directed at Title I. But perhaps even more significant was the absence of any solid opposition to urban redevelopment. Conservative organizations denounced it, but without much vigor or conviction. Ideological consistency required them to attack any further expansion of federal activities, yet self-interest tempered the assault; they questioned details, not the legitimacy of the program. Urban redevelopment, unlike some of the other liberal-sponsored measures, offered readily visible benefits to many segments of the business community. As never before in national politics, diverse urban interests joined together to support a city-oriented program.

Beneath this surface unity, however, lay deep divisions. Redevelopment succeeded where other Fair Deal projects failed, concluded Catherine Bauer, "because different groups of people, like the blind men feeling the elephant, made entirely different assumptions as to the essential nature and purpose of this legislation." Social welfare-minded individuals viewed Title I as a simple extension of the campaign to get rid of bad living conditions and provide everyone with a good home in a good neighborhood. Businessmen saw it as a way to bolster waning property values and open up valuable but decayed central sites for private investment. City planners hoped to use it to rationalize the physical structure of the metropolis. Elected municipal leaders wanted to restore the financial health of the cities by enticing affluent suburbanites back into downtown shopping and residential areas. "Seldom has such a variegated crew of would-be angels," Bauer observed, "tried to sit on the same pin at the same time." [85] Vaguely written, Title I was broad enough to hold all of them—for a while.

On a quick reading, the statute seemed to favor the social welfare groups the most. The "Declaration of National Housing Policy," which served as the preamble to the 1949 Housing Act, affirmed the nation's commitment "to remedy the serious housing shortage, to eliminate slums and blighted areas, and to realize as soon as feasible the goal of a decent home and a suitable living environment for every American family." Title I, itself, referred repeatedly to slum clearance and spoke often of residential districts; it also required that localities assume responsibility for taking care of displaced families. Coupled with Title II, which authorized 810,000 additional units of low-rent housing, the "community development and redevelopment" section adhered to most of the public housers' specifications for city rebuilding.

Despite some strong misgivings, businessmen too could find much to savor in the bill's provisions. They regretted that the measure expanded public housing and kept urban redevelopment tied to the agency that supervised this "subversive" program, but, on the other hand, Title I did assign priority to private reconstruction of blight-cleared neighborhoods. The law instructed localities to afford "maximum opportunity for the redevelopment of project areas by private enterprise." And unlike many of the state statutes, Title I set no limits on profits; the only bridle on individual initiative was the rule that projects be approved by local governments. Thus, despite having lost custodianship of the program they had fathered, the realtors and other businessmen were pleased to discover that the "encouragement to enterprise" label Wagner had attached to the 1943 ULI bill still applied to the 1949 W-E-T version.

Even planners had reason to be happy with Title I. In spite of its failure to see the entire metropolitan region as a single organism and to separate housing from the job of city rebuilding, the bill had positive attributes from the planners' perspective. For the first time, federal legislation established "the development of well-planned, integrated residential neighborhoods and the development and redevelopment of communities" as national objectives. At last, the planners believed, the Federal Government had recognized that the welfare of the country was bound up with the welfare of its cities. Although the planning requirements of Title I fell distressingly short of what the professionals would have liked, the planners took some solace from the fact that the 1949 act demanded a modicum of local preparation before any project could receive federal aid. "General plans for the development of the locality as a whole" was a politicians' phrase that left the technicians confused, but never before had Washington granted this kind of acknowledgment to city planning.

Title I's success in satisfying these disparate groups only pointed up the measure's ambiguities and inconsistencies. There was, as the act's Policy Declaration proclaimed, a "serious housing shortage," thus, removing the slum dwellers' houses—bad as they might be—could only exacerbate the problem. Similarly, the bill's requirement that all displaced tenants be supplied with "decent, safe, and sanitary dwellings" could not be met, since the statute itself said that such accommodations were not available. Public housing might help make up the deficit, but the law contained no provision that cities must accept the low-rent program if they wanted urban redevelopment assistance. While Title I's "predominantly residential" requirement appeared to uphold the housing reformers' position that the primary purpose of the section was "to remove the impact of the slums on human lives," the act's frequent mention of "community development and redevelopment" threw considerable doubt on the issue. Title I could be used in full conformity with the law to tear down slums and replace them with good tax-producing and profit-making projects like office buildings, convention halls, and luxury housing. The imprecision of "predominantly residential" was matched by the obscurity of "general plan." What was the plan to be: some maps and statistics or a detailed blueprint for urban development? Would reconstruction await its completion or would rebuilding begin while the plan was still being drawn up? On these and many other subjects, Title I was silent, doubtful, or contradictory.

The task of resolving the act's uncertainties and the conflicting views of Title I's sponsors fell most heavily on municipal politicians. Administrators and bureaucrats in Washington were involved in this process, but as the Housing Act emphasized local determination many of the important decisions had to be reached at the city level. Almost immediately, these local leaders found themselves engaged in the tricky job of satisfying ill-housed voters and profit-seeking private developers, while at the same time looking to the city's long-term interests and their own political futures. The mayors quickly learned that everyone—the public housers, realtors, planners, and Congress—had underestimated the full responsibilities and implications of the assignment before the nation. For up to now, no one had asked, much less answered, the most crucial question of all: how did the people want to live? The tests of urban development's roadrunning abilities were not over; they were, in fact, just beginning.

5

Marking Time—
The Eisenhower Years

We charge that [the Democrats] have weakened local self-government which is the cornerstone of the freedom of men.

Republican Party Platform (1952)

You can't build houses out of slogans or in the middle of the road.

Adlai E. Stevenson (1955)

After two decades under Democratic control of its national affairs the American electorate decided in 1952 that it was "time for a change." Exhausted by a generation of unrelieved crisis, the nation looked to new leadership to give it a respite from the rigors of advancing democracy at home and abroad. Dwight D. Eisenhower was swept into the White House by an avalanche of voters searching for a return to "normalcy." The general's personality overshadowed old partisan divisions, and if Eisenhower received any mandate from the populace it was to pursue a course of placidity and moderation. Eisenhower did not disappoint his supporters, but after eight years of "dynamic conservatism" metropolitan voters were ready to return to the Democratic fold.

I

At mid-century the large American city presented a mixed picture of robust vitality and creeping senility. The total population of municipalities with over 250,000 people rose by 4.6 million in the 1940s, more than three times the growth figure for the Depression decade. But the central cities lost ground to their suburban competitors in the 1940s. In the nation's 168 metropolitan districts, central city population increased by 13.9 per cent, slightly less than the national average of 14.5 per cent. By comparison, suburban population soared by 35.5 per cent, and the proportion of residents of metropolitan areas living outside the core cities went from 32 per cent in 1940 to 41 per cent in 1950.[1] Housing starts followed similar lines. Most large cities experienced big construction booms in the late 1940s and early 1950s. Chicago, for example, which had not built more than 4800 units in any one year from 1929 to 1940, averaged 9000 new dwellings annually from 1946 to 1952. But again, the suburbs did even better: while central-city housing inventories climbed 19 per cent, that of the suburbs jumped 44 per cent.[2] Retail trade distribution reflected the spreading population patterns. Central cities had accounted for approximately 70 per cent of metropolitan area retail sales in 1939; by 1948, despite a 60.1 per cent increase in total sales, the cities saw their share of the retail dollar slip to 68 per cent. The core-cities' position deteriorated much more rapidly between 1948 and 1954; with the trend toward huge suburban shopping centers well under way, central city sales fell to 58 per cent at mid-decade.[3] Assessed valuations in big cities, after the disastrous deflation of the 1930s, showed a healthy growth in the post-war era, rising 21.4 per cent from 1946 to 1950. Yet tax rates went up too: 7.2 per cent in the same period.[4]

The unsettled state of the urban economy in the decade after World War II brought forth a burst of civic reform activity not seen since the Progressive era. As with the earlier reform wave, this movement for change was led by businessmen concerned with the safety of their investments and a new breed of politicians seeking to unseat the old-style power brokers. The slogans were also the same: an end to corruption, more efficient administration, greater home rule, and the "city beautiful." Missing was the harsh rhetoric against entwining national and local politics, but there was still no great call for federal assistance to deal with outstanding problems.

Restructuring municipal government often served as the starting point in the hunt for stability. Only one big city, San Antonio, chose to make the dramatic switch to a city manager system; nearly all the other cities that overhauled their governments during this period opted for the strong mayor format. Philadelphia's new charter, approved by the voters in 1951 to replace the one that had been in operation since 1885, was typical. It stripped the City Council of its administrative duties and vested them in the mayor, who was also given great powers of appointment and removal. The Council still retained firm control over the budget, but the mayor's hand was strengthened here too. In a number of the largest cities, expert administrators were placed in the mayor's office to oversee the operations of city services. New York, for example, named Luther Gulick, a member of Roosevelt's Committee on Administrative Management and director of the prestigious Institute of Public Administration, as its first city administrator in 1954. Writing in 1957, an editor of *Fortune* observed: "Today the big city must rank as one of the most skillfully managed of American organizations—indeed, considering the problems it has to face, it is better managed than many United States corporations."

Besides enlarging the powers of the office of mayor, urban voters elected "as competent, hard-driving, and skillful chief executives as ever sat in the high-backed chairs behind the broad mahogany desk." [5] The late 1940s and early 1950s saw the defeat of Boston's James Curley and the retirement of Edward Kelly in Chicago, as well as the demise of other lesser known scandal-ridden régimes; even the long reign of Frank ("I am the Law") Hague in Jersey City came to an end, although in this instance the citizens merely exchanged one boss for another. But, in general, the people turned to a new type of leader, one concerned less with the spoils of authority than with exercising that authority to move their cities out of the economic doldrums. Some of the mayors, like St. Louis's Raymond Tucker, an engineer by trade, had little experience in politics; others such as the Philadelphia team of Joseph Clark and Richardson Dilworth, two Mainline corporation lawyers, had been campaigning against corruption for years. Along with De Lesseps Morrison of New Orleans, Albert Cobo of Detroit, and many more, these men brought municipal government out of the shadows into a place of respectability.[6] It was not accidental that Philadelphia's monumental City Hall received its first thorough scrubbing in decades during Clark's tenure.

Once through with the job of municipal house cleaning, the mayors turned their attention to expanding their cities' economic base. Better street lighting, improved garbage collection, more playgrounds, and greater fire protection were important, they realized, but these amenities could be paid for in the long run only if the city was economically healthy. Almost to a man, the nation's big-city mayors equated their cities' prosperity with the well-being of their downtown commercial districts and set about rebuilding these areas to make them more attractive, profitable, and competitive with suburban shopping and office complexes. Reminiscent of the "city beautiful" spirit of the Progressive era, the mayors' programs emphasized massive construction and physical layout: skyscrapers, convention halls, parking garages, freeways, pedestrian malls. "Cities all over America," noted *Newsweek* in 1954, "are busy getting their shapes changed, their faces lifted, and their downtown hearts replaced." A year later *Time* commented on the same phenomenon: "Across the nation, the sound of jackhammers and heavy earth movers told of large-scale building projects under way in the hearts of scores of U.S. cities." Thanks to this vigorous civic action, the Urban Land Institute's Central Business District Council claimed somewhat overoptimistically in 1954, "the forces which have been called 'decentralization' are being routed." [7]

The mayors' efforts to give their downtown areas a new lease on life thrust them into an alliance with the leaders of their cities' business community. Close ties between politicians and the local chambers of commerce dated back to the early days of most municipalities, but these links had become strained with the rise of urban political machines in the last quarter of the nineteenth century. Strong enough to rule the city alone, these political organizations were able to choose which companies and individuals they wished to favor with their franchises and contracts; most of the time they picked marginal operators who were anathema to the local business establishment. It was the members of this élite—the well-to-do merchants, manufacturers, and bankers—who led the revolt against bossism around the turn of the century, but this civic impulse had run its course by 1930. The inherent difficulties of sustaining a reform drive over an extended period of time explains, in part, the movement's decline; just as important, however, was the change in the structure of American business. With the trend toward increasing consolidation, local firms were swallowed up by national corporations that cared little about the well-being of particular cities. The Depression taught many the lesson of survival, and big firms thought nothing about closing down a plant in one city to move to a cheaper labor market or about shutting a retail store in the central city and opening a new outlet in a suburban shopping center.[8] However, the law of diminishing returns caught up with this policy of running and chasing in the late 1940s. Business executives realized that profits could best be maximized by imposing order. Since investments were still concentrated in the central cities, businessmen decided to make their stand for the maintenance of values there. The entrepreneurs' plans for protecting their stake in urban real estate and retail trade dovetailed nicely with the politicians' schemes for redeeming downtown districts. Party labels were easily forgotten as Democratic mayors and Republican boards of trade joined together to help themselves and save their cities.

This strange coalition first appeared in Pittsburgh; it reached its apogee in New Haven. The Democrats had seized control of Pittsburgh's City Hall in 1933 for the first time since the Civil War by attacking the Mellon family-controlled Republican machine.

They retained power for the next twelve years by continuing to use the town's business élite as whipping boys for the hardships of the Depression. All the while Pittsburgh's environment and economy deteriorated. Smog cast an oppressive pall over the city; traffic was bottlenecked in the city's narrow, old downtown streets; no new buildings had been constructed in the commercial Triangle district since the 1920s; obsolescent steel mills were being closed and replacements built elsewhere. Afraid that his family's fortune might be jeopardized if Pittsburgh's decline was not reversed, and unhappy with the sad state of the town he called home, Richard Mellon inaugurated a study of what had to be done to save the city. Uniting Pittsburgh's business leaders behind him, Mellon formed the Allegheny Conference on Community Development. Plans were outlined in 1945 for an ambitious project to replace the ugly warehouses on the site of Fort Duquesne with a park, to relieve strangled downtown traffic with new expressways, and to reduce air pollution. To the surprise of both his political friends and enemies, the Democratic candidate for mayor that year, the unusually astute David Lawrence, endorsed the conference's program. Lawrence, as aware as Mellon of Pittsburgh's ills, recognized that the businessmen's cooperation was necessary if the city was to be prosperous again and his own political future secure. Winning the election in 1945, Lawrence worked closely with Mellon and the conference to push through their initial proposals. In 1947 plans were released for privately financing the redevelopment of the blighted railroad yards near the Point into the $50 million Gateway Center of office buildings, and the Pittsburgh Renaissance was on its way. Taxable values of the cleared and rebuilt properties rose four to five times, giving the city an excellent return on its small outlay of time and money. The Renaissance also made Lawrence unbeatable; he was re-elected in 1949 and in 1953 by successively bigger margins that established him as the undisputed leader of the Democratic party in the Keystone State and a power to be reckoned with in national politics.[9]

Pittsburgh's comeback saga neared its close just as New Haven's began. New Haven, the nation's seventh oldest city, clearly showed its age in the 1940s. A third of its housing was substandard, its factories were outdated, its downtown retail shopping area dilapidated and clogged by traffic. Overvaluation of commercial properties encouraged demolition of existing buildings and blocked the construction of new ones. Apathy was rife in both entrepreneurial and political circles. Businessmen simply accepted New Haven's decline as a fact of life and adjusted to it by moving their firms and families out of town. Democrats and Republicans alike glossed over the city's broad problems, dealing instead with small issues such as constructing a playground in one neighborhood or a new school in another. Richard C. Lee's first two campaigns for the mayor's chair in 1949 and 1951 did not break from this mold. He attempted to out-promise the Republican incumbent and tie his foe to corruption. These tactics brought Lee within two votes of victory, but on his third try in 1953 the candidate decided to base his appeal on a pledge to rebuild New Haven. Backed by independent voters and an improved party organization, Lee finally won, by a margin of 3,500 ballots. Drawing upon Lawrence's experience in Pittsburgh, Lee actively sought the help of the business community in the execution of his plans; unlike the Steel City, however, these plans were always to be the mayor's, not the businessmen's. New Haven did not have a Richard Mellon to provide initiative and direction for the undertaking. Lee stepped in and furnished it, and after some early hostility mobilized the city's financial leaders, as well as the town's most distinguished institution, Yale University, behind his program. The mayor also proved adept at winning federal and state cooperation. Lee received state approval for a highway to run through New Haven's Oak Street slum, and gained federal funds to renew the area. By 1957 over $12 million of private money had been invested in this project and plans were well advanced for private redevelopment of the downtown Church Street district at a cost of $35 million. Richard Lee's re-election pluralities also grew: 20,000 in 1955 and 23,000 in 1957. New Haven became the mecca for mayors hoping to learn from Lee's success, federal officials looking for hints on how to operate their assistance programs, and magazine writers intrigued by the "rebirth" of a city.[10]

Like their Progressive forebears, most of the municipal reformers of the late 1940s and early 1950s did not envision much of a role for the Federal Government in their endeavors. A few had ideological reservations about seeking and accepting federal aid, but the majority simply felt no great need for it. With their emphasis upon income-producing, tax-paying physical construction rather than welfare-oriented social action programs, cities experienced little difficulty in finding enough private capital to push through their projects. Pittsburgh's Renaissance, Philadelphia's Penn Center, Boston's Prudential Center, and Chicago's Lake Meadows were all underwritten by corporate and insurance investors. Municipalities did not reject federal funds available under Title I, but they were slow to make use of it.[11] New Haven's dependence upon federal urban redevelopment aid—due to the city's comparatively small size (165,000) and grandiose schemes—was uncommon in the first half of the 1950s. Only later in the decade, after the opportunities for profitable private rebuilding had narrowed, did urban politicians and businessmen begin to push aggressively for larger federal subsidies.

A comparative improvement in the municipal financial balance sheet also reduced the tendency to look to Washington. After the nightmare of the Depression, the war years had turned out to be a "fiscal utopia" for municipal officials. Cities were forced to hold spending to a minimum because of supply restrictions; manpower shortages cut relief rolls to a fraction of 1930s' norms; and tax money flowed in as never before—even delinquent taxes left over from the previous decade were collected. Blessed with this bonanza, local governments reduced their debt loads: the combined debts of states and municipalities dropped 21 per cent between 1941 and 1945. This pleasant interlude for city controllers ended on V-J Day. The backlog of public works carried over from the 1930s and the war period combined with a greater demand for municipal services and the inflationary pressures present in the national economy caused municipal expenditures to jump 64 per cent from 1945 to 1949. City revenues increased by only 45 per cent; the difference was made up by issuing bonds. The previous peak of municipal borrowing had been reached in the 1920s when the yearly average was $1.5 billion; in the late 1940s, the figure approached $3 billion. Even with this heavy reliance on long-term credit, many municipal ledgers were splattered with red ink. But the reaction of city politicians during this time was not to ask Washington for grants, but to request greater taxing powers from their states. Most states assented, and sales and income taxes took their place alongside property levies as the main sources of municipal revenues. City finances stayed tight throughout the 1950s, but no sense of crisis, such as that which had pervaded the 1930s, prevailed, and there was no demand for across-the-board federal assistance.[12]

The waning of municipal interest in federal aid was reflected in the declining fortunes of the U.S. Conference of Mayors. Organized during the darkest days of the Depression to deal with an emergency of unprecedented proportions, the USCM performed admirably in the 1930s as the cities' representative in Washington. In large measure this was due to the intimate ties between La Guardia and Roosevelt. But both men were gone after 1945 and their replacements were unable to maintain this relationship. The "Little Flower" was succeeded by a string of short-term presidents who lacked his charisma and complete faith in federal solutions to municipal problems. Similarly, Harry S. Truman was not the leader of Congress his predecessor had been, and he often had to turn away from domestic matters to give his attention to foreign developments. Paul Betters, the conference's executive director since its birth, held on to that office until his death in 1957, but the last decade of his tenure was far less happy than his first. The director's attempts to fill the leadership vacuum created by La Guardia's retirement antagonized many of the mayors and led to damaging friction within the organization. Another crippling blow came in 1953 with the switch in national administrations. Dozens of Betters's contacts in the federal bureaucracy were relieved or transferred from their posts and replaced by Republicans not overly friendly to the Democratic-dominated USCM.[13]

The American Municipal Association showed signs in the late 1940s of wanting to step into the void resulting from the USCM's troubles. Back in the 1930s the AMA had abstained from pressure group activity on the grounds that this type of activity was incompatible with its federation-type structure. As late as 1947 the association's director was telling a joint congressional committee that the AMA could take no stand on pending housing legislation, because its membership had "such varying opinions as to the extent of federal responsibility and the economic and welfare questions of federal policy." The association's preponderantly small-town composition also made it highly suspicious of the propriety of federal aid. Addressing a conference on urban problems sponsored by the United States Chamber of Commerce in 1947, the AMA director explained that "federal grants are not desirable nor, frankly, are they wanted." These sentiments, notwithstanding, the AMA revised its constitution later that year to enable the association "to speak with a single voice" in Washington for municipalities. Realizing that federal grants were here to stay and resentful of USCM's ability to influence their administration, the AMA decided to allow cities of over 100,000 people to hold direct membership, and to issue an annual statement of "National Municipal Policy" containing the association's recommendations for action by local, state, and federal governments. It was not until 1954, however, after the selection of a new director and the shift of the association's headquarters from Chicago to Washington that the AMA seriously challenged the USCM as the cities' spokesmen in the nation's capital.[14]

Significantly, both the USCM and AMA focused their limited activities in the early 1950s on civil defense. The problems of urban survival in the nuclear age overshadowed all other federal-municipal cooperative contacts at mid-century. Russia's successful testing of an atomic device in 1949 and the outbreak of hostilities in Korea the following year fueled municipal demands for $600 million in federal civil defense grants. Unimpressed by the mayors' pleas, the Congress authorized only $75 million, required recipients to match the federal funds, and placed administration in the hands of the states. The two urban organizations raised a howl over these arrangements, but to no avail.

International tensions continued to dominate federal-municipal relations throughout Eisenhower's first term. The President called a special conference of mayors at the White House in December 1953 to brief the municipal chief executives on national security affairs and to give some stimulus to the lagging civil defense effort; similar meetings were held in 1954 and 1956. Addressing the USCM's regular convention in 1954, Eisenhower placed the issue of national defense and city protection at the top of the federal-municipal agenda. The administration's omnibus housing bill passed by Congress that year instructed the Housing and Home Finance Administrator "to promote the reduction of the vulnerability of congested urban areas to enemy attack" in carrying out the agency's programs. Little was actually done along these lines, but the threat of nuclear war continued to cast a dark shadow over many city halls. A House committee survey released in 1957 found "widespread" support among mayors for proposals to give cabinet rank to the Federal Civil Defense Administration. It is suggestive of the cities' priorities that mayoral opinion about plans to elevate the Housing and Home Finance Agency to similar status was not as definite.[15] In any case, neither idea would come to fruition during an Eisenhower administration dedicated to stemming "the heedless stampede to Washington."

II

Dwight D. Eisenhower entered the White House in 1953 eager to achieve a "revolution" in the national government: "to make it smaller rather than bigger and finding things it can stop doing instead of seeking new things to do." Five terms of Democratic misrule, he believed, had seen the government in Washington assume functions it had "no business performing," threatening the country with "the rise of a centralized national state in which the seeds of autocracy can take root and grow." Reversing the New Deal-Fair Deal policy of "creeping socialism" also meant clamping down on federal largesse. "Getting control of the budget," the President declared in his first State of the Union Message, "requires that State and local governments and interested groups of citizens restrain themselves in their demands upon the congress that the federal Treasury spend more and more money for all types of projects." After twenty years of slow but growing intimacy, the federal-municipal relationship faced difficult strains.

Eisenhower's selection for administrator of the Housing and Home Finance Agency (HHFA) offered unmistakable evidence of the President's wish to loosen Washington's ties to localities. HHFA was responsible for the two federal programs—public housing and urban redevelopment—most closely connected to the municipal economy; unlike other federal grants-in-aid, both activities were conducted jointly by the federal authorities and local officials without intervention by the states. Throughout the 1940s, HHFA had steadfastly supported the omnibus housing bill that eventually became the Housing Act of 1949. The man Eisenhower nominated to head HHFA, Albert Cole, had, however, voted against that measure. Indeed, as a four-term (1945–53) congressman from a farm district in Kansas, Cole had acquired a reputation in building circles as a staunch foe of liberal housing legislation. He bitterly attacked public housing as a giant step toward the "destruction of private homes and private business" and proposed an amendment in 1949—that was defeated—to bar appropriations for urban redevelopment unless the national budget was balanced. The designation of Cole, bemoaned Minnesota Senator Hubert Humphrey, "is like putting the fox in charge of the chicken coop." "If the President," the St. Louis *Post-Dispatch* commented, "had conducted a search for the appointee most likely to kill the 1949 Housing Act by administrative strangulation, he could hardly have come up with a better choice." [16]

The President's political instincts and preference for moderation, however, kept him from delivering the deathblows his critics expected. In few places was this soft touch more evident than in Eisenhower's handling of public housing. From an ideological point of view, the low-rent program represented everything Eisenhower detested about the New Deal: it was socialistic and paternalistic; it bypassed the states; and it put a burden on the federal budget.[17] Yet, he also felt that the government had a "moral" obligation to help people get out of the slums, and he realized that it would hurt his party in urban areas, especially among blacks who made up a large segment of the public housing population, to halt the program completely without finding a substitute.[18] The White House and HHFA searched in vain throughout Eisenhower's eight years in Washington for a private enterprise alternative to the 1937 act; in the meantime, however, they allowed the public housing effort to deteriorate. While Eisenhower refused to go along with the archconservatives in the Republican party who wished to destroy the program outright, neither did he lend support to those who wanted to see the promises of the 1949 act fulfilled. That act authorized the construction of 135,000 units a year; Eisenhower cut this down to 35,000 units annually and administered the program in such a way as to make it difficult for the cities to take good advantage of even that number.[19] Public housing would still be alive when the Democrats regained power in 1961, although just barely.

Another graphic illustration of Eisenhower's "dynamic conservatism" (his phrase for his political philosophy) at work was the President's maneuvering on urban redevelopment before 1957. Liberals in the Democratic party had been the strongest advocates of slum clearance-redevelopment in the late 1940s and their votes finally put the program on the statute books in 1949, but their traditional foes in the housing field—the realtors, home builders, and mortgage bankers—were not at all unhappy with what the reformers had wrought. Although the businessmen may have disliked some details of Title I, they found nothing wrong with the measure's "principal" theme: reliance upon and assistance to private enterprise. Thus, while the 1952 Republican platform said not a word about subsidized low-rent housing, it did promise to "aid slum clearance with local cooperation." The general's victory in November, however, found the Republicans confused and divided about what kind of housing policies to pursue. More than a few of the G.O.P.'s big contributors in the construction industry talked of getting the Federal Government completely out of housing; just as large a group urged a more selective approach—maintaining some programs and dropping others. This lack of a consensus hindered Eisenhower in his search for an HHFA administrator; none of the business people he talked to wanted the post given the unsettled future of federal housing activities.[20] The job finally went by default to Cole who, having been defeated for re-election to Congress in 1952, had campaigned hard for the position. But when he announced Cole's appointment in February 1953, Eisenhower also created a President's Advisory Committee on Government Housing Policies and Programs. The committee's mission was to find a way out of the impasse that had arisen in Washington as to the proper route to take on housing. High on the list of sensitive questions to be tackled was what to do with Title I.

The urban redevelopment program that the Republicans inherited in 1953 "lay in the dumps." [21] Congress, in 1949, had authorized the HHFA to make $500 million in grants to localities over the next five years for "slum clearance and community development and redevelopment"; by the end of 1953, only $105 million had been committed and less than a tenth of that figure actually had been spent. Over two hundred communities had expressed an interest in participating in the program, but just sixty had reached the land acquisition stage and scarcely half-a-dozen had begun to rebuild.[22] Urban redevelopment's snail's pace was due largely to the obstacles customarily faced by a novel program. Staffing proved to be a problem both in Washington and in the municipalities, because of the shortage of qualified people in this new field. There was a great deal to learn about setting property values in condemnation proceedings and about relocating people. Bureaucratic red tape also wasted time, as localities learned the ropes of drawing up project plans and preparing detailed applications for assistance. Legal challenges to the basic laws under which the program operated occurred in nearly every state, adding to the delays. The Korean conflict, with its mobilization of manpower and goods, disrupted the program still further.

Other difficulties surfaced as actual work started. Municipalities discovered that it was not easy to find private investors who were willing to build on cleared blighted and slum properties. The economic risks were too high, especially since the Federal Housing Administration refused to issue mortgage insurance in those areas. City officials found that providing for the displaced was a bigger burden than they had anticipated. But aside from some extreme conservatives, no one else demanded the scrapping of Title I, although few on the urban scene denied it could use an over-hauling.[23]

The contours of such a repair job were presented in a book that appeared in the spring of 1953 entitled *Renewing Our Cities.* Published by the Twentieth Century Fund, the monograph was written by Miles L. Colean, a respected housing economist with strong ties to the private building sector. Colean's key recommendation called for a changeover from urban redevelopment to what he labelled "urban renewal." Urban redevelopment was limited to specific projects involving the assembly, clearance, and preparation of land within a designated area for rebuilding. According to Colean this was a narrow concept, restricted merely to the physical improvement of slum districts. Urban renewal, on the other hand, was "the comprehensive process of maintaining urban vitality." This entailed augmenting police and fire protection, upgrading educational opportunities for city residents, improving recreational facilities, providing quicker transportation, greater public health measures, action against all types of pollution, metropolitan planning, and political reorganization, as well as increasing the supply of decent housing. On this last point, Colean criticized Title I for its exclusive reliance on the "root-and-branch approach" (that is, total clearance) to rebuilding; conservation and rehabilitation of existing dwellings, he argued, had to be considered as equal partners in the renewal task. Unless steps were taken to halt the deterioration of good housing, slums would continue to grow at a faster rate than the nation's ability to destroy them. But, in general, Colean wished to keep the battle on the slums independent of the renewal program:[24]

The renewal problem is primarily one of how to construct, maintain and rebuild the various parts of the urban structure so that the city as a whole remains at all times in a sound economic condition from the point of view of both the private and public interest. Many other factors—social, aesthetic, political, and so on—enter into the consideration of the renewal problem, but these are incidental or supplemental to its fundamentally economic characteristics.

Colean's proposals received a friendly reception in business and administration circles. Both the private entrepreneurs and the federal officials liked his suggestion for a shift in stress from clearance to rehabilitation; the new format was expected to be a lot less expensive than the current demolition and reconstruction procedures. They also appreciated the economist's demand for more efficient municipal housekeeping; if the cities straightened out their own shortcomings, there would be a decreased need for federal assistance. Soon after Colean's book was released, HHFA started cracking down on local governments for their failure to enact and enforce building and health codes as required by the 1949 Housing Act. The realtors and bankers were particularly pleased by Colean's description of urban renewal in economic terms. Title I had lumped social and economic goals together; urban renewal would give definite precedence to the latter. Profits, not the amelioration of the pathology of the slums, were to be the goal of the revised program.

Eisenhower's Advisory Committee on Housing accepted the main points of Colean's thesis. Chaired by Cole and dominated by representatives of the private construction industry, the committee also counted Colean among its members.[25] The committee's report, submitted in December 1953, urged the replacement of urban redevelopment by a "broadened program of urban renewal" that would permit federal assistance to localities for conservation and rehabilitation, as well as clearance. In return for this aid the report recommended that the Federal Government insist that the "cities help themselves" by requiring the submission of a Workable Program detailing how the locality expected "to attack the problem of urban decay." This Workable Program would have to include rigorous code enforcement, plans for the rehabilitation of existing structures and neighborhoods, plans for the relocation of displaced residents, plans for the widest possible citizen participation in the renewal process, and comprehensive plans for the renewal of the entire city. As part of this change in focus from the slum to the city as a whole, the committee warned against an "overemphasis on housing for reuse," urging instead that "cleared land be put to its best industrial, commercial, institutional, public, and residential use." Among the other proposals contained in the report were suggestions for two new FHA-insurance programs to promote investment in renewal areas and to facilitate the construction of relocation housing, and a recommendation that federal grants be given to states and metropolitan area governments for regional planning.

The President adopted the Advisory Committee's findings as his own. For all of his campaign rhetoric about curtailing federal activity, he was not prepared, in his first term at least, to mangle any program enjoying the wide backing of his supporters in the business community. Urban redevelopment fell into this category; the private builders liked urban renewal even better. Eisenhower could also disarm his more doctrinaire conservative critics by pointing out that rehabilitation was supposed to give the Federal Government greater results for its money, and that the Workable Program would place a larger part of the burden on localities.[26] He forwarded the committee's proposals to Congress in January 1954 with a special message asking for their speedy enactment.

Public housing, as it had every time for the past decade, generated the fireworks at the congressional hearings on the omnibus measure, but urban renewal provided some sparks, too. Cole led off the proceedings with a short description of rehabilitation and conservation, pointing out that up to now deterioration of housing had advanced faster than the cities' ability to clear slums and replace them with new structures. He was followed to the witness table by a parade of representatives from business groups, the U.S. Chamber of Commerce, the Mortgage Bankers Association, the National Association of Real Estate Boards, the National Association of Home Builders and the United States Savings and Loan League, who lauded the urban renewal strategy. This chorus of praise was broken by the testimony of housing reform organizations and spokesmen for the mayors. The public housing-oriented National Housing Conference (NHC), while agreeing that conservation and rehabilitation could play a useful role, cautioned against the tendency to view them as a panacea for all the cities' ills. Baltimore's much-touted successes along these lines had been exaggerated; there was no evidence that strict code enforcement and repairs could reverse the blight process once it had started. Furthermore, the NHC contended, unless substantial amounts of new housing were supplied, rehabilitation would run into the same problems of relocation that had stymied urban redevelopment. Neither renewal nor redevelopment could make any real progress until a much larger number of public housing units had been constructed. The National Association of Housing and Redevelopment Officials (NAHRO), whose membership was composed mainly of local administrators responsible for operating the public housing and Title I programs, warned that unless the Workable Program regulations were framed rather loosely, cities would not be able to participate in the endeavor. It would take several years, NAHRO advised, before municipalities could bring their codes and other rules up to acceptable standards. Witnesses for USCM and AMA echoed these sentiments, adding also that they hoped renewal would not totally replace redevelopment and that more funds would be authorized to get renewal underway.

Urban renewal duplicated urban redevelopment's experience in the legislative arena, only much more quickly. The administration's amendments to Title I emerged from committee without any significant changes and were then almost completely ignored in floor debate as the Congress fought over public housing. Eisenhower had left everyone confused as to how he wished to handle the low-rent program; his Advisory Committee had been divided on the issue, as were both political parties. When the President finally decided on his keep-it-but-starve-it policy for public housing, Congress passed the Housing Act of 1954 in July with the urban renewal provisions intact.

Like its 1949 ancestor, the 1954 act raised more questions than it answered. Cities were given additional tools to work with, but the manner in which they were to be used was as obscure as ever. By enlarging the dimensions of project areas, the 1954 measure weakened the efficacy of the "predominantly residential" requirement; although not entirely free of its connections to housing, Title I had lost a great deal of its welfare characteristics. Cole and other administration spokesmen professed concern for the families displaced by renewal, yet let the public housing enterprise—in many cases, the only hope for a decent home these people had—be emasculated. The Workable Program represented a bold attempt to make cities face up to their own deficiencies, but it remained to be seen whether the Washington bureaucrats could keep the pressure on their local counterparts once the inevitable charges of federal interference began to be voiced. And while the 1954 revision broadened Title I, it did not embrace the non-physical elements Colean had identified as crucial to the renewal process: crime control, better educational opportunities, and political reorganization.

The 1954 Housing Act marked the peak of Eisenhower's attentiveness to urban needs. Although amendments would be added almost yearly, the 1954 revision of Title I remained the basic law of urban renewal for the rest of the decade. The measure demonstrated a growing sophistication in the federal approach to urban ills. Adding rehabilitation and conservation to the redevelopment arsenal provided the cities with subtler weapons with which to remake their physical environment. The grants for metropolitan planning indicated an awareness that urban problems did not stop at city limits. But these matters did not really interest the President. Knowing little about cities and caring less about them, he went along with his Advisory Committee's recommendations because his political aides, upon whom he relied heavily in his first term, thought it would help the party. Urban renewal was the Republican professionals' gift to the G.O.P.'s business friends in the cities; the White House sweetened the pot in 1955 by getting a $400 million two-year authorization from Congress to move urban renewal into high gear. Yet by 1956 there were already signs that Eisenhower was beginning to have second thoughts about the program. That year's Republican platform referred to urban renewal only in the past tense, and the President never mentioned Title I in any of his campaign speeches. The President's "dynamic conservatism" would lose much of its dynamism during his latter four years in the White House.

III

One interest of Eisenhower's that spanned both of his terms was the subject of intergovernmental relations. A believer in tightly structured organization, the President wanted to put federal-state-local contacts on a regular and businesslike basis, to end the chaotic practices of his predecessors. At his request, Congress set up a special commission in 1953 to look into the problem. While awaiting the group's recommendations, Eisenhower, in January 1955, added an administrative assistant to his already large White House staff to handle, among other tasks, liaison with the other levels of government. Later, when the Commission on Intergovernmental Relations' report urged the naming of "a special assistant in the Executive Office to serve with a small staff as the President's chief aide and advisor on state and local relationships," Eisenhower raised this person to the status of deputy assistant and instructed him to devote exclusive attention to issues of intergovernmental concern. The following year, in a demonstration of the importance the President attached to this mission, Eisenhower requested and received his cabinet's blessing of the new arrangement.

To fill this position, Eisenhower chose Howard Pyle. A radio personality turned politician, Pyle was a former governor of Arizona and a Taft supporter in 1952. His experience on the state level and his personal opposition to greater federal power made Pyle, in the White House's view, a perfect choice for the intergovernmental post. A cabinet paper, prepared in June 1956, spelled out eight detailed assignments for Pyle, the most important of which were:[27]

to act as a focal point for advice and coordination in the Executive Office on policy matters affecting state and local government; to keep in touch with the Council of State Governments, the American Municipal Association, and similar organizations; to create, as needed, *ad hoc* committees of departmental representatives to work out specific interdepartmental problems involving relations with state and local governments.

In none of them would Pyle leave much of a mark.

As adviser and coordinator, Pyle at no time possessed adequate staff assistance. The commission that had suggested the creation of Pyle's post had also proposed that a separate office be established to help Pyle develop "guidelines for determining the conditions and circumstances justifying national action." No such aid was forthcoming, however, and without it Pyle found himself restricted to operational duties. He acted as a "troubleshooter," ironing out the misunderstandings to which a system of divided sovereignty is heir. In that role, Pyle participated in the redrafting of the bill granting congressional consent to the Great Lakes Basin Compact, befriended the City of Cleveland in its efforts to obtain special federal appropriations so it could hold the Pan-American Games, and expedited the resolution of a conflict between San Diego and the Navy Department over airports. Pyle's services were useful, but working on a case-by-case basis, he could not construct an orderly framework for the disposition of intergovernmental differences.[28]

Nor was his counsel followed in 1957 when Eisenhower decided to reduce federal participation in urban renewal.[29]

Pyle fared little better in his role as liaison with organizations of state and local officials. His job here, as he saw it, was to preach the Eisenhower gospel of the dangers of centralization of power and the necessity for the states and their subdivisions to assume greater burdens. "I cannot believe," Pyle told one gathering, "that our state, county or municipal governments want a continuous extension of federal authority over their affairs . . . which can only reduce them to the status of satellites and mere administrative units of a federal bureaucracy." [30] His ties to the Council of State Governments proved amicable, but unproductive. The governors and state legislators who composed this group listened politely to Pyle's description of the administration's efforts to cut the size of the Federal Government, applauded his defense of states' rights, and then ignored his call for reform in the forty-eight statehouses so that the cities would not come running to Washington for help.

If Pyle made a scant impression on the states, he failed even more miserably with city leaders. Coming from a region still relatively free of the troubles encountered by the older, larger cities, Pyle did not really understand the urgency of the mayors' pleas in the second half of the 1950s for increased Title I aid. His Western orientation was reflected in his belief that most municipal dealings would be with the Department of the Interior.[31] Picked for his post more for his political background than for his ability to come up with new ideas, Pyle shied away from the heavy reading and long discussions that would have permitted him to speak on urban issues with some authority. Pyle's last two years in the White House before he left in 1959 to join the National Safety Council were taken up defending administration cut-backs in urban renewal funding. This chore hardly endeared him to the mayors, one of whom summed up Pyle's role this way:[32]

Governor Pyle is supposed to be the man to look after local governments. Well, we get lectures on various subjects when we go see Governor Pyle, and he is a nice gentleman and a fine man, but we just don't get results. By the way, he is a former governor, not a local official at all.

Pyle's departure from Washington and the abolition of his office was no occasion for mourning at City Halls.

One initiative Pyle did take before leaving the White House was to create an *Ad Hoc* Interagency Committee on Metropolitan Area Problems, but this, too, produced meager results. The Commission on Intergovernmental Relations' Advisory Committee on Local Government (1955) had identified metropolitan districts as the "most important focal points for intergovernmental relations":

In the metropolitan areas, the relations between the Federal and local governments are numerous and intense. . . . The metropolitan areas have a special significance in the study of intergovernmental relations. They are more concerned than other areas about the broad range of Federal and State grants-in-aid. There is much reason to believe that most of the problems of intergovernmental relations would disappear if it were possible for the metropolitan areas to finance their activities from the resources they possessed but cannot tax for legal or economic reasons.

Seconding its committee's diagnosis, the full commission urged the states "to assume leadership in seeking solutions for the problems of metropolitan government," declaring also that "the National Government has an obligation to facilitate state action" in this field. The federal authorities might begin, the commission noted, "by analyzing the impact of [their] activities on metropolitan areas and by working with the states for better coordination of National and State policies and programs in such areas." [33] Characteristically, more than two years elapsed before Pyle acted upon this recommendation. Finally, in October 1957, he invited representatives from the Departments of Commerce, Defense, Health, Education and Welfare, Justice, and Treasury; HHFA; General Services Administration; Federal Civil Defense Administration; Office of Defense Mobilization; and the Bureau of the Budget to a meeting to discuss "problems arising in Federal relationships with metropolitan areas." Everyone present at the session agreed that better communication was necessary among the various agencies operating in urbanized regions and that the *Ad Hoc* committee had the potential to operate as the instrument for interagency cooperation.[34] Pyle, however, failed to carry through on this promising beginning and did not call another meeting in the remaining fifteen months of his stay in Washington.

The work of Robert E. Merriam compensated, in part, for Pyle's undistinguished record. First as assistant director of the Bureau of the Budget (1955–58) and then as deputy assistant to the President for Inter-Departmental Relations (1958–61), Merriam was the only high-echelon member of the administration possessing familiarity with urban affairs. Merriam's presence in Washington was somewhat fortuitous, for until 1954 he had been a New Deal Democrat. The son of Charles E. Merriam and holder of a master's degree in political science, Robert Merriam entered politics in 1947, winning election to the Chicago City Council from the Hyde Park ward formerly represented by his friend Paul Douglas who was on his way to the U.S. Senate. In contrast to his colleagues, Merriam was an exceptionally energetic alderman, keeping himself informed about pending legislation and voting an independent line. He easily won a second term in 1951. Over the next four years, Merriam's occasional policy differences with the Cook County Democratic organization turned into open revolt as he sought to expose the machine's ties to the criminal syndicate alleged to be running Chicago. In November 1954, he bolted his party to accept the Republican nomination for mayor in the following spring elections, declaring that no one could fight for good government in Chicago wearing a Democratic label. Forty-two years before, the older Merriam had waged a similar battle. To counter Robert Merriam's reform image, the Democrats dumped the lackluster incumbent mayor in favor of a new face, County Clerk Richard J. Daley. Backed by Douglas and Adlai Stevenson, for whom Merriam had written speeches in 1952, Daley turned back Merriam's spirited challenge in the closest mayoral contest since 1943. Embittered by the defeat, Merriam broke all his ties to the Democratic party and two months later accepted the President's offer of the Budget Bureau position.[35]

Once settled in at his new job, Merriam quickly immersed himself in federal-local problems. His formal duties at the bureau did not regularly involve him in such issues; it was at Merriam's own request that he took on the added assignment of "back-stopping" Pyle's office in 1956.[36] Almost at once he tried to engage Pyle in an examination of metropolitan areas, whose efficient management had been the subject of one of Charles Merriam's research projects in the early 1930s. The older Merriam had advocated statehood for such regions as the way to get federal action on metropolitan problems; Robert Merriam steered clear of the city-state idea but felt that the Federal Government had some responsibility for assisting in the search for a solution to the governmental tangle in these areas. Three-fifths of the nation's population lived in the 174 Census Bureau-defined Standard Metropolitan Areas in 1956; a decade later this figure was expected to reach 70 per cent. For this reason alone, Merriam wrote Pyle in 1956, "the Federal Government has a recognizable and proper interest in the problems of metropolitan governments, especially as they relate to our grants-in-aid and other financial programs." It was only Merriam's constant prodding that led Pyle to convene the *ad hoc* committee. Merriam hoped the committee would provide a forum for assessing the impact of national activities on metropolitan life, pull together "the huge and diverse operations of multifold government agencies into a unified approach," and encourage states and localities to cooperate more closely with one another.[37] But Pyle let the committee wither, and although Merriam called three meetings in 1959 and 1960 after moving to the White House, his other responsibilities prevented Merriam from vitalizing the committee.[38] Based upon this disappointing experience, Merriam recommended to President-elect Kennedy in 1961 that he appoint a full-time adviser—with staff help—on federal-metropolitan relations.[39]

Yet, for all his Resources Board inheritance, Merriam was not out of place in Eisenhower's service. Among the first in the 1950s to characterize "the acute growing pains of our metropolitan areas"—central-city deterioration, transportation snarls, haphazard land usage, air and water pollution, inadequate educational and recreational facilities, and racial conflicts—as "a national crisis," Merriam was also certain that "the answer to what ails us will never be found in Washington." Merriam insisted, true to the spirit of the Eisenhower years, that the states and localities face up to their own shortcomings instead of following "the easy trail to Washington." [40] Like the "good government" people of the Progressive era, he believed that administrative improvements, not new programs, would solve the metropolitan mess. The very fact that Merriam usually referred to "metropolitan problems" rather than "urban problems" is indicative of this frame of mind, for the solution to the former required, above all, structural readjustments, while the latter required infusions of money. [41]

But even with his "reform as efficiency" outlook, Merriam proved far more daring than the rest of the administration in wanting to bring metropolitan issues to the fore. In December 1956, he submitted a paragraph on metropolitan problems to the President's speech writers for inclusion in the following month's State of the Union Message. "A major phenomenon of twentieth century life in this country," Merriam wrote,

has been the movement of people to urban areas. . . . All signs point toward even greater expansion in and around our great central cities as well as the smaller urban communities. Urban and regional planning are presented with greater challenges than ever before. The problems are many and difficult, for the needs of the cities are complex. . . . In all, it is a pressing situation wherein there exists an outstanding opportunity for governments at all levels to work together toward a common solution.

Merriam's draft amounted to nothing more than a bare assertion of well-known facts, but it apparently raised too many embarrassing questions for an administration determined to keep out of local affairs. [42] Not until January 1960, on the eve of a Presidential campaign where Republican neglect of urban areas was shaping up as a Democratic target, did Eisenhower use the annual address to Congress to draw attention to the "staggering roster of urban problems." Typically, he coupled this with a warning:

In meeting these [problems] we must, if we value our historic freedoms, keep within the traditional framework of our Federal system with powers divided between the national and state governments. . . . [W]e must realize that nothing is really solved and ruinous tendencies are set in motion by yielding to the deceptive bait of the "easy" Federal tax dollar.

To the end, Eisenhower resisted all suggestions that the national government provide leadership for the growing movement to improve the urban environment.

IV

The federal-local partnership proceeded remarkably smoothly during Eisenhower's first term. For the first time since the inauguration of direct federal-municipal links in 1933, the nation's big-city mayors, overwhelmingly Democratic by party affiliation, were forced to deal with a Republican administration. Suspicions existed on both sides, but a working relationship was established. Eisenhower disappointed the city officials by not moving aggressively on civil defense; their sense of urgency on this matter was diminished somewhat, however, by the President's success in winding down the fighting in Korea and achieving a rapprochement with the Russians at Geneva. Similarly, the mayors' feeling of betrayal at Eisenhower's refusal to carry out the 1949 act's mandate on public housing was tempered by their own difficulties in finding sites on which to construct the low-rent projects.[43] The anguish they experienced as a result of Eisenhower's rhetoric about eliminating federal programs was eased considerably with the passage of the Highway Act of 1956 which launched the 41,000-mile Interstate and Defense Highway System on a very generous 90-10 federal-state sharing basis. Complain as they might about federal meddling through the

Workable Program requirements, urban leaders were quite happy to take the additional money the President and Congress had authorized for renewal. The 1956 campaign saw the Democratic mayors rally behind their party's standard-bearer, but the city electorate voted to extend Eisenhower's leasehold on the White House. Even Chicago, the bastion of the Democracy, followed Merriam into the President's camp.[44]

But if "peaceful co-existence" aptly describes federal-city relations during Eisenhower's first term, then "cold war" sums up what happened during the second. Mutual satisfaction with the status quo gave way to deliberate moves by the White House and the mayors to get the pendulum of change swinging again in their respective directions. It was not long before the President's obsession with a balanced budget ran head on into the desire of civic groups to increase the pace of urban revitalization. Convinced that they had achieved all that could be gained by internal reform and that time was running out for the cities, mayors besieged Washington with demands for vast new sums of money to execute their ambitious renewal plans. Eisenhower, on the other hand, a lame-duck President free of any personal political worries and increasingly surrounded by conservative advisers, grew ever more determined to halt the "deadly drift" toward socialism and overcentralization, even at the risk of G.O.P. losses. Just as in 1932, the mayors and a Republican President were on a direct collision course.

The focus of the dispute was urban renewal. Compared to public housing, the program to give new vigor to the cities had enjoyed, at least until 1957, a charmed life, winning support from Democrats and Republicans alike. Firmly within the American tradition of government assistance to private enterprise, urban redevelopment-renewal twice passed Congress without the need for a roll-call vote. After making some important changes in Title I in the Housing Act of 1954, the administration put its stamp of approval on urban renewal the following year by asking for a doubling of the program's funding authorization. Mayors generally approved of the switch away from slum clearance to economic renewal, although they feared that the additional paperwork of the Workable Program would delay local projects. Indeed, the laborious task of tooling up both the federal and municipal bureaucracies kept city demands upon the federal Treasury at low levels for most of Eisenhower's first term. By 1957, however, the cities, their application-filling machinery well-oiled (among those projects in the pipeline at this time were New Haven's Church Street development and Philadelphia's renewal of the Society Hill area), were ready to launch a big offensive against decay, and they expected Washington to supply the financing.

The President's January 1957 Budget Message gave no hint of the fight that was to follow. With the $900 million previously authorized by Congress almost totally allotted, Eisenhower routinely requested $250 million for urban renewal in fiscal 1958. While local officials felt this covered only "the bare minimum" of what the cities could use—"anything less," the National Association of Housing and Redevelopment Officials cautioned a House committee, "will seriously jeopardize the progress the program is now making"—this figure did represent an increase of $50 million (or 25 per cent) over former expenditure rates.

But the President's endorsement of an expanded war against urban deterioration proved short-lived. Intimidated by the prediction of his secretary of the Treasury that continued high government spending could lead to "a depression that will curl your hair," Eisenhower ordered his aides to cut his own budget.[45] Nothing, not even military appropriations, was exempt from the White House paring knife, but in the end domestic programs bore the brunt of the economy drive. Urban renewal, extremely vulnerable because of its suddenly larger outlays, took a particularly deep slash; in March, the Budget Bureau recommended to Eisenhower that the HHFA request be reduced to $100 million. Administrator Cole protested sharply.[46] As a congressman in the 1940s, Cole had opposed any money for urban redevelopment in times of budget stringencies, but now that he was in the Executive Branch, Cole, like every other bureau chief, felt a proprietary interest in the program he directed, and resisted attempts to decrease its spending authority. The Kansan also believed in what his agency was doing. Addressing a mayors' meeting in 1956, Cole had warned:[47]

Unless improvements [in cities] are made across the board, they will be wasted. There is still time. A year remains, perhaps two or three years. But if we lag and postpone, if we have not by 1960 begun to take across-the-board action, it may be too late. The people of any city without a comprehensive plan of action underway within the next five years will face municipal bankruptcy in 1965.

Appealing the Budget Bureau's decision, Cole succeeded in having $75 million restored, for a total request to Congress of $175 million.

Not since the darkest days of the Depression had City Halls been so disturbed by announcements coming from Washington. Coupled with other HHFA actions, the tightening of the purse strings appeared to herald the "scuttling" of urban renewal. Just a week before releasing its revised budget, HHFA, wanting to spread its limited money around, had issued stiff new regulations that practically called a halt to the huge projects most city officials preferred. This lowering of expectations, in both appropriations and renewal areas, threatened, in the mayors' eyes, to "slow the program to a walk" and shrivel it into "an ineffectual dribble." Afraid that this "temporary fund curtailment" might become a permanent change in policy, the AMA and USCM recruited mayors from all over the country to personally plead the cities' case in the nation's capital. Pyle attempted to assuage them with solemn declarations that the cutbacks denoted "no change of heart about urban renewal," but only an audience with the President would satisfy the mayors. In April a joint AMA-USCM delegation finally got to see Eisenhower. The nation would be in a "whale of a mess," they warned, if the full $250 million were not restored to the budget. Like Hoover before him, Eisenhower listened sympathetically to his visitors' tales of woe, but rejected their appeal. Any escalation in the battle against blight, he explained, would have to be financed by the cities themselves or by the states; he could find no room in an already cramped federal budget for increased aid.[48]

Rebuffed by the White House, the mayors sought help on Capitol Hill. The predominantly Democratic contingent of municipal chief executives, led by Richard Lee of New Haven, Richardson Dilworth of Philadelphia, and Richard J. Daley of Chicago, quickly established close ties with the Democratic chairmen of the housing subcommittees that handled urban renewal legislation. Senator John Sparkman and Representative Albert Rains, both from Alabama and both firmly within the New Deal-Fair Deal tradition of government aid for slum clearance, shared the local officials' fear that the administration's proposals would "cripple the program." Important additional support for urban renewal came from commercial and industrial concerns that were finding the federally subsidized program very profitable. This alliance of big-city Democratic politicians and local businessmen, which had made Lee, Daley, and others practically unbeatable at home, survived the transition to Washington without any measurable loss in effectiveness. Thus, despite the general clamor for less federal spending, urban renewal was spared from the budget-balancers' axe. With scarcely any debate in either chamber, Congress not only restored the President's $75 million cut, but also tacked on an additional $100 million. Eisenhower criticized the legislature for its "excessive" generosity, but dared not veto the $350 million authorization because it was part of an omnibus bill that also extended the lending capacity of the very popular Federal Housing Administration.[49]

The 1957 budget struggle taught the mayors a number of lessons. For one, they learned that urban renewal commanded strong backing in Congress. Never before had the program been tested in the legislative arena; Congress had devoted its attention to public housing, while allowing the Executive Branch to hold the initiative on Title I. This time was different, and urban renewal proved its mettle. Public housing was kept alive only by the dedicated efforts of a small band of congressmen and reformers who cared about the silent poor; Title I, in contrast, drew the favor of influential business groups with powerful political clout. Unsure of themselves in this initial encounter, the mayors limited their demands to the $250 million that Eisenhower had originally asked for, even though their own surveys indicated that the cities could use twice that figure. However, emboldened by their success in 1957, the mayors lost their inhibitions. When Congress reconvened in 1958, the AMA presented a ten-year $5 billion plan. The lawmakers met the mayors only part way, but they blocked the White House's attempts to move in the opposite direction.

Municipal groups came away from the fight convinced more than ever that protection of urban interests required structural changes in the Federal Government. In contrast to the Executive departments, HHFA had been forced to accept exceptionally deep cuts in its fiscal requests. The mayors blamed this, to some extent, on the administrator's lack of stature in the organizational charts and his consequent inability to bargain with the budget director on equal terms. Representation at the cabinet table appeared to be imperative. Other urban analysts felt that an urban adviser in the White House might be better. This person, backed up by a capable staff, would have easy access to the President, and would be able to acquaint him with the metropolitan viewpoint. But whether it was a cabinet secretary or a White House aide, an increasing number of city organizations believed that they needed a friend high in the Executive Branch to present the urban perspective when broad questions of public policy were being settled.[50]

Lastly, the budget imbroglio created a sense of camaraderie among mayors not felt since the Depression. Economic prosperity in the 1940s and early 1950s had cooled the officials' fervor for joint action; they might, on occasion, as in respect to civil defense, get together to demand some federal action, but their individual city problems took precedence. For most of this period, city leaders felt their towns could make do without additional federal programs, that they possessed enough local resources (with state help) to fix up their downtown areas, build their schools, dispose of their sewage, and successfully counter the lure of the suburbs. But by mid-decade, this optimism was beginning to fade. The outward rush beyond central city limits had continued, renovated commercial districts were not keeping up with the shopping centers on the fringes, the costs of providing municipal services were rising, causing tax rates to climb, thus further encouraging the suburban exodus. Tired of and frightened by complaints from property owners about onerous realty levies, and despairing of ever getting their fair share of aid from the states, the mayors looked more and more to the federal Treasury for relief.[51] Then, just as the cities began putting forth tentative schemes for widening the sphere of federal grants-in-aid to municipal government, Eisenhower announced his intention to retrench on urban renewal. Alarmed by this threat to the federal-municipal partnership, the mayors revived the dormant AMA and USCM and made ready to repulse any further White House aggression.[52]

Indeed, speeches delivered in the summer of 1957 by the nation's top two elected officials indicated that the mayors were in for a fight. Appearing before the Governors' Conference in June, President Eisenhower, for the first time since becoming Chief Executive, addressed himself to the "glaringly evident needs of our cities." He did so, however, in a manner profoundly disturbing to municipal leaders. While observing that "urban problems will soon almost defy solution unless action is prompt and effective," Eisenhower showed less concern about mobilizing national resources to clear them up than in making sure that "the powerful Federal Government [is] confined to its proper role." Primary responsibility for meeting urban wants rested with "the government nearest the people," not with "the far-off, reputedly 'rich uncle' in Washington, D.C." The safety of the Republic depended on the transfer of various federal programs to the states so as to "lighten the hand of central authority." The twin themes of economy and freedom also ran through Vice-President Richard Nixon's remarks to the U.S. Conference of Mayors' annual convention in September. National defense requirements, he told the gathering, would continue to make heavy drains on the federal Treasury for years to come. This meant that "less amounts can go for the purposes of grants-in-aid than previously had been the case." Instead of looking to Washington for help, the cities should henceforth direct their energies toward their state capitols. Thus, as summer gave way to autumn, another showdown between the administration and the mayors was taking shape. "The budget-firsters," exclaimed the AMA in its call to battle, "are now threatening the programs upon which America's urban areas depend for survival." [53]

A preliminary skirmish occurred over the Joint Federal-State Action Committee. This body, composed of high-ranking administration aides and a group of governors, had been created at the President's suggestion to "designate functions which the States are ready and willing to assume and finance that are now performed or financed wholly or in part by the Federal Government." Mayors reacted angrily to the Joint Committee's formation, fearing that it would lead to the abandonment of vital federal programs; urban renewal had been prominantly mentioned as a likely target. The local leaders felt defenseless; strictly a two-level affair, the committee barred municipal officials from its deliberations. But the mayors need not have worried: the governors wanted no part of Eisenhower's "historic venture." Despite persistent prodding by the federal members of the panel, the gubernatorial representatives refused to consider any major overhaul in the existing division of powers or duties. In the end, the committee recommended the shifting of only two insignificant programs: municipal water-treatment plants and vocational education. As for urban renewal, the committee's December 1957 report simply urged more state assistance to supplement, not supplant, federal aid.[54] The cities had won another round from the President.

Bloodied, but undaunted, Eisenhower kept up his campaign. Determined to save the cities and states from the dangers of overcentralization even if they did not want to be saved, he threw political caution to the wind by proposing a drastic change in the financing of urban renewal. Under the 1949 Housing Act, the Federal Government covered two-thirds of project costs while the locality picked up the remaining third. Conservative organizations, such as the National Association of Real Estate Boards and the United States Savings and Loan League, had favored a 50-50 matching formula, but Title I's architects, notably Senator Taft, felt the cities would not be able to participate on that basis. The 1954 Housing Act, a product of Eisenhower's more moderate period, continued the 2:1 arrangement.[55] In the spring of 1957, however, searching everywhere for places to cut federal spending, Eisenhower ordered a review of this setup. It was necessary, he told a news conference in a clear reference to urban renewal, that

> this country take a much stronger and longer look than we have in the past as to the proper role of the Federal Government in so many of the projects that are essentially local in character, which produce for the locality a greater value than they do for the nation.

The President hoped that the Joint Action Committee would provide him with a rationale for Washington's graceful exiting from the program; instead, it had implicitly endorsed the present format. But Eisenhower was not to be diverted from his chosen course. Claiming that "the time has come when States and local communities should assume a share of the financial costs more nearly commensurate with the benefits which their citizens receive," he asked Congress in his January 1958 Budget Message to require municipalities to pay 50 per cent of urban renewal expenses.[56]

The President's decision ran directly counter to the advice offered by the two men most intimately connected with the program: HHFA Administrator Cole and intergovernmental relations specialist Pyle. Still smarting from the criticism he had taken from the mayors and Sparkman and Rains for knuckling under to the "penny-pinchers" in the 1957 battle, Cole begged Eisenhower to leave urban renewal as it was. A switch to 1:1, he warned, "would virtually halt" the program. Most cities were already at their financial "breaking point"; only a lucky few would be able to continue under the new ratio. How, he asked, could the administration defend its policy in view of the Joint Action Committee's disinclination to support "a precipitous transfer of urban renewal responsibilities"? Besides, the proposal stood "little chance of passage." It would "generate the strongest kind of political opposition from many powerful quarters," thereby "jeopardizing many other of our legislative objectives in housing." Adoption of the President's idea, Cole concluded, would benefit no one, not the administration, the states, the cities, nor, especially, "the national welfare." [57] Pyle, looking at the issue from a strictly political angle, agreed. He may not have known much about urban problems, but he could count heads: "Any action that might appear to indicate that we are suggesting abandonment of the urban renewal program would almost certainly mean trouble." [58] Both men's appraisals proved to be accurate, but Eisenhower, steeled in his resolve by an economy-minded budget director and Treasury secretary, was putting principle above party.

With defense of the dollar and national security in the wake of Sputnik I uppermost in Eisenhower's mind, all domestic programs underwent retrenchment in the President's budget for fiscal 1959. Farm subsidies, hospital construction, public welfare grants, and aid to veterans joined urban renewal as victims of the campaign to curtail non-military spending.[59] To soften the blow on Title I, Eisenhower did propose that urban renewal be put on a firmer foundation by substituting a six-year commitment for the practice of one- or two-year authorizations. But the total sum Eisenhower asked for, $1.3 billion, fell far short of what the cities wanted. HHFA spokesmen, obliged once again to defend a measure they did not like, conceded during Senate hearings that the budget request was "not geared to anticipated need but rather to what is felt can be made available for this program in the light of other demands upon the Government." Urban renewal seemed fated for the same benign neglect to which public housing had already been consigned.

Alerted by the previous year's events, the mayors and their friends prepared themselves for this latest administration offensive. Indeed, Representative Rains had scheduled hearings on urban renewal in early 1958 even before the President's recommendations were known on the "certainty that they will be pitifully inadequate." The White House, Rains declared, "if left to its own resources would cripple our essential domestic programs." The testimony his subcommittee heard demonstrated the cities' new aggressiveness: the USCM and AMA pushed for a ten-year, $5 billion plan with Washington picking up 80 per cent of the entire cost.[60] Steering a middle route between the two sharply divergent proposals, the Democratic majorities on the House and Senate panels decided to retain the federal share at two-thirds. They rejected the President's program because they believed it would stall urban renewal; the mayors' plan was turned down because it would give the cities a "free ride." The committees also compromised on the money issue: the Senate group approved a six-year, $2.1 billion program; the House unit a two-year, $1 billion measure. All of this work came to naught, however, when the conservative-dominated House Rules Committee, acting with Eisenhower's blessing, refused to clear the omnibus housing bill for floor consideration. Advance planning for urban renewal projects would have come to a halt in 1958 if it had not been for the economic recession that forced the President to release $100 million of previously authorized funds he had bottled up by Executive order. All of this money, however, was allocated by the end of the year.

The battle of numbers resumed as soon as the new, Eighty-sixth Congress convened in January 1959. Eisenhower's electioneering during the fall against "spendthrift" Democrats had been convincingly rejected at the polls, but the President stuck to his restrictive budget policies. He resubmitted the same urban renewal package the housing committees had turned down the year before. The mayors, in turn, distressed by the loss of momentum resulting from legislative inaction in 1958, upped their request to $6 billion over ten years. Congress, now overwhelmingly Democratic in composition and already looking ahead to the 1960 Presidential contest, showed itself to be more generous than ever. With orthodox Republicans standing by powerlessly, a $900 million, two-year authorization was soon on its way to the White House for the President's signature. But

Eisenhower vetoed the measure instead, claiming that the omnibus bill was "extravagent and inflationary" and the urban renewal provision "excessive." Unable in the face of this increasingly common exhibition of executive power to muster the necessary two-thirds majority to override, the Democrats passed a new bill allocating $650 million for urban renewal for the next fiscal year. Again Eisenhower killed it for "going too far." Failing once more to reverse the President's action, Congress accepted a compromise that spread the $650 million over two years.[61] This was still $150 million above what Eisenhower asked for, but $550 million below the mayors' requests. Eisenhower failed to reduce federal participation in urban renewal, but neither did the cities succeed in significantly increasing it. It was a standoff so typical of the Eisenhower era.

As Eisenhower's second term came to an end, practically all ties between the mayors, both Democratic and Republican, and the administration had been severed. More than three years of constant haggling over money for urban renewal had destroyed each side's faith in the other. City officials, declared New York's Robert F. Wagner, Jr., "are tired of being treated as special pleaders seeking unwarranted assistance to meet purely local problems, instead of what we really are: the field grade officers who must daily and at first hand direct the battle against the nation's prime domestic problems." Federal officials, on the other hand, rejected the idea of some "that almost any problem common to localities is to some extent a national problem and therefore subject to federal 'responsibility.' " [62] Programs continued but dialogue ceased. HHFA bureaucrats still attended AMA and USCM conventions to explain procedural changes, but no high-ranking administration spokesmen appeared before either group after Vice-President Nixon's address to the USCM in September 1957.[63] The organizations' invitations went rather to congressional friends of the cities' cause, to men like Senators Joseph Clark of Pennsylvania, Hubert Humphrey of Minnesota, and John Kennedy of Massachusetts. For most advocates of federal-municipal cooperation, the Eisenhower years could not end too soon.

V

The politics of the center that characterized the 1950s barred the fostering of important new federal-municipal contacts. Old ones were retained, and in urban redevelopment's case even broadened, but no additional links forged. More self-confident after their recovery from the Depression, cities were slow to enlarge the foothold in Washington the New Deal had given them. Lack of good information about their communities' needs kept municipal leaders home; so did the political atmosphere in Washington. Untouched by the progressive influences that led his two predecessors to expand the realm of federal intervention, Eisenhower pulled the Executive Branch back from the frontiers of social change. He was more concerned about holding the line on government spending, about returning responsibilities to the states, about giving free enterprise free rein, than about correcting the imbalances in society. Congress, while somewhat more liberal with the purse strings at the end of the decade, could not fill the leadership void. Itself controlled by a conservative-moderate coalition reluctant to confront the nation's domestic shortcomings, the legislature acted mainly as a restraining force on Eisenhower's disposition during his second term to balance the budget at any cost.

As the politicians marked time, the cities began to slip noticeably. The 1960 Census did have some bright spots for the core cities, but the general picture was gloomy. No less than ten of the fifteen largest municipalities lost population during the decade; the proportion of people in metropolitan districts living in the central cities dropped from 59 per cent in 1950 to 51 per cent.[64] This decline in residents returned at least one beneficial dividend in helping to ease the housing shortage, but its effect on retail trade was disastrous. Every one of the ten biggest central cities saw their share of total metropolitan sales fall; 95 of 109 central business districts actually experienced a loss in receipts between the 1954 and 1958 business censuses. Just as depressing were the employment figures. From 1954 to 1958 the forty largest central cities had an average annual loss of nearly 3000 manufacturing jobs. Gains in the wholesaling, retailing, and service industries partially offset these losses, but after 1958 even these categories showed net declines.[65] On the municipal finance side, the story was one of higher spending and higher taxes. Per capita expenditures of city governments, which had been just under $100 in 1952, were nearly $200 in 1960; per capita property tax revenues rose from less than $50 to $75 over the same period. State grants-in-aid increased almost 60 per cent during this stretch, and while direct federal assistance to big-city governments jumped 300 per cent (from $40.9 million to $168 million), the federal contribution to local budgets was only 1.2 per cent of total municipal receipts.[66]

Perhaps the most significant development in the cities during the 1950s was the changing racial composition of urban centers. Negroes had been leaving the South since after the Civil War so that by the turn of the century, sizeable Negro populations lived in many large Northern cities. But it was not until World War I that the out-migration became substantial. The Depression slowed the north-ward flow in the 1930s; World War II, the increasing mechanization of agriculture, and the need for manpower in Northern and Western factories speeded it up again in the 1940s. More than 1.59 million blacks joined the exodus from the South in that decade; another 1.45 million followed them in the 1950s. As Negroes moved into central cities, and that is where nearly all went, middle-class whites moved out. Eleven of the fifteen largest non-Southern cities had a net loss of whites in the 1950s; all fifteen had a net gain of blacks, ranging from 22.6 per cent to 189.1 per cent. In only one city, Washington, did Negroes comprise a majority of the population, but in a score of others they were a very visible presence.[67] Somewhat overcautiously, a leading demographer told a 1958 Conference on Metropolitan Growth sponsored by the U.S. Chamber of Commerce: "The urbanization of the Negro [is] probably the most important social problem that faces metropolitan areas today." [68]

When Eisenhower left office in January 1961, the streets were still quiet and the welfare centers relatively empty, but the pressures for change were building. Prosperity had not solved the governmental problems of administering the metropolis; it had added to them. Urban assets and political authority were now more scattered, making it more difficult to bring them to bear on the deficiencies in public services. Nor had unprecedented affluence eliminated poverty or the dilemmas of race. For these issues Eisenhower had little interest and even fewer answers. His successors would suffer the consequences for the lost time.

6

Federal Programs and the Cities—
Patterns of Three Decades: 1933–60

The many Federal programs affecting metropolitan areas today are initiated from various sources and generally without reference to their impact on the areas to which they are directed.

> Bureau of the Budget Staff
> Memorandum—November 1960

The federal-municipal partnership neared its thirtieth birthday in 1960. Much to Eisenhower's chagrin, the helping hand the New Deal had hesitantly held out to urban government and urban residents in the 1930s was now an established feature of American political life. As one mayor told a House subcommittee investigating federal-state-local relations in 1957, big-city officials and interest groups knew their "way around fairly well down in Washington." The Federal Government, however, had by then become far different from the pre-Depression institution of that name. In the nation's attempt to cope with the challenges of modern industrial society and world peace, the authorities in Washington had greatly expanded their range of activities and administrative apparatus. Just as in the first half of the nineteenth century, cities again found federal decisions on such matters as internal improvements (for example, grants for airport construction), and contracts and installations (for example, military procurement and bases) important determinants of local economic health. But if practically everything the central government did—from giving price supports to agricultural products to fostering collective bargaining—affected metropolitan development, four federal programs instituted after 1933—public housing, urban renewal, home mortgage insurance, and large-scale highway building—left the greatest mark on the urban landscape.

I

No federal endeavor in large cities aroused more political controversy than public housing.[1] Initiated as a recovery measure in a period of economic depression, the low-rent program represented one of the most radical legacies of the New Deal. Unlike social security, for example, which served the middle class, operated on actuarial principles and was immune from partisan criticism by 1952, public housing entailed government subsidies to the bottom third of the population and, consequently, never won wide popular support. The private American city could not take public housing to its heart.

Public housing met opposition in both Washington and the cities. Hardly a year passed between 1935 and 1960 without a congressional vote on public housing's fate; only the farm program could match that track record. Those fighting public housing at the national level fell into two groups: rural conservatives who disliked federal spending, especially in urban areas; and urban businessmen —particularly realtors and home builders—who felt government aid to the poor raised their property and income taxes and reduced their profits. The rural congressmen provided most of the votes against the program, but the financing of the intense anti-public housing lobbying campaign was assumed by the urban elements of the coalition. This alliance succeeded in virtually halting the program from 1939 to 1949 and keeping appropriations far below authorized limits from 1950 to 1960. The program's foes had also been able to add debilitating amendments to public housing legislation. What they could not accomplish in the national arena—killing the program completely—the realtors and home builders sought to bring about on the local scene. They supported candidates pledged to reject offers of federal housing aid, forced popular referenda on the question of proposed public housing construction, and encouraged neighborhood groups in their efforts to prevent the placement of projects in their midst. Thanks to these tactics, less than 440,000 public housing units, about one-tenth of the number needed to satisfy the housing requirements of the urban poor, were completed between 1939 and 1960.[2]

Those units actually built did not return their highest possible dividends to the cities. Crippling regulations in the law, unsatisfactory and often unsympathetic administration, community hostility, and socio-economic changes significantly reduced public housing's ability to help the poor and the cities. The program represented a net plus to the urban environment, but by 1960 few of its friends—social workers, labor unions, liberal mayors and congressmen—doubted that it could use an overhaul.

Typical of the statutory limitations on public housing were the curbs on construction expenses and tenant income. Proponents of the program had to accept these restrictions to blunt their opponents' allegations of extravagance with the taxpayers' money and competition with private enterprise. These concessions to America's laissez-faire heritage did not stop the local housing authorities (LHA) from building sound structures with provisions for air and light far superior to what private firms had constructed, but it did prevent the LHAs from supplying some basic amenities. Closets without doors, elevators that did not stop at every floor, bare lobbies and hallways were the penalty the poor paid for public landlordism. Compared to what they had left behind in their dark and dirty hovels this price was indeed small, but the psychological costs of the big, skyscraper-type projects (building large and up was supposed to be more economical) that were characteristic of public housing in Eastern and Midwestern cities could sometimes be overwhelming.

"Visually they [i.e., projects] may be no more monotonous than a typical suburban tract," Catherine Bauer wrote in 1957,[3]

but their density makes them seem much more institutional, like veterans' hospitals or old-fashioned orphan asylums. The fact that they are usually designed as islands—"community units" turning their back to the surrounding neighborhood, which looks entirely different—only adds to this institutional quality. Any charity stigma that attaches to subsidized housing is thus reinforced. Each project proclaims, visually, that it serves the "lowest-income group."

The drabness of the projects' milieu—one critic likened it to a well-kept cemetery—continuously reminded possibly forgetful tenants of their dependent position in society. To both resident and taxpayer, public housing became the "modern symbol of the poorhouse." [4]

Public housing's rules on income further isolated its beneficiaries from the rest of society. Families faced eviction once their earnings exceeded federally prescribed levels; after 1949, these limits were kept very low to avoid the charge of interference with the private housing market. Although this made more public housing available to the desperately poor, stricter enforcement of the income regulations also had some less positive results. The crackdown on over-income tenants deprived projects of their most successful residents and natural leaders; continued dislodgements obstructed the emergence of replacements. For those compelled to leave, the next move was often back to the slums. Their incomes might be above the public housing limits but far from the minimum necessary for decent private housing; for those remaining, the income limits slapped a "cast-iron top" on the incentive to improve. "Nothing," one housing official noted in 1956, "could be more murderous to the simple earthly American pattern of bettering oneself by little ingenious ways than the present regulations and rigmaroles on income eligibility." [5] A person had to refuse to earn more or to cheat to stay in public housing. In 1948, the median income of public housing families was 44 per cent below the median for all urban families; nine years later, the figure was 58 per cent.[6] Public housing was achieving its goal of serving the poverty-stricken, but in the process it was making itself more unpalatable to the rest of urban—and affluent—America, which associated the poor with rising crime rates and lower property values.[7]

The problems of race also burdened the public housing effort. Thanks to the dedicated work of Harold Ickes, the program's first director and a former president of the Chicago branch of the National Association for the Advancement of Colored People, Negroes had fared exceptionally well in the beginnings of the public housing endeavor. Ickes required localities to give blacks an equitable share of the new dwellings his agency constructed—about 30 per cent were so reserved—and inaugurated the practice of appointing racial relations advisers whose job was to protect minority group interests in all phases of the public housing venture. His successors continued these policies.[8] This unusual record did not go unnoticed: "The United States Housing Authority," declared Gunnar Myrdal in his classic study, *An American Dilemma* (1944), "has given him [the Negro] a better deal than has any other major federal public welfare agency." By the 1950s, however, public housing was so closely identified with Negro housing that the program could not be sustained in some big cities and could be continued in others only if public housing was kept away from white neighborhoods. Because of the large post-war migration of Negroes to Northern central cities and the blacks' inability to match the income gains of whites in this period, Negroes accounted for an increasingly large proportion of the population eligible for public housing. In Detroit, for example, 90 per cent of the people who fell within the law's income limits were black; in Chicago, 80 per cent. As the presence of blacks in projects became more marked, poor whites tended to shun public housing. By 1960, Negroes occupied nearly 50 per cent of all public housing units, and in cities like Los Angeles and Chicago 80 per cent of the tenants were non-white.[9]

The identification of public housing in the middle-class mind with overcrowded projects, the culture of poverty, and the invasion of racial minorities made the location of subsidized dwellings a volatile issue in local politics. Cities that rejected the realtor-home builder arguments about taxes and socialism—and most of the big ones did—were still divided about the best place to put these unpopular but necessary projects. The social workers and planners who staffed many of the LHAs favored vacant land sites. These offered the advantage of being cheaper and quicker to build on than slum properties; furthermore, with housing in short supply, it appeared to make no sense to destroy existing homes, slum or otherwise. But since vacant land was usually to be found only in outlying working- and middle-class neighborhoods, the LHAs' schemes were unacceptable to a majority of politically active city residents. They would support public housing only on the condition that it remained out of their communities. Elected municipal officials accepted these terms and set up informal arrangements for their implementation. In New York City, for example, no project could be approved by the Board of Estimate unless the borough president of the area involved gave his consent; the approval of the local alderman was required before the Chicago City Countil would agree to a LHA proposal. The winning candidate in the 1949 Detroit mayoralty election rode into City Hall on his pledge to build public housing "where it is needed—in the slums." And that was where it was constructed in most large cities, thus helping to perpetuate the segregation of the poor and the Negro ghetto.[10]

Public housing's capacity to improve the central city environment was also diminished by the mechanics of the federal system. After 1937 the Federal Government itself did not build another public housing unit; it merely supplied funds for that purpose to those communities that wanted it. This change occurred in response to lower court decisions that had brought up the issue of the legality of Washington's use of its eminent domain powers to raze slums and construct low-cost housing. Afraid that a hostile Supreme Court might declare the entire PWA operation unconstitutional in adjudicating appeals of these cases from the lower courts, Roosevelt decided to rely upon the well-recognized police powers of the states and municipalities in the housing field. Good politics also dictated the switch. Conservatives who opposed the extension of national power might be appeased, and the reformers who chafed at Ickes's tight centralized direction of the program could be satisfied. Local control undoubtedly eased public housing's path through the courts and Congress, but it fostered the dichotomy between core cities and their suburbs in metropolitan areas. Most of the large central cities joined the program; very few of the suburbs, however, followed suit. Unlike the older core areas, the vast majority of suburbs had no serious slum problem and very few people below the poverty line. Constructing public housing, suburbanites believed, would only encourage other impoverished families to move in, driving up taxes and making their communities less attractive. Thus, at the same time that public housing and other federal programs were influencing many in the middle class to flee beyond the city limits, suburban zoning laws and the non-existence of public housing kept the poor bottled up in core cities, away from the growing job market in the suburbs and on the municipal welfare rolls.[11]

Yet for all its troubles and deficiencies, public housing helped most of the people it reached. The living accommodations might be spartan, but at least they were clean, decent, and safe. An elevator apartment may not have been the most desirable place to raise a family, but public housing was free of rats, and the playgrounds and open spaces the projects provided were a vast improvement over the dangerous, heavily trafficked slum streets. Anti-social behavior did not disappear, but the slum mores, which had glorified such actions, lost some of their strength in the green surroundings of public housing. The income eligibility rules were not always enforced wisely, but until enough public housing could be built to meet the needs of all those who could use it, the regulations helped keep the program open to families in most dire want. Public housing was hardly the panacea its advocates had suggested,[12] but the low vacancy rates and long waiting lists offered good evidence that the Federal Government was putting out a basically worthwhile product.[13]

Beginning in the mid-1950s, public housing's friends attempted to eliminate the program's weaknesses, but an unsympathetic Eisenhower administration frustrated their efforts. Among the reformers' proposals were plans to drop the large-scale project format in favor of small, scattered site developments more in tune with other types of housing in local neighborhoods; proposals to modify eligibility rules to allow over-income families to remain as tenants, thereby maintaining a more diverse population in public housing; and suggestions to provide residents with such social services as family and job counseling, community centers, and health clinics. With this kind of unified approach, the public housers believed, they could enhance the program's value to the poor and make it more palatable to the average urban dweller.[14] But restoring vigor to public housing would cost money, and the Republican régime in control of the Executive Branch cared little for the goal and even less for the means. Further progress in supplying cities with more and better low-cost housing would have to await a new decade and a new administration in Washington.

II

Urban redevelopment-renewal, the first national legislation to deal explicitly with the central city, generated little of the political bitterness that plagued public housing in the 1950s, but it, too, had its human problems. The financial stringencies that kept the low-rent program from fulfilling the hopes of its sponsors also hindered the renewal effort; although in the latter instance, it was not a shortage of public funds so much as a lack of private capital. Federal subsidies were available, but the cities found it difficult to use them profitably and, at the same time, equitably. "Architecturally or socially," admitted Title I's supporters at the editorial board of *Architectural Forum* in 1958, urban renewal's accomplishments "do not match the political ingenuity that made them possible."

At the close of the 1950s, what stood out most about urban renewal was how little it had changed the face of American cities.

When Title I cleared Congress in 1949 "there was a widespread expectation that a great redevelopment blitzkrieg was going to hit the country, that the scent of Federal money would nerve local planners and builders to undertake great things." [15] And, indeed, some startling transformations did take place. The grimy St. Louis riverfront received a thorough housecleaning in preparation for the construction of the graceful Gateway Arch and a new sports stadium; Philadelphia's historic downtown area, thanks to some imaginative federal-municipal cooperation, regained some of its former elegance; and New Haven's rat-infested Oak Street slum gave way to a gleaming complex of modern office buildings and fancy apartment houses. But behind the glitter, stark figures told another story. After more than a decade of action, less than ten square miles of blighted land had been acquired and only three square miles redeveloped. At urban renewal's "death-step pace" the job of salvaging the hundreds of square miles of slums would take centuries and even then might not be finished since new blight was forming at least as fast as the old disappeared. Instead of a blitzkrieg, the cities found themselves in a war of attrition, which they appeared to be losing.[16]

Urban renewal lagged for a variety of reasons. An important cause of the delay was the very complexity of the task. The demolition and rebuilding of entire city districts could not be done overnight; it required extensive consultations and deliberations at the local level. What was to be ripped down? What was to be put up in its place? Who would do it? How was it to be paid for? These questions all had to be decided before the city could begin protracted negotiations with the federal bureaucracy. Detailed and cumbersome procedures did nothing to ease the agony. As one mayor complained to a Senate committee in 1958, referring to the 1949 act and the scores of amendments to it, the law "is so full of 'provided thats' and 'notwithstandings' that it is a nightmare to track down just what is provided for." The paperwork entailed was stupefying, the steps in the planning and review process endless. On the average, more than two years elapsed between receipt of an application in HHFA offices and final approval of the federal grant. Total time consumed on projects, from beginning to completion, often ran as high as six to nine years.[17]

This dilatory schedule reduced the program's appeal to private investors. Yet their capital was essential to the success of the endeavor. Under the law, federal funds were available only for the purchase and clearance of blighted properties; rebuilding was to be the task of private enterprise. Realtors and construction firms had fought for this arrangement, but they proved hesitant in taking advantage of it. Although government subsidies in the form of "write-downs" made urban renewal a potentially lucrative outlet for investment, the long and uncertain incubation period scared many people away. "Redevelopment is a fine opportunity for profits served on a silver platter," observed a leading mortgage banker, "but the platter has a tight lid and is surrounded by mousetraps." [18] In 1960, over 5,000 acres of the 7,700 acres acquired by local renewal agencies remained unsold.[19]

Important consequences flowed from Title I's dependence upon a small pool of private funds. The 1949 act had been worked out as a compromise between those housing reformers who wished to use the new device to "help remove the impact of slums on human lives," and businessmen interested in restoring central city property values. As passed by the Democratic-controlled Congress, the measure seemed to favor the reformers: it contained a "predominantly residential" requirement to insure action against the slums and vested administration with the Housing and Home Finance Agency. Title I had been purposely drawn flexible so that it could contribute to city betterment, but in HHFA's mind, "the dog was slum clearance and the tail was community development." [20] Urban redevelopment's troubles in getting started in the early 1950s, however, gave businessmen a chance to reverse these priorities. Using their influence with the Eisenhower administration, they succeeded in easing the "predominantly residential" rule and converting urban redevelopment into the more economically oriented urban renewal whose goal was to rebuild the cities. Also, the Republican-led HHFA was philosophically inclined to allow local authorities greater discretion on how to proceed.[21]

Municipal officials quickly turned urban renewal to their own advantage. They found it politically profitable and financially expedient to channel the federal largesse into ambitious programs to revive downtown shopping and business centers and build conveniently located luxury housing so as to attract middle- and upper-class families back from the suburbs. They had little choice, given the realities of the electoral and real estate marketplace. Bankers could be induced to risk their money only if the rewards were to be large and reasonably secure; providing housing for the slum dweller obviously met neither of these standards under existing legislation. Furthermore, the reconstruction of central business districts and the erection of expensive apartments promised to add to the cities' sorely pressed property-tax base. And as an extra dividend, redevelopment permitted politicians to forge close ties with their communities' financial leaders; both groups possessed a common interest in fostering their city's image as a dynamic, vital, and growing metropolis. Instead of helping the ill-housed, urban renewal was used to enhance political reputations, provide profitable investment opportunities for lending institutions and builders, and indirectly improve the cities' economic foundations.[22]

Severe distortions were created in the slum clearance process by the subordination of urban renewal to the laws of supply and demand. Areas that could not objectively be called blighted were nonetheless demolished because their desirable locations made them ripe for "higher uses," such as office buildings and civic centers. Stable and decent neighborhoods, like Boston's West End and Los Angeles's Bunker Hill, fell below the wrecker's ball while truly deteriorated districts were allowed to stand because no one saw a way of making money out of them except as slums.[23] Urban renewal carried out beneath the banner of city betterment only aggravated the agony of being poor. In ten years, Title I was responsible for the destruction of over 140,000 units of housing, some standard, most substandard, but nearly all low-rent. Over that same period, in contrast, the redevelopment program built less than 40,000 units, of which only about 5 per cent were within the means of a low-income family.[24] Private, unsubsidized developers could not service this market, and by a quirk in the law, public housing was virtually excluded from renewal areas.[25] At a cost of hundreds of millions of dollars, urban renewal succeeded in materially reducing the supply of low-cost housing in American cities. Just as the liberals had feared, slum clearance cleared the slums without helping the slum resident.[26]

New York City provided a classic example of urban renewal gone awry. Its program was run by Robert Moses, "the man who gets things done." In one respect his reputation was richly deserved, for under his leadership the City of New York accounted for one-third of all urban renewal construction started before 1960. But Moses carried out his mission with the man of action's contempt for all planning and planners; he belonged to the school, a student of his activities had observed in the 1940s, that believed "the way to solve problems is to attack the sorest spots at dawn without presuming to try to plan in terms of the whole community." [27] His Slum Clearance Committee operated without the benefit of professional planners on its staff and coordination with the City Planning Commission was practically nonexistent. The only pattern to his projects, claimed one critic, was that they were "tailored mainly to serve or assist special designs of the moment, institutions or favored sponsor organizations, with only enough slum clearance to assure Federal assistance." [28] Along with his disdain for planners, Moses lacked any faith in the public. "People," Moses declared, "always stand in the way of progress." [29] Despite the federal law's requirement of the widest possible citizen participation at all stages of the urban renewal process, the first notice seen by New Yorkers living or conducting business on a site designated for Title I demolition was generally a story in the newspapers.[30]

Many cities copied Moses's techniques. The initiative for urban renewal usually rested with business-dominated redevelopment authorities who looked for "show" projects—eyesores that could be converted into attractive and profitable developments. Rarely did the local agencies let the public know what they were doing. They kept the general populace in the dark about their operations for as long as they could, because they feared, as one city official admitted, that the voters "would not like it if they understood it." [31] Even in New Haven, where community involvement was championed, the citizens' role tended to be ritualistic rather than substantive.[32] The results were a program that rewarded the strong and punished the weak.

Urban renewal's treatment of those it displaced reflected its diversion from the welfare path laid out by many of Title I's architects. As written, the 1949 act represented a tremendous advance in the Federal Government's attitude toward the people it uprooted while engaging in public works. Property owners necessarily received compensation for buildings condemned for slum clearance, but until 1949 the national authorities refused to assume responsibility for the inconveniences and hardships caused tenants and small businesses. The PWA Housing Division and the USHA sometimes paid the moving expenses of evicted families, but this was done only to expedite demolition. Although the 1937 Housing Act made no specific reference to relocation, it did allow city officials flexibility in fulfilling their obligations under the equivalent elimination section (which required the demolition of one substandard dwelling for every public unit constructed), in cases of an acute local housing shortage. This was a significant first step. But even with liberal interpretations by USHA, public housing programs often forced families to leave one slum for another.[33] Dissatisfied with public housing's performance in this field and alarmed by signs that urban redevelopment would only add to the already huge deficit in the housing supply, reformers demanded that future federal redevelopment laws contain safeguards for the rights of those required to vacate their homes. "Without statutory provisions," Catherine Bauer had warned in 1943, "the pressure for placing high rental apartments in redevelopment areas and neglecting to provide for displaced low-income families will be too overwhelming to withstand." While

Congress turned down suggestions that site residents be given preference in new housing built in the project area (there were good planning reasons for this rejection), it did insist that localities draw up "a feasible method for the temporary relocation of families displaced," and show that "there are or are being provided . . . decent, safe, and sanitary dwellings . . . at rents or prices within the financial means of the families displaced . . . equal in number to the numbers of and available to such displaced families." Congress, apparently, had viewed relocation as an integral part of the whole renewal process and a crucial element of the comprehensive package it enacted to fulfill the National Housing Goal of "a decent home in a suitable living environment for every American family." There could be no rationale for federal aid for urban redevelopment, explained the program's first director, "unless it results in improving conditions of living for the families now subjected to blighted and blighting surroundings." [34]

Holding urban renewal to this commitment would have been difficult under the best of circumstances; it proved to be impossible during the 1950s. While the gigantic suburban building boom of the post-war years solved most of the housing problems of middle-class families, it left those of the moderate- and low-income group relatively unchanged. Standard housing relinquished by families leaving the cities for new homes on the outskirts filtered down and allowed some in this category to escape the slums, but millions were still confined to dilapidated dwellings. Urban renewal's slum clearance operations only added to the deficit and to the problems of displaced families. [35]

The cities' answer to this dilemma was to ignore the relocation requirement. Viewing urban renewal as little more than a real estate enterprise, local agencies saw the rule as a burden and a barrier to profitable ventures rather than a major tool for the implementation of national policy. Finding vacant, decent housing for poor people in an era when such low-rent dwellings had virtually ceased to exist took time and money that municipal leaders felt they could ill afford. In case after case, cities filed in Washington the necessary and bulky forms that detailed how they would take care of the unhoused and then went ahead and, as one federal official described it, "gave the families a few dollars and told them to get lost." [36] HHFA bureaucrats were aware of this deception but adopted a hands-off policy, knowing that to do otherwise would jeopardize the program. The consequences were predictable: further overcrowding of the slums; intense pressures on "gray areas," which hastened their decline to the slum level; and higher rents. To a large extent, redevelopment was possible only because of the "hidden subsidies" provided by the residents of the district to be cleared: small businesses folded up; rent consumed a bigger part of family income; social and psychological dislocation became more common. [37]

No group suffered as much as did racial minorities. From the start, black leaders had feared that urban renewal might turn into "Negro removal." "Under the guise of 'city planning' and under the name of a 'reclamation' program," a black expert on housing wrote in 1940, "minority groups may be forced to relinquish areas in which they have established themselves at considerable sacrifice." [38] Urban redevelopment presented a triple threat to the Negro: it could be used to displace him from desirable neighborhoods; it could force the break-up of integrated neighborhoods; and it could reduce the supply of living space open to black occupancy. The policies followed in tenanting the nation's first redevelopment project, New York's Stuyvesant Town, built immediately after the end of World War II under state law, sharpened the Negroes' anxiety. Acting on the premise that "Negroes and whites don't mix," the life insurance company that owned the property barred Negroes as "a matter of business and economics." If similar considerations guided future projects, then Negroes would find themselves shut out from all the benefits of the pending federal subsidy. To prevent this, Negro spokesmen demanded inclusion of a non-discrimination clause in the 1949 legislation; they also urged that site occupants be given first preference in renewal areas. [39] Neither proposal received much support in Congress, however; few in the civil rights contingent on Capitol Hill wanted to imperil urban redevelopment by burdening it with the explosive racial issue.[40] Title I was thus silent on this crucial matter, but HHFA officials recognized that the measure's relocation requirements obliged them to find a solution to the "important and delicate minority housing problems which will arise in connection with the great majority of redevelopment projects." [41]

HHFA did not find that solution in the 1950s. Housing Administrator Albert Cole delivered numerous speeches arguing that the success of urban renewal depended upon the fair treatment of minorities, and the agency laid down several regulations for the protection of Negro rights. The talk and the rules, however, accomplished practically nothing, because an honest commitment to the protection of black interests might lead to a slowdown in the pace of the program.[42] Federal officials stood idly by as local authorities converted slum clearance into "Negro clearance" along the very lines minority leaders had predicted. Non-whites accounted for over two-thirds of those uprooted; Southern and border cities demolished integrated slums for reuse only by Caucasians; Northern communities constructed new housing far beyond the rent-paying capabilities of most blacks. Relocation arrangements, inadequate to begin with, degenerated still further when minorities were involved. Low incomes plus residential discrimination confined Negroes to the ghettos, placed severe strains on transitional areas, and tipped the shaky racial balance in public housing. Urban renewal, concluded the Commission on Civil Rights in 1959, "is accentuating or creating patterns of clear-cut racial separation." [43] Those opportunities urban redevelopment had presented initially for improving the living conditions of Negroes vanished in the cause of "municipal progress" and private property.

The twisting of Title I's social aims was facilitated by the adherence of federal officials to the principle of local autonomy. Just as in public housing, Washington left the "fundamental decisions as to the nature and direction" of the program to the communities.[44] The planning of projects rested entirely with the locality; the national agency could initiate nothing, it could only review what the community had decided to do. While in theory this review power should have enabled HHFA to force cities into compliance with the law's commands on type of projects, relocation, and citizen participation, in practice it did not. HHFA lacked enough trained staff to give each of the applications it received a thorough going-over. Even when discrepancies were uncovered, HHFA showed little eagerness to have them corrected. Like most institutions, the agency was most concerned with self-preservation and expansion. Requests to Congress for larger appropriations could be justified only if the program showed results; tangible signs of action, such as new buildings and cleared slums, were consequently much more important than the quality of the finished product. HHFA's enforcement of the much publicized Workable Program—Eisenhower's plan "to make cities help themselves"—became a well-known farce. A city could receive certification simply by promising to meet the program's requirements; in most cases, promises were about as far as cities went. New York City, for example, did nothing about drawing up the requisite master plan, but the federal dollars continued to flow in all the same.[45] Rather than risk embroilment in nasty political fights with municipalities and their congressmen, HHFA emphasized technical instead of substantive program supervision. Examining HHFA's procedures in 1960, one Bureau of the Budget management analyst found that the agency operated on the premise that, "provided a project is feasible and reasonable in its financial dimensions, the locality has as much right to undertake a bad one as a good one." [46]

New Haven provided the outstanding case of urban renewal's accomplishments and failures. Under Mayor Richard Lee's aggressive leadership, the Connecticut city received more per capita aid through Title I with the exception of Washington, D.C. than any other community with a population over 100,000. Slums were cleared out, new highways built, glass skyscrapers put up, luxury apartments constructed, and abandoned buildings in the old downtown shopping district levelled. Working closely with the mayor's office, Yale University launched its own expansion program that added to the town's architectural assets and payrolls. Yale's holdings were tax-exempt, but the town's construction pushed property levy revenues high enough to allow Lee to hold the tax rate constant from 1954 to 1959 despite an increase of nearly 45 per cent in his budget. Dimming this bright picture were the vacant, rubble-strewn lots that marked the year-delayed Church Street project. Legal battles held up reconstruction, adding significantly to interest charges and development costs. The misfortune of the downtown investors was apparent to everyone; few saw the hardships of those displaced by Lee's ambitious schemes. New Haven destroyed more than ten times the number of low-rent units it built in this period. Not until the "hot summer" of 1967 would the city learn of the frustrations and anger of its poor, black residents.[47]

Those riots in New Haven and other cities were still in the future in the 1950s, however, and the placidity of that decade provided no occasion for a searching scrutiny of urban renewal's techniques and objectives. Virtually all energies were devoted to getting the program off the drawing boards and past the administration's budget-cutters; clearing up these practical day-to-day difficulties left little time for a look as to where urban renewal was headed. Only a few people seemed aware that urban renewal was only a half-program, both geographically and functionally. It dealt with only the central city and some old suburbs, not the entire metropolitan area. Core areas would regain their strength only after a new partnership had been forged with their neighbors; instead of fostering cooperation, urban renewal promoted competition. Similarly, urban renewal's attacks on physical deterioration obscured the underlying sources of urban distress: poverty, lack of education, discrimination. The program could not assist cities in meeting these problems and in many instances exacerbated them. Until urban renewal could be expanded politically and socially, its services to the cities would be limited.[48]

Nevertheless, the 1950s did see some of the program's more flagrant wrongs corrected. With relocation shaping up as the program's "Achilles' heel," Congress, in 1956, authorized the payment of moving expenses for families and businesses displaced by Title I. In 1959, the tenth anniversary of urban redevelopment, Congress cleared the way for the construction of public housing on renewal sites. That same year new policies were inaugurated to halt the project-by-project approach to rebuilding and to force municipalities to compile long-range inventories of their needs and assets. Changes also took place on the local level. Under heavy civic pressure, Robert Moses finally resigned in 1960 as head of New York's Slum Clearance Committee. The days of the bulldozer strategy that ignored community wishes were numbered; in the future neighborhood participation and rehabilitation would be seen as the core of the renewal process.

III

Whereas a combination of politics and economics determined the shape of urban renewal, economic considerations were paramount in the metropolitan mortgage insurance operations of the Federal Housing Administration. For urban centers this proved unfortunate, because FHA, designed and run as a profit-making enterprise, cared little about the cities' welfare. FHA's interests went no further than the safety of the mortgages it secured; if protection of these investments encouraged new building on the suburban fringes and discouraged renovation in the inner city, then that was, as one critic of the agency's policies put it, "just too bad for the city." [49] Moreover, by adopting the financial community's skeptical view of the future prospects of the central city, FHA sharply reduced the effectiveness of the urban redevelopment endeavor. FHA's banker mentality also added to the cities' racial problems by promoting residential segregation. Many of the racial troubles cities experienced in the post-World War II period occurred independent of FHA policy, but that policy certainly compounded the difficulties.

FHA began in 1934 as a New Deal pump-priming device. The crucial home-building sector of the economy had practically shut down with the onset of the Depression, throwing thousands out of work and sending shock waves throughout the credit world. Eager to start the derricks moving again, but unwilling to have the Federal Government become directly involved in the construction or financing, Roosevelt chose a middle course: government insurance of private mortgages. The National Housing Act contained both recovery and reform features. By taking much of the risk out of home finance, the measure gave strong encouragement to builders to build and bankers to lend. At the same time, the act helped establish a more rational nationwide mortgage-lending pattern by making second and third mortgages unnecessary. Aside from a general interest in providing more and better housing, however, FHA was not imbued with any social consciousness: the principle of "economic soundness" guided its conduct.[50]

FHA's faithful adherence to bankers' standards had serious consequences for the cities. Right from its inception, the agency "red lined" vast areas of the inner cities, refusing to insure mortgages where the neighborhoods were blighted or susceptible to blight. This action practically guaranteed that these districts would deteriorate still further and drag the cities down with them. After more than twelve years of government aid to home construction and repair, not one dwelling unit in Manhattan had FHA coverage. In addition to writing off large sections of the old cities, FHA also cast a jaundiced eye at the predominant form of central city accommodations: rental housing. The agency considered rental housing, in comparison to private home construction, a very risky form of investment. Profits could be realized only over the long term; the real estate asset was relatively nonliquid; rent control always presented a threat; and maintenance and operation of the property raised personnel and tenant problems. Thanks in part to FHA policies, new rental units as a percentage of total new starts fell from 43.9 per cent in 1927 to 8.3 per cent in 1956.[51]

FHA's preference for sales housing helped spur the post-war mass exodus from the central cities. Americans had been moving to the suburbs since the early days of urban settlement, but at no time in the numbers that did so between 1945 and 1960. Various trends were at work encouraging this migration. Sustained post-war prosperity and higher incomes created a large consumer class able for the first time to fulfill the deep-seated American desire for a private home.

The jump in the birth rate reinforced this urge: families with children in cramped apartments wanted more rooms and outdoor space. These were usually not available in the central city. Discriminatory tax policies also added to the attractiveness of home ownership. By allowing deductions for interest and property levy payments in the computation of the federal income tax, Congress gave a tremendous hidden subsidy to the single-family dwelling.[52] Federally aided highway construction had the same effect: the home ownership boom would not have been possible without the roads that made large tracts of inexpensive land more accessible. Practically all this land was, of course, situated in the suburbs, outside the legal and taxing limits of the core city. FHA policies worked in tandem with these developments. For the most part, builders and prospective buyers could take advantage of FHA-induced reductions in down payments, lower interest rates, and extensions of amortization periods only if they located themselves beyond the inner city. Statistics can only hint at the dramatic switch in construction sites. In the Chicago metropolitan area, for example, 74 per cent of new home building in 1927 was within the boundaries of the central city and 26 per cent in the surrounding suburbs; in 1954, FHA's twentieth anniversary, the figures were almost completely reversed: 28 per cent inside Chicago and 72 per cent elsewhere.[53]

FHA's underwriting of the outward middle-class migration hurt not only the cities but the suburbs as well. Few suburban communities were prepared for or equipped to handle the problems that FHA helped dump on their doorsteps. In the 1930s FHA had exerted a striking and constructive influence on the quality of local residential development by forcing builders to adopt new and better forms of design. But as FHA matured and concentrated its efforts on increasing the flow of mortgages, the Land Planning Division lost its veto over the issuance of insurance. Hence, "what was once a new high ceiling became an old low floor" [54] of unimaginative architecture striving for minimal costs and maximum profits. The "FHA town," acre upon acre of ground-hugging monotony, was the trademark of the post-war building boom. Although these subdivisions gave their residents decent housing, the general metropolitan area suffered. Many communities lacked adequate zoning laws to prevent the intrusion of industry; still others, by contrast, did not have sufficient industry to provide a stable and sound tax base. FHA's neglect of regional planning resulted in the expansion of an environmentally destructive urban sprawl "laced with helter-skelter transit routes." [55]

Attempts in the mid-1950s to redirect FHA's energies to city rebuilding met with little success. Disturbed by the slow pace of urban redevelopment, the President's Advisory Committee on Government Housing Policies and Programs proposed, in 1953, a brand new FHA program to spur housing construction in renewal areas. Unlike earlier programs, Section 220 was to be administered on an "acceptable risk" rather than an "economic soundness" basis, thereby signalling to FHA that greater insurance risks should be taken in the interest of rescuing the cities from internal decay. Congress included this section in the 1954 Housing Act, but in spite of its liberal terms it stimulated little building. Part of the trouble was that Congress had not been liberal enough; investors needed still more incentives to run the gauntlet of government bureaucracies that redevelopment entailed. FHA's attitude aggravated the situation. The agency still held serious doubts about the safety of mortgages in central cities, especially when they involved high-rent apartment houses bordering on slum areas. As one FHA official explained: "The urban renewal program requires a willingness to take a chance. But FHA's whole background is built on getting the facts and making large percentage loans based on the facts." [56] With facts in short supply due to the experimental nature of urban renewal, FHA, eager to keep its default record low, made it difficult for developers to take full advantage of Section 220's aids. Not until the 1960s would there by any significant reorientation of FHA's activities. [57]

In addition to shortchanging the cities, FHA's banker outlook also intensified their racial problems. Like most government agencies, FHA adopted the professional beliefs and prejudices of the interests it served. The real estate trade, the building industry, and financial institutions supplied FHA with most of its personnel and guidelines, and each of these groups accepted, as an iron law of economics, the concept that racial homogeneity was essential if residential districts were to retain their stability and desirability. The official code of ethics of the National Association of Real Estate Boards until 1950, for example, prohibited participating brokers from introducing into an area "members of any race . . . whose presence will be clearly detrimental to property values in the neighborhood." [58] FHA embraced this doctrine without any hesitation; its *Underwriting Manual* for the agency's first fifteen years, observed the lawyer and social critic Charles Abrams, "read like a chapter from Hitler's Nuremberg Laws." [59] Insurance would be granted only if steps had been taken to "prevent the infiltration of adverse influences." Pigpens and "inharmonious racial groups" were considered equally objectionable. The *Manual* suggested racial zoning and physical barriers as useful tools for keeping out the wrong kind of people, but FHA liked the restrictive covenant most of all. Covenants had been used prior to 1934, but FHA helped perfect them and virtually made them mandatory; due to FHA, racial restrictive covenants spread throughout the country and became a regular part of the common form of deed. In the name of sound business principles, FHA put the stamp of federal approval on residential segregation and strengthened the walls around the black ghetto.[60]

The post-war climate of opinion forced some changes in FHA's racial policies, but the substantive impact of the agency's program remained essentially the same. In 1926, the Supreme Court had upheld restrictive covenants as private agreements not violating any provision of the Constitution, but in 1948 the high tribunal ruled that such covenants could not be enforced by the courts since this would be state action incompatible with the equal protection of the laws guarantee of the Fourteenth Amendment.[61] Although the Justice Department had filed an *amicus curiae* brief siding with the NAACP in the 1948 case, it took FHA nearly two years to align itself formally with the Supreme Court's decision. Only after the White

House applied strong pressure did FHA finally announce in December 1949, that it would not insure mortgages on property covered by restrictive covenants recorded after February 1950.[62] This new policy could not, however, undo the damage already done, and it said nothing about barring aid to builders who practiced discrimination by other means. FHA grudgingly agreed, again only after Presidential intervention, in 1949, to drop its flat ban against integrated projects, but that did not signify that it encouraged open occupancy; rather, it let each developer decide for himself how he wished to treat the racial issue. Most chose the path of segregation: less than 2 per cent of the housing financed with federal mortgage assistance from 1946 to 1959 was available to Negroes.[63]

Increasing civil rights agitation in the late 1950s failed to alter FHA's "neutral" stance. Unlike the 1940s, Presidential indifference provided the buffer that allowed FHA to continue with business as usual.[64] Eisenhower and his aides spoke often of the need "to assure minorities equal opportunities to acquire good and well-located homes," but they did not follow up their words with deeds. Besides convening a widely publicized White House conference on Negro housing and launching an unsuccessful voluntary program to make more mortgage money accessible to minorities, the administration showed no desire to get involved in what it considered a matter for local determination. Rejecting demands that FHA require open occupancy in its insured projects,[65] administration officials emphasized that "the role of the Federal Government is to assist, to stimulate, to lead, and sometimes to prod, but never to dictate or coerce, and never to stifle the proper exercise of private and local responsibility." [66] They also warned that any move toward a policy of nondiscrimination would cause a serious depression in the supply of new housing.[67] As if to allay such fears, HHFA Administrator Cole scuttled his agency's Racial Relations Service, replacing the dedicated career civil servants with mediocre political appointees. What once had been a strong advocate of racial equality, Charles Abrams lamented, "degenerated into an official apologist for official acceptance of segregation." [68] Freed of social responsibilities, FHA continued to tighten the white suburban noose around the growing black cores in the central cities.

IV

No federal venture spent more funds in urban areas and returned fewer dividends to central cities than the national highway program. In the same manner that FHA financed houses without concern for sound community development, the Bureau of Public Roads (BPR) laid down expressways without regard for their effects on the urban landscape. If the standards of the banker guided FHA's operations, then the values of the engineer were supreme at BPR. FHA measured its success by the amount of insurance issued; BPR was interested only in moving vehicular traffic as economically and rapidly as possible. FHA had no social purpose beyond the mortgage, BPR none beyond the automobile. One championed the single-family home, the other the private passenger car. Together they helped push the central cities further along the road of decline.

Significantly, federal aid for highways started as a program to help rural districts. While most important city streets were already paved by the end of the first decade of the twentieth century, all but a few rural roads were still dirt covered, making them impassable during rainy seasons. The agitation that finally resulted in passage of the Highway Act of 1916 was directed at bringing the quality of country road transportation up to that of urban areas. Under the measure federal funds were to be used solely for the improvement of rural postal roads. Besides lodging administration of the program with the Department of Agriculture, the act also barred any expenditures in municipalities of more than 2,500 people.[69] The federal-aid highways system continued in this fashion until the 1930s when the Depression forced a broadening of the program's objectives. Expanded road construction offered employment opportunities for many of the millions of men out of work; to be an effective pump-priming tool, however, highway building would have to take place in cities where most of the idle lived. Rising to the occasion, Congress enacted emergency legislation lifting the ban against urban highways, but to satisfy the rural bloc it also provided for a new and extensive secondary road network to serve farm regions. The program thus remained essentially rural in character; although the transfer, in 1939, of the BPR from the Agriculture Department to the just created Federal Works Agency indicated that urban economic needs would receive greater consideration in the bureau's work.

Once having established itself in urban areas, BPR campaigned aggressively to enlarge its foothold. In two reports, the first published in 1939, the second in 1944, BPR recommended to the President and Congress that city highways become the main focus of its activities. The BPR's 1939 study, *Toll Roads and Free Roads*, suggested an interregional system of highways to link all the nation's large cities. America's most pressing traffic problem, BPR declared, was the congestion in cities resulting from the tremendous number of cars trying to get downtown. Outmoded street patterns, curb parking, and the failure to separate pedestrians from the flow of traffic had created an intolerable mess that hurt business and cost lives in every big city. BPR's interregional highway proposal would end that disorder by constructing superhighways directly into the city center. The 1944 report reaffirmed these conclusions. Acting under Roosevelt's orders to prescribe a system of national highways designed to meet the requirements of national defense and improved interregional transportation, BPR [70] again requested that precedence be given to modern highways serving the central business district:

Twenty years ago when the Federal Highway Act prohibited the expenditure of limited Federal funds for [transcity connections], the prohibition was not unreasonable. It was instead a necessary and logical recognition of the superior need of rural highway improvement. Now, with the congestion of transcity routes replacing rural highway need as the greatest of traffic barriers, emphasis needs to be reversed and the large expenditures devoted to improvement of the city and metropolitan sections of arterial routes.

Noting that post-war travel by motor transport was expected to soar,

BPR warned that the future economic viability of central cities depended on the building of inner city expressways.[71]

Congress reacted cautiously to BPR's sudden interest in urban highways. The United States Conference of Mayors and city-based, automobile-related groups endorsed BPR's plans to concentrate federal aid in metropolitan areas, but the powerful farm bloc naturally opposed diversion of funds from rural districts. After much haggling, a compromise formula was devised that maintained the rural orientation of the program but opened the door for federal grants for city routes. The Highway Act of 1944 not only continued the original numbered system of rural primary roads but also placed the Depression-born rural secondary and urban programs on a permanent basis. Under the allotment plan worked out, the urban part received 25 per cent of the total appropriations, rural primary 45 per cent, and rural secondary 30 per cent. By practically every criteria of "traffic need" cities were entitled to almost twice as much as they actually won, but the 1944 act represented, nonetheless, the first legislative recognition of urban transportation requirements.[72] State administration, however, wiped out all but the symbolic gains. While federal law demanded that the states spend a quarter of the national grants in urban areas, most rural-dominated state highway departments funnelled the funds to fringe locations and small towns. Federal assistance to urban highways was still, the BPR commissioner noted sorrowfully in 1950, "pitifully small." [73]

Cities quickly realized that relief for their traffic problems could not come through the regular federal-aid highway program but only by way of BPR's proposed interregional system. This special network set aside nearly 4,500 of its 33,920 miles for urban roads and made solution of metropolitan area congestion one of its prime targets. Congress, in 1944, had authorized the designation of a National System of Interstate Highways, but did not earmark funds for its construction. Thus, for its first decade the National System existed only on paper. Prospects for completing the job fell to their lowest point during the early months of the Eisenhower administration. In keeping with his philosophy of decentralization, the President gave serious thought to abolishing the federal gasoline tax and handing complete responsibility for highway building over to the states. But as in so many fields, studies showed that the states could not or would not pick up the burden. With highway construction and user groups demanding that something be done to modernize the nation's overloaded roads,[74] Eisenhower reversed his stand and in a message to the Governors' Conference in July 1954, suggested a "grand plan" of federal-state cooperation to clear up all the country's highway deficiencies.

To fill in the details, the President appointed an Advisory Committee on a National Highway Program, headed by retired General Lucius D. Clay. Working with dispatch, the Clay Committee had its report on Eisenhower's desk by January 1955. While recommending that the traditional federal-aid program be continued, the committee urged that "top priority" be given to the Interstate System, which it found would carry 15 per cent of all the nation's traffic even though it included but 1.2 per cent of total road mileage. Since national security and the health of the national economy were dependent upon the rapid construction of the Interstate System, the Clay Committee suggested that instead of the 50-50 matching arrangement utilized in the regular program the Federal Government "assume principal responsibility" for the cost of Interstate highways. The Clay Committee's substantive findings received practically unanimous acclaim from the President, the various automobile-connected trade associations, and the mayors. Final congressional approval, however, was delayed until 1956 because of a dispute over how to meet the projected $27 billion price tag.

In sharp contrast to the two BPR investigations that preceded it, the Clay Committee report completely ignored the impact of highways upon the complex urban organism. The 1939 study postulated the close connection between expressway construction and downtown revitalization and stressed the need for city plans to coordinate slum clearance and redevelopment with new highway construction. The 1944 report dealt with this matter at some length.

Describing the process of urban growth and decay and the stimulus the automobile gave to the suburban migration, BPR had advised that the interregional network "will exert a powerful force tending to shape the future development of the city." It is "highly important," the report went on, "that this force be so applied as to promote a desirable urban development." Toward that end, BPR urged that urban routes be selected only after intensive discussion had taken place between state highway departments and local planning officials; for best results, it recommended that planning be on a metropolitan area-wide basis.[75] BPR kept harping throughout the 1940s on the theme of the highway's role in saving the city as part of an unsuccessful attempt by the Federal Works Agency to wrest administration of the proposed urban redevelopment program away from HHFA. Well-situated highways, BPR insisted, provided "an unparalleled opportunity for rebuilding [cities] along healthy and functional lines." [76] But after its transfer to the Department of Commerce in 1949, BPR lost its interest in the broad implications of the highway in the city and concentrated its attention exclusively on making travel by automobile and truck quicker and less expensive. These same aims directed the deliberations of the industry-domi-nated Clay Committee. Except for the obvious observations that "our cities have spread into suburbs, dependent on the automobile for their existence" and that the car "has brought city and country closer together," its report was silent on the social effects the spending of billions of federal funds for highways in urban areas would have.

Unfortunately, the two years of congressional hearings and debates that followed release of the Clay Committee study produced little new important information about the urban sections of what was now the 41,000-mile National Interstate and Defense Highway System. Administration spokesmen never went beyond bland gen-eralities on how badly the country needed a modern highway network, on how the program would cut the number of accidents and save hundreds of millions of dollars in operating costs, on how high-speed expressways were essential to the rapid evacuation of cities in case of nuclear attack. The delegations of mayors that flocked to Washington to testify in behalf of the legislation had little more to offer. They simply pointed to the daily crush of traffic in their business districts and demanded that the Federal Government put up the funds for highways to relieve the congestion. Hardly a word was uttered about requiring regional plans, about what was to happen to the families and businesses uprooted by construction, about insuring adequate coordination with public transportation.

Congress was so engrossed in devising a painless method to finance the system that it totally overlooked the inherent contradiction in the program. Municipal leaders made it very clear that they expected to use the system to solve their commuter rush-hour problem; since local traffic would generate most of the revenue to pay for the venture, they felt this was only fair. But the Clay Committee sold the Interstate System to Congress as a carrier of long-haul traffic, bypassing downtown areas, with only a limited number of feeder routes to link the highways with central cities.[77] This difference was crucial, but no one on Capitol Hill bothered to consider its implications.

The legislature passed the Highway Act of 1956—and thus set into motion "the greatest man-made physical enterprise of all time with the exception of war"—in a near total vacuum.[78] As far as the 1956 act was concerned, one urbanologist has observed, "there is no form of transportation but the automobile and no objective save providing more room for it." [79] Unlike the comprehensive housing bill passed just two years before, the 1956 measure lacked the slightest bit of planning-conscious language. It handed responsibility for the major decisions over to the highway engineers who by training and education were not prepared to do anything more than build sound highways cheaply. While the law did require state highway departments to hold public hearings to consider the "economic effects" of the routes they had selected, there was no compulsion whatsoever for the departments to listen to what was said. Nor was there any stipulation that local officials be consulted. Urban renewal had the statutory obligation to relocate those it displaced, but Congress imposed no such handicap on road construction. Indeed, Congress seemed to have forgotten that there was an urban renewal program; the 1956 Highway Act made no provision for coordinating these complementary endeavors. All the principles BPR had expounded in the 1940s were quietly ignored as the President and Congress rushed to serve what Lewis Mumford has called that "mistress that exists in every household right alongside the wife—the motor car." [80]

The fruit of the federal money tree proved to be very bitter. Of the $27 billion to be spent over the next decade, $15 billion was allocated for urban areas. Since Washington had agreed to cover 90 per cent of this amount, most cities could not resist the temptation to get as many miles of freeway as they could squeeze out of their state highway departments. For the most part, the state agencies proved quite accommodating, realizing that the much travelled urban roads would supply the needed gasoline tax receipts to construct the rural sections of the system.[81] Interstate routes were soon cutting massive concrete ribbons right into the core of the nation's large cities. But instead of solving the traffic problem, the new roads only added to it: "In a variation on Parkinson's Law that expenditures rise to meet income," one critic has noted, "congestion rises to meet highway capacity; the supply of highways creates a demand for its use." Making automobile commuting more attractive diverted riders from public transportation and into their cars, thus wiping out the expected gains.[82] Not only did the paving over of vast stretches of urban land remove valuable properties from the municipal tax rolls, but, by dumping huge numbers of cars downtown, the expressways produced an insatiable thirst for more parking space that disfigured central business districts. Highway construction also dislocated thousands of families and compounded the cities' housing dilemma. Good neighborhoods as well as bad ones felt the effects of what *Architectural Forum* characterized as the "highwaymen's single-minded urge to drive freeways through a city by the most convenient engineering routes without regard for the city's tissue and fabric of life." [83] Middle-income families could make a new start elsewhere, but for the poor, and especially the minorities, eviction meant a desperate search for shelter in the overcrowded slums. And while urban renewal tried to attract the well-to-do back to the central city, the Interstate System made suburbia that much more accessible.

Pleas that something be done to stop this carnage were not long in coming. They started, in fact, about the very time the 1956 act was passed. A Brookings Institution study entitled *The Metropolitan Transportation Problem*, published that year, warned that extensive road construction "could have highly damaging effects in urban areas unless it is carried out as part of an area-wide community development plan." Urging that federal aid for highways be made contingent on "their relation to over-all transportation objectives and to comprehensive community planning," the Brookings report observed that "transportation development that merely helps us to move more expeditiously through areas of urban decay misses the mark." Professional planners echoed these thoughts in 1957. It was a mistake, the planners argued, to base route location decisions, as the 1956 act did, almost entirely on traffic surveys and costs: "Just as war is too important to leave to the generals, so highways are too important to leave to the highway engineers." Projected land uses, population trends, and preservation of open space had to be considered along with countless other variables before a sound highway network could be laid out.[84] Planners received an excellent opportunity to express their fears and hopes at a symposium in September 1957, sponsored by an insurance company, on "The New Highways: Challenge to the Metropolitan Region." Over fifty leading businessmen, government officials, transportation specialists, and highway builders participated; all agreed that the Interstate System could "make or break the future of our burgeoning cities." [85] A few of the more daring suggested that a two-year moratorium be declared on road building so that the planners could have additional time to find the most suitable sites. HHFA Administrator Cole gave implicit encouragement to the idea with his statement that "there cannot be separate solutions to the problems of providing a decent environment for urban dwellers and the allied problem of moving urban people and their goods from place to place," but the chief of the federal highway agency rejected it out of hand. There was a need to coordinate the two programs, he admitted, but "wholly impractical schemes" should not be permitted to impede either urban renewal or highway construction; to force the Interstate System to comply with regional plans "would result in no highway program at all." [86] The highway administrator's position prevailed, and the program continued as before; indeed, when a recession struck the economy in 1958, Congress authorized a speedup in construction.

Critics of the 1956 act received unexpected support from none other than the President himself. What disturbed Eisenhower in 1959, naturally enough, was not the lack of adequate safeguards to protect the urban environment, but the cost and possible illegality of running the Interstate System into metropolitan areas. Urban roads were far more expensive than rural highways, with costs sometimes as high as $40 million per mile, and Eisenhower worried that the Trust Fund set up to finance construction would be depleted before the entire job was done. He also questioned the propriety of having the Federal Government pay 90 per cent of the bills incurred building expressways intended to solve local commuting problems. Sending Interstate routes through the congested parts of cities, the President argued, had not been contemplated in 1956, because the national interest extended only to long-distance travel.[87] In April 1960, he issued guidelines to the Commerce Department that declared that amelioration of the rush-hour traffic mess was not to be considered a function of the Interstate System. This action had little effect. State highway departments possessed great autonomy in route location decisions and, like the mayors, they opposed a reduction of activity in urban regions. BPR, which looked to its clientele for direction as much as it did to the President, permitted the inner-city construction to proceed as scheduled.[88]

But even if Presidential orders could not halt the highwaymen's assault on the cities, the late 1950s did witness a resurgence of interest in mass transportation. Public transit had made the spread of large cities possible in the late nineteenth century, and during World War II, with gasoline and rubber rationed, public transit was virtually the only means of getting to and from work. In the post-war period, however, automobile registrations skyrocketed, jumping 75 per cent between 1946 and 1954. By 1955, over two-thirds of all consumer units in the nation owned a car. As Americans settled down behind the wheels of their private cars, public transportation patronage fell off precipitously. The number of mass transit passengers slipped from 23.4 billion in 1946 to 11 billion in 1956. With this drop in riding came a sharp decline in profits: $149 million in 1945 to $41 million in 1955. "Among U.S. industries," observed *Business Week* in that latter year, "none has a darker future than municipal transit." It was caught in a vicious cycle of traffic losses, rising costs, higher fares, less frequent service, and further loss of business. By the end of the decade, however, efforts were underway to break that circuit and have mass transit play an important role in straightening out the metropolitan transportation tangle.[89]

City planners and downtown businessmen were among the first to stress the need for improving mass transit. Planners do not like to put all their eggs in one basket, and so, almost by instinct, they proposed a mix of private and public transportation. "I am willing to stake my reputation," the executive director of the American Society of Planning Officials said in 1948, "on the forecast that building of expressways will not solve the traffic and transportation problems of any community." Only public transit, he claimed, could effectively move the vast numbers of people who earned their livelihoods in the big cities. Other experts voiced similar ideas over the next decade, but their words were lost to most in the din of blaring car horns.[90] Two groups that did hear the message were the merchants and real estate managers of the central business districts. Like practically everybody else in the immediate post-war era, these two groups saw the transportation problem originally in terms of how to make travel by car easier. Their proposals for reviving central areas emphasized downtown freeway construction and off-street parking. But they soon discovered that their woes could not be eased by placating the motorist: "Freeways beget more freeways, garages more garages, and the streets, however wide, are somehow never wide enough." [91]

The suburban shopping centers obviously could not be beaten at their own game, so after about 1950, an increasing number of inner-city chambers of commerce turned to mass transit as the answer to their problems. With businessmen in the lead, cities like Chicago and San Francisco began serious studies into public transportation expansion.[92]

Few in the mid-1950s considered enlisting federal aid for this purpose. While practically no one doubted the wisdom of federal appropriations for highway construction, government subsidies for public transportation posed several difficult questions. The federal road program seemed to be just an ordinary—if exceptionally huge—public works endeavor no different than the Army Corps of Engineers' flood control projects or the Bureau of Reclamation's irrigation projects. Federal assistance to mass transit, on the other hand, immediately raised the spectre of socialism since many of the transit systems were still in private hands and run for a profit, and even those that were municipally owned were operated, in theory at least, on a break-even basis. The private firms did not want government subsidies, federal or local, because they related government subsidies with even greater public supervision of their activities; they preferred to sell out completely. Most municipal officials were as automobile-minded as the people who elected them; thus while they had no qualms about using the taxpayers' money to subsidize the car, tapping the same source to restore the health of mass transit seemed financially unwise and politically unrewarding. Appearing before the congressional committees conducting hearings on the Interstate System in 1955, spokesmen for the American Transit Association urged restoration of the balance between the automobile and public transportation in downtown areas, but asked for nothing more than an exemption from federal gasoline and tire taxes for mass transit operations. The mayors who testified failed to mention mass transit altogether.[93]

The crisis on the commuter railroads supplied the impetus for change. No segment of the transit industry had suffered so badly in the post-war period as the suburban lines of the large common carriers; in the New York region alone, deficits surpassed $20 million annually. When the 1957 recession threatened to send many of the big companies into bankruptcy, Congress responded to their pleas for relief by approving the Transportation Act of 1958, which made it easier for the railroads to drop their unprofitable passenger train service. Hardly had the ink dried on Eisenhower's signature when a number of lines announced plans to eliminate their commuter runs. Municipalities had previously blocked such action through the courts, but that mode of attack was no longer possible under the new law; only generous subsidies could keep the commuter trains operating. Lacking funds of their own with which to succor the railroads, the cities looked to Washington for help.[94]

The groundwork for this appeal had been laid in the mid-1950s by the chief executives of Philadelphia. The two commuter lines that served the City of Brotherly Love transported over 100,000 riders daily, and the unusually capable City Planning Commission feared that continued deterioration in service would send many of these people on to the already overcrowded highways. Preservation of the central business district, the commission felt, depended upon a balanced system of rail and rubber. Mayor Joseph Clark accepted the commission's recommendation of public assistance for mass transit facilities but pointed out that the Federal Government alone had the financial resources to do an adequate job. As early as 1955, therefore, Clark had tried to get the American Municipal Association behind his proposal for federal aid, but that organization was interested only in the rapid passage of the Interstate Highway Act. Clark moved on to the Senate the following year, but his successor and close associate Richardson Dilworth stepped up the campaign to win national recognition for the plight of urban public transportation. Not only did he lobby with his fellow mayors, but, in addition, Dilworth worked closely with the presidents of the major railroads.[95] Progress was slow, however, until the 1958 Transportation Act brought the commuter crisis to a head. Municipal leaders who had previously ignored Dilworth's warning that total reliance on freeways would ruin the cities were shaken out of their complacency by figures showing that it would cost the five metropolitan areas with extensive rail networks $17 billion to construct roads with the carrying capacity of the endangered transit lines. For a little over $3 billion these same lines could be completely modernized and made into attractive alternatives to automobile commutation. Dilworth found the going rougher with the railroad executives who preferred to drop passenger trains altogether rather than become enmeshed in the tricky business of government subsidies. After a year of hard negotiations, Dilworth finally worked out a program acceptable to AMA and the big Eastern railroads. Instead of advocating the grants Clark and Dilworth desired, the joint AMA-railroad policy statement, announced in December 1959, called only for $500 million in long-term, low-interest federal loans to cities for intra-metropolitan mass transit improvements. This was a far cry from the aid extended the automobile, but it was a start on the public transportation problem.[96]

But if the mayors were tardy in awakening to the need for encouraging mass transit, the Federal Government was even slower. The last year of the Eisenhower administration was simply not the time or the place to come in search of additional federal funds. The President had already tried to withdraw from urban renewal and he was in no mood for more local "raids" on the national treasury. Resolution of the rush-hour mess, he felt, was purely a community matter, far outside the proper sphere of federal responsibility. The certainty of a Presidential veto doomed the AMA proposal from the day it was dropped in the congressional bill hopper, but the desire of Senate Democrats to establish an image of concern for cities enabled the mayors to get a full-scale hearing for their measure. Three days of testimony from municipal leaders, railroad spokesmen, and urban specialists built up an "impressive case" for federal intervention to save public transportation. After perfunctory debate the bill passed the Senate by a voice vote, but that was as far as it got. Lacking an influential sponsor in the House, it died in committee. This roadblock in mass transit's path would not be cleared until the mid-1960s.[97]

V

Privatism had built the cities and subsequently abetted their decline; government programs inaugurated after 1933 contributed to that latter process. The values federal officials adopted in fulfilling their responsibilities were those of the taxpayer, the banker, the home-owner, and the automobile driver. This is only natural in a democratic society since the government should reflect the dominant mood of the country, and these were the preeminent values. Unfortunately for the cities, these beliefs were antithetical to the urban way of life. Public housing would always look stark because the voters who paid taxes insisted upon it. Urban renewal's capacity to improve community development was severely hampered by the program's need to return a reasonable profit to its financial investors. Privacy and security held priority with the typical homeowner; this usually meant keeping different kinds of people out of his neighbor-hood and finding new enclaves once the old walls had been breached. The desire of the car operator to take his vehicle wherever he went no matter what the cost led to the pouring of millions of tons of concrete without any consideration of the side effects. Unwittingly, the Federal Government served those same narrow interests.

Political value systems hindered movement toward reform. Ameri-can federalism has always made a virtue of decentralized decision-making; the New Deal-Fair Deal paid homage to this ideal by establishing cooperative programs that left most of the basic determinations up to the localities. Some of the weaknesses of this approach were apparent by the 1950s, but Eisenhower declined to make the necessary adjustments. The rather bold Workable Program concept put forth by an administration eager to cut federal spending was subverted by the same administration by its refusal to tell another level of government what to do. State and local autonomy remained sacrosanct—at times, it appeared more sacrosanct than individual rights, particularly for those individuals in racial minori-ties. Urban renewal and highway programs were undermined because few in the nation's capital dared suggest that the Federal Government make states and municipalities realize that metropolitan problems could only be solved on a metropolitan basis.

Institutional arrangements within the Federal Government also shaped Washington's response. Both congressional committees and executive agencies were organized along functional lines, and each was accustomed to thinking in terms of houses and highways rather than communities. So-called "urban programs" were actually the by-products of more limited functional goals whose pursuit happened to require federal spending in heavily populated areas. Even urban renewal emphasized the project-by-project approach that served to obscure the regional interests. Constant exposure to urban issues did educate some members of the Banking and Currency panels in the House and Senate in the late 1950s, but the efforts of these committees to broaden urban renewal's perspectives were overwhelmed by the highway legislation handled by the Committees on Public Works, which knew next to nothing about the momentous consequences of road building in urban areas. This lack of coordination on Capitol Hill was mirrored downtown in the Executive Branch. The BPR took its signals from the transportation-minded Department of Commerce and tried to steer clear of the residential-oriented Housing and Home Finance Agency. HHFA, itself, was hardly the paragon of harmony. Each of the three main constituent units, FHA, Public Housing Administration, and Urban Renewal Administration, was run as an independent fiefdom, more attuned to the wishes of the particular clientele it served than to the supervisory power of the HHFA administrator. FHA sabotaged urban renewal while URA went ahead with its projects oblivious of what PHA was doing. This leaderless, alphabetical troika rambled all over the urban landscape adding to the metropolitan disorder.

Since administrative structures are usually more malleable than a complex of values, efforts in the late 1950s to improve the operation of federal programs in urban areas concentrated almost exclusively on correcting procedural and administrative techniques and defining agency goals and responsibilities. Hence, instead of asking what kinds of cities people really wanted or should aspire to, the businessmen, political scientists, planners, managerial experts, mayors, agency heads, and bureaucrats focused their energies on increasing efficiency and securing a place in the Federal Government for the presentation of the urban viewpoint.

A Cabinet Department for Cities—
Ideas and Proposals: 1937–60

Metropolitan growth is posing one of the greatest challenges of the second
half of the 20th century. We cannot meet this challenge with government
machinery designed for the 19th century.

Joseph S. Clark (1957)

On a hot July afternoon in 1954, with Congress just days away from
adjournment, an obscure freshman representative dropped the draft
of a bill into the hopper next to the clerk's desk in the House
chamber. The ten thousand and thirty-second bill introduced during
the 83rd Congress attracted no special attention on Capitol Hill, and
like the vast majority of other measures that preceded and succeeded
it, it never went beyond this first step in the law-making process. But
if H.R. 10032, "to create a Department of Urbiculture," passed into
history without ever passing into law, it did mark the initial blow in a
twelve-year struggle to give America's cities recognition and representation at the highest councils of the Federal Government.

I

Organizational arrangements within the Federal Government are
not neutral. The bewildering maze of departments, agencies, bu-

reaus, services, boards, commissions, and so forth, that characterizes Washington was not shaped in a vacuum. Organization is one way of expressing national commitment, influencing program direction, and ordering priorities. As Presidential advisor Richard Neustadt has pointed out: "In political government the means can matter quite as much as the ends; they often matter more." The structure of administration often tends to give certain interested parties, with certain perspectives, more effective access to those with decision-making authority, no matter whether those decision-makers be in the Congress or in the Executive Branch.[1]

By practically every yardstick of power and responsibility, the Executive department ranks highest in the formal Washington political order. It is the only form of administrative organization mentioned in the Constitution—if only obliquely—and department heads have traditionally had the easiest access to the White House and the chairmen of influential congressional committees. The secretaries of the executive departments receive a salary that is exceeded only by that of the President himself. They are also the only appointed officials who stand in the line of Presidential succession. In addition, each departmental chief is automatically a member of the cabinet. Different Presidents have used the cabinet differently: some made it an integral element of the program-making process, while others ignored it. But if the American cabinet legally possesses none of the power entrusted to its British counterpart, legend had invested it with the ultimate power to determine national policies.[2]

The growth of the cabinet has been, a student of that institution observes, "a faithful record of the growth of the nation. It reflects our westward expansion, our industrialization, the burdens of world responsibility, the concern for social justice." [3] George Washington could govern effectively with three Executive departments: State, Treasury, and War. Later Presidents felt the need for more help. In the hundred-year span following Washington's retirement, five additional departments were established: Navy (1798), Interior (1849), Justice (1870), Post Office (1870), and Agriculture (1889). The first two decades of the twentieth century saw the creation of two more: Commerce and Labor (1903—in 1913 it became the Department of Commerce) and Labor (1913).

Some common threads can be detected in the legislative histories of the various departments. For one thing, Congress was usually very deliberate in its examination of proposals for departmental status; thirty-three years elapsed between President Madison's recommendation for a "Home Department" and congressional approval of the Interior Department. The merits of a Department of Agriculture were debated for thirty-seven years, those of Commerce for thirty-nine years, and those of Labor for over forty years.[4] An important reason for this slow pace was the type of opposition the departmental plans encountered. No matter what the nature of administrative reorganization, defenders of the status quo could be expected to denounce it as a threat to the safety of the Republic. Thus, John C. Calhoun was "overcome with apprehension" at the "monstrous and ominous bill" to set up a Department of the Interior since the creation of such a department would surely lead to federal domination of the states; this in spite of the fact that the bill merely brought together well-established activities under a new head, adding nothing to functions long accepted.[5] Similarly, bills for a Department of Agriculture met resistance as "dangerous pieces of class legislation, opening the door to demands of other great economic groups for departments protective of their interests." Furthermore, critics claimed, the fostering of agriculture was not within the proper sphere of federal operations.[6] The Labor Department suffered through the same arguments during its long gestation period. What finally broke the back of obstruction in each instance, but particularly in the cases of Agriculture, Commerce, and Labor was strong organized political support for departmental status. It took time for large numbers of farmers, businessmen, and union members to rally behind their respective campaigns for national recognition, but when they did they won the battle. Clearly, popular support, and not any set of administrative standards, has been the determining factor in the composition of the cabinet.[7]

The cabinet's membership had remained constant for twenty-four years when Franklin D. Roosevelt began his second term as President in 1937. Not since the division of the Department of Commerce and Labor into two separate units in 1913 had any change occurred in the upper reaches of the administrative structure. In 1923 President Harding had urged the consolidation of the War and Navy Departments into a single Department of National Defense and the creation of a new Department of Education and Welfare, but these proposals did not receive congressional attention. The 1920s were simply not the time for a thoughtful re-examination of the Federal Government's commitment to the health and well-being of its citizens or for a look at the nation's military establishment. Executive and legislative interest in the entire question of administrative reorganization was, for that matter, very slight during the decade since the Federal Government seemed more likely to contract than to expand.[8] With the coming of the Great Depression and the New Deal that situation was transformed dramatically. Bureaus blossomed forth everywhere. Washington appeared to be overrun with agencies that had no names, only initials. The mushrooming growth of the federal bureaucracy disturbed officials at both ends of Pennsylvania Avenue. Roosevelt feared that this haphazard proliferation would undermine White House control of the Executive Branch, while Congress worried about duplication, inefficiency, and the legislature's ability to maintain its financial reins on the bureaucracy's activities. Thus, in 1936, the President and Congress commissioned separate panels of experts to study the problem of reorganization; both groups finished their tasks early the following year. Although the subject of federal relations with the cities did not figure prominently in either investigation, the two reports nevertheless had important consequences for the future of federal-urban ties.

The President's Committee on Administrative Management (PCAM) focused its attention on strengthening the Presidency. All three members—Louis Brownlow, Charles Merriam, and Luther Gulick—had close ties to the municipal reform movement and believed deeply in a strong mayor-type government for cities. They carried these same ideas into their analysis of the federal executive. The President, they concluded, needed help if he was to fulfill his constitutional duties as "administrator-in-chief." Toward this end, PCAM recommended the formation of a White House Office composed of six Presidential assistants, with a "passion for anonymity," who would serve as the President's liaison with the agencies carrying out national programs. It also advocated transferring the Bureau of the Budget (BOB) from the Department of the Treasury to the Executive Office of the President where it could more effectively aid the President in monitoring the policies and procedures of Federal bureaus. In addition, PCAM suggested that all independent boards and commissions be brought within one or another of the ten existing Executive departments or the two new departments—Public Works and Social Welfare—that it proposed to create. By this reshuffling, the committee sought to reduce to an absolute minimum the number of people reporting directly to the President. Just where the cities and their programs would fit into this new arrangement was far from clear; despite their previous championing of expanded federal-municipal links, Brownlow, Merriam, and Gulick neglected to make explicit provisions for some kind of agency to deal particularly with urban communities.[9]

The study prepared for Congress by the Brookings Institution, in contrast, faced this question. Interested less in building up the power of the President than in eliminating wasteful overlapping of responsibilities, the Brookings staff devoted its energies to preparing plans for the realignment of bureaus. Discussing the general factors that had to be considered in this reorganization, the institution's report noted that "much administrative significance attaches to the division of the population into rural and urban." There has been, it went on, "the reasonable tendency to give the Department of Agriculture broad functions relating to rural life. If this tendency is recognized as sound, a Federal Department of Welfare, if one is created, must in some important respects, serve largely, if not exclusively, the urban population." This city-oriented department would include the relief, public health, and education agencies, as well as the Housing Division of the Public Works Administration and the Resettlement Administration of the Department of Agriculture.[10] Urban dwellers, whose unemployment problems had caused Washington and the municipalities to work together for the first time in 1933, would get representation at the cabinet table through a department charged with a variety of social and economic tasks.

Congress, however, responded unenthusiastically to both reports. Roosevelt's plan to "pack" the Supreme Court, announced soon after the release of the reorganization studies, so poisoned the atmosphere in Washington that the President's administrative proposals were widely attacked as a further step toward executive dictatorship. It took three years of hard fighting before Roosevelt was able to win congressional consent for the White House Office and the repositioning of the Budget Bureau. He never won his Department of Public Welfare. Adamantly opposed to institutionalizing the relief features of the New Deal, conservatives from both major parties refused to admit Social Security and Roosevelt's other programs to the prestigious and select circle of Executive departments.[11] Roosevelt had to settle for the establishment in 1939 of three sub-cabinet agencies to take care of his New Deal progeny. The Federal Security Agency (FSA) included all the bureaus originally headed for the Welfare Department under the Brookings plan except the United States Housing Authority (USHA), which went instead to the Federal Works Agency (FWA) where it was joined by the Bureau of Public Roads and the Public Works Administration. The Federal Housing Administration and the other housing boards were placed within the Federal Lending Agency (FLA) along with the remains of the Reconstruction Finance Corporation.

This division of activity authorized by Congress in 1939 made sense to a country preoccupied with reviving a faltering economy, but it hindered the development of an urban outlook in the national government. No single agency had enough city-based functions to label it a logical candidate for elevation to a federal Department of

Urban Affairs. Support for such a step was growing as a corollary to the increasing discussions on proposals for federal aid for urban redevelopment, but everyone seemed to favor a different agency as the nucleus for the new cabinet department. Some people, like the economist Guy Greer, thought that a "Department of Urbanism" should be built around FWA since its responsibility for public works, public roads, and public housing gave it vast influence over the shape of community improvements.[12] For others, like the sociologist Louis Wirth, the Department of the Interior, with a few alterations, appeared most appropriate for this role. In a memo to Merriam, written in the summer of 1941, Wirth explained that Interior[13]

comes closest to any of the government departments to having the greatest experience with the problem of reclamation, which is essentially the problem of our cities, and through its considerable control over the power projects of the Federal Government, is likely to have one of the most crucial weapons at its disposal for determining the pattern of urban development in the areas of the United States which are likely to see the greatest degree of urbanization in the next few years.

Still others thought that a merger of FSA, FWA, and FLA into one Executive department offered the best way of focusing federal leadership in a broad-based attack on urban ills.[14] All these formulations were, however, nothing more than academic exercises since there was absolutely no hope politically for an urban department in the period 1939–41; the proposals were significant, though, as being representative of the divergence of opinion that would plague the campaign for a cabinet department in the decades ahead.

The exigencies of war helped clear up some of this initial confusion. By late 1941, approximately twenty different federal agencies, each operating entirely on its own, were engaged in building or financing defense housing. These arrangements produced more bickering and congressional investigations than new homes. Worried that this anarchy in the housing field would imperil the mobilization effort, Roosevelt, in October, asked his top troubleshooter, Samuel I. Rosenman, to look into the problem. After three months of discussions with spokesmen for the many sectors of the housing industry, Rosenman recommended the consolidation of all the various federal housing activities into one National Housing Agency (NHA).[15] Such a step had been out of the question in 1939 because of the sharp animosity between the public housers and the private home builders, but in this period of emergency both groups were willing to suspend their hostility in the name of national security. Consequently, Roosevelt's creation of NHA in February 1942, by Executive order, permissible under his wartime reorganization powers, aroused little opposition. By the President's action, FLA was abolished and most of its constituents—notably FHA and the Federal Home Loan Bank Board (FHLBB)—were transferred to the new NHA, which also took over the direction of USHA from FWA. After a decade of separation on federal organization charts, the nation's housing agencies were now together under the same roof.[16]

Proponents of an expanded federal role in urban affairs greeted NHA's establishment warmly. While some were disappointed that a full-fledged "Department of Urbanism" had not been set up, there was general concurrence that the cities had, at last, found a home.[17] Residential structures covered about 60 per cent of built-up urban land, and any well-conceived endeavor to increase housing production would certainly have to be based upon a solid understanding of the urban environment. Recognizing this, the NHA administrator, John B. Blandford, Jr., formed a Division of Urban Studies within his office "to assist in relating the total programs of NHA to the other elements of city building and city rebuilding and urban life as a whole." [18] Although the division never grew very big, it helped shape NHA policy on the crucial issue of urban redevelopment. Except for those in the planning fraternity who supported FWA's unsuccessful attempt in the late 1940s to wrest control of the urban redevelopment program from the housing agency,[19] no one who favored a cabinet department for cities doubted NHA's primacy in the urban arena.[20]

The future of NHA remained a question mark, however, as victory overseas came closer to fruition in the early months of 1945. As a wartime agency NHA was due to expire six months after the cessation of hostilities; in order to continue after the return of peace, NHA would have to gain the sanction of Congress. But while the fighting was winding down abroad, old conflicts that promised to make getting that approval extremely difficult were building up again at home. Public housing, as usual, was at the center of the controversy. Liberal groups, such as the National Public Housing Conference and the Congress of Industrial Organizations, wanted to expand the low-rent program and keep it together with the other housing programs in a cabinet-level "Department of Housing and Community Development." [21] The National Association of Real Estate Boards (NAREB) and its allies—the savings and loans associations, the mortgage bankers, and the home builders—showed some interest in the department idea, but demanded that public housing be stopped before any permanent consolidation take place. They claimed that any government agency charged with administering aids for both public and private construction would inevitably give greater encouragement to the former.[22] Just as the battle over public housing had prevented immediate action on urban redevelopment legislation, so too, did the public housing struggle delay administrative reorganization. By the time of V-J Day, the fate of NHA was a subject of intense political debate in Washington.

Not until two-and-a-half years after the Japanese surrender were the President and Congress finally able to agree on what to do with NHA. Truman had put himself on record early in favor of a permanent NHA, but as with other matters in the housing field, he deferred in the beginning to the legislature. The first congressional statement came in August 1945 with the release of the Taft Subcommittee report. In line with the Ohio Senator's generally progressive stand on housing, the study called for continuation of public housing and permanent status for NHA, noting that the agency's "excellent performance during the trying conditions of wartime has been demonstrative of the value of unification and coordination." Having adopted the liberals' position on these points, Taft attempted to appease the conservatives by diluting the power of the administrator. Under the Executive order that created NHA, Blandford had exercised substantial control over the policies and operations of the bureau chiefs who ran FHA, USHA, FHLBB, and so forth. Opposed to centralization wherever and whenever it appeared, Taft wished to vest only "general supervisory and coordinating" powers in the administrator; his role would be essentially that of a mediator: to reconcile those differences that might arise among the constituent units, each of which would maintain its autonomy. This arrangement, Taft insisted, would preclude any possibility of favoritism toward public housing.[23] The Taft formula was incorporated in the Wagner-Ellender-Taft bill that passed the Senate in 1946; conservative resistance to public housing, however, ruled out House action.

With the comprehensive housing bill obviously dead for the 79th Congress, Truman decided to assume the offensive, using his reorganization powers to establish a permanent NHA. According to a 1945 law, Congress could halt such a step only if both Houses registered their disapproval within sixty days of the submission of the Presidential plan. Truman's plan, drafted by management specialists in the Budget Bureau, drew heavily upon Taft's bill but contained one significant change: instead of giving the administrator "rather limited authority of a coordinating nature," BOB Director Harold D. Smith explained to a Senate committee in June 1946, Reorganization Plan No. 1 of 1946 would make the NHA boss "in fact, the directing head" of his agency. Afraid that this shake-up would destroy the close and profitable relationships they had forged with FHA and FHLBB, realtors, home builders, and bankers lobbied vigorously to defeat the plan. The House actually needed little inducement; by a large margin it voted down Plan No. 1, as well as two other Presidential reorganization proposals. In the Senate, the enemies of the Wagner-Ellender-Taft bill and public housing picked up the decisive support of Robert Taft in their fight against the Reorganization Plan. Charging that Truman's suggestion

of "a unitary agency" might permit the public housers to "dominate" the privately oriented FHA and FHLBB, Taft called for the
rejection of NHA and its "king-pin" administrator. The Senate did
just that, humiliating the President by a 45–31 vote.

Events went differently in 1947. Taft reintroduced his version of
the NHA bill when the new 80th Congress met, but the power of
conservatives in the House doomed the Taft-Ellender-Wagner
measure from the start. Still eager to put the consolidated housing
agency on a permanent footing, Truman again resorted to the
reorganization route; this time, however, he capitulated to Taft on
the authority of the administrator. In addition, the revised Truman
plan gave NHA a new name: the Housing and Home Finance
Agency (HHFA); this title, the President hoped, would carry none
of the centralizing connotations the agency's foes found in NHA.
Truman's pacificatory approach failed in the House but worked,
thanks to the assistance of Taft, in the Senate. On July 27, 1947,
HHFA became a statutory member of the federal bureaucracy.

Establishment of HHFA fell far short of the goals of the original
supporters of an urban-affairs department. While the step heralded a
continually active governmental housing policy, the Reorganization
Plan provided no mechanism for constant review and evaluation of
that policy at the highest decision-making levels. HHFA was a
second-echelon agency, one of the many narrowly based independent agencies vying for White House attention and congressional
understanding. Its budget was relatively small and its scope of
operations limited. In prestige-conscious Washington, the HHFA
administrator was just another faceless functionary. Nor was the
administrator master of his own house. The agency's last administrator called HHFA a "bureaucratic monstrosity," and most managerial specialists would have agreed.[24] Legal responsibility for nearly
all of HHFA's programs was lodged with the chiefs of the
constituent units, not with the administrator; two of the bureau
commissioners held direct Presidential appointments. The administrator was boss of HHFA in name only and incapable of providing
direction or coherence to the agency's often contradictory programs.

Besides these structural weaknesses, HHFA also lacked a close identification with cities or their myriad problems. The inauguration of urban redevelopment in 1949 solidified HHFA's position as the most important federal agency dealing with urban communities, but nothing in the Housing Act of that year hinted at an urban policy or a special role for HHFA in urban areas. HHFA's job was to build as many houses as it could—not to make cities better places to live, work, and play. The decision, in 1948, to dismantle the Urban Studies Division reflected this lack of concern for relating home building to city building. At mid-century, America's cities still had not found a niche for themselves in Washington.

II

The early 1950s offered no opportunity for reopening the case for an urban department. After the outbreak of hostilities in Korea, the production of defense housing took precedence over plans for well-integrated community development, and the vigorous conservative counterattack against public housing forced liberals into a defensive posture. With the Eisenhower-G.O.P. sweep of the 1952 elections the very future of HHFA was again thrown into doubt. The realtor-builder-banker complex had not reconciled itself to HHFA, and continued to use its close contacts with the new President's staff to press for the agency's abolition. Since Eisenhower had, during the campaign, indicated a desire to curtail federal intervention in the housing sector, the outlook for HHFA appeared bleak as the Republicans took control. But following discussions with Taft, Eisenhower decided to maintain the status quo; although his appointment of an ex-congressman from rural Kansas, Albert Cole, who had voted against NHA-HHFA in 1946 and 1947, to the post of administrator made it clear that the time was not ripe for a move to give HHFA greater stature.[25]

Eisenhower's unexpected support for the comprehensive housing package that became the Housing Act of 1954 changed that situation dramatically. Instead of the slow death by atrophy that seemed in store for HHFA, the agency now found itself with enlarged responsibilities for the conservation and renewal of America's cities. The Workable Program requirement, grants for metropolitan planning, and more generous FHA aids for rental housing all signified a bigger federal role in urban development. With HHFA finally assured of a long lease on life, Budget Bureau administrative experts and a committee of Presidential advisers began a joint study of the agency's organization and purpose. And on Capitol Hill, on July 23, 1954, just three weeks after President Eisenhower signed the 1954 Housing Act, H.R. 10032, "to create a Department of Urbiculture," was introduced.

Sponsorship for this measure came from an unlikely source: Republican Congressman J. Arthur Younger of California. A sixty-one-year-old first-term conservative representative from San Mateo County, a wealthy suburban district just south of San Francisco, Younger had not distinguished himself as an avid spokesman for urban interests prior to H.R. 10032. On the outstanding urban issue of the 83rd Congress—public housing—Younger almost always joined his G.O.P. colleagues in opposing further appropriations. By his record in Washington, Younger seemed an improbable advocate of a bill to establish an "executive department to develop methods of dealing with pressing social, economic, and civic problems growing out of inadequate knowledge of the principles of using and developing urban land."

Despite his instinctively conservative politics, Younger was drawn to his "Urbiculture" proposal by a variety of personal experiences. He had worked for the FHLBB in the 1930s and had been an executive with a California savings and loan association since 1937, and thus, he possessed a special knowledge of the problems of the home-building industry. Most of them, Younger believed, "originated from our faulty techniques in the development and use of urban real estate." Thanks to the long-established scientific studies conducted by the Department of Agriculture, America was making full and excellent use of its farmlands; but "there has been no consistent research done to discover how best to 'cultivate' urban land so as to produce maximum yields in monetary terms and amenities," Younger argued. The results were "slum-ridden, traffic-strangled, and income-starved cities."

The Agriculture Department had been created, Younger pointed out, when 80 per cent of the nation's population lived in rural areas; now with "85 per cent *[sic]* of the people concentrated in urban communities," the nation needed a corresponding Department of Urbiculture to bring "the science of urban land economics out of its nebulous state." [26] Besides spurring research, the Urbiculture Department would also "coordinate the sprawling, frequently conflicting activities of the dozen or so federal agencies which deal independently with the various city problems." [27] As chairman of the San Francisco Municipal Conference, a civic group composed of the city's largest taxpaying organizations, Younger had seen at first hand the difficulties of making federal programs operate in unison; as a politician and resident of San Mateo County, one of the fastest growing suburban counties in the country—its population jumped nearly 90 per cent between 1950 and 1960—Younger knew how importantly federal policies influenced community life.[28] "I became interested in the cabinet idea," Younger reminisced in 1961,

when I learned that municipal officials coming to Washington were unable to find out the various places to go where the Federal Government was already interested in municipal affairs. A farmer comes to Washington and he goes to the Department of Agriculture and they direct him to all of the various things that the Government does in regard to farming. But the Federal Government's urban activities were scattered all over in five or six departments and without any central direction or without any direction so far as a cabinet department is concerned.

Younger did not seek additional federal programs, but he wanted all of the existing ones brought together.[29]

Beyond the usual disabilities associated with proposals advanced by junior congressmen, Younger's bill also suffered from another major weakness: the lack of pressure group support. Although the National Housing Conference (NHC) had been recommending cabinet status for HHFA in its annual policy statements since 1952, this issue took a back seat to NHC's perennial struggle to maintain the vigor of public housing.[30] Prompted by Younger's bill, the National Association of Housing and Redevelopment Officials (NAHRO) endorsed an Executive department for housing and urban affairs in the fall of 1954, but it, too, depleted its limited political influence on behalf of public housing.[31] The research-minded Urban Land Institute, which in 1953 had urged a "Department of Urban Affairs" that would "parallel the long and constructive interest of the Department of Agriculture in the nation's rural economy," found "logic and merit" in Younger's plan; but in contrast to its trade association affiliate, NAREB, the institute carried little weight on Capitol Hill.[32] A few leading realtors and home-builders were known to favor raising HHFA to cabinet rank, but neither NAREB nor the National Association of Home Builders (NAHB) indicated sympathy for such a move.[33] H.R. 10032 and its successor in the 84th Congress, H.R. 1864, also failed to interest the mayors' organizations; both the 1954 and 1955 meetings of the American Municipal Association (AMA) and the United States Conference of Mayors (USCM) ignored the question of urban representation at the cabinet table.

Despite the absence of enthusiasm for the Younger proposal, the Californian's bill did receive a hearing in the House during the first session of the 84th Congress. Younger owed his good fortune to the fact that the Committee on Government Operations, which handled reorganization matters, was chaired by a liberal, big-city congressman, William Dawson of Chicago. The chief of the Democratic machine in Chicago's black South Side ghetto, Dawson supported closer federal-urban ties and thought the Younger measure would promote action along these lines. Dawson's committee held hearings in July 1955 on H.R. 1864, but given the dearth of interest they were far from comprehensive: testimony consumed only two-and-one-half hours and filled just fifty-two printed pages. Nevertheless, the congressmen heard enough to rule out the possibility that H.R. 1864 could serve as the vehicle for the creation of an urban department.

The remarks of the two administration witnesses spotlighted the bill's deficiencies. Both HHFA Administrator Cole and Assistant Budget Director Percy Rappaport indicated interest in the "general objectives" of the measure, but criticized its vagueness. They were "not quite sure of [H.R. 1864's] scope and breadth." On the one hand, the bill seemed "overly limited and restricted." As drafted, H.R. 1864 appeared to confine the new department to mere research and education on the development of urban land. HHFA's activities, Cole and Rappaport pointed out, "have already gone far beyond the types of programs outlined by this bill." "It would be difficult," they argued, "to justify placing the constituents of HHFA now charged with administering action programs in such a department." Yet while Cole and Rappaport found H.R. 1864 too narrow in this respect, they found it was too broad in another. Younger had proposed to transfer HHFA to the Urbiculture Department along with all other agencies "the President deems appropriate." The Californian thought that civil defense, smog control, juvenile delinquency, and small business programs, as well as all the other programs that "deal solely with cities," were prime candidates for inclusion in the department. To the two administration spokesmen, Younger's grandiose plans would cause the Urbiculture Department to "expand indefinitely," possibly engulfing all the already existing departments with the exception of State, Defense, and Agriculture. Before any department could be established, they maintained, it would first be necessary "to determine exactly over what areas it might have jurisdiction." The "complexities of urban living are such," declared Cole, "that we could find ourselves floating in an ethereal atmosphere, and not put our feet solidly on the ground." This difficulty of defining the Urban Department realm would continue to plague the cabinet department idea in the years ahead.

Another controversial issue brought to the fore by the hearings was the matter of a name for the department. Establishment of the Department of Health, Education and Welfare, which was finally achieved in 1953, had been held up for many years by, among other things, a dispute over its title, and already sharp differences were shaping up over what the Urban Department would be called. Younger preferred "Urbiculture," which he defined as "an art, or a science, of developing and cultivating urban land to its best and highest use," arguing that as a new word not found in the dictionary it was bound to attract publicity for the department. Furthermore, he explained, "Urbiculture invited comparison with agriculture and would emphasize the effort to provide a square deal for the city fellow." Others, however, felt Younger's handiwork was too clever.[34] The American Society of Planning Officials (ASPO) claimed that the success of the department would depend upon popular understanding of its purposes and the public's lack of familiarity with the term "Urbiculture" would hinder its acceptance. It urged a "Department of Municipal Affairs." "Urbiculture" also came under criticism from housing groups, public and private, which were afraid that the housing functions of HHFA might be submerged in an urban department. They wanted the word "housing" prominently in the title; NHC, for instance, proposed the name "Department of Housing and Urban Affairs." Over the next decade more than a dozen different titles would be presented for serious consideration.

Besides the administration spokesmen, the committee heard from four other witnesses. Younger outlined his reasons for devising the bill and conceded that passage was still some time off. Representatives of NHC and the American Institute of Planners conveniently avoided discussing specific details of H.R. 1864 but spoke out in support of the creation of an Executive department to improve coordination of federal programs in urban areas. An official of the AMA reported that his organization had not yet taken a position on the matter, but was eager to be involved in any future planning for a department. NAHRO and ASPO wrote letters to Dawson commending the principles of Younger's measure. No group that might be expected to be against establishment of another department, such as the U.S. Chamber of Commerce, bothered to make an appearance. Nor were the views of the powerful NAREB and NAHB elicited.

The close of hearings marked the end of the road for the Younger bill. Poorly conceived and amateurishly drafted, H.R. 1864 could not even withstand the scrutiny of those predisposed to look at it positively. The consensus of the testimony was that the subject of a department for cities needed a good deal more study. With the defects of the Younger bill now well publicized and with the Executive Branch showing little enthusiasm for correcting them, Dawson undoubtedly recognized that it would be futile to push for further action on H.R. 1864. Not known as a fighter for lost causes, he dropped his identification with the cabinet idea; no bill for this purpose would be reported out of his committee for the remainder of the 1950s.

But if the Younger bill had reached a legislative dead end, the hearings did return dividends by stimulating discussion. Three days after the hearings were held, Representative Martha Griffiths, Democrat from Detroit, introduced a measure (H.R. 7731) to establish a "Department of Urban Affairs." "There is a need," declared the bill's statement of findings, "for a central place in the Federal administrative structure to assess the overall results of the numerous Federal programs having a vital impact on local communities and metropolitan areas, to help coordinate these activities, and to represent the needs of urban areas at the national level." In February 1956, at the start of the 84th Congress's second session, a bill to create a "Department of Housing and Urban Affairs" was presented to the Senate by Herbert H. Lehman (D.-N.Y.) and eight co-sponsors.[35] This proposal was a companion measure to Lehman's reform housing bill, both of which had been written by NHC. While neither the Griffiths bill nor the Lehman departmental bill was accorded hearings, their very existence was enough to arouse NAREB. Afraid that a rearrangement of housing agencies would impair FHA's ability to serve realtors' interests and that a new department would mean greater federal spending, NAREB, at its 1956 meeting, denounced cabinet suggestions as leading to "more and more Federal controls and more and more programs." [36] But as NAREB moved into open opposition the cabinet idea received a boost from AMA. Prodded by Philadelphia Mayor Richardson

Dilworth, the AMA, in November 1956, urged a "new Federal executive department for urban affairs." The Association's resolution, adopted over the protests of small municipalities, observed that

unlike the other segments of our political economy, such as industry, labor and agriculture, local governments have no one place to turn in their many dealings with the Federal Government. . . . The growth and development of our cities requires a comprehensive and unified administrative organization at the Federal level.[37]

The by-now familiar mayor-public housers versus realtors battle lines were beginning to take shape.

When the 85th Congress assembled in January 1957, a new champion stepped forward to carry on the battle for a cabinet department for urban affairs. Younger reintroduced his "Urbiculture" bill, but the mantle of leadership passed to a freshman senator, Joseph S. Clark of Pennsylvania. A liberal Democrat, Clark was much more closely allied with the housing and urban groups that were the bulwark of support for an Executive department than was the conservative Younger. Clark came from a well-to-do Philadelphia Republican family, but early in his political career he had left the party of his ancestors to join the Democrats and vote for Al Smith in 1928, declaring, "You can't get anything done in the Republican Party." After more than two decades of fighting the entrenched and corrupt Republican machine and the regular Democratic organization, Clark, with the close collaboration of Dilworth, was elected in 1951 mayor of Philadelphia, the first Democrat to win that post since 1884. Clark cleaned up city government and launched a massive public works program; it was under his direction that the big Penn Center urban renewal project in downtown Philadelphia was started. Leaving City Hall in 1955 so that his associate Dilworth could take his place, Clark ran for the Senate the following year; almost buried by the Eisenhower landslide, he managed to pull off an upset victory over the incumbent.[38]

Once in the Senate, Clark quickly established himself as the logical successor to Lehman, who had inherited the role from Robert Wagner, as the foremost advocate of urban problems on Capitol Hill. Clark, noted one magazine,[39]

exemplified a new type of U.S. Senator—the urbane, urban legislator. His interests are not farm supports, but city supports, not subsidies for corn but more money for urban renewal, not public power but public housing, not help for the American Indian but aid for the American slum dweller.

"I don't know whether the American city has a future or not," Clark told an interviewer. "The problem of the city is the most enormous and pressing one we face domestically insofar as the difficulty of its solution is concerned. The experts are baffled by it and so am I. But we must keep trying." [40]

For Clark, establishing an Executive department seemed a good way to start solving urban problems. In May 1957, along with eight other senators, he introduced legislation, S. 2159, to create a "Department of Housing and Urban Affairs." [41] The bill was essentially the NHC measure Lehman had presented the year before embellished with a new preamble, which declared, in part, that

the general welfare and security and the living standards of its people require that the Federal Government adapt its administrative organization to provide those programs which will be of the greatest assistance to the States and local governments in meeting the problems caused by the continuing growth and concentration of population.

"A visitor from outer space," Clark later explained,[42]

looking at the structure of our Federal Government, would surely conclude that America is still a rural nation, with rural problems its dominant concern. We have a Department of Agriculture, which devotes itself to the problems of the farm; we have a Department of the Interior, which reflects the interests and needs of the more sparsely settled states; but there is no department with responsibility for the problems of the tens of millions of people living in forced congestion in metropolitan areas. . . . City people, too, need an advocate in Washington. . . . We must re-orient a Federal

Government superbly equipped to deal with the 19th century problems of agriculture and natural resources, and hardly equipped at all to deal with the urban society which today it largely represents. . . . A Federal Government which does not pay as much attention to urbiculture as to agriculture, to the conservation of cities as to the soil, to the movement of people and goods within as well as between cities, is not adapted to today's America.

Clark's impassioned advocacy of a cabinet-level urban affairs department added virtually nothing to its political appeal within Congress. As a senator, Clark enjoyed somewhat greater access than did Younger to the mass media where he could popularize his views, but like the Californian, Clark suffered from the disability of low seniority, intensified by Clark's estrangement form the rural, conservative bloc of senators who controlled the flow of legislation in the upper chamber. Cut off from the inside contacts that might have allowed him to move S. 2159 along, Clark was also denied the aid that might have come from the outside from NHC and AMA. They were much too busy struggling with the administration over Eisenhower's plan to reduce urban renewal authorizations to give Clark any help.[43] Just like its predecessors, S. 2159 died a silent death.

III

At the same time that Congress was quietly burying bills to establish an urban department, the idea of giving cities representation at the cabinet table was receiving serious study at the staff level in the Executive Office of the President. Eisenhower, who had learned the virtues of sound administrative arrangements as Supreme Allied Commander in Europe during World War II, had created a President's Advisory Committee on Government Operations (PACGO) shortly before his inauguration to work with the Budget Bureau on improving the operating efficiency of federal agencies. Although PACGO, whose members were Nelson Rockefeller, chairman, Arthur S. Flemming, and Milton Eisenhower, remained more or less active throughout Eisenhower's two terms, it never produced a coherent organizational doctrine. What it did do, however, was provide the framework for an impartial review of the merits of cabinet department proposals.[44]

PACGO turned its attention initially to the internal structure of HHFA. As it functioned under Reorganization Plan No. 3 of 1947, HHFA departed radically from the axiom of the First Hoover Commission on the Organization of the Executive Branch (1949) that[45]

the heads of departments (or agencies) must hold full responsibility for the conduct of their departments. There must be a clear line of authority reaching down through every step of the organization and no subordinate should have authority independent from that of his superior.

But the HHFA administrator exercised only "general supervisory and coordinating authority" over the constituent units. Albert Cole, as a congressman in the 1940s, had fought for this kind of setup, but now as administrator he chafed at these strict reins on his powers.[46] Management experts at BOB agreed with Cole's complaints, and at PACGO's request they drew up a Reorganization Plan that would make the administrator the true boss of HHFA. The plan was ready for submission to Congress in the spring of 1954, but at the last minute Eisenhower decided not to send it. A move toward a consolidated housing agency at this time would jeopardize the support of conservative Republicans Eisenhower needed to pass his 1954 housing program.[47] Rebuffed in this attempt to reform the HHFA, Cole would never again find the White House open to a reconsideration of the issue. Indeed, the President kept silent as the savings and loan associations pushed a bill through Congress, in 1955, taking the Federal Home Loan Bank Board out of HHFA and giving it independent status.[48] HHFA continued to be "a bureaucratic monstrosity" for the remainder of Eisenhower's tenure.

Besides looking into HHFA's structural defects, PACGO also re-examined the agency's mission. It soon concluded that the

"Housing and Community Development Agency" would be a "more fitting designation" than HHFA for its operations since, with the 1949 and 1954 Housing Acts, the Federal Government was "no longer concerned exclusively with the financing or construction of dwellings, but rather with the development of wholesome neighborhoods and well-planned cities." This recommendation was laid to rest with the abortive 1954 Reorganization Plan.[49]

Introduction of the Younger, Griffiths, and Lehman bills rekindled PACGO's interest in the matter, however, and in November 1956 the committee's executive director, Arthur Kimball, asked its members to study the question of departmental status for housing and community development functions. Kimball's memorandum noted that the "Federal Government's activities in this field are with us to stay and will grow in importance." Cabinet representation, he went on, "now includes the interests of health, education, agriculture, natural resources, commerce, labor, etc. There is no logical reason to exclude activities of such widespread and growing national import as housing and community development." Furthermore,

the presence in the cabinet of a Secretary of Housing and Community Development could better assure that housing and community development views would be brought to bear on such policy matters as the budget, interest rates, treatment of minorities, highway and construction programs, etc.

In addition, "the greater prestige, as well as the more effective access to the President, which cabinet status would afford, would undoubtedly facilitate the effective accomplishment of the programs [HHFA administers]; also it would probably attract better men." Against these arguments in favor of a cabinet department, Kimball cited only two objections from an administrative standpoint: first, a new department would result in a larger cabinet; and second, it would increase the number of people normally reporting directly to the President.[50]

Before PACGO could discuss the substance of Kimball's memorandum on its own merits a complicating factor intruded. The main topic on PACGO's agenda when Kimball raised the subject of departmental status for HHFA was the desirability of cabinet rank for the Federal Civil Defense Administration (FCDA). Few on the BOB-PACGO staff believed that FCDA deserved the promotion, but Rockefeller, who in the early 1960s would make national headlines with his call for a massive bomb-shelter program, was strongly in favor of it. Eager to dispel the doubts of his colleagues about bringing civil defense to the cabinet table, Rockefeller seized upon the Kimball memo as a way of strengthening FCDA's standing; he proposed that HHFA and FCDA be merged into a single Executive department. Flemming and Milton Eisenhower received Rockefeller's suggestion with some interest, but since it raised some new issues they urged that the idea be sent to the staff for study.[51] More than six months elapsed before PACGO was ready to pass on any recommendation to the White House.

In a memorandum handed to Presidential Assistant Sherman Adams in early July 1957, PACGO advised that "a Department of Urban Affairs is already needed and that the need will rapidly become more urgent." "The problems of planning, building, and conserving our cities and metropolitan areas have become increasingly acute in recent years," PACGO reported. Creation of an Executive department would give leadership and direction to federal efforts in this area and provide for the presentation of the urban perspective in cabinet deliberations on national policy issues. As for civil defense, PACGO felt that the reduction of urban vulnerability was closely related to the existing functions of HHFA and should be integrated with them in a single department. PACGO concluded by urging that a reorganization plan establishing a Department of Urban Affairs be prepared for submission to the next session of Congress.[52]

Adams's "off-the-cuff" reactions to the PACGO study proved favorable, although he was seriously troubled by the term "urban affairs." Discussing the matter with Flemming in July, Adams said he believed that "urban affairs" in the new department's title "would imply the potential assumption of increased Federal responsibilities with regard to urban areas." This, he felt, "would be contrary to Administration policy" and the theme of the President's recent address to the Governors' Conference in Williamsburg where Eisenhower called upon the states to take over many federal grant-in-aid programs, most notably urban renewal. Adams suggested that "Department of Rehabilitation and Development" might be more appropriate.[53]

PACGO-BOB staff spent the rest of the summer searching for a suitable title for the department. Adams's proposal did not seem descriptive enough, so it was dropped quickly from contention. After much hesitation, Kimball and his aides decided that "urban affairs" would have to go, too. Besides Adams's political arguments against its use, they noted that some of HHFA's programs, such as its loans for community facility construction, operated in rural as well as urban areas; thus, any use of that phrase would be "misleading and unduly restrictive." Finally, in September, they found a name that would accurately identify the scope of the department's realm and "minimize fears or expectations that the Federal Government will assume increased responsibilities in regard to the cities and communities of the nation." Their discovery: the "Department of Housing and Community Development." [54]

But having settled on a name PACGO found that the rest of its recommendations were encountering stiff resistance. The director of the Federal Civil Defense Administration was adamantly opposed to having his agency swallowed up by HHFA; so vehement were his criticisms of the merger idea that PACGO was forced to withdraw its endorsement of the scheme pending further study.[55] Then, in a meeting with the committee in October, the President announced that he could not support the creation of an Executive department for housing. Eisenhower was already preparing a message for the next Congress requesting that a number of programs handled by HHFA be curtailed or that a large degree of responsibility for them be shifted to state and local governments; to go before this same

Congress to ask for an upgrading of HHFA was simply out of the question. The mere request for a new department, no matter how innocuous its title, would seem to suggest further federal involvement in local affairs, something that Eisenhower definitely did not want to do.[56]

The first public statement of the administration's negative stand on an urban department came in a speech Rockefeller gave to the American Council to Improve Our Neighborhoods (ACTION) that same fall. Up to now the Executive Branch, in letters to congressional committee chairmen and in testimony on the Younger bill, had been careful not to deprecate the possible merits of such a department; it simply took the position that the various bills before Congress were technically deficient and that further study was required. But in line with Eisenhower's renewed offensive against the overcentralization of power in Washington, Rockefeller used his address to ACTION, an organization of businessmen and civic leaders favoring increased spending on urban renewal, to label proposals for a federal agency on city affairs "appalling." To establish a department to bring order to the numerous federal activities influencing metropolitan development would mean, Rockefeller claimed, the creation of a "Frankenstein monster" that would run roughshod over state governments; "home rule would become a memory." [57] After that outburst, it would be two years before there was anyone in PACGO, BOB, or HHFA with the temerity to press for a reconsideration of the issue.

IV

Even as Eisenhower closed off discussion within the administration on a cabinet department, another debate was shaping up outside on what form an urban agency should take. The political scientists, managerial experts, planners, and municipal leaders who agreed that cities were entitled to recognition in the Federal Government's structure had different answers to two key questions: what functions should be included in the department? Would, indeed, the cities be better served by an Executive department or by a staff agency in the Executive Office of the President?

Advocates of an urban department held widely variant opinions on which activities should be directed by this new member of the cabinet. While there was virtual unanimity that the department would be built around HHFA, there were a variety of suggestions on what else might be added. Some people believed civil defense ought to be linked with HHFA;[58] others wanted to put the highway program in the department;[59] still others thought that the air and water pollution control programs, as well as the airport construction program, belonged in the Urban Department.[60] Younger's proposal to transfer all bureaus dealing with city problems to a single department enjoyed considerable support among municipal officials who looked forward to the "one-stop service" this setup would afford. Coordination of the myriad federal programs operating in metropolitan areas could best be achieved, they argued, if they were all housed under the same roof.[61]

Whatever the common sense appeal of bringing all urban-directed federal activities together into one department, the idea possessed little attraction administratively. A "Department of Urban Miscellany," declared political scientists Robert H. Connery and Richard H. Leach, would be "an organizational misfit." They argued that the insertion of "an executive department based on a geographical pattern into a system primarily organized functionally would make for more, rather than less, confusion in the administrative structure." [62] As other critics pointed out, long-established agencies such as the Public Health Service and the Bureau of Public Roads carried on their work in both urban and rural areas; according to some plans for an urban department, each would be split along territorial lines that ignored the essential unity of its mission.[63] Furthermore, there was no evidence that throwing all of the various agencies into a single department would really improve coordination. The Department of Health, Education and Welfare was hardly a model of harmony, and an even larger and more heterogeneous urban department promised to be "so unwieldy" as to become "a hopeless morass." [64] Difficult political fights could also be expected if wholesale transfers of bureaus were attempted. No bureau outside of HHFA was particularly anxious to move to an urban department, and the combined strength of their respective clienteles would surely be enough to kill urban department legislation should it ever reach the floor of Congress.[65]

Recognizing the impossibility of "combining the sum of the Federal Government's interests in cities into any single Federal Department," most of the department's supporters set their sights on the simple elevation of HHFA to cabinet rank. William L. C. Wheaton, professor of city planning at the University of Pennsylvania and the leading advocate of the department idea within NHC, contended that the magnitude and importance of HHFA's activities alone were enough to warrant Executive department status. Despite this restricted operational base, Wheaton insisted, the new department, which he preferred to call the "Department of Housing and Urban Development" (HUD) would be able to coordinate all of the federal programs in metropolitan areas. "Today we have had coordination between unequals," he wrote in 1960. "Like the traditional rabbit stew, composed of one horse and one rabbit, we have asked the representative of an independent agency [HHFA] to sit down at a coordinating table with cabinet officers of easily greater prestige, power, and influence." The result was "an urban policy that has been dictated to the HHFA Administrator by the Secretary of the Treasury or the Secretary of Commerce." Raising HHFA to the cabinet level would end that disparity and insure that the urban point of view was presented when national policies and programs were being hammered out.[66]

Not everyone, however, shared Wheaton's optimism about HUD's ability to direct federal activities in urban districts. Robert Merriam, whose efforts at coordination through an interagency committee had failed,[67] observed that HUD would be the "junior member of a very elite society." "Historically," he told the AMA, no cabinet officer has yet effectively coordinated the work of other co-equal (and in this case senior) cabinet heads. And unless *all* activities of the Federal Government affecting urban areas are poured into a new department (and I doubt that anyone is seriously suggesting this), the basic problem we now face will inevitably still be with us. That problem is symbolized by the fact that under our Constitution only one person can make final decisions; only one person can resolve differences of opinion and judgement between his various departments and agencies. Only one man can determine national policy relating to urban areas, and that man, under any administration, will not be an agency head or cabinet officer—it will be the President.

Whether or not a cabinet department was created, Merriam argued, there would have to be a staff agency in the Executive Office of the President to keep the Chief Executive abreast of present problems and to plan ahead for future programs.[68]

The most elaborate case for a staff agency as an alternative to a cabinet department was presented by Connery and Leach. In a series of articles and a book, they attacked "the false belief that simple organizational change will provide the answer for urban and metropolitan problems." Creation of a department

would beg the most important question of all: What is the Federal Government's proper role in urban areas? The answer is not merely to assign urban affairs to a single organizational unit. It is a matter of principle and philosophy, not of method. To establish a method without first having established a philosophy to base it on is to put the proverbial cart before the horse.

More than "organizational reshuffling," the Federal Government needed "a national policy toward metropolitan areas." Development of such a policy would be the task of a three-member Council on Metropolitan Areas, backed up by a professional staff, comparable to the Council of Economic Advisors. An urban department might eventually prove useful, Connery and Leach concluded, but for the present, "when the basic issues of intergovernmental relations in metropolitan areas are still unresolved, such a proposal is clearly premature." [69]

Underlying the split between proponents of a staff agency and supporters of a cabinet department was a fundamental difference in priorities. As much as Connery and Leach were interested in improving the effectiveness of federal activities in metropolitan districts, they were still more concerned about strengthening the hand of the President. Inheritors of the Brownlow-Merriam-Gulick tradition of administrative management, Connery and Leach wanted to provide the Chief Executive with the staff help he needed to run the bureaucracy and formulate policy. As political scientist Robert Wood, the first undersecretary of HUD, later pointed out, in terms of "administrative precision and tidiness in organization arrangements," the Connery-Leach position "would have won hands down"; but Wheaton and Clark were not debating on this level. Rather, they rallied around "the simple concept of a spokesman for urbanites"; the realities of political power, not administrative theory, formed the basis of their thinking.[70] "The cities of America," Clark declared, "need a voice at the summit equal in status to the voice of agriculture." Wheaton agreed:[71]

The primary reason for a Department of Urban Development is to secure a seat at the bargaining table in the White House where the Federal pie is cut up and divided. In Washington, unfortunately, the flaming sword of truth is a poor substitute for the broad axe of influence. In Washington, influence is largely measured by prestige, payrolls and budgets, and only a cabinet officer commanding ample amounts of these can represent urban people.

Representation and equity were to be the main themes of the political campaign for an urban department.

The sharp, but friendly divisions over how the national government ought to deal with a new urban constituency impaired the prospects for action on a department bill. In 1959, for instance, three different bills were introduced that would have established open-ended departments of urban affairs or urbiculture. This type of imprecision only lent credence to the administration's claim that the entire matter needed more study.[72] Similarly, the failure of such respected managerial experts as Brownlow and Gulick[73] to endorse a department for cities deprived the cabinet idea of the scholarly foundations it could have used to compensate for its lack of a strong political base.

V

Recognizing the futility of pushing for a cabinet department bill in the face of administration hostility and division in his own ranks, Clark decided on a new strategy when the 85th Congress met in 1959. The departmental measure was in want of two crucial elements essential to the passage of most reform legislation: a sense of national urgency; and a consensus on what should be done. Clark hoped to remedy these defects by a tried and true method: a federal study commission. The joint Presidential-Legislative Commission on Metropolitan Problems he wished to establish would focus public attention on the problems of urban governments and make recommendations for their solution. Clark was confident that a well-informed and impartial commission would see the wisdom of a cabinet department for cities.[74]

Clark's proposal was not original, but it received a different reception than that of its predecessor. In 1957 an upstate New York Republican congressman, Harold Ostertag, had introduced a similar bill, which had subsequently been referred to Dawson's Committee on Government Operations, where it died without a hearing.[75] That this would not be the fate of the Clark bill (S. 1431) was made apparent the very day it was presented to the Senate. Majority Leader Lyndon B. Johnson of Texas, who usually had no use for Clark's brand of liberalism, interrupted the Pennsylvanian's lengthy introductory speech to announce his support of S. 1431 and to pledge prompt action on the measure. Johnson's sudden interest in metropolitan problems was stimulated by the approach of the 1960 Presidential elections. Eager to embarrass the Republicans on domestic issues, Johnson felt a study commission would highlight the administration's failure to come to the aid of local government.

Also, by identifying himself with this type of urban legislation, Johnson believed he might get rid of his image as a Southern agrarian politician, an image that hindered his drive for the Democratic nomination. With Johnson behind the bill, S. 1431's prospects looked bright.

The unexpected Johnson-Clark alliance greatly upset the administration. Back in 1957 the White House had written approvingly of the Ostertag bill, secure in the knowledge that it was not going anywhere.[76] But S. 1431 was an entirely different matter. With twelve of the commission's eighteen members to be appointed by the Democratic leadership in Congress, the commission seemed likely to produce a partisan document; furthermore, it would probably call for increased federal spending, a policy the President could not accept. To formulate the administration's counterattack against S. 1431, Robert Merriam reactivated, in May 1959, the *Ad Hoc* Interagency Committee on Metropolitan Area Problems, which had not met in nearly two years. The group drafted a letter to the Senate committee holding hearings on the bill contending that a commission was not necessary. "The Executive Branch," it declared, "has been increasingly active in exploring and attempting to deal with the problem areas to be studied." In addition to the *Ad Hoc* committee, the letter cited the Public Works Planning Unit in the White House, BOB, HHFA, and the Joint Federal-State Action Committee as examples of Executive agencies addressing themselves to the ills of metropolitan districts. Besides, the administration claimed, since most big urban centers had already started their own studies, a national commission would be superfluous.[77]

Despite the White House's antagonism, S. 1431 made excellent progress in its course through Congress—up to a point. Committees in both chambers conducted hearings on the Clark bill and similar measures during the summer of 1959; only friends of the proposal took the trouble to testify. By Labor Day the two panels had reported favorably to their respective houses. On September 10, Johnson, delivering on his earlier promise, gained Senate approval of S. 1431 without any debate. But that was as far as the bill went.

Unmistakably labelled as a piece of liberal legislation, S. 1431 ran into a solid wall of conservative opposition in the House Rules Committee. Enough rural Democrats joined the firm Republican minority to prevent future action on the bill.[78] This would not be the last time the rules unit served as a roadblock to cabinet status for the cities.

VI

But just as the department idea lost its momentum in Congress, it picked up new force in the Executive Branch. The impetus came from HHFA. That agency clearly stood to gain the most from the addition of another seat at the cabinet table. The men in HHFA's top echelon keenly felt their lack of influence at the White House. Cole was rarely consulted on such national policies vital to home-building as the setting of interest rates; nor did he do as well as the department heads in resisting BOB's efforts to cut their spending during Eisenhower's second term. On those infrequent occasions when Cole was invited to cabinet meetings, the rules of protocol did not allow him to forget his secondary position. Only the President, Vice-President, and the cabinet secretaries had high-backed chairs with their names on engraved plaques at the table; Cole and other agency chiefs were forced to find seats elsewhere in the big cabinet room. Once Cole was seated in the back row against the wall, Eisenhower completely forgot he was there, even though a matter directly involving HHFA was under discussion.[79] Personal as well as bureaucratic considerations demanded a change in this situation.

While loyalty to the administration prevented Cole from endorsing the bills for a new cabinet department, Cole had been careful not to discourage thinking along these lines. Thus, in the same letter, written in July 1956, in which he opposed the Younger, Griffiths, and Lehman bills because of their technical deficiencies, Cole also wrote that "the country can expect the growth of our urban areas over the next fifty years to pose problems of ever-increasing magnitude and national significance within the sphere of major interest and responsibility of a department of housing and community development." The "time will likely come, and may indeed come very soon," he continued, "when the principal functions of the Federal Government in this field ought to be organized into a new executive department." [80] The next month Cole asked the White House to weigh the merits of departmental status for HHFA,[81] but in October 1957, Eisenhower rejected the PACGO plan. Cole never again raised the matter during the sixteen months before he left HHFA in February 1959, to accept a job in private industry.

Norman P. Mason, Cole's successor as administrator, seized upon the cabinet issue almost immediately upon taking office. A prosperous lumber dealer and commissioner of FHA at the time of his promotion to HHFA's top spot, Mason was familiar with the arguments of the big home-builders for a department of housing. This group had been hurt by the tight money policies pursued by the administration from 1955 to 1957; they blamed the absence of the administrator from high executive councils for their plight.[82] In language reminiscent of that used by Wheaton and Clark, the president of NAHB demanded that "the economic and social voice of housing in all its ramifications be heard on equal terms at the cabinet level with those of commerce, of agriculture, of labor, and of the Treasury." [83] Mason was also under pressure from his own staff to exert greater leadership in the general area of urban affairs. Convinced that there was "a vacuum with respect to dealing with the dramatic national problem of a sweeping increase in urbanization," members of HHFA's Office of Program Policy wanted the agency to seek a new legislative policy directive that would expand the limited purposes of the 1949 Housing Act to cover metropolitan development. They expected cabinet status to follow inevitably.[84]

Eager to change his title from administrator to secretary, Mason worked assiduously to build up HHFA's credentials. As a first step, he resurrected the National Housing Council in May 1959. Created by the 1947 Reorganization Plan, the Council had been intended to serve as a medium for coordinating HHFA's housing programs with those of the Veterans' Administration and the Agriculture Department; the Council had performed this function well for a couple of years, but by 1952 it had fallen into disuse. When Mason restored the council, it was "to provide a forum to deal with the urban problems of America"; thus, he invited the many other agencies and departments with programs in metropolitan areas to participate. Little of substance came out of this first session or another one in December 1959, but the meetings aided Mason's publicity campaign.[85] Mason also established an Advisory Committee on Housing and Community Development composed of leading businessmen and students of urban society; and a Mayors Advisory Committee to consult with him on urban renewal.[86] By early 1960, Mason was ready to ask the White House to reopen discussion of the cabinet question.[87]

Mason's request caused a brief flurry of activity at the Budget Bureau, but in the end Mason received the negative reply Cole had. BOB staff went back to their files to retrieve the two-year-old memoranda they had written endorsing cabinet status for HHFA; slightly revised, they were forwarded to BOB Director Maurice Stans for submission to PACGO.[88] But Stans, Eisenhower's last and most conservative budget chief, rejected the recommendation of his subordinates, and in a sharp letter to Mason explained why the administration could not support changing HHFA into a department of urban affairs. As was customary by now, Stans cited the need for more study. Further analysis might show, he claimed, that HHFA's problems could be overcome better by "strengthened internal management than by regular attendance at the Cabinet." And even if the need for a department should be demonstrated, it would still be necessary to decide what functions it should include. These preliminaries out of the way, Stans then expounded his material objections to Mason's proposal. "Almost alone of Federal agencies," he noted,

HHFA deals directly with local governments rather than working through the states. Safeguards will have to be developed to insure Federal-state cooperation; and to facilitate the role of the states in providing leadership and financial aid to local governments in meeting urban problems.

Without such safeguards, Stans warned,[89]

there is a serious danger that a new department may become a clientele-oriented agency, concerned exclusively with the municipality and the urban resident. It would be unfortunate if any department should develop, as a policy, a pattern of direct national-local relationships at the expense of the state governments, and thus provide a focal point for interest groups rallying in support of additional Federal expenditures.

Stans was turning his back on almost three decades of federal-city ties as well as the entire history of the cabinet.

Stans's emphatic "no" placed Mason in an embarrassing position when Clark switched back to direct espousal of a cabinet department during the second session of the 86th Congress. With the study commission bill bottled up in the Rules Committee, Clark decided to introduce legislation creating a "Department of Housing and Metropolitan Affairs" (S. 3292) in the hope of making an Executive department for cities a campaign issue in the approaching Presidential election.[90] To speed action on the measure, Clark had it referred to the more sympathetic Banking and Currency Committee instead of the Government Operations panel, which normally handled reorganization proposals. A Banking and Currency Subcommittee conducted hearings on S. 3292, along with other liberal-sponsored general housing legislation in May 1960. In its letter to the Senate unit, the Budget Bureau emphasized once again that additional study was in order: "the basic structure of the Federal Government should not be altered until the soundness of specific plans has been carefully explored." S. 3292, it insisted, was too vague as to what activities would be located inside the department and what powers the secretary would have.[91] Clark's bill and BOB's rejection of it posed a dilemma for Mason: S. 3292 would set up the department he desired, but he did not want the Democrats to get credit for it or to have himself appear at odds with the White House. His testimony reflected his predicament: Mason had no "disagreement with the broad considerations of policy suggested by the bill"; his objection "related solely to its timing and to the method of attack." The President, he argued, should have "the initiative and responsibility to establish organizational arrangements; this is the philosophy of the Reorganization Act, and this is how the Department of Health, Education and Welfare was created." [92]

But besides putting Mason on the spot, the Clark bill achieved its primary purpose of projecting the cabinet issue onto the national political stage. S. 3292 won the unqualified endorsement of the full Banking and Currency Committee, whose report declared that "there is no longer any serious question about the need for, or the desirability of, establishing a Department of Housing and Metropolitan Affairs." Doubts about the measure's ability to withstand a parliamentary challenge from the Government Operations Committee kept Clark from bringing the bill up for floor consideration, but three thousand miles away a truly significant victory was being won. The Platform Committee of the Democratic party, meeting in Los Angeles, wrote a plank calling for the creation of an Executive department for cities. When its Republican counterpart failed to do the same, it was clear that the fate of the cabinet idea now rested upon the outcome of the Presidential contest.[93]

VII

By the fall of 1960, the cabinet department proposal was an issue politicians in Washington could no longer ignore. While not holding the same priority on the liberal agenda as such items as civil rights, medical care for the aged, aid for economically depressed areas or even bigger appropriations for urban renewal, the topic of cabinet representation for cities was attracting more and more interest. During Eisenhower's first Congress, the 83rd, only one bill on this subject had been introduced; ten times that number were lying in the bill hoppers when the 86th Congress adjourned in August 1960.[94] And with the Democratic and Republican platforms on opposite sides of the question of a "Department of Urban Affairs," that matter shaped up as an important point of contention between two Presidential candidates most observers likened to tweedledum and tweedledee.

8

The Emergence of an
Urban Consciousness:
The 1950s

Events since World War II have inescapably involved the national government in metropolitan problems. . . . Not only scholars and high-minded politicians seem agitated. While the "metropolitan complex" and "open spaces" are not yet as popular terms as "missile gap" and "growth rates," here, most Washington officials now nod knowingly when the whisper of "gray areas" runs through a cocktail party.

Robert C. Wood (1960)

In the late 1950s, American government, on all three levels, began to acknowledge that the United States was a metropolitan nation. No single event accounted for this recognition; indeed, the big "happenings" of the period—Sputnik, integration at Little Rock Central High School, the downing of the U-2 inside Russia—all served to hinder the development of a national urban consciousness. Rather, it was the product of the sheer weight of numbers and the activities of businessmen, academicians, and practical politicians.

The 1960 Census merely confirmed what the more alert knew from personal observation. America's population had grown tremendously over the past ten years, by nearly 28 million or 18.5 per cent, the biggest absolute gain in the nation's history and the largest percentage jump since the first decade of the century, when European immigration was at high tide. Fully 97 per cent of this unprecedented swelling of the population occurred in metropolitan areas; in 1920, less than 40 per cent of the people lived in metropolitan districts; by 1960, this figure was nearly two-thirds.[1]

Journeying by car or airplane, a traveler could hardly fail to be impressed by the expanding urban complexes transforming the face of America. As the decade ended, almost 50 per cent of the people in metropolitan districts lived outside the boundaries of the central cities. Plagued by the ravages of old age, rising crime, and racial prejudice, the core cities were widely recognized to be in decline. But the burgeoning suburbs had their problems too: poor transportation, overcrowded educational and recreational facilities, and tightly circumscribed revenue bases. For the entrepreneurs, scholars, and municipal officials who lived in and presided over metropolitan America, the plight of the cities and suburbs was a daily annoyance and a long-term threat. With the 1960 Presidential election, these annoyances and threats became national campaign issues for the first time.

I

Although the problems of metropolitan area government were by no means new, the response of the America of the 1950s was. Serious debate over multiple jurisdictions, limited home rule powers, and divided taxing authority had been going on at least as early as the 1850s. But as the twentieth century passed the half-way mark the issue took on greater urgency. The post-war flood of home buyers threatened to inundate the ill-equipped suburbs and quicken the decline of the core cities. Suggestive of the country's growing concern with the metropolitan muddle was the interest shown by the Governors' Conference. Antiquated state laws on annexation and incorporation presented nearly insurmountable obstacles to order in urban regions, and in 1955 the Commission on Intergovernmental Relations called upon the states to take the lead in finding answers to the riddle of metropolitan government. With unaccustomed vigor, the Governors' Conference adopted a set of recommendations the following year urging each state to provide legal authorization for the creation of general metropolitan units and to establish an agency "to aid in determining the present and changing needs of metropolitan areas." Due to legislative inertia, rural intransigence, and suburban hostility, however, few of the states implemented the suggestions.[2]

Before the decade was over, the more urbanized states would take some action. Four states created study commissions on metropolitan government, and New York established an Office of Local Government to handle state-municipal contacts. Perhaps most significantly, the Democratic governors of New York, New Jersey, Massachusetts, Connecticut, Rhode Island, and Pennsylvania and the Democratic mayor of New York City convened a Conference on Metropolitan Area Problems at Arden House in September 1957. Presentation of papers by various experts on administrative theory kept partisanship to a minimum, but the opportunities for making the metropolitan mess a political issue were unmistakable.[3] Ironically, New York's governor, W. Averell Harriman, the leading organizer of the conference, was defeated for re-election in 1958 by his Republican opponent, Nelson Rockefeller, who charged that he had not done enough to solve metropolitan problems.[4]

The states' record of dilatory behavior fostered unprecedented proposals around mid-decade for federal intervention. "Our traditional literature on the government of metropolitan areas," observed an official of the Institute of Public Administration in 1955, "has little or nothing to say about the part to be played by the Federal Government." [5] The resolution on "Metropolitan Area Problems" passed by the American Municipal Association that year reflected this heritage. It focused almost completely on the tasks of states and localities, mentioning Washington's role almost as an afterthought: "The Federal Government must be concerned with metropolitan areas which cross state borders and with the problems of coordinating metropolitan civil defense." But when communities found themselves unable and the states unwilling to deal with the burdens of metropolitan civilization, important elements of the urban population started turning to the Federal Government for assistance.

Among the first groups to request federal aid in solving the metropolitan puzzle was the National Planning Association (NPA). An organization of businessmen and labor leaders interested in current economic and social issues, NPA had published, in 1941, the Hansen-Greer pamphlet on urban redevelopment that led to Title I of the 1949 Housing Act. Sixteen years later, in February 1957, NPA continued its pace-setting ways with the proposal for a White House Conference on Metropolitan Areas. Despite clear signs of the "serious obsolescence" of the country's urban matrix, NPA complained, "there is but limited awareness, and our piecemeal programs, Federal, state, and local, are only nibbling at the growing shortages." It urged that a White House Conference be conducted "to kick off a ten-year urban planning project to deal with the rising tide of urbanism and metropolitan growth." The conference, to be followed by regional meetings and another national session in five years to review the progress being made, would bring together "the best present thinking on what America needs to begin to modernize the urban centers of this land by 1975." [6]

NPA's proposal was widely distributed in business and government circles. The immediate reaction by some White House staffers was that the NPA conference would merely go over ground already covered at the National Conference on Metropolitan Problems held the previous spring in East Lansing, Michigan.[7] That gathering, sponsored by nearly a score of the country's foremost civic, professional, and business organizations, had covered most of the subjects commonly placed under the heading "metropolitan problems," although its treatment of the Federal Government's responsibilities in this area was relatively scant.[8] Presidential Assistant Howard Pyle, the man in charge of Executive Office contacts with state and local governments, argued that a White House conference would be sure to highlight the federal role and thereby would engender additional federal programs and spending.[9] While the

White House did not publicly say "no" to the NPA proposal, the President's June 1957 speech to the Governors' Conference asking the states to step into the metropolitan vacuum and the subsequent formation of the Joint Federal-State Action Committee were clear signs that the project was dead.[10]

Another businessmen's group working in the mid- and late-1950s for greater federal recognition of metropolitan problems was the American Council to Improve Our Neighborhoods (ACTION). Interestingly, ACTION owed its creation to a White House report. The December 1953 study of the President's Advisory Committee on Government Housing Policies and Programs recommended the formation of "a broadly representative private organization outside the Federal Government with congressional and/or Presidential sponsorship to mobilize public opinion in support of vigorous and responsible action by communities in urban renewal activities." A proposed "President's Conference on the Modern City" to launch the group was not held, but Eisenhower did address ACTION's first meeting in November 1954.[11] The leadership for ACTION's organization was supplied by the influential publishers of the Washington *Post* (Phillip Graham) and *Time* (Roy Larson); among the others on ACTION's board of directors were Senator Joseph Clark and the big urban redeveloper, James W. Rouse. During its early years ACTION seldom ventured beyond advertising campaigns promoting "patch and paint" rehabilitation of marginal residential districts, but as it matured ACTION started serving as an important generator of discussion on broad questions of urban affairs. With the aid of such giant corporations as General Electric and Sears, Roebuck, it set up clinics and conducted discussion groups around the country on the subject of the businessmen's stake in sound community development. Grants from the Ford Foundation allowed ACTION to complete a scholarly eight-volume examination of government and housing in metropolitan areas. In May 1959, ACTION held its first National Conference on the American City, with Adlai Stevenson as a featured speaker.[12]

The field of urban studies, which Robert Park had launched at the

University of Chicago in the early 1920s, blossomed in the late 1950s. A number of prestigious universities, including Harvard and M.I.T., set up special research institutes to explore urban topics. In the nation's capital, private monies were raised to establish an independent Washington Center of Metropolitan Studies. Grants from such business groups as ACTION and the Committee for Economic Development helped end the post-war "drought" in scholarly examinations of "the impact of urbanization on our governmental institutions and political life." [13] The U.S. Chamber of Commerce sponsored a National Conference on Metropolitan Growth, and the Connecticut General Life Insurance Company convened a symposium on "The New Highways—Challenge to the Metropolitan Region." "Metropolis in Ferment," a volume of the *Annals* of the American Academy of Political and Social Science published in 1957, contained articles by anthropologists, sociologists, economists, planners, builders, mayors, and political scientists expressing their "hopes and fears and images of our urban future." All of this activity, noted the British periodical, *The Economist*, "yielded a crescendo of warnings about the dire effects of unplanned growth and brought metropolitan disintegration into the national spotlight." [14]

Politicians responded to all this advice from academicians by undertaking studies of their own. In the fall of 1957, Congress created a Joint Committee on Washington Metropolitan Problems to look into how the Capitol District could more comfortably co-exist with its neighbors. [15] Two years later, the National Association of County Officials held the First Urban County Congress to explore ways of bridging the gap between core cities and the surrounding suburbs. Technical talks on such topics as water pollution control and long-range planning were on the agenda, along with speeches by prominent national officeholders. Looking ahead to the world of the 1960s as 1959 drew to a close, *Newsweek* predicted that "the one great, overriding physical change will be the spread of urbanization." The periodical approvingly cited the statement of New York Mayor Robert F. Wagner to the November National

Municipal League convention that "the biggest challenge of the 1960's is to awaken fully to the fact that we are an urban nation." [16]

Four Tennessee cities acted decisively in 1959 to make the political system adjust to this reality. Their immediate target was the pattern of legislative malapportionment that deprived metropolitan centers of equitable representation in forty-six of the forty-eight statehouses. In the Volunteer State, for example, the four largest urban counties accounted for 38 per cent of the state's population but elected only 22 per cent of the members of the assembly and 20 per cent of those in the senate.[17] Other states, such as Georgia, Florida, and California, presented even more extreme cases of urban underrepresentation, but in Tennessee the situation had led the state to appropriate annually $225 to rural counties for each child attending school while allowing only $90 per pupil for urban school children.[18] Finding it difficult to balance their budgets because of this unequal distribution of state funds, officials in Memphis, Nashville, Knoxville, and Chattanooga decided to contest legally the legislature's failure to reapportion itself, as required by the state constitution. A three-judge federal panel threw out the cities' suit, in December 1959, relying upon a 1946 Supreme Court opinion that held such suits to be of a "peculiarly political nature" and thus outside the courts' jurisdiction. Undaunted, the plaintiffs, with aid from the National Institute of Municipal Law Officers, carried their case to the high court; in November 1960, the Supreme Court agreed to hear their appeal.[19] While two more years would elapse before the Court adopted the doctrine that the judiciary could grant cities relief and still another two years would pass before the Court ruled affirmatively on the principle of "one man, one vote," the cities were clearly unwilling to accept their subordinate status any longer as the 1950s came to an end.

This awakening of an urban consciousness was greatly aided by private philanthropies. Local groups, such as the Haynes Foundation in Los Angeles, financed metropolitan surveys on the possibilities and alternatives for regional integration in particular areas. Others, like the Edgar Stern Family Fund, underwrote wide-ranging analyses of "the governmental problems thrust to the fore by the revolutionary expansion of urban populations in the United States." [20] The Russell Sage Foundation, which in the 1920s had spurred thinking about metropolitan developmental problems with its support of the Regional Plan of New York and its Environs, sponsored the research and writing of the monumental *Governing New York City* (1960). Perhaps the best-known project of foundation-backed research started in the 1950s was the examination of the Northeastern seaboard megalopolis stretching from Boston to Norfolk that French economic geographer Jean Gottmann conducted for the Twentieth Century Fund. Published in 1961, *Megalopolis* illustrated the common problems faced by the widely scattered parts of this giant urban agglomeration.

By and far the most ambitious program in urban studies was carried out by the Ford Foundation. City problems were overlooked during the foundation's formative years in the early 1950s, but after some internal organizational changes around 1955, urban subjects became the motif of the foundation's Public Affairs Program directed by Paul N. Ylvisaker. A social scientist who had served for two years as executive secretary to Philadelphia Mayor Joseph Clark before coming to the foundation, Ylvisaker concentrated first on conventional research projects. Initial grants went to universities in Boston and St. Louis for studies of these metropolitan areas; to ACTION for its series on housing and community development; to Columbia University for investigation and training in the government and politics of New York; and, in conjunction with the Rockefeller Foundation and others, to the Regional Plan Association of New York, for an exhaustive inquiry into the economic and demographic characteristics of that region. Ford Foundation funds financed the creation of the Harvard-M.I.T. Joint Center for Urban Studies in 1958. As the 1950s ended, Ylvisaker began showing a preference for innovative, experimental schemes. An especial favorite of his was the idea of an urban extension service; a grant went to Rutgers in June 1959 "to adapt the research, educational, and extension techniques of the land grant colleges from an agricultural

to an urban setting." Seven more universities were later added to this
program. Another project, still in the planning stage in 1960, sought
to organize the residents of "gray areas" so that they might
effectively participate in the rejuvenation of their neighborhoods. In
the years 1957–63, the foundation handed out $30 million under the
explicit label of "Urban and Regional Affairs." [21]

The report of the President's Commission on National Goals,
submitted in November 1960, confirmed the rising prominence of
metropolitan problems in discussions among business and academic
leaders. Financed by private foundations but sponsored by President
Eisenhower, the National Goals Committee was charged with the
task of defining the country's priorities for the decade ahead. In
planning its work, the committee concluded that "no domestic issue
is more puzzling or intricate than improving our rapidly growing
cities and suburban areas," and it enlisted the always provocative
pen of Catherine Bauer Wurster to write a background paper on the
"Framework for an Urban Society." Wurster recommended a
sevenfold increase in public spending for urban renewal; the
transformation, through strong local government and effective
regional planning, of suburbs from scattered enclaves into mature,
balanced cities; a 60 per cent increase in the average annual output
of housing to provide a wider range of choice for all income groups
and minorities in both central and peripheral areas; transportation
patterns to maximize convenience rather than mobility; the acquisition and preservation of open spaces in urbanizing areas; and a
federal "agency to help cities and larger regions fit the pieces of
specialized federal aid and policy together in order to create a more
efficient and desirable framework for living and working." [22]

But as with the *Social Trends* and *Our Cities* studies of the 1930s,
the National Goals report had no measurable impact on policy.
Released with great publicity from the White House, it was
immediately tagged as the valedictory of a lame-duck administration
that had just been repudiated at the polls. Those people who
bothered to read what Wurster had to say found that events had
already overtaken her professional musings. For in the fall of 1960

urban affairs had come out of the library, the classroom, and the conference session into one of the rings in that circus called Presidential politics.

II

Despite the increasing concentration of the nation's wealth and population in the big metropolitan complexes, urban issues had not figured prominently in Presidential elections during the first six decades of the twentieth century. Party differences over labor legislation, social security and health programs, immigrant restriction, economic policy, and even farm prices were, of course, of vital concern to the city dweller, but these matters did not bear directly upon his place of residence. Harry Truman's sharp and frequent attacks in the 1948 campaign on the "do-nothing" 80th Congress for its failure to enact low-rent housing and slum clearance bills represented a direct appeal to the urban voter on the basis of where he lived, but even Truman rarely, if ever, used the terms "city," "urban," or "metropolitan." Four years later the magic personality of Dwight Eisenhower overshadowed nearly everything else. The big cities since the days of the New Deal had been the core of Democratic strength. In 1948 Thomas Dewey had won but four of the thirty-seven largest cities; Eisenhower's score in 1952 was a remarkable twenty-one out of thirty-nine. Without speaking once about the future of America's cities, the Republican standard-bearer from Kansas reversed a two-decade trend in urban voting.[23]

Eisenhower, the man, was still the crucial consideration for a large number of Americans in the 1956 elections, but metropolitan problems began attracting some attention. New York Governor W. Averell Harriman, a contender for the Democratic Presidential nomination, became the first national figure to endorse a cabinet-level Department of Housing and Urban Affairs. The new department, he declared, "should view housing as part of the larger problem of urban growth—instead of urban decay." [24] Adlai Stevenson, who eventually gained the dubious honor of opposing Eisenhower again, said nothing about the cabinet idea, but in a November 1955 address to the American Municipal Association, had bitterly attacked the Republican administration for cutting back on public housing and hamstringing urban renewal. "I suspect," Stevenson told the municipal leaders, "that we face today no more basic need, surely none requiring bolder thinking and more aggressive action, than to make the American city a decent place in which to live and raise a family." Little of this "bolder thinking" was apparent, however, in the 1956 Democratic platform; it proposed merely to raise the federal share of the cost of urban renewal so that communities would find it easier to participate in the program, and to aid urban and suburban planning, something already provided for in the 1954 Housing Act.[25]

For their part, the Republicans thought even less about the cities. Their platform, in fact, mentioned urban renewal only in the past tense, noting that the party "has supported measures that have reduced urban slums." [26] Officials at the Housing and Home Finance Agency, greatly upset at this slighting of the administration's "good record" in a potentially decisive area (a Gallup poll found that people ranked housing only behind the farm problem and unemployment as important issues facing the country), registered their complaint. They pointed out to White House officials that while the G.O.P platform devoted a grand total of thirty-five words to housing, "the subject of 'Fisheries,' so dear to the hearts and minds of the rank and file of the American people, is given half a page, over three times as many words, and a separate title." Confident that it was Eisenhower, and not so much his performance or promises that the electorate would be judging and voting for, the President's counselors ignored HHFA's advice to put special stress on housing; that topic appeared, and then only in passing, in but three of Eisenhower's campaign speeches.[27]

Stevenson's inability to generate enthusiasm among the electorate seemed to bear out the Republican strategists' decision to rely on the "Peace and Prosperity" slogan; but in late October the chief White House aide, Sherman Adams, received a plea for a reconsideration.

The appeal came from Senator Clifford Case, a liberal Republican from New Jersey, the most urbanized state in the union. Case wrote:

The physical, economic, and social decay of our cities is one of our most urgent domestic problems. . . . The problem is just as important and just as big as the farm problem, for example, or roads, natural resources, and others. And it directly affects even more people. Yet we haven't really tackled it at all.

States and localities, he observed, "aren't doing and probably can't do the job without federal help." Suggesting that "we make this an Administration program and give it top priority," Case warned that "if we don't you can bet your bottom dollar the Democrats will, and their solution will in all likelihood involve more centralization of authority in Washington and still further lessening of local, state, and private initiative and responsibility." To forestall the Democrats, he requested that the President use one of his remaining speeches to announce the formation of a blue-ribbon commission "to investigate the problem in all its aspects and to make detailed recommendations for meeting it." Adams discussed Case's memo with several White House staff members who were favorably impressed by it, but before action could be taken fighting broke out in the Middle East and Soviet tanks entered Budapest. Charting administration policy on these foreign crises took precedence over all else in the last weeks of the campaign and the Case proposal was put aside.[28] As war clouds darkened abroad, the voters re-elected Eisenhower in a landslide; improving upon his 1952 performance, the President carried twenty-eight of the thirty-nine largest cities.

Eisenhower's disputes with the mayors and Democrats in Congress throughout his second term over the size of the urban renewal program helped make the metropolitan mess an issue in the 1960 Presidential contest. The problems presented by physical obsolescence, the flight to the suburbs, inadequate community facilities, and other dislocations that provoked the massive response from academia and progressive businessmen in the late 1950s were not strong enough, alone, to make an impression on the ambitious politicians aiming for the White House. Everyday annoyances such as poor transit, crowded parks, and dirty air did not command the same newspaper space or television time as rising unemployment rates, missile launchings, or the dangers of Communism in Cuba. Politicians assumed correctly that a citizen did not make up his mind how to vote for President while sitting in a car stalled in traffic or while cleaning out his clogged sewer; but Eisenhower, by his hard line on spending for local improvements, turned these petty, individual nuisances into important matters of principle and equity. Pushed to the end of their patience by a string of executive vetoes of housing, public works, airport, and stream pollution control authorization bills, the staff of *Architectural Forum* gave expression to this growing consciousness of geographic discrimination in a stinging editorial, published in September 1959, entitled "Cheating the Cities." A million more people lived in urban slums than on farms, they noted, and while the average farm family received $3000 in federal benefits a year, the average slum family saw only $84 in federal largesse. The $300 million Eisenhower wished to spend annually on urban renewal, the magazine complained, "is slightly larger than the price support program on potatoes or about one-eighteenth of the Department of Agriculture budget. . . . When the huge wasteful farm surplus program is added to other urban burdens, the cities are being cheated on the vastest scale in history."

No one felt this disparity more keenly than the mayors, most of whom were Democrats. Eisenhower's decision to balance the national budget at the expense of city projects had forced these mayors to request higher local taxes and take the political consequences. In their frequent complaints during the late 1950s about being neglected by the national government, *The Economist* noted, "the mayors talked a language that was almost reminiscent of the farmers' protest movements which set the prairies ablaze nearly a century ago." Employing a phrase that would gain wide currency the following year, Richardson Dilworth of Philadelphia told the American Municipal Association in 1959 that "the real frontiers of

America are inside the big cities. But the Administration in Washington is still living in a 100-year-old dream world of wide Kansas prairies." [29]

Beginning in 1959, a group of Democratic mayors, led by New Haven's Richard Lee, worked diligently to give their party an urban outlook. Lee, whose ability to gain and apply effectively the entire range of existing federal grants-in-aid for his city had already won him national recognition, scored a significant victory in September when the Democratic Advisory Council (DAC) appointed an Advisory Committee on Urban and Suburban Problems. The council, which was created in early 1957 to formulate party positions while the Republicans held the White House, had previously set up separate committees on economic, foreign, and labor policy, and on science and technology when Lee suggested the urban-suburban group. Dominated by "urban intellectual liberals," [30] the DAC eagerly adopted the proposal, choosing Lee as chairman and Dilworth as vice-chairman. Among the other members of the twenty-three-man panel were Mayors Robert Wagner of New York and Ben West of Nashville, urban redeveloper James Scheuer, planner William Wheaton, political scientist Robert Wood, and Catherine Bauer Wurster. The group's secretary was Edward Logue, Lee's chief tactician in his fight to make New Haven a slumless city.[31]

Lee's efforts started paying dividends almost immediately. The DAC's version of the State of the Union Message, released in December 1959, contained a section called "To Help the Cities of America Meet Problems Beyond Their Means." "A nation once predominantly rural," declared the council,

is now 85 per cent [sic] urban, with an ever-growing need for urban services. Yet our cities and their suburbs, overwhelmed by problems of growth, are finding the elemental needs of urban life—like pure water, easy transportation, opportunities for wholesome recreation, even law and order—increasingly difficult to provide with the financial resources and administrative structures which are available to them.

And while localities suffered through this agony, the council noted in disdain, "the National Government has no plan, no program, not even a philosophy as to what, if anything, should be done about it. Yet, these problems are a meaningful area for federal action." The council recommended, as an initial step, "the establishment of a comprehensive national commission to survey the needs of the country's metropolitan areas and determine whether the Federal Government should take a more active role." In the meantime, "the Federal Government should strengthen rather than weaken programs of aid now in operation . . . and start new ones in the fields of education and juvenile delinquency control." [32] Although still falling short of an imaginative policy for urban America, the DAC pronouncement represented a big advance over the party's 1956 platform.

The Advisory Committee's own report appeared in two sections, in March and June 1960, as part of the DAC pamphlet series, "Domestic Policies for a Growing and Balanced Economy." Other tracts had discussed the farm mess, better utilization of natural resources, and the crisis in education; the Lee's groups findings were published under the titles "The State of Our Cities and Suburbs in a Changing America" and "Urban Growth in the Decade Ahead." Largely Logue's handiwork, the report elaborated upon the predicament described in DAC's December declaration and proposed a "ten-year action program" in housing, urban renewal, pollution control, transportation, and recreation to remedy it. "Just as the Marshall Plan restored the cities of Western Europe from the devastation of war," the committee wrote, "so our program will restore urban America from the ravages of spreading slums and disorderly growth." The Advisory Committee's criticism of the régime in Washington was especially sharp:

The President and his Administration are either uninformed or unconcerned with the mounting urban and suburban problems around them. Eisenhower and his party have turned their backs on cities and suburbs all across America. From the lack of sympathy and concern in the White House, it seems to us quite clear that the President and his budgeteers have neither seen nor heard the plight of the 22 million American slum dwellers. And with 50 million Americans already in the suburbs, and with 50 million more on the way, it is folly indeed to say that suburban problems are none of the Federal Government's concern.

Solution of the urban-suburban tangle would require national leadership, the committee concluded, and only the Democratic party could supply it.

As Lee, Logue and other municipal officials labored to attune the Democratic party to the needs of metropolitan areas, each of the serious candidates for the party's nomination sought to identify himself with the cities. All had a genuine interest in solving metropolitan problems, but there were also good political reasons for championing the cities' cause. Urban bosses, after all, wielded vast influence in the big state delegations, such as those from New York, Pennsylvania, and Illinois, states whose support was essential for success at the convention. Strong ties to urban dwellers would be useful in November, too; nearly 65 per cent of the population lived in the 216 Standard Metropolitan Statistical Areas according to the 1960 Census.

Hubert Humphrey, the first hopeful to announce his candidacy formally, probably possessed the strongest emotional links to the cities. He had served as mayor of Minneapolis in the mid-1940s and had worked hard for urban legislation since his election to the Senate in 1948; he had, for example, co-sponsored the Lehman and Clark bills for an urban department. It was as much passionate conviction as good rhetoric that prompted Humphrey to tell the U.S. Conference of Mayors in June 1959 that "the problems of the American city are the problems of America." In that speech, delivered just days after a meeting with his advisers where it was decided to seek the White House, Humphrey lambasted Eisenhower for "treating the cities as step-children or poor relations." "I am unable to understand," he went on, "the philosophy of government which treats the cities as beggars at the back door; rather they should be brought into the inner councils of policy and administration." But defeats in two primaries short-circuited Humphrey's campaign to impress the Eastern big-city leaders with his political prowess, and he withdrew from the contest even before the Democrats gathered in Los Angeles.[33]

Lyndon Johnson waited until five days before the convention opened to throw his hat into the ring, but his planning for this day stretched back many months. The Senate majority leader knew that only by shedding his Southern label did he have any chance of capturing his party's nomination. His main goal was to have himself portrayed as the candidate of the West, but he was anxious for support wherever he could find it, even within the metropolitan complexes of the Northeast. Smoothly directing the upper chamber's operations, Johnson had guided a $1.9 billion urban renewal bill to quick and easy passage in early 1959, although two Presidential vetoes eventually cut this figure in half. Johnson had also won Senate approval for two urban measures—Clark's 1959 bill to create a Metropolitan Study Commission and the AMA's 1960 bill for federal loans for mass transit—but in each case the conservative bloc in the House had prevented further action.[34] Disappointment would also mark Johnson's efforts to woo the cities, for at the convention their votes went to someone else.

Nobody projected an urban image as sharply as did John F. Kennedy. Grandson of a Boston mayor, congressman from a metropolitan district, and senator from a state with old, deteriorating cities, Kennedy had a firsthand acquaintance with urban problems. But while Senator Kennedy could be counted on to vote for the expanded housing and community development programs liberals like Clark had tried to push through the legislature and past Eisenhower, he had no record of participation in writing these bills or in participating in their debate on the floor. His committee assignments—Labor, Government Operations, and after 1957, Foreign Relations—shaped and then reflected his primary interests; his not very distinguished Senate career is best remembered for his labor rackets control measures and speeches on the nation's diplomatic and military posture. It was only after setting his sights on the White House and seeing how important urban votes would be in achieving that goal that Kennedy began to speak out on city issues and seek out local politicians.

An attack on malapportioned state legislatures formed Kennedy's initial thrust into urban affairs. This was the topic of an address he was scheduled to give to the Conference of Mayors' 1957 annual meeting, but sudden illness kept him away; his brother Robert took his place and discussed the Senate's investigation of corrupt union practices. Not one to waste opportunities, Kennedy turned the speech into an article, which the *New York Times Magazine* published under the title, "The Shame of the States." Citing Lincoln Steffens's turn-of-the-century exposés of municipal corruption, Kennedy declared that "the shame of our cities today is not political; it is social and economic." Local governments were run efficiently, but they lacked the resources to deal with advancing blight, juvenile delinquency, traffic congestion, inadequate recreational facilities:

The burden for coping with these problems rests—logically or illogically, fairly or unfairly—upon our municipal governments primarily. But the harsh facts of the matter are that these local governments receive all too little help and cooperation from Washington and the state legislatures. They are refused sufficient federal and state funds for the programs they need so badly, and for which they have paid so heavily. They contribute the lion's share of federal and state taxes, but an equitable share is rarely returned to them. They have been pre-empted by the federal and state governments from the best sources of tax revenue.

As Kennedy viewed it, the root of the cities' dilemma was their underrepresentation in the statehouses, and to a lesser extent in Congress. "Of all the discriminations against the urban areas," he wrote, "the most fundamental and the most blatant is political. Our legislatures still represent the rural majority of a half century ago, not the urban majority of today." Under these circumstances, he argued, it was ridiculous to propose, as Eisenhower repeatedly had, that many federal programs, including urban renewal, be turned over to the states:

For all of its limitations, Congress stands in shining contrast to many state legislatures in responding to the needs of the city and its people. . . . Congress cannot yield vital public functions affecting our metropolitan majority to state legislatures dominated by rural minorities. To do so would consign almost two-thirds of a nation to second-class citizenship.

But the cities were not entirely blameless for their predicament. "If there is a 'shame of the cities' today," Kennedy concluded, "it is the failure of our urban dwellers and their spokesmen to be aware of this discrimination—and to press more vigorously for its elimination." [35]

The Massachusetts senator returned to this theme in his talk at USCM's 1958 session. He presented a seven-point "urban Magna Carta," which would give municipalities greater home rule and guarantee them fair treatment in representation, taxes, and appropriations. Touching on an issue that had special meaning for himself, Kennedy told the mayors: "I think it is high time that this nation eliminated the written and unwritten restrictions on the influence of urban areas and urban politicians in our public life which have resulted largely from ancient prejudices and unwarranted suspicions." He expressed confidence that the cities' cause would ultimately prevail, predicting that as "urban populations grow, suburban populations [will] realize that their needs are intermingled with those of the city, and leaders and opinion-makers [will] recognize the justice of our struggle."

Urban-suburban cooperation was the message Kennedy brought to the First Urban County Congress in March 1959. "No more difficult challenge than the problems of metropolitan areas," he said, "confronts us on the domestic scene." For too long the central cities and their neighbors had emphasized the differences that divided them instead of the common interests—overcrowded schools and poor transportation, for example—that united them. The federal authorities should do everything they could to ease the localities' burdens, Kennedy declared, but it would all be in vain unless municipalities and state governments adapted themselves to the realities of the mid-twentieth century. In a way, Kennedy was doing his own adapting. The suburbs were beginning to overtake the core cities in voting strength, and by focusing on metropolitan rather than strictly big-city problems Kennedy was reaching out for this new power bloc in American politics.

Kennedy completed his rounds of municipal officials' assemblies with an appearance at the AMA's Convention in November 1959. His speech, coming from a probable but as yet unannounced candidate, struck observers as being notable for the frank political vein in which it was pitched.[36] "I think it is fair to say," Kennedy began,

that the overall outcome of the 1960 campaign is going to be decided in the cities of the United States. Most of the delegates will come from the great urban areas in both parties. Most of the votes in the electoral college will be represented in those states of great urban areas and the urban areas will have the greatest strength.

In his travels around the country so far, however, he noted, how rarely he had been asked "what we should do about the cities." This, Kennedy claimed, "is the great unspoken issue in the 1960 election." But to slight it would be disastrous, he answered, for "unless our cities move forward our country will not move forward; therefore the problems of our cities should be attacked on a national basis." Going down the list of likely topics for debate between the two major parties in 1960, Kennedy urged that similar consideration be given to urban problems:[37]

We should be concerned about the 21 million Americans who now live on our farms. But we should be concerned about the 22 million Americans who live in our cities in sub-standard housing, and who live without hope of tomorrow and with a gloomy past in their childhood.

We should be concerned about the comparison of American defenses to those of the Soviet Union. But we should also be concerned about the rising rate of blight and decay in our cities which are destroying in many of our cities more areas than were destroyed by the Nazi bombers in London in World War II.

The staggering growth of federal expenditures will obviously be a subject of discussion in the next campaign. But neither can we ignore the fact that, while the federal budget may have increased 13 per cent in the last five years, the annual costs of municipal budgets have increased 55 per cent in the last five years.

New reclamation projects are vitally needed in the Western United States—but wise land use policies are equally needed in our cities where mass-produced housing developments are being built on a helter-skelter basis, without in too many cases real zoning and constructive vision, that is destroying 5000 acres of our land every day.

From Kennedy's perspective the time for study of the urban problem had passed; what was required now was action: "Most of us know what needs to be done, and I think we know that most of what needs to be done requires one ingredient—and that is money." Since the cities did not have it and the states would not give it to them, the Federal Government must increase its aid; as a starter, he proposed that Washington allocate $600 million a year for urban renewal, twice the amount Eisenhower was willing to spend. "We are engaged in a difficult and trying period in the history of the United States," observed Kennedy in closing.

It is quite important in these great urban areas, where a great majority of our people live, that life become better and more promising for them. As we reach a population double what it is today in the next 50, 60, 70 years, the problems of today in our cities will become more complicated. We must look into space and look abroad, but we must also defend our own.

Five weeks later he formally announced his candidacy.

Despite these brave words, Kennedy scarcely mentioned urban issues in the six months before his nomination. Neither of the two important primary states, Wisconsin, the "Nation's Dairyland," nor West Virginia, the "Mountain State," were politically appropriate places to raise questions of this sort. Kennedy spent most of his time answering allegations about his religion, his youth, and his inexperience in foreign affairs. But if the mechanics of the primary system kept Kennedy out of states with pressing metropolitan problems, his success in what were considered inhospitable regions was enough to convince the big-city bosses that he was a winner. New York, Pennsylvania, and Illinois supplied one-third of the votes Kennedy amassed to become his party's choice for President.[38]

Besides selecting a "big-city boy" as their candidate, the Democrats also gave the mayors the·urban platform they wanted. In a spirit of harmony that would grow in the years ahead, AMA and USCM had pooled their talents and drafted a "comprehensive urban plank," which they had then presented to both national parties. The Democrats adopted virtually every part of it. To a large extent the mayors owed their good fortune to the fact that Ed Logue was a close associate of Chester Bowles, the Platform Committee chairman, and that the committee's secretary was James Sundquist, Senator Clark's administrative assistant.[39] Under the heading "Cities and Their Suburbs," the platform pledged:

A new Democratic Administration will expand federal programs to help urban communities clear their slums, dispose of their sewage, educate their children, transport suburban commuters to and from jobs, and control juvenile delinquency.

We will give the city dweller a voice at the Cabinet table by bringing together within a single department programs concerned with urban and metropolitan problems.

"The United States is now predominantly an urban nation," declared the platform. "The efficiency, comfort, and beauty of our cities and suburbs influence the lives of all Americans." Yet, it went on, echoing the Advisory Committee's report, "the Republican Administration has turned its back on urban and suburban America. The list of Republican vetoes included housing, urban renewal and slum clearance, area redevelopment, public works, airports, and stream pollution control." In contrast to the G.O.P.'s record of negativism, the Democrats proposed a five-point "ten-year action program to restore our cities and provide for balanced suburban development." They promised "the elimination of slums and blight within the next decade"; federal aid for metropolitan area planning and community facility projects; federal aid for "comprehensive metropolitan transportation programs"; federal aid in combating air and water pollution; and "expansion of park systems to meet the recreation needs of our growing population." [40] Here was a platform perfectly tailored to fit Kennedy's campaign strategy of concentrating on the industrial Northeast.[41]

The Democrats ran away with the urban issue with practically no resistance from the Republicans. As early as 1957 members of the White House Public Works Planning Unit, whose responsibilities often brought them into contact with metropolitan area problems, were warning that the Democrats could be expected to use their charges of administration "do-nothingism" in this field to good political profit in 1960.[42] But Eisenhower's stand against greater federal spending stiffened as his second term rolled along, and there was no one in the G.O.P. high command who saw any reason to challenge the President's position. The report of the Republican Committee on Program and Progress demonstrated the insignificance the G.O.P. attached to urban issues. That committee had been created in the wake of the Republican debacle in the 1958 congressional elections to furnish the party with an identity and some long-range objectives; its chairman was Charles Percy, a young successful Chicago businessman who desired a progressive image for the G.O.P.[43] Dividing the group's wide mandate into four broad categories, Percy assigned "housing" to the Task Force on Human Rights and Needs. In sharp contrast to the makeup of the DAC Advisory Committee on Urban and Suburban Problems, the Republican Task Force included no mayors, no experts on urban polity, and no urban redevelopers; only the State's Attorney for Cook County, Illinois, of the six-member panel had any sort of familiarity with the operations of municipal government.[44] Not surprisingly, the G.O.P. study, released in the fall of 1959, read quite differently than the DAC statement, which appeared at about the same time. Whereas the Democrats referred constantly to the Federal Government's responsibilities to help localities meet needs beyond their means, the Percy report hardly mentioned the Federal Government. It spoke of building millions of more homes, preserving the cores of cities from "urban rot," and better planning for parks and transportation needs, but aside from continuing the mortgage credit programs of HHFA and further federal encouragement of research into new techniques of low-cost construction, the committee urged that cities rely on private enterprise and community effort to achieve these goals.[45] Modern Republicanism had still not recognized the cities.

The G.O.P. platform in 1960 was little more than a rewrite of the Percy report. A delegation of Republican mayors was dispatched to the convention by USCM and AMA to present an urban plank, which the Democrats had already accepted, but unlike the group sent to Los Angeles, the Chicago-bound group met only rebuff and disappointment. None of the Republican mayors possessed anything like the political power and influence wielded by Chicago's Richard Daley, Pennsylvania's David Lawrence, or even New York's Robert Wagner; except for Norris Poulson of Los Angeles, who could not even use the G.O.P. label in that city's non-partisan elections, no Republican mayor came from a big population center. They also lacked the personal contacts of the kind supplied by Logue and Sundquist which had been so important at the Democratic gathering. Squeezed in between Republican promises to help the Indians and aid medical research, the 225-word section on "Housing" was a far cry from the impressive 500-word Democratic exposition on "Cities and Their Suburbs." It is only in comparison with the 1956 G.O.P. platform that the 1960 document can be said to recognize the urban revolution sweeping the United States. At last, after eleven years, the Republican party accepted as its own goal the 1949 Housing Act's declaration of a national objective of "a decent home in a suitable environment for every American." From there the Republicans went on to make general commitments "to promote rebuilding, rehabilitation, and conservation of our cities," to sponsor research into ways of reducing housing costs, and to aid urban planning. Each of these programs would be "designed to supplement and not supplant private initiative." [46]

To carry their message of balanced budgets and private enterprise to the country, the Republicans selected Richard M. Nixon. Brought up in a suburb of Los Angeles, Nixon had been swept into Washington in 1946 on the conservative tide of that year. While in Congress, Nixon lined up with the majority of his Republican colleagues in opposing the New Deal-Fair Deal social program. In 1949 he backed attempts to kill public housing and shelve the entire Housing Act. As Eisenhower's Vice-President, Nixon's only significant contact with municipal officials came in September 1957 when he delivered Eisenhower's message to USCM that the military's demands upon the federal budget would require cutbacks in urban renewal. Much more comfortable discussing foreign affairs than domestic ones, Nixon neglected to examine the changes going on in metropolitan America in any of the speeches he gave in the two years before his nomination.[47] He did not expect to alter his ways in the contest against Kennedy: "If you ever let them [the Democrats] campaign only on domestic issues," he told aides on the night he was picked to succeed Eisenhower as the G.O.P.'s leader, "they'll beat us—our only hope is to keep it on foreign policy." Whereas Kennedy aimed his appeal at the big urban states, Nixon was determined to project himself as the "national" candidate, the man of "experience" and "peace and prosperity." [48]

Yet, it was Nixon who first made a major address on housing once the intensive campaigning began after Labor Day. Kennedy struck often and hard during these opening weeks at the Republican responsibility for the persistence of slum conditions in the cities and Eisenhower's vetoes of housing legislation as part of his theme of the need to get the country moving again, but nowhere did he dwell upon the Democratic platform's promises.[49] Then, in late September, while on a tour through Long Island, Nixon unveiled what the *New York Times* characterized as "a broad new Republican program for improving housing conditions in the nation, particularly in urban areas." [50] The Nixon statement opened with a reference to the massive population explosion in the suburbs, noting that 80 per cent of the nation's post-war growth had occurred in the suburbs and that by 1965, suburban voters would outnumber their urban neighbors. Reviewing the many difficulties created by the movement and congregation of people, Nixon adopted the middle-of-the-road position that was so typical of his approach to domestic issues:

Obviously we need a general Federal policy to deal with these dynamic developments. As to this, I realize that some are tempted in matters of this kind to say that this problem is so complicated that we must set up a great new Federal bureaucracy, appropriate billions of dollars, and have the whole thing dictated from Washington. I say that we must avoid this at all costs. On the one hand, we must block Federal dictation; on the other, we must assure the progress we want and urgently need.

To retain local control and yet provide the necessary federal leadership, Nixon outlined a seven-point program calling for metropolitan planning, new criteria for urban renewal assistance, more liberal credit to spur private home-building, stabilization of the housing economy, reform of public housing, better handling of relocation, and equal opportunities for minorities in housing. Nixon ignored the Democratic endorsement of a cabinet-level Department of Urban Affairs but did cite the advisability of "converting HHFA into a fully integrated agency, with operating authority clearly vested in the Administrator, reporting directly to the President." With a combination of federal initiative, private investment, and state and local responsibility, Nixon concluded, "we can meet the housing crisis of the 1960's in the city and in the suburb." [51]

Nixon's remarks received a mixed response. Some reporters felt that his stand moved him "beyond the Republican platform and his own voting record" and closer to the Democratic position. But they also noted that his ideas were couched in very general terms and without any reference to cost.[52] Democrats were quick to attack these inconsistencies and ambiguities. The Nixon plan, claimed David Lawrence, governor of Pennsylvania and former mayor of Pittsburgh, "was released as filler material on a day in Queens when the campaign crowds were thin, and the contents of the statement are as thin as the crowds." According to a group of twelve incumbent Democratic mayors, Nixon's program was "too little and too late." Charging that cities had received "only ineffective crumbs from Washington over the past eight years to meet pressing needs," they argued that "it took a Presidential campaign and a desperate candidate to realize that the Administration could no longer play ostrich where the well-being of millions of its citizens is affected." Republicans, Lawrence chimed in, "pay lip service, or in this case mimeograph service, to housing and slum clearing every four years." [53]

Having stuck his neck out as far as his strong beliefs in private enterprise and states' rights would allow, Nixon did not again return to the urban issue during the remainder of the election campaign. One of his advisors, Robert E. Merriam, had a speech prepared for the candidate that expressed Nixon's "deep personal concern for the problems which are facing our cities and which seriously affect our ever-increasing number of urban citizens," but Nixon did not use it. While the Merriam draft paid the requisite homage to individual and local responsibility in coping with urban distress, it may have been unacceptable to Nixon because it called for a White House Conference on Metropolitan Area Problems and the creation of "a corps of metropolitan area agents, comparable to our agricultural agents, to serve as the necessary conduits between the Federal Government and the states, counties, and urban areas." [54] In the last five weeks of the campaign, Nixon mentioned housing only to praise the administration's achievement in helping home-building starts reach new high levels and to laud the Republican platform; except for a brief summary presented to the Association of Business Economists, Nixon did not again refer to his seven-point program.[55] What he did do was flaunt his "kitchen debate" with Nikita Khrushchev as proof of his rival's lack of seasoning in foreign relations, and try to wrap himself in the mantle of Dwight D. Eisenhower.[56]

As Nixon moved away from domestic issues in general and urban ones in particular, Kennedy acted decisively to fill the vacuum. Cutting short a trip through the South in mid-October, he flew to Pittsburgh (The Renaissance City) to address an Urban Affairs Conference, which had assembled at his request. Plans for the conference had been hatched much earlier, in discussions between Richard Lee, Edward Logue, and Adam Yarmolinsky, a liberal lawyer who did consulting work for foundations and who was the chief of the Kennedy campaign organization's Urban Affairs Section. Stressing the theme that the "urban issue is new and fresh and waiting to be dramatized," they persuaded the candidate to deliver an urban equivalent of the traditional farm policy speech and that a special conference would provide the most appropriate forum.[57] Lee was named chairman of the organizing committee of six mayors, and over 450 municipal officials, almost all of them Democrats, showed up for the four panel sessions on "what needs to be done about the urgent human problems of American cities and suburbs" and Kennedy's oratory.[58]

His speech on the "new urban frontier" followed the pattern of most of his talks: an attack on the "do-nothing" policy of the Eisenhower administration and Nixon's role in it, accompanied by a pledge to use the full resources of the Federal Government to remedy the country's failings. It began with a quote from Aristotle: "Men come together in cities in order to live; they remain together in order to live the good life." But, Kennedy declared, "the good life is still just a dream for too many of the people who live in cities." The reason for this was not lack of ability to produce consumer goods; rather it was the failure of public action to deal effectively with "bad housing, poverty, recessions, discrimination, crowded and obsolete schools and hospitals and libraries, inadequate recreation, the breakdown of mass transportation, polluted air and water, juvenile delinquency." All were matters of national concern, insisted Kennedy,

but when the cities turned to Washington for help, how have they been received? The Republican Administration has taken a position as consistent as it is negative. You know their record:

On urban renewal—stall it.
On low-rent public housing—kill it.
On moderate-income private housing—bury it.
On aid for public schools—block it.
On aid for hospitals—reduce it.
On mass transportation—ignore it.
On control of stream pollution—abandon it.
On air pollution control—study it.
On alleviating juvenile delinquency—research it.

This is the eight-year Republican record of neglect. It is a shameful record. It is a record that we must bring to an end on November 8.

For Nixon, Kennedy had nothing but ridicule. Kennedy contrasted his vote for the 1949 Housing Act with the Republican's negative ballot and denounced his opponent for advocating higher interest rates—"as though increasing the monthly payment for homebuyers is the way to build and sell more homes." Terming Nixon's "urban program" an "empty shell," Kennedy advised the public "to buy the genuine Democratic article and not the counterfeit that Mr. Nixon suddenly coined in the middle of the campaign." [59]

In a more positive vein, Kennedy put his stamp of approval on the ten-year program for urban renewal, housing, mass transit, pollution control, and recreational facilities outlined in the Democratic platform. "These are five areas," he said, "in which a new partnership of community and National Government can lead us across the urban frontier." Kennedy also threw his support, for the first time, behind proposals for an Executive department for urban development and metropolitan planning: "The cities and suburbs of America deserve a seat at the cabinet table. The Department of Agriculture was created 98 years ago[60] to serve rural America. It is time the people who live in urban areas receive equal representation." In an ironic twist, Kennedy referred to that old agrarian, Thomas Jefferson, to make his last point. It was the Sage of Monticello, he reminded his audience, who told us that our "laws and institutions must go hand in hand with the progress of the human mind." But "in this area of urban affairs," Kennedy concluded,[61] our laws and institutions have lagged behind what our minds tell us we can do. There is a civic renaissance, an awakening of public spirit and will, throughout our cities. We see it in the Golden Triangle in Pittsburgh, at Lincoln Center in New York, at Charles Center in Baltimore. Let us hope that spirit of confidence and enterprise now arising in the cities of America will sweep next year into the Capitol of the United States. Then the Federal Government will join in partnership with its States and its cities—and together we will move forward to realize in our cities the good life that can be ours.

The party of Jefferson was pinning its future on megalopolis.

Despite Kennedy's determined efforts to highlight the differences between Nixon and himself in respect to cities, the urban issue never caught on. Charges and countercharges on the missile gap, Quemoy and Matsu, Castro, recession, and religion, not on slums and sewers, captured the headlines. Most newspapers totally ignored Nixon's housing statement, and those papers that carried stories on Kennedy's Urban Affairs Conference usually buried them in articles on the chances for a fifth "great debate." [62] In the debates themselves, housing came up for discussion just once. In response to a question during the fourth and final confrontation, Nixon, as he was doing regularly now on the stump, accused Kennedy of "running America down," of constantly attacking her schools, her space accomplishments, her homes. Just as routinely, Kennedy replied that the "country had to do better," that there were too many slums and too few classrooms and that Eisenhower's vetoes of crucial legislation were to blame. No screaming bannerheads resulted from this exchange.[63]

But if the media tended to overlook the urban issue vote, Kennedy in his personal appearances did not. Relying on the city bosses to firm up the traditionally Democratic ethnic blocs inside municipal boundaries, he campaigned extensively in the great suburban belts in the large states. Throughout October and early November, in shopping center after shopping center, Kennedy appealed to young married couples to join his drive to get the nation moving again. He placed particular emphasis on the shortage of educational facilities since this was usually the problem of greatest concern in these children-rich, tax-poor new communities. In what turned out to be the closest election of the century, that effort may have provided the slim margin of victory.[64]

Kennedy's regional strategy prevailed over Nixon's national one. Whereas the Republican candidate spread himself thin and wasted valuable time fulfilling his promise to visit all fifty states, Kennedy concentrated on taking the big Northeastern states. New York, Pennsylvania, New Jersey, and Massachusetts plus Illinois and Michigan supplied him with half the electoral votes he actually amassed and nearly 60 per cent of the total he needed to win.[65] With Eisenhower's name not on the ballot, Kennedy brought twenty-seven of the thirty-nine largest cities into the Democratic fold; he came out most poorly in the growing metropolises of the South where civil rights was an explosive issue. But Kennedy's greatest gain came in the suburbs; in the suburbs of the top fourteen metropolitan areas he was able to increase the Democratic percentages from the 38 per cent netted by Stevenson in 1956 to 49 per cent in 1960.[66] Thrilled by the electoral returns, New Haven's Richard Lee excitedly proclaimed: "Kennedy is more than anything else the President of the cities." [67]

III

The cities stood on the threshold of a new era as John F. Kennedy prepared to assume the Presidency. Slowly, almost imperceptibly, they had forced their way into the national consciousness. Thanks to imaginative foundation executives like Ylvisaker, politically active academicians like Robert Wood, the civic-minded businessmen in ACTION, and vigorous municipal officials such as Lee and Logue, the cities and their problems were firmly established on the agenda of liberal reform. Aside from the highly excitable mayors no one as yet spoke of "the urban crisis"—this would come later with the outbreak of racial disorders—but that the Federal Government had a stake in the welfare of the cities was no longer in question.

Kennedy was pledged, as was none of his predecessors, to make Washington a generous partner with the cities and suburbs in a joint effort to clean up the mistakes of the past and guard the metropolitan future. That the new President was more interested in what happened in Havana, Berlin, and Saigon than what took place in New York, Chicago, or Los Angeles would not be apparent for some months; in the immediate afterglow of the Democratic success at the polls, the nation's cities could justly believe that they were indeed the new frontier of American life.

9

Cities Along the New Frontier

We will neglect our cities at our peril, for in neglecting them we neglect the nation.

John F. Kennedy (1962)

The special vulnerability of those living within the cities was made crystal clear to John F. Kennedy on the eve of his Inauguration. Since late fall Washington and other cities along the Northeastern seaboard had had frequent and heavy snowfalls; it was with some apprehension then that the residents of the nation's capital greeted the white flakes that began drifting down early in the afternoon of January 19. By dinnertime, the "already crisis situation" created by the arrival of thousands of Inauguration visitors was further aggravated by the accumulation of 7.5 inches of snow and the continued presence of low temperatures. Ill-suited to heavy automobile traffic in the best of weather, the snow-covered Washington road network soon became a vast parking lot; an estimated 10,000 vehicles were stalled and abandoned. With the city virtually paralyzed, the heavy schedule of Democratic celebrations had to be curtailed. Two-thirds of the sellout audience for the National

Symphony's Inaugural Concert at Constitution Hall and sixty of the orchestra's one hundred musicians, as well as the featured soloist, failed to show up. Only a special escort and the use of emergency detour routes enabled the President-elect to make his rounds of galas and private parties.

By the next morning, however, a semblance of order had been restored. Working through the night, a sanitation crew of 3,000 men and 700 pieces of equipment cleared Pennsylvania Avenue and East Capitol Plaza. The outgoing and incoming Presidents motored down the broad avenue under a bright, if not particularly warm, sun whose rays made the huge mounds of snow glisten. A large crowd was on hand to see Kennedy take the oath of office and hundreds of thousands of chilled citizens lined the sidewalks to enjoy the spectacle of the Inaugural Parade. The night of confusion and anxiety had given way to a day of hope and promise. Washington had demonstrated it could overcome natural adversity. Whether the new administration could deal as effectively with the human problems of the urban environment would take longer to determine.

I

The manner and nature of Presidential appointments often provide clues to an administration's intentions in a given field; so it was with Kennedy and urban affairs. Eisenhower, uncertain about the Federal Government's proper relationship to the home construction industry, had not found a man to fill the top post at the Housing and Home Finance Agency until a month after his Inauguration. In contrast, Kennedy, who had spelled out his views on federal-city ties lucidly during the 1960 campaign, was ready with his HHFA nominee nearly a month before assuming the Presidency. Most of the early speculation on possible candidates for the job focused on Democratic mayors, such as New Haven's Richard Lee, who had labored so strenuously to give the party an urban image. One of the more prominent aspirants for the office was Joseph P. McMurray. A former staff director of the Housing Subcommittee of the Senate and

New York State commissioner of housing during the mid-1950s, McMurray had close friends both in Congress and among home-builders.[1] But as with so many of Kennedy's other appointments, the choice of HHFA administrator was a surprise: on December 31, 1960 the President-elect announced the selection of Robert C. Weaver.[2]

Weaver's background differed significantly from that of his three predecessors at HHFA. Since its creation in 1947, HHFA had been led by men intimately linked to the *private* housing sector of the economy; two had served as commissioners of the Federal Housing Administration before advancing to the HHFA top spot, and the third—Albert Cole, Eisenhower's first administrator—had acted as one of the principal spokesman in the House of Representatives for the realtor-homebuilder-banker lobby. Weaver's experience, on the other hand, was almost entirely in the area of *government* construc-tion. A Harvard-trained economist, Weaver had joined the Public Works Administration soon after its creation in 1933. He took a special interest in PWA's subsidized housing program and when the United States Housing Authority was established in 1937 he transferred to that agency. After working for the War Production Board and the War Manpower Commission during World War II, Weaver left federal service, but through his writings and other activities continued to champion the role of public housing in meeting the needs of the poor. At the time Kennedy picked him to head HHFA, Weaver was vice-chairman of the New York City Housing and Redevelopment Board, a three-member body Mayor Wagner had set up to replace Robert Moses's one-man urban renewal drive.[3]

Another distinguishing characteristic of Weaver's probably figured in his designation: he was black. Negro votes had been crucial to Kennedy's victories in many Northern states and the President-elect was under pressure to return the favor by awarding Negroes good posts in his administration. The mishandling of an offer of the postmaster generalship to black Chicago Congressman William Dawson in mid-December made it even more imperative that Negroes receive suitable recognition.[4] Kennedy's diligent talent hunters compiled a long list of possible Negro appointees; ranking high on the list was the name of Robert Weaver. His academic credentials were impressive. The economist's two books, *Negro Labor* (1946) and *The Negro Ghetto* (1948), had been praised by reviewers, and he was a frequent contributor to scholarly journals on racial topics. Furthermore, Weaver had the kind of moderate civil rights record the Kennedy administration wanted; in 1960, he was chairman of the board of directors of the National Association for the Advancement of Colored People. There does not seem to have been a conscious decision by Kennedy or his advisers to single out the Housing Agency, with its urban programs, as the appropriate place for a Negro to enter the top ranks of American government; indeed, they tended to see the civil rights problem as basically Southern and, in many respects, rural in location. Rather, Weaver appears to have been chosen because he was an exceptionally capable black, and then put in the HHFA spot because of his expertise in housing.[5]

But whatever the role of race in his appointment, Weaver held some very definite ideas about federal responsibility for the protection of minority rights in housing. His assignment as Racial Relations Advisor at PWA and USHA in the 1930s had been to safeguard the interests of blacks and other minority groups in the public housing program. Weaver enjoyed some success in this task, having drafted regulations that required the setting aside of a reasonable percentage of federally subsidized units for Negroes and the employment of minority labor as a condition for federal funding.[6] Racial integration had not been a politically feasible policy in the 1930s for the black bureaucrat to advocate, but in the 1940s and 1950s Weaver, now out of the Federal Government, began demanding an end to all federally supported props to segregation and discrimination in housing. He urged the Public Housing Administration to prohibit separate projects for different races, insisted that the Urban Renewal Administration stop the use of Title I as a vehicle for "Negro removal," and backed attempts to bar the

Federal Housing Administration from insuring mortgages for suburban developers who refused to sell or rent to Negroes on an equal basis.[7] As chairman of the NAACP and the National Committee Against Discrimination in Housing, Weaver was in the forefront of the fight in the late 1950s for an Executive order on open occupancy covering all federally assisted public and private housing.

Predictably, there was a dispute over Weaver's confirmation. Both Senators A. Willis Robertson (D.-Va.) and John Sparkman (D.-Ala.), the respective chairmen of the full Banking and Currency panel and the Housing Subcommittee, preferred to see McMurray, whom they knew well, at the helm of HHFA.[8] But more important, neither wanted a strong proponent of integration running the agency. Previous administrators had helped blunt the drive for open occupancy by claiming that an anti-discrimination order would decrease new housing construction. The Southerners wanted to fill the job with someone who would continue to furnish this type of aid in the future. Adding further to their discomfort was the strong possibility that Weaver might join the cabinet if HHFA, as seemed likely, was raised to departmental status. Kennedy had made no public comment on this matter, but it was widely assumed that whoever held the HHFA post would be in line for promotion to secretary.[9]

When hearings opened on Weaver's qualifications in early February, the HHFA administrator-designate became the first Kennedy nominee to meet senatorial delay and defiance. Alluding to rumors, baseless as it turned out, that connected Weaver to Communist front groups during the 1930s, Robertson refused to hear testimony until the President gave his committee written assurances of Weaver's loyalty. After this red herring had been disposed of, the panel pressed Weaver for his opinions on open occupancy. While holding firm to his belief that all federally aided housing should be available to everyone, Weaver drew back from his exposed position by pointing out that the timing of an Executive order was the President's, not the HHFA administrator's, decision.[10] With the open occupancy matter thrown back into the White House's lap,

Weaver won a 11–4 vote in support from the committee and was confirmed by a voice vote in the Senate. On February 11, 1961, Weaver was sworn in as HHFA administrator, the highest post in the Executive Branch ever held by a Negro.

Weaver brought a new list of priorities to HHFA. The agency could not deal effectively with the problems of housing and home finance, he argued, unless it saw its final goal as improving urban life. Unlike many of his associates in government and construction circles, Weaver not only saw the problem of housing as how to build more homes but how to increase housing along orderly lines and how to supplement it with transportation, jobs, and welfare programs, to create a rational urban complex. Taking his predecessors to task for their definition of priorities, Weaver argued that people, not interest rates, should be the determinants of community organization; to help him understand how society operated, he took the unprecedented step of adding an urban sociologist to his staff.[11] A resident of big cities his entire life, Weaver knew and loved the metropolis. "Those of us in the present administration," he wrote,[12]

have certain basic convictions about what the American people want in their urban environment. One of our convictions is that the small-town atmosphere of the nineteenth century has disappeared from our major cities and cannot be reclaimed. We believe that the city is a good place, that life in it can and should be desirable, and that what people like about it is the challenge of its concentration.

"Putting [his] money where [his] mouth is," Weaver rented an apartment in the southwest Washington urban renewal area.[13] While not antagonistic toward the suburbs, which since the 1930s had been the chief beneficiaries of federal housing programs, Weaver was, above all, "a central city man." [14] "Americans are not interested in living in a series of suburbs surrounding the ruins of their old central cities," he declared in 1964. "To abandon our central cities would be to forsake the cornerstone of our culture. The central city is the cultural, commercial, and political nerve center of our metropolitan civilization." [15]

To give substance to his rhetoric, Weaver felt he had to shake up HHFA. The agency he inherited was composed of many fiefdoms that operated with very little central control. Programs run by different bureaus sometimes worked at cross-purposes, coordination was slight, and duplication rife. Elevation to cabinet rank was supposed to put an end to this feudal system but in the meantime, Weaver used the limited powers at his command to gain greater control over personnel, budgets, and legislation. A key element of his strategy was getting the right people to fill the top posts. The commissioners of FHA and PHA held direct Presidential appointments, but Weaver was given a role in the selection process. The FHA job went to Neil Hardy, an old HHFA hand with excellent contacts with the big developers whom Weaver hoped to interest in planning and entice into urban renewal. For PHA the President, with Weaver's blessing, chose Marie McGuire, executive director of the San Antonio (Texas) Housing Authority. The first housing professional to take over at PHA, Mrs. McGuire had won wide acclaim in housing circles for the innovative project her city had built for the elderly.

Weaver's hopes for improving urban renewal's treatment of minority groups were almost short-circuited at the start by the White House. In private life Weaver had been a persistent critic of the program's treatment of the poor; as HHFA administrator he intended to keep a close watch over this aspect of Title I's performance, but he wanted an expert in the planning-development field to manage the agency's technical operations. Instead of finding a specialist for the post, however, the administration's patronage dispensers selected a politician, ex-Mayor Thomas D'Alesandro of Baltimore, who had helped in Kennedy's campaign. Afraid that D'Alesandro might not be tough enough in negotiations with his friends at City Halls across the nation, Weaver balked at the appointment. After more than a month of haggling, the White House placed D'Alesandro in another job and allowed Weaver to nominate his own choice: William L. Slayton, a former aide at the National

Association of Housing and Redevelopment Officials and an associate of William Zeckendorf, the nation's biggest urban renewer.[16]

II

His staff collected, Weaver began putting together a housing program. Speed was of the essence as Weaver wished to take advantage of the traditional honeymoon a new President enjoys with Congress. The HHFA administrator and his aides had plenty of material to draw upon; besides the promises in the Democratic platform and Kennedy's Pittsburgh speech, there were the comprehensive proposals put forth by the U.S. Conference of Mayors-American Municipal Association, the National Housing Conference,[17] and the President-elect's own special Task Force on Housing and Urban Affairs.

Task forces represented a new device in Presidential transitions. Altogether, Kennedy appointed twenty-nine task forces, in such areas as space, defense, the economy, social welfare, and education to prepare briefing papers for the incoming administration. Some antedated the election, but most were set up in December 1960 with instructions to report by Inauguration Day.[18] The Housing and Urban Affairs group was created on December 6 and handed in its recommendations on January 7. Academicians and Kennedy supporters with previous government experience, rather than political celebrities, served on the various task forces. Joseph McMurray chaired the Urban Affairs panel; two bankers, the staff director of the House Subcommittee on Housing, and M.I.T. political scientist Robert C. Wood were the other members. A few of the reports, such as the ones on depressed areas and the recession, were released with great fanfare to draw public attention to certain issues Kennedy was particularly concerned with, but most were held for background use. Only a very abbreviated summary of the McMurray group's findings reached the press.[19]

Assembled in New York and Washington hotels during two snowbound weekends, the eighty-five-page report of the Housing

and Urban Affairs task force was essentially "a Noah's Ark of
everybody putting in their own piece." [20] The bankers merely offered
some technical amendments to the FHA legislation. McMurray
discussed the woes of public housing, suggesting that such reforms as
greater local discretion, use of rent certificates, and raising income
limits, be given tryouts. The sections on mass transit and orderly
suburban development, which were drafted by Wood, similarly
called for demonstration programs of federal assistance to localities
for open lands acquisition and urban transportation improvements.
Increased expenditures for urban renewal and urban research were
also endorsed.[21] But while the 1960–61 task force report was the
most complete review of urban needs yet prepared for the confiden-
tial use of an American President, it was, nevertheless, a "slapdash"
product, still more a collection of programs than a well-thought out
urban policy statement.[22]

This first essay into "task forcing" met a cool response from
HHFA, but, significantly, the agency's own subsequent proposals
followed fundamentally the same lines. Weaver had played no part
in the McMurray group's establishment and was understandably
eager to stake out his primacy in the housing and urban affairs field.
But the task force's recommendations had encompassed practically
all the ideas to improve urban society that big-city liberals had
formulated during the bleak Eisenhower years, and Weaver, acutely
aware of the administration's precarious majorities in Congress, felt
he could not safely go beyond these familiar prescriptions. Hence,
the omnibus housing bill the HHFA sent to the White House in
February bore a close resemblance to the programs outlined by the
task force in January. Weaver's major accomplishment was not in
blazing a strikingly innovative federal approach to urban problems,
but in translating the vague reform remedies into detailed legislation.[23]

Weaver aptly described the HHFA program as "a blend of the old
and the new." [24] To assist low income families, HHFA urged that
Congress appropriate funds to start the remaining 100,000 public
housing units authorized by the 1949 Housing Act.[25] Besides asking

for a reversal of the Eisenhower's régime's policy of phasing out the low-rent endeavor, HHFA also requested additional money to experiment with new techniques for sheltering the poor, such as buying privately built housing and having local public housing authorities rent private accommodations in the moderate price range for re-leasing to low income families. In a further break with tradition, HHFA asked that the rule requiring the eviction of over-income tenants be relaxed.

Changes were also propounded for urban renewal, which the agency felt had been previously too narrowly conceived: "We must do more than concern ourselves with bad housing—we must reshape our cities into effective nerve centers for expanding metropolitan areas." HHFA wanted Title I reoriented from slum clearance and slum prevention into a positive program for "economic and social regeneration." [26] As a means to this end, HHFA urged broadening the exemption from the "predominantly residential" requirement and replacing the "project-by-project" approach with the formulation of community plans that realistically appraised long-term city needs and opportunities. Liberalized relocation aids, a new FHA program of subsidized low-interest loans, and more efficient rehabilitation procedures, were supposed to ease the agony of the displaced and spur investment in renewal areas. So as to make the Federal Government's commitment to reviving the central cities unmistakable, HHFA advocated a four-year, $2.5 billion authorization—a figure three times larger than Eisenhower's request.

Greater federal spending and additional programs were also HHFA's advice for directing metropolitan development along desirable lines. The agency recommended expanded assistance under the metropolitan planning title ("701") of the 1954 Housing Act, and the inauguration of a $100-million-grant program to preserve open spaces. "Land is the most precious resource of the metropolitan area," HHFA noted. "The present patterns of haphazard suburban development are contributing to a tragic waste in the use of a vital resource now being consumed at an alarming rate." [27]

On the subject of urban transportation, HHFA pointed to the lack of expert knowledge in the field and suggested that federal action be held off until a joint HHFA-Department of Commerce study could be completed.[28] Indeed, HHFA concluded, the necessity for understanding all phases of urban life required a mobilization of the nation's intellectual talent, and the agency called for a sharp rise in federal spending for research.

Kennedy adopted the Weaver package as his own without significant modification. The broad outlines of the HHFA proposals were very familiar to the President; he had endorsed all the basic concepts during the 1960 campaign. In general, the New Frontier housing program placed its emphasis on getting more out of the existing machinery, rather than inventing novel devices. Although the 1961 recommendations to Congress carried a higher price tag than any previous Presidential statement in this area, they were essentially a repetition and widening of the landmark Housing Act of 1949.[29]

This basic continuity helped move the HHFA housing bill swiftly through the legislative obstacle course on Capitol Hill. Kennedy's special message to Congress on housing and community development, the first by a President since 1954, was sent up March 9; a month later, before the administration bill had been printed, the Senate Subcommittee on Housing started hearings. Of the eight days of testimony taken before the Sparkman group, Executive Branch officials consumed two; other witnesses, complained one banker, were "rushed through like the lineup in a public reception." The procedure was repeated on the House side. Subcommittee Chairman Albert Rains of Alabama, who had worked in vain for liberal housing legislation during the Eisenhower years, prodded his fellow congressmen to speed up their interrogation of witnesses so the panel could begin marking up the bill. One observer called the two weeks of House hearings the "worst railroad job I've ever seen." [30]

Some changes in the legislation, however, did result from the committee hearings and subsequent floor action. The greatest controversy centered around the provisions for an FHA-operated, no down payment, forty-year-mortgage insurance program to house low- and moderate-income families. Liberals were split on the plan, with some fearing that the poor would be tied down by the long amortization period; conservatives were worried about the possibility of widespread defaults and depletion of FHA reserves. A compromise was worked out that required some money down.[31]

Due to the "stem-winding" oratory of Senate Minority Leader Everett Dirksen (R.-Ill.), the administration's proposals for orderly suburban development fared less well. The bill's "open spaces" title would have started two programs: 1) federal aid to municipalities for the purchase of land for parks; 2) federal aid to municipalities for the acquisition of land to be kept undeveloped until local authorities had drafted plans for its use by private builders or public agencies. While conservatives were not enthusiastic about the park-buying scheme, they concentrated most of their fire on the second, or "land bank" idea, which they felt seriously endangered the prerogatives of free enterprise. With Dirksen applying his expert talent for ridicule ("This title represents a new dimension in space," he declared. "It should have come from the Committee on Aeronautics and Space Sciences, instead it has come from the Committee on Banking and Currency."), opponents of the measure succeeded in striking the "land bank" section and restricting park spending to $50 million.[32]

But if the Congress found the "land bank" too radical, it proved to be more adventurous than the White House in the field of mass transit. At the prodding of Senator Harrison Williams (D.-N.J.), the legislators spurned Kennedy's recommendation that action in this area be held off until the joint HHFA-Commerce Department study on urban transportation could supply needed information on the dimensions of and solutions to the problem, and they allotted $25 million in grants for demonstration projects and $50 million for loans.[33]

Two old programs, urban renewal and public housing, encountered little difficulty. The modifications in Title I, especially the weakening of the "predominantly residential" requirement, won easy approval, although proponents of "fiscal responsibility" were able to slash $500 million from the $2.5 billion HHFA had requested. More remarkable was the comparative ease with which public housing cleared its legislative hurdles. Few issues had been more bitterly fought in the 1940s and 1950s than public housing appropriations; in 1961, by contrast, Congress allocated funds for the full 100,000 units after a short, perfunctory debate. This dramatic change was due in part to a shift in tactics by realtors and private builders. They had begun to tire of their battles against the small but organized public housing lobby in Washington and now believed their best chance for halting the low-rent program to be at the local level. Some old-fashioned political logrolling also smoothed public housing's passage. Addressing the National Housing Conference in March, Representative Rains bluntly explained the situation: "You cannot pass a housing bill with the votes of the big cities. You can't even come close. The housing bill has to have a little bit of sugar in it for Congressmen whose towns don't have renewal and public housing programs." [34] Rains's sweetener was an amendment providing $500 million in new funding for the community facilities program serving small localities. On the crucial teller vote in the Committee of the Whole House, public housing survived by the relatively comfortable margin of 168–141. In 1949 the low-rent endeavor had squeaked through by five votes.

With a display of speed unusual for the 87th Congress, the legislature had the Housing Act of 1961 on the President's desk on June 30 for his signature. The men on Capitol Hill operated with such haste and comparatively little divisiveness (the votes on final passage were 235–178 in the House and 64–25 in the Senate),[35] because omnibus housing bills that had something for everybody were a popular commodity among politicians. The previous Congress had wanted to enact many of the provisions of the 1961 law, but Eisenhower had thwarted these attempts with vetoes and threats of vetoes. A shift in the occupancy of the White House allowed these legislative frustrations to be relieved and harnessed for the cities' advantage. The New Frontier also provided the environment for the adoption of reform proposals that had been bandied about in the 1950s without much effect on the Republican administration. A number of these liberal suggestions were written into the 1961 act, and the reformers were on hand in the bureaucracy, or in close contact with it, to see that they were carried through. Although passed at the beginning of a new decade and a new administration, the 1961 Housing Act really reflected the ideas of the previous era and sought to rectify the mistakes of its predecessors.

As it turned out, the 1961 Housing Act was the only important piece of urban legislation added to the statute books during Kennedy's tenure in the White House. Authorizations were expected to last for three to four years, and a new bill was planned for the Presidential election year of 1964, but an assassin's bullet removed Kennedy from the scene before the HHFA proposals were ready. The administration's troubles with its mass transit bills in 1962 and 1963, however, indicated that the President might have had difficulty getting anything innovative or specially designed for metropolitan regions through an increasingly hostile and budget-minded Congress. Following the release of the HHFA-Commerce Department study in early 1962, Kennedy endorsed a bill providing for $500 million in grants for mass transit projects. The housing subcommittees in both chambers reported the measure favorably, but a conservative roadblock in the Rules Committee prevented further action before 1964.[36] As in so many other areas of domestic concern, the New Frontier for the cities had been stalemated by the fall of 1963.

III

Kennedy's unsuccessful attempt to establish a cabinet department for cities demonstrated vividly the problems the President faced in trying to lead Congress across the urban frontier. Although some tactical errors contributed to Kennedy's humiliating defeat, the basic predicament was that there were not sufficient votes on Capitol Hill in the early 1960s, particularly in the House, to enact an exclusively urban, or perhaps more accurately, big-city piece of legislation. The omnibus housing bill encountered little real trouble because it pumped federal money into all parts of the country and aided communities of all sizes; even agricultural regions benefited from the 1961 omnibus legislation through its funding of the farm housing program. But the Urban Department measure lacked this universality and, despite the administration's efforts to blur the cabinet proposal's big-city image, a Congress still very reflective of America's rural heritage refused to buy it.

According to the 1960 Census, nearly 66 per cent of the United States population was urban, but this impressive-looking figure obscured the small city or even town surroundings in which a majority of Americans dwelled. By defining as "urban" any community of more than 2,500 persons, the Bureau of the Census lumped together in a single category such different localities as Philadelphia, Mississippi with 5,017 people and Philadelphia, Pennsylvania with 2,002,512. Except for a tag placed on them by a government agency, these municipalities had little in common, especially in terms of life styles or political cultures. If instead of "urban" the Census Bureau's description of an "urbanized area" (a central city of at least 50,000 population plus the communities with high population densities near it) is utilized, then the enumeration of 1960 revealed that 46.5 per cent of the American people resided outside these 213 districts in isolated towns or rural settings. Among the half that could be classified as urbanized, there were further disparities. Muncie, Indiana, the "Middletown" of the 1920s, was in 1960 the core of an urbanized area of 77,500 people, but it was still a far cry from New York, Detroit, Milwaukee, or St. Louis. The congestion, inadequate housing, and rising welfare rolls that plagued these larger and older municipalities were much less common in Muncie and the 175 other urbanized districts of under 500,000 total population. At every election but one since 1946, Muncie had helped send a conservative Republican to Congress who regularly voted against "urban" programs. The giant metropolitan complexes produced their share of conservative Republicans, too. Most came from the suburban counties that ringed the great core cities; divided up into a multitude of small, often homogeneous communities, these areas had developed from the influx of people who found big-city living conditions distasteful and wished to combine the best of the rural and urban worlds. To some extent these migrants had succeeded, but they were often as antagonistic to the needs of the ultimate source of their prosperity—the central city—as farmers had been. Each of the four congressmen representing the counties immediately to the north and east of New York City in 1961, for example, possessed a long record of opposition to an expanded federal role in domestic affairs. Less than 190 of the House's 435 seats could be classified as central-city or suburban, and even fewer of their occupants could be labelled urban liberals.[37]

The new President, however, was an urban liberal, and one prepared to exercise the powers of his office to cement the federal-city partnership. Kennedy's victory in 1960 had rested heavily upon the votes of metropolitan centers, and the President wanted to reward his urban supporters not only with additional federal programs, but also with representation at the cabinet table. Although Kennedy grasped the coordinating and policy-making benefits likely to result from upgrading HHFA, it was the symbolic gesture of giving urban concerns the same high-level recognition afforded agricultural problems that most appealed to him.[38] The task of awakening the nation to "the opportunity—and the responsibility—to remold [its] cities and to improve [its] patterns of community development," [39] he believed, would be facilitated by establishing an urban Executive Department. But after fourteen years in Congress, Kennedy knew that this act of creation would not be easy. Cities may have become the socio-economic and intellectual heart of the country, but on Capitol Hill rural politicians were still in control. For a cabinet bill to pass, Kennedy realized, he would have to rely upon the party loyalty of the Democratic majority.[40]

Resisting constituency pressures in the name of fealty to the President would have been difficult for a large number of Democrats in the best of circumstances; an early decision of Kennedy's intensified their dilemma. The choice of Robert Weaver to be HHFA administrator added the inflammatory racial issue to the already bitter urban-rural discord. While it was a fact that Kennedy had said nothing publicly at the time of the Weaver appointment indicating that the housing chief would become the urban secretary if the department was set up, Weaver seemed the logical man for the job.[41] He thus would become the first Negro in the cabinet.[42] In 1961, few men of power in the South found acceptable the prospect of a black man on the most prestigious Executive council in the Federal Government. Civil rights agitation in the South was gaining momentum, and the region's whites feared that raising a Negro to such an exalted position would lend strength to the fight against segregation. There was also the danger that Weaver might use his new role to lobby more effectively for a change in the Federal Government's racial policies. With Weaver in the picture, it was clear that Kennedy would have a hard time holding the Democratic lines firm.

During his first year in the White House, Kennedy followed a cautious strategy on the departmental question. As much as he supported the idea of urban cabinet representation, other matters had higher priority on the Chief Executive's agenda; one of these was the omnibus housing bill. Both HHFA and the President's close advisers agreed that quick passage of the housing legislation was of the utmost importance. Weaver needed a new statutory authorization to keep many of his programs running, and the White House counted upon the expected increase in housing construction to aid the anti-recession drive.[43] Not wanting the dispute over cabinet status, which was almost certain to be very heated, to spill over and endanger the housing bill, the administration delayed sending its special message on the Executive department until the housing measure seemed safely on its way through Congress.

The form of the proposal submitted to Congress also illustrated Kennedy's desire to reduce possible points of friction with Congress. Under the Reorganization Act of 1949 the President held the initiative in restructuring the Executive Branch; Presidential plans could not be modified, and they took effect automatically within sixty days unless either chamber of Congress voted them down. But the proud men on Capitol Hill were not happy with this arrangement, and so to appease Senator John McClellan (D.-Ark.), the powerful chairman of the Committee on Government Operations, Kennedy had his staff prepare a bill that would have to go through the normal legislative processes.[44] Unable to interest the rural-based and conservative McClellan in introducing the measure, the White House had to be satisfied with the much less influential Joseph Clark (D.-Pa.) as S. 1633's sponsor in the Senate.[45]

In a further attempt to enhance the departmental bill's prospects, Kennedy tried his best to keep Weaver out of the limelight. The administration sought to discourage speculation about who might be named secretary, and did not send Weaver up to Capitol Hill to testify on the legislation even though it was his agency's future that was being decided. Weaver, who sympathized with Kennedy's quandary, cooperated by maintaining a low profile on the issue and referring all inquiries to the Executive Office of the President.[46]

The administration bill accomplished what Presidential Adviser Richard Neustadt called "the trick of 'creating' something bigger and broader than HHFA with respect to urban development without actually taking anything away from anyone else and, at the same time, permitting a housecleaning in HHFA." [47] On the delicate subject of a title for the new department, Kennedy chose to go with "Urban Affairs and Housing." The first part, with its connotations of a wide area of responsibility, was a repayment to the mayors for their strong support, while "Housing" was meant to allay the fears of home-builders who believed their interests would be neglected by a department serving cities.[48] The administration also hoped to appease conservatives and avoid trouble with entrenched bureaucrats running programs in urban areas by restricting the new department to the agencies presently included within HHFA. But HHFA would not be elevated just as it was; the secretary would be given full operating authority over the constituent bureaus, with the power to shift programs around.[49] Perhaps even more significantly, S. 1633 contained a strong "Declaration of National Housing and Urban Affairs Policy":

The Congress hereby declares that the general welfare and security of the
Nation and the health and living standards of our people require, as a
matter of national purpose, sound development and redevelopment of our
urban communities in which the vast majority of our people live and work.

Included among the comprehensive list of objectives were: a decent
home in a suitable environment for every American family; additional employment opportunities; adequate transportation, educational, and recreational facilities; and establishment of larger and
more stable tax bases for localities. It would be the secretary's duty
to exercise leadership in coordinating federal activities affecting
urban areas and "to provide for full and appropriate consideration,
at the national level, of the needs and interests of urban areas and of
the people who live and work in them."

Testifying before the McClellan Committee on behalf of S. 1633,
Senator Clark repeated the familiar arguments for a Department of
Urban Affairs and Housing (DUAH). Management of federal
programs in housing and community development would be improved, he claimed, by "conferring status" on HHFA. "In government as elsewhere, the importance of status cannot be ignored,"
declared the former mayor of Philadelphia. "A major, no matter how
able, cannot do a major general's job." Raising HHFA to cabinet
rank would enable it to bring some order and direction to the many
federal programs operating in metropolitan areas. Municipal leaders
would have somewhere to go with their complaints: "A local official
with an inquiry will be able to get 'one-stop service' instead of being
bucked around from one federal agency to another." The new
secretary could not dictate to other departments, but he would be in
a position to bring problems to their attention and, when necessary,
to alert the White House to the difficulty. Up to now, Clark
observed, "the health of the cities has been no one's concern." The
mass transit dilemma, for example, was considered not from the
standpoint of the cities' well-being, but from that of the transportation industry, with results—decline of service—detrimental to the
urban economy. "If a crisis develops in rural America," the senator

said, "the Department of Agriculture automatically has jurisdiction. When this bill passes, a Department will automatically have a corresponding jurisdiction over the crises that develop in urban America."

Bureau of the Budget Director David Bell, the administration's spokesman on S. 1633, attempted to give the term "urban" the broadest possible definition in the course of his testimony. Nowhere in the bill it had drafted did the Budget Bureau explain what it meant by "urban communities." This omission appears to have been deliberate. The impetus for a cabinet department for cities had come from groups located in the large central cities, and when Kennedy referred, as he did in his 1961 State of the Union Message, to the need for an Urban Department to turn back the "squalor engulfing our cities," he undoubtedly perceived the great metropolitan complexes as the department's key constituency. But the President's advisers also realized that a departmental proposal presented in that way stood no chance of passing; rather than irritate the idea's old advocates or risk the loss of potential new backers by delineating just what localities would be assisted by the department, BOB tried to obfuscate the issue by having the bill remain silent. Under hostile questioning by non-metropolitan congressmen at the hearings, however, Bell found he could not avoid making a choice. He opted for the chance to widen the department's base of support by stressing that smaller cities and towns had a special stake in DUAH's establishment. The big cities, he declared, "often experience little difficulty in finding their way around Washington and gaining a hearing for their views." With a DUAH, the small communities would have a friend in the nation's capital to represent their interests.

Bell's remarks failed to dampen the enthusiasm of veteran champions of an urban department. S. 1633 received the endorsement of the USCM, AMA, National Housing Conference, National Association of Housing and Redevelopment Officials, American Council to Improve Our Neighborhoods, American Institute of Planners, and the AFL-CIO. A number of senators and congressmen from metropolitan districts also testified in favor of the department.

Opposition to the proposal was varied and sometimes intense. Realtors, home-builders, and bankers feared the subordination of the housing agencies in an Executive department for urban affairs. DUAH, they claimed, would be the "mayors' baby," [50] with the result that the interests of the private construction industry would be overlooked. The National Association of Home Builders and the Mortgage Bankers Association of America indicated a willingness to go along with the bill if it was amended to guarantee the operation of FHA in its current form,[51] but the National Association of Real Estate Boards was in no mood to compromise. Going through one of its more conservative periods, NAREB demanded that the Federal Government get out of public housing and urban renewal and sell FHA to private groups.[52]

The subcommittees also heard charges raised about S. 1633's deleterious impact upon the federal system. The Council of State Governments, an organization of elected state officials, argued that a cabinet department for cities would weaken the ties between states and their political subdivisions and "accelerate the dependency of local government upon the National Government." [53] A group of seventeen Democratic governors joined in a statement backing DUAH,[54] but the Advisory Commission on Intergovernmental Relations, a federal body composed of officials from all three levels of government, suggested that language be added to the bill emphasizing that the department's creation did "not connote any disregard or diminution of the constitutional powers and responsibilities of the States." [55]

Evidence of metropolitan and urban disunity was clearly visible. The National Association of County Officials, which was controlled by its suburban members, opposed S. 1633 because it feared the department would strengthen the hands of the core cities, due to their close ties with the Federal Government, and make them dominant over their neighbors in metropolitan districts.[56] Similar anxieties were voiced by congressmen from outside the giant metropolitan complexes. The remarks of Representative Glenn

Cunningham (R.-Neb.) were especially illuminating. An ex-mayor of Omaha, a municipality of 300,000 people, Cunningham spoke for nearly 100 million Americans who lived in rural areas or in urbanized regions of less than a half-million population and abhorred the apparent hegemony of the great metropolises. He challenged the Conference of Mayors' right to present itself as the cities' agent in Washington. Reviewing his own experiences with the conference, whose presidents between 1957 and 1960 had been the chief executives of New York, Los Angeles, Chicago, and Philadelphia, Cunningham claimed that the organization was "dominated by a group of about six mayors from the huge metropolitan areas, and all the rest of us [were] just bystanders." According to the Nebraskan, the troubles of the few big cities paled in comparison with those of the hundreds of more moderately sized communities; small towns, he declared, were "dying on the vine." Rejecting Bell's bid for support, Cunningham called upon Congress to kill the big-city-oriented DUAH and to create instead a Department of Small Towns and Rural Affairs.[57]

The Declaration of Policy generated the greatest fireworks. Authors of the measure had included it to make DUAH something more than just a cabinet-level HHFA.[58] Although the Declaration conferred no specific new responsibilities on the secretary, it did give him a very broad mandate in urban affairs. Senator Clark felt the policy statement was "the heart of the bill: Without it, all we have done is to give status to HHFA. You had made a major general out of your major, but you haven't given him many of the functions of the major general." But to those not thrilled by a cabinet department for cities in the first place, the declaration seemed to leave the door open to a great expansion of federal activities in metropolitan areas and DUAH's intrusion into the operations of other agencies. Critics charged that the mayors would use the declaration to justify wholesale raids on the federal Treasury. The Advisory Commission on Intergovernmental Relations urged that "any declaration of national policy by Congress in this legislation should avoid language giving any impression or interpretation as a *carte blanche* for direct action [by DUAH] on any and all subjects involving or affecting urban areas." If Congress desired to widen the federal role in urban affairs, the commission counseled, it should consider the question carefully and in separate legislation.[59]

The administration persisted in its conciliatory approach as the subcommittees went into executive sessions. With the Budget Bureau's acquiescence, the department's friends agreed to let FHA retain its name and primary functions, although its commissioner would be under the direction of the secretary. To satisfy rural interests, the subcommittees added a definition of urban areas ("all communities, regardless of size, whether incorporated or unincorporated, eligible to participate in the Department's programs") that made it clear that DUAH would serve smaller localities. New language was also inserted requiring the secretary to give attention to these communities' special problems. Finally, the panels decided to delete the expansive Declaration of Policy and replace it with a less provocative Declaration of Purpose. Contented that the modifications did no damage to the bill and even enhanced its chances for passage, the administration welcomed the subcommittees' actions.[60] The full Government Operations Committees in both chambers were finished with their work by mid-September 1961.

But no further progress was achieved during the first session of the 87th Congress. Preliminary headcounts convinced legislative leaders that they did not have the votes to pass the bill. The conservative Republican-Southern Democratic coalition, which had already blocked the President's Medicare and federal aid to education proposals, seemed to have also marked the departmental measure for defeat. The tone of the minority views filed by Senators McClellan, Mundt (R.-S.D.), Curtis (R.-Neb.), and Ervin (D.-N.C.) was extremely sharp. S. 1633, they declared, would "violate the principles of the federal system, usurp authority vested in state governments, crumble the walls of self-determination, demolish local leadership, and build ever higher the stronghold of Central Government." Their report continued:

We will, in one sweeping gesture, create a goliath which will drain our Treasury and which will keep a watchful, police eye on every urban community and its citizens, planning, spending, directing until citizens will not call city hall when streets need repair, or a water main needs replacing, but will notify their Congressmen to contact the Cabinet member handling such problems, seeking repair and service.

Despite all the administration's assurances about taking care of small towns, the dissenters insisted upon referring to DUAH as a "big city" department. For good measure, the minority report repeated the old allegation that federal aid would help perpetuate corrupt machine control of large city politics.[61] Faced with this spirited opposition, the administration decided to avoid a showdown in 1961 and rethink its strategy for the next congressional session.

By the time the legislature reconvened in January 1962, the White House knew the departmental bill was lost. Rural-urban-suburban animosities had threatened S. 1633 from the start; the racial issue now sealed its doom. Kennedy had always known that DUAH would stand no chance of passage unless it received the backing of Southern moderates, such as Sparkman of Alabama, who had traditionally voted for liberal housing legislation. The President also understood that their support was endangered by the possibility of Weaver's designation as secretary; thus his non-committal public stance on Weaver's future. But in the highly charged atmosphere of Southern politics in the early 1960s, with the region feeling itself under attack from the courts, the Executive Branch, and outside agitators, this silence was not enough to quiet the fears of the South's elected representatives. They demanded a private pledge from the President not to appoint the Negro. This Kennedy could not do, concerned as he was about the Northern black electorate. Rebuffed by the White House, Sparkman reversed his earlier tacit encouragement of the Urban Department idea and announced his opposition to S. 1633. In the absence of a miracle, the bill was dead.[62]

The Republicans on Capitol Hill were in no mood to act as S. 1633's savior. Few in the G.O.P. contingent came from big central cities, and except for a handful of mavericks, congressional Republicans were uniformly hostile to the New Frontier's spending policies. Passage of the departmental measure, the Republican leadership believed, would only secure the Democrats' domination of urban politics; on the other hand, if Kennedy could be tagged with another defeat alongside his setbacks on Medicare and education, then the President's image would be severely tarnished. For both ideological and political reasons, the Republicans wanted S. 1633 beaten.[63]

Realizing that his year-old policy of pacification had failed to mollify Southern Democrats or conservative Republicans, Kennedy accepted the G.O.P. challenge in early 1962 for a partisan fight. If he could not recompense his urban allies with a cabinet department, then he would make it perfectly clear to them that it was the Republican party that was blocking their recognition. Similarly, if he was unable to satisfy black aspirations for a cabinet member from their race, then he would saddle the G.O.P. with the blame. Enactment of S. 1633 was impossible, but Kennedy figured he could reap the same political dividends that he would have gained in victory with a well-engineered defeat.

Both the G.O.P. and Kennedy rushed eagerly into their first engagement in the House Rules Committee. Back in January 1961, the President had expended a large amount of his political capital to enlarge the committee so it could be "packed" with friends of the administration, but in the January 1962 vote on the DUAH bill the intrusion of the racial matter nullified this triumph. Four Democrats, all of them from the South,[64] joined the five Republican members of the panel to refuse, by a 9–6 margin, a rule for the departmental measure.

Having expected this result, Kennedy launched his counterattack on the very afternoon of the Rules vote. Replying to planted questions at his scheduled news conference, the President proclaimed his intention to send a reorganization plan up to Congress "right away" and to appoint Weaver to the DUAH post if it was created. Kennedy fixed the culpability for S. 1633's rejection squarely on the G.O.P.: "I thought," he declared, "the Republicans shared our concern for more effective management and responsibility of the problems of two-thirds of our population who live in the cities. These cities are expanding. They face many problems—housing, transportation, and all the rest—which vitally affect our population." Defending his designation of Weaver to an as yet non-existent position, Kennedy explained to a later news conference that Weaver's selection was well known on "the Hill" and "the American people might as well know it." The President was laying down the gauntlet to his enemies. "Imagine them [the Republicans and Dixiecrats] claiming that the bill was bad bureaucratic organization," he told a close aide. "They're against it because Weaver's a Negro and I'd like to see them say it." [65]

Political analysts awarded the preliminary skirmish to Kennedy. Instead of killing the DUAH proposal, the Rules Committee vote gave the initiative back to the President by forcing him to use his reorganizational powers. "If there was any political trap in all this," commented Walter Lippmann, "the Republican leaders laid the trap into which they have fallen. They should not have forgotten the Reorganization Act of 1949." Giving free rein to "their reflexes, which takes it for granted that any new proposal to deal with the changing world is automatically undesirable," the Republicans had afforded Kennedy the opportunity to tell a nationwide television audience that the G.O.P. was anti-urban.[66] Kennedy's promise to nominate Weaver also labelled the Republicans as anti-black. One Republican lamented: "It is going to take another Emancipation Proclamation to get Negroes to vote Republican again." [67] The 1962 and 1964 election campaigns were underway.[68]

To gain maximum political advantage, however, Kennedy had to complete a difficult scenario. Congress had sixty days to veto the Reorganization Plan; a negative vote in either house would be sufficient to kill it. There was an outside chance the Republicans might reverse direction and back DUAH, but the President's advisers believed, correctly as events demonstrated, that the G.O.P. opposition would be even more intransigent. With the Plan's defeat "a foregone conclusion" [69] in the House, the administration hoped to put the Republicans on the spot by forcing a vote first in the Senate where the chances for approval were greater.[70]

The hearings were a portent of the misfortune to come. McClellan and other conservatives challenged the administration's right to create an Executive department by a reorganization plan. Mayors from small cities charged that the AMA and USCM resolutions in support of a cabinet department had been rammed through by the large cities and did not accurately reflect urban thinking. The Home Builders Association withdrew its support for the department because the plan, due to legal technicalities, downgraded the role of housing. Disturbed by the fact that under the plan the new department would have no more responsibilities than the old HHFA, J. Arthur Younger (R.-Cal.), who had introduced the initial legislation back in 1954, called for the defeat of the President's proposal. Other long-time advocates of an urban department endorsed the Reorganization Plan, but they had a difficult time convincing the panels that there was substantial grass-roots enthusiasm for the idea. The departmental question, noted one newspaper, was a matter of "technical organization with as much human interest and political appeal as an argument over a cash versus accrual system of keeping the books." [71]

A breakdown in Democratic communications and Republican aggressiveness prevented the clear-cut votes on the issues Kennedy sought. The House Government Operations Committee finished its hearings and report before the Senate panel, in part because of McClellan's unhurried management of his group's affairs. The Arkansan had little interest in helping Kennedy meet his schedule of having the upper chamber act first.[72] Seizing upon this foul-up in the administration's timetable, the Republicans took the White House by surprise on February 19 by announcing their intention to force a quick vote in the House. In order to hold to his original design, Kennedy had to resort to a discharge resolution in the Senate to free DUAH from McClellan's clutches. But the proud Senate was not to be pushed around so easily. With impassioned speeches about "orderly procedure" and "insulting treatment" of the distinguished chairman of the Government Operations Committee ringing in their ears, the Senators defeated the White House-sponsored resolution, 58–42.[73] The next day the House delivered the *coup de grâce*. After three hours of lethargic debate, the House did as expected: it killed the Reorganization Plan, 246–150. A nearly solid phalanx of Southern Democrats joined with the almost monolithic Republican minority to inter, at least temporarily, the DUAH idea.[74]

Kennedy's great political stroke had turned into one of the administration's most humiliating tactical reverses. The White House, one magazine observed, "maneuvered with all the finesse of third-rate precinct captains." [75] The President himself admitted later that the matter had been mishandled: "I played it too cute," he told a reporter. "It was so obvious it made them mad." [76] Newsmen found a subdued Kennedy at his press conference on the afternoon of the House vote. "There will be an urban department some time," he said. "There isn't going to be one now, but there's going to be sooner or later. It is as necessary and inevitable as the Department of Agriculture or HEW." Administrator Weaver, the President declared, "will get along all right; it is the people in the cities who have been defeated."

With those remarks, the cabinet department idea practically disappeared from the agenda of the New Frontier. Kennedy referred to the 92 per cent Republican vote against DUAH in three fall campaign appearances in behalf of Democratic candidates for Congress, but the Cuban missile crisis overshadowed all other national issues in November. The President's 1963 budget message contained a recommendation for the creation of DUAH, but its legislative prospects were so bleak that no effort was made to hold hearings.[77] In the eleven months before his death, Kennedy never brought up the topic in a public gathering.

IV

While Congress debated HHFA's future, Weaver worked to strengthen his agency's programs. His goals were to correct the errors of the past and prepare HHFA for the responsibilities of a real urban department. Using the limited means at his disposal—the 1961 Housing Act and the general supervisory powers of his position—Weaver achieved some measure of success.

To help break down central city-suburban walls, in both HHFA and the urban complexes, Weaver established the Office of Metropolitan Development. Its job was to coordinate HHFA activities within metropolitan areas and to cooperate with other federal agencies in encouraging a common approach to planning and development of urbanized regions. Restricted to acting primarily in an advisory capacity, the office did, however, have some statutory support. The Open Spaces and Mass Transit titles of the 1961 act conditioned federal assistance upon the local formulation of comprehensive proposals for metropolitan land use and transportation. But public housing, urban renewal, and FHA were not covered by these regulations, and HHFA was unable to have these crucial programs utilized within a metropolitan framework.[78]

Freed from the annual battles over funding and infused with fresh leadership, the public housing program showed some signs of vitality in the early 1960s. Washington loosened its control of local authorities and cities were encouraged to experiment; under the demonstration program authorized by the 1961 act, new techniques in design and construction were tried out, rent supplements were studied, and various types of tenure besides tenancy were explored. In line with this emphasis upon improving the environment of public housing projects, Weaver and PHA Commissioner McGuire reached an agreement with the Department of Health, Education and Welfare providing for the whole range of HEW services—homemaking, job placement, counseling, day care centers—to public housing's residents. But the joint enterprise never truly got off the ground due to a shortage of funds and an abundance of red tape; it would, however, offer some useful lessons for the more comprehensive Model Cities program that got underway later in the decade.[79]

Concentrating upon social improvement, Weaver and McGuire faltered in the production aspects of public housing. Annual new starts in the last three years of the Eisenhower administration had averaged 22,300 units; the figure for 1961–63 was only slightly higher, 26,600 units. Application and review remained a cumbersome process, and PHA's promotion of scattered sites put local housing authorities (LHAs) in a bind. Lower- and middle-class white neighborhoods resisted attempts to locate projects in their midst; LHAs were able to soften this hostility only by limiting these projects to the elderly. By the end of 1964 more than a quarter of low-rent apartments were occupied by people over 65 years of age. Unable to stand the political heat of finding public housing sites, some municipal leaders took their cities out of the program. Baltimore, Boston, Cleveland, and Detroit were among the cities that failed to start any new projects from 1962 to 1964. Small towns replaced them as recipients of PHA aid. Between 1961 and 1968, the number of LHAs increased from 1,174 to 2,738; most of the newcomers were in communities of less than 10,000 population with tiny programs. For many of the urban poor, the quest for decent accommodations would continue to mean long periods on public housing waiting lists.[80]

In contrast to public housing's sluggish building performance, urban renewal helped fuel one of the biggest construction booms in metropolitan history. It took Eisenhower's URA commissioners eight years to authorize $1.6 billion in Title I grants; Slayton approved a similar sum in just two years. Congressional largesse in the 1961 Housing Act eased the task of the commissioner, but URA also contributed to the spurt of activity by speeding up its handling of applications. The legislature's generosity and URA's reforms paid off in increased private investment in urban renewal projects. Giant companies such as Alcoa, U.S. Steel, and General Electric thought the tax advantages and cash flow benefits to be gained from putting their profits into urban real estate too great to pass up.[81] This demonstration of faith in the urban future by the business community fostered a new spirit of municipal optimism. "The battle against blight," declared *Time* in 1962, "is slowly being won." [82]

Besides accelerating the pace of the program, Weaver and Slayton also began rectifying some of its faults. To improve URA's performance in finding homes for those it displaced, Slayton created the post of assistant commissioner for relocation and appointed the able director of rehousing operations for the District of Columbia's Redevelopment Land Agency, James Banks, to this sensitive job. At Banks's prodding, URA started cracking down on local renewal authorities, demanding better statistics on available accommodations and keeping a closer eye on how municipalities cared for the uprooted. Closer coordination with PHA and FHA helped these efforts. Localities were encouraged to take advantage of the public housing program; some cities used Title I sites for low-rent units for the first time.[83] To cut red tape, URA and FHA reached an understanding whereby the two agencies utilized the same price figures in determining the amount of federal aid for renewal areas. URA also established closer working ties with the Bureau of Public Roads to insure that the highway construction venture and city rebuilding endeavor did not conflict.[84]

Yet as in public housing, serious problems remained. The requirement of citizen participation in the planning process was rarely enforced; URA did not have the resources or the patience to advance community organization or to accept the consequences of popular scrutiny of developers' designs. White House-HHFA support for additional exemptions to the "predominantly residential" rule moved Title I further away from its welfare origins. Its main focus was no longer on housing, but more on the "best use" of available land. Civic centers and shopping complexes continued to be more appealing to politicians and investors than high-risk rental apartments; this demolition of housing in the name of "sound planning" hindered progress along the relocation front.[85] Those in the social work and race relations fields who complained about the handling of the displaced were joined in their criticism of urban renewal by a segment of the business world. The big leap in Title I spending and the greater use of eminent domain powers frightened small storeowners who came to associate urban renewal with higher taxes and rentals, and the disruption of their neighborhood retail trade.[86]

FHA, too, presented a mixed record of reform. The Kennedy administration believed, Weaver wrote, that "FHA is a governmental agency designed to serve the public as well as the building and mortgage industries." Promoting the general welfare in FHA's case meant accepting the possibility of financial losses: "There is no justification for an insurance system," declared the HHFA chief, "unless it takes risks." [87] The 1961 Housing Act extended FHA's risk-taking role in two areas: rehabilitation of dwellings and housing for moderate income families [Section 221(d)(3)]. Both were designed to increase FHA's contribution to urban renewal. To demonstrate the new importance FHA attached to central-city housing, FHA Commissioner Hardy established the position of assistant commissioner for multifamily housing operations. But legislation and administrative realignments could not immediately overcome decades of indifference to urban needs and the inexperience of potential sponsors in utilizing the programs' benefits. By the end of 1963 work had begun on less than 13,000 units under 221(d)(3), about one-quarter of the number of annual starts Weaver had hoped for.[88] Adding a social dimension to FHA's traditional business activities would be a long and difficult task.

V

Aside from the departmental issue, the White House kept aloof from housing and urban topics. No one on the President's personal staff had a professional background in these areas; 1600 Pennsylvania Avenue's contacts with HHFA were handled by Assistant Special Counsel Lee White, whose responsibilities ranged widely over the domestic field. What to request of Congress in the 1961 housing legislation was determined by HHFA, and it was Weaver and his aides who worked out the modifications on Capitol Hill, although they did coordinate their tactics with Kennedy's congressional liaison team. The Executive Office had no means to formulate its own ideas; the "urban affairs brains trust" put together during the 1960 campaign and the interregnum did not survive the inauguration. Yet if the President preferred to raise HHFA to cabinet rank and let it take the helm in helping the cities, urban groups and other agencies were not so ready to forego the advantages of strong Presidential leadership.

A perennial question for Executive determination was the holding of a White House Conference on Urban Affairs. The post-election 1960 convention of the AMA had urged such a conference, calling it "a further step in focusing national attention on the vital problems of our urban areas." Getting the new administration underway delayed consideration of the mayors' suggestion until early spring when it was joined and overshadowed by a proposal from the American Council to Improve Our Neighborhoods. In conversations with White and Weaver, ACTION spokesmen suggested a one-day briefing of the President and his advisers on "The American City" by leading urban businessmen in June 1961; the appointment by the President of a National Commission on Urban Problems; and the assembling of a full-scale White House conference in the fall of 1962 to review the commission's recommendations.[89] Weaver had mixed reactions. He desired the publicity a conference and commission report would bestow on the cities' dilemmas but doubted that a citizens' group could offer constructive suggestions. Furthermore, Weaver feared that the one-year study by the commission would give opponents of the departmental bill an excuse to request a delay in congressional approval.[90] With prospects for the DUAH measure uncertain in mid-1961, the White House decided to take no chances. It shelved the ACTION scheme. After the humbling defeat of the Reorganization Plan in February 1962, 1600 Pennsylvania Avenue was not the place for a further airing of urban woes.

But the mayors continued to press their case. Visiting the President in January 1963, a delegation from the USCM pleaded for the convening of a White House conference later that year. They did not receive a firm commitment, but the Budget Bureau began some preliminary studies.[91] At the USCM's June convention, which

Kennedy addressed, USCM President Richard Lee happily revealed that the go-ahead had been given for a White House Conference on Community Development[92] to be held that December. Plans called for a national commission, composed of government and private members, to organize the sessions; observers expected the conference to supply Kennedy with an attractive election-year program for urban areas. The original prospectus also envisioned regional hearings by the commission as a prelude to the national meeting, but these were cancelled because of the danger that civil rights activists might use them as a forum for attacking segregation.[93]

In the end the conference was not held either. No public announcement was made prior to the President's assassination, but the decision to cancel had been reached before the trip to Texas. An Executive order creating the commission was prepared but never signed. Lack of enthusiasm for the conference at both HHFA and the White House was responsible for its undoing. Preparing his own legislative proposals for 1964, Weaver wanted no competition from a group of outsiders.[94] The White House, too, was leery about what might emerge from the conference; unrealistic spending recommendations could place the administration in the unpleasant position of having to choose between upsetting its budget or damaging its reputation as a friend of the cities.[95]

One problem the White House could not avoid so easily was discrimination in housing. During his campaign for the Presidency, Kennedy had noted that it would take just "a stroke of the presidential pen" to end racial bias in all federal housing programs, and he promised to make that stroke.[96] But once elected, Kennedy moved slowly. As the controversy over Weaver's nomination to HHFA demonstrated, open occupancy was a volatile issue that threatened to deprive the administration of the Southern Democratic support it needed to enact its program.[97] Rather than risk major Southern desertions in his first year, Kennedy kept the Executive order bottled up. The fight over DUAH in early 1962 prevented quick action that year too. Weaver made it clear that he felt the Executive order was more important than the department proposal, but the White House believed it could get greater political mileage out of the latter.[98] After DUAH went down to defeat, Kennedy realized that the patience of the civil rights groups was wearing thin, but salvaging the rest of his legislative program, such as the Trade Expansion Act, took precedence. The approach of the mid-term congressional elections provided still another occasion for delay: political analysts figured Kennedy stood to lose more in the South than he could gain among blacks in the North if he issued the order.[99] But once the returns were in the President redeemed his two-year-old pledge and barred discrimination in the sale of federally assisted housing. Even then, however, Kennedy went only part way: the ban applied only to new housing, not to existing facilities, and did not cover homes financed by savings and loan associations that operated under Federal Home Loan Bank Board supervision.[100] Moreover, the Presidential edict was administered so unsympathetically that little progress was made knocking down the walls of segregation that were the cause of so much metropolitan distress.[101]

Civil rights street protests in Southern cities spurred Kennedy to move further in the equal opportunity field in 1963. The use of police dogs against anti-segregation demonstrators in Birmingham, Alabama, the bombing of black residences and businesses, and brawls between black and white citizens convinced the President that the nation faced a great moral crisis.[102] Addressing the USCM convention in Honolulu in early June, Kennedy asked the mayors' help in ending racial discrimination. Through local administrative and legislative action, he declared, "we can move these disputes off the streets and into the courts, and give all Americans a fair chance for an equal life." His five-point municipal program called for: establishment of bi-racial human relations committees; repeal of all ordinances supporting segregation; a policy of non-discrimination in public employment; enactment of equal opportunity laws covering jobs, housing, and public accommodations; and provision of summer jobs for teenagers and concerted efforts to keep students in school. Two days later, in a televised address to the nation, Kennedy threw his support behind an omnibus federal civil rights bill encompassing most of the items he had suggested to the mayors. As in so many other areas, however, passage of this legislation would not come until Kennedy's successor had taken up residence in the White House.

Besides committing the Executive Branch's resources to the civil rights struggle, the Kennedy administration also joined the campaign for more equitable apportionment of state legislatures. During the last months of the Eisenhower years, the Justice Department had shown some interest in a Tennessee case contesting the state's failure to redistribute seats in the legislature to reflect population shifts as required by the Tennessee constitution,[103] but it had failed to take positive action. The Supreme Court's decision in November 1960 to hear the plaintiff's appeal was made without any indication of the department's attitude.[104] By contrast, one of the first steps taken by the new attorney general, Robert F. Kennedy, was to request the Court's permission to enter the case as *amicus curiae*.[105] This intervention may have been crucial to the outcome. The department's briefs and oral presentation tended to shape the Court's perception of the issues; the majority opinion in *Baker v. Carr* (1962) ignored the arguments of the plaintiff's counsel and relied heavily upon those of the solicitor general in finding a federal constitutional right to challenge state apportionment systems in the courts.[106] Two years later the Justice Department was back in court urging the high tribunal to adopt the principle of "one man, one vote." "A rural voter is not entitled, by reason of that fact alone," declared the Government's brief, "to have greater or less representation than an urban resident." [107] A six-judge majority of the Court agreed: "Legislators represent people, not trees or acres. Legislators are elected by voters, not farms or cities or economic interests. . . . A citizen, a qualified voter, is no more nor no less so because he lives in the city or on the farm." [108]

VI

The New Frontier that had begun so hopefully in cold, snow-blanketed Washington in January 1961 ended suddenly and tragically in sun-drenched Dallas in November 1963. Instead of the eight years he expected to have to move and lead the nation, John Kennedy was given less than three. But if death cut his tenure short and left his record incomplete, Kennedy did leave his mark on urban America.

The making of that imprint came slowly, however. During his thousand days in the White House, the President's mind was preoccupied with foreign affairs. Not a single item of domestic concern was identified in his Inaugural speech. Determined to restore America's prestige abroad and reduce the risk of nuclear holocaust, Kennedy expended much of his energies on seeking new relationships with our friends and enemies overseas. Crisis followed upon crisis: Cuba, Berlin, Laos, Cuba again, and Vietnam. The last was still hanging in the fire that fateful November, but after the successful resolution of the Cuban missile crisis and the signing of the test-ban treaty, the President could feel more confident about the direction in which the winds of change were moving and give more attention to domestic developments.

Kennedy's troubles with Congress reinforced his tendency to look abroad. He had more freedom of action in foreign than in domestic policy. On paper his party commanded sizable majorities in both chambers, but in reality a conservative coalition controlled the legislature. Rejecting the advice of those who wanted him to appeal over the head of Congress for public support, Kennedy tried to work with congressional leaders. It was a job for which he was temperamentally unsuited. Kennedy did gain an important new foreign trade bill, some tax reform, public works funds, and other liberal measures, but almost always at the price of some crucial concessions. For two of his most controversial proposals, Medicare and federal aid to education, Kennedy could do nothing. The Urban Department fiasco was just another in a long list of White House failures to persuade Congress to enter the second half of the twentieth century. This inability to lead the legislature had its impact on everything the administration did and did not do. Commenting on the cancellation of the White House Conference on Community Development a month before the President's last trip to Texas, one architectural critic wrote:[109]

It is sad and symptomatic of the New Frustration on the New Frontier that our urban philosophers must cruise to Greek islands to discuss the city, while at home, what with civil rights unrest, growing opposition to urban renewal and other headaches, a national conference seems at the moment too hot to handle.

At the time of Kennedy's death, Congress appeared almost as paralyzed as Washington's traffic had been on the eve of Kennedy's inauguration.

Interest in foreign affairs and the stalemate in Congress had kept Kennedy from delving deeply into urban matters. With respect to the 1961 housing legislation, for example, Weaver saw Kennedy just twice: in February to get his approval for the agency's proposals and in June when the President signed the measure.[110] Aside from his messages to Congress on housing, the Urban Department, and mass transit, Kennedy never used the White House as a forum for an in-depth public discussion of urban topics. Two issues that did receive some special Presidential attention were the strategy for the departmental bill and the timing of the Executive order on open occupancy; the former was a legislative disaster and the latter a triumph of political expediency over morality.

Yet if Kennedy devoted little of his time to urban subjects, that did not mean he was ignorant of what was going on. For Kennedy was, as one admiring member of the White House team has observed, "unregenerately a city man, deeply anxious about the mess and tangle of urban America."[111] In a period when city problems were hardly a "ringing issue," even the limited considera-tion he gave them was remarkable.[112] The President, unlike most of his predecessors, understood the difficulties involved in making cities habitable and was prepared, within the bounds set by foreign and other domestic commitments with prior call, to help out.[113]

In many small ways and a few big ones, the Kennedy administration came to grips with the large city on its own terms. Weaver had put together a very capable team at HHFA, and with the tacit encouragement of the White House, he and his aides strove to improve program performance. Thanks to their efforts, for example, the Interstate Highway Act of 1956 was amended to give displaced families the same type of assistance provided those uprooted by urban renewal. While these relocation indemnities remained inadequate under both programs, there was, at least, recognition that injustices had been perpetrated and an earnest attempt to redress them. Similarly, HHFA's endeavors to make renewal project architecture bolder and more attractive demonstrated a growing sophistication about the dynamics of urban life. Yet, as with the reforms in public housing, this advice was often rejected by localities as expensive and disruptive of community patterns. The New Frontier put some grease on the aging and creaky federal-local bureaucratic machinery, but it could not retool it completely. Federal legislation for cities still read better on paper than in fact.

The big advances on the urban front were only beginning to take shape at the time of Kennedy's death. After months of piecemeal administrative actions, the President in mid-1963 decided to strike decisively at the roots of segregation and discrimination through legislation. Events in the South precipitated Kennedy's switch and the main thrust of his proposals was directed at the South, but his show of support for the civil rights revolution had significance for all regions of the country and especially for metropolitan areas. Kennedy's concern for the nation's poor also broadened in the closing months of his administration. The downtrodden and unemployed in rural Appalachia had captured his attention during the 1960 campaign and held it while the President pushed through an area redevelopment bill. But if Kennedy continued to associate indigency with the countryside, officials at the Council of Economic

Advisers, the Justice Department, which was running an experimental program aimed at stemming juvenile delinquency, and at other agencies were focusing on the urban dimensions of poverty. By the fall of 1963 schemes for a "war on poverty" were well advanced and awaiting the President's review.[114] The interrelated problems of race and poverty would occupy the nation's headlines for the remainder of the decade.

Kennedy would not be alive to witness or guide these developments, but he did leave a valuable legacy for America's cities. In terms of substantive achievements, the Kennedy record was very slim: a housing act that widened well-worn paths and a strengthened housing agency that still experienced great difficulties in translating the fine generalities of federal legislation into sound, workable programs. Perhaps the biggest step forward of the Kennedy years as far as the cities were concerned was taken not by the legislative or Executive Branches, although the latter did lend a helping hand, but by the Supreme Court when it struck a mortal blow against malapportioned state legislatures. In the end, however, the New Frontier's contribution cannot be measured by a short list of acts and actions; rather, it must be gauged by intangibles. After a decade of drift, the New Frontier started the wheels of change moving again; the sharp and sometimes bitter debate of 1961–62 stood in contrast to the academic musings of the 1950s. Thanks to Kennedy, a seat at the cabinet table for cities was an idea whose time had come. Symbolically, the articulate and urbane young Chief Executive made the country more appreciative of its metropolitan future, just as his predecessor had represented the nation's rural past. "Kennedy will be remembered for many things," observed a political scientist a few months after the President's death, "but in the long run, it may well be that he will be best remembered as the first President to understand the implications of the metropolitan revolution in the United States and as the first to try to do something about it." [115]

10

Cities in the Great Society

The modern city can be the most ruthless enemy of the good life, or it can be its servant. The choice is up to this generation of Americans. For this is truly the time of decision for the American city.

Lyndon B. Johnson (1965)

It was a pleasant September morning and the White House Rose Garden was filled with the 150 distinguished guests the President had invited to attend the bill-signing ceremonies. "We are bringing into being today a very new and needed instrument to serve all the people of America," declared Lyndon B. Johnson. "The America of our Founding Fathers was, of course," the country-reared President observed, "a rural America, and the virtues and values of our rural heritage have shaped and strengthened the American character for all of our 189 years. Our debt to this heritage is deep and abiding, and we shall honor it always." But the day when "America was the land of the farmer, the woodsman, the hunter and mountaineer" was gone, never to return. "In less than a lifetime"—in less than the President's own fifty-seven years—America had become "a highly urbanized nation" and it was up to this generation to "face the many meanings of this new America." The United States confronted physical and spiritual challenges of awesome dimensions; these challenges had to be met, Johnson claimed, if "our cities and our new urban age [were not to become] symbols of a sordid, nightmare society." And then with more than a score of pens, the President affixed his signature to the act establishing the Department of Housing and Urban Development.

I

Intense despair and widespread apathy characterized public discussion of urban topics in the first half of the 1960s. Most of the academics drawn into the urban studies field since the late 1950s tended to paint a gloomy picture of the future. "The approved way to talk about cities these days," Paul Ylvisaker of the Ford Foundation declared in 1961, "is to speak solemnly, sadly, ominously, and fearfully about their problems. You don't rate as an expert on the city unless you foresee its doom." [1] Justifying their decision to dedicate the Winter 1965 issue to "Urban Problems and Prospects," the editors of *Law and Contemporary Problems* observed:[2]

Even a casual glance at back and current numbers of the nation's journals of opinion and at recent publications of both trade and scholarly books reveals that a great amount of attention has already been devoted to the "urban crisis" in the United States, and much of it in the past several years.

But this growing volume of literature struck a responsive chord with only a very limited audience. Noting that "practically any five-point list of the Great Problems of our Contemporary Civilization is likely to include, in one cryptic variation or another, a reference to the problems of urban living," the Harvard economist Raymond Vernon commented:[3]

For all the chorus of protest, however, most Americans seem strangely unaroused. Each year, they buy a few hundred thousand more picture windows, seed a few hundred thousand more lawns. The decay of the central cities barely concerns them; the cries of strangling congestion stir them only briefly; even the subject of mounting taxes, an exposed nerve in the structure of local politics, does not seem to have the capacity to bring them shouting into the streets.

The differing perceptions of the intellectuals and the general populace help explain this paradox. Social critics were inclined to see the flaws of the metropolitan system: the maze of overlapping governments; the waste of resources; the lack of planning; and the obvious signs of deterioration in the environment. Committed to high standards, these academics and urban professionals were distressed by what they felt was the gap between what the nation could do and what it was actually doing with its cities; they were unimpressed by the findings of a Twentieth Century Fund study that the population of the Northeastern megalopolis was "on the average, the richest, best educated, best housed, and best serviced group of similar size in the world." [4] Rather, many intellectuals subscribed to the view that "by any sane and humane criterion, the quality of life in American cities is a disgrace." [5] Beyond the sad physical state of the city, there was the disheartening spiritual decline of urban society. Instead of serving as the center of a dynamic civilization, cities were responsible for the sterile, homogenized nature of American thinking and behavior. "The Greek dream of the city as a teacher of men," lamented one writer, "is not merely unfulfilled: it is forgotten." [6]

The academics often spoke in cataclysmic terms. Publication of Lewis Mumford's massive *The City in History* (1961) provided a renewed hearing for those who warned that the growing trend toward large urban agglomerations was hastening the day of final judgment. "We have reached the point," declared a sympathetic reviewer of Mumford's tome, "where the absolute extinction of the city is conceivable on a global basis. After Megalopolis the final Spenglerian stages of cultural disintegration are Tyrannopolis, the city of parasitic Caesarism, and Necropolis, the city of death." [7]

Praising a book entitled *Sick Cities* (1963), one social critic claimed that the author's recital of "horror" stories about air and water pollution, traffic congestion, poor educational opportunities, and crime was enough "to make any lay reader instantly and passionately concerned with questions of his own survival." [8] So unmistakable was the cities' desperate predicament, contended a leading city planner in 1963, that "today there is unanimous agreement that a severe urban crisis exists." [9]

In fact, there was no such consensus. National opinion polls indicated little public anxiety about or even awareness of the alleged "urban crisis." [10] To the mass of citizens the harsh opinions and dire predictions of the intellectuals seemed incomprehensible. Instead of decline, the majority of urban Americans believed that living conditions had improved over the past two decades. Since the end of World War II, urban dwellers had had reasonably secure employment, enlarged opportunities to buy their own homes, and a chance to send their children to college. The highways might be crowded, but at least the typical urban dweller now possessed his own car and the vacation time to enjoy it. The air might be dirty and the nearby streams polluted, but how often did the smog and odors really become offensive? Schools on double- and triple-sessions were intolerable and the feeling was that something had to be done; yet new schools were rising everywhere to accommodate the baby boom. It was difficult for urban residents to get greatly excited about prophecies of impending doom when the personal experiences of most pointed to greater and greater material acquisition. [11]

The professional and the man-on-the-street each saw ample justification for his portrayal of the urban scene. For the average citizen, the dramatic comeback of central business districts, for example, seemed to offer concrete evidence that the old metropolises would have bright futures. Fueled by the longest economic upswing on record plus increased federal spending under Title I, the "urban renaissance" had picked up momentum in the early 1960s. "As a result of combined private and public efforts," noted *Business Week* in 1964, [12]

shiny new towers thrust skyward in nearly every major city. Massive efforts
to spruce up and rehabilitate are beginning to pay off. More attention is paid
to esthetic values, to good design and planning, to light and air, and green
spaces. Cultural, recreational, and educational complexes play an important
role in reshaping Downtown U.S.A. Profitable commercial and residential
ventures have raised assessed values and tax revenues for many a sorely
strained budget.

About a third of Boston was in some stage of the urban renewal
process; Philadelphia had seventy separate projects underway; and
Houston was planning to rebuild 10 per cent of its downtown area
without a cent of federal aid. To some commentators this surge of
new life appeared to be "the most remarkable chapter in the
remarkable history of the modern city." [13] "Whatever its defects in
practice," the American correspondent of *The Economist* reported,
"the vision of urban renewal is a noble one and on a continental
scale; there is nothing like it anywhere else." [14]

But there was another, far less radiant side to the urban picture.
Although the new construction added to municipal tax rolls, it could
not by itself relieve the stresses on local budgets. Urban government
spending in the mid-1960s was double that of a decade earlier;
inflation and the demands of affluent Americans for better and
greater municipal services were primarily responsible for this jump.
From coast to coast it was the old story of narrow local revenue
bases, tightfisted state governments, and occasional taxpayer revolts.
Acute financial stringency was not common, but as the 1960s
progressed there was growing interest in revenue-sharing schemes.[15]

Suburbs, as well as the central cities, suffered from these
budgetary woes, but while the capacity of the fringe areas to cope
with these difficulties rose over time, that of the core districts
declined. By 1965 the suburbs had replaced the central cities as the
place called home by the largest number of Americans, and
increasingly these people did their shopping and found employment
in the suburbs too.[16] In general, the suburbs attracted the more
prosperous segment of the population: whereas 59.9 per cent of
metropolitan families with incomes under $3,000 lived in core cities,

54.8 per cent of those with incomes over $10,000 lived in suburbs.[17] Due to the size of the core cities and their more fully developed network of services, central-city per capita expenditures were, over-all, 21 per cent higher than those of the suburbs, but in the crucial area of education, the fringe districts were outspending the core cities by $125 per pupil ($574 to $449).[18] As the preponderance of disadvantaged children who needed special attention lived in the cities, this difference in spending highlighted the deficiencies and inequities in the administration of metropolitan areas. Declared the Advisory Commission on Intergovernmental Relations in 1965: "In twentieth century America—urban America—good fences do not make good neighbors."

A further cloud on the urban landscape was the changing racial complexion of central cities. Negro out-migration from the South dropped significantly in 1960–63, but the movement of whites from the central cities picked up. By 1966 non-whites accounted for about 23 per cent of the population of cities over 250,000, nearly double the figure for 1950.[19] Unskilled, discriminated against in the hunt for jobs and housing, and often unable to adjust to urban conditions, many minority group members ended up on municipal relief rolls. Welfare spending showed the largest percentage increase of any item in the budgets of the nation's forty-three largest cities between 1960 and 1966; Aid for Dependent Children caseloads in 121 urban counties rose 31 per cent between 1960 and 1964.[20] Complaints about rising welfare costs were frequently voiced on the local level, but there was little national discussion of this issue or that of poverty among urban blacks before 1964. The civil rights drive of the first half of the 1960s focused on clearing away the legal barriers to Negro social and political equality in the South, not on the obstacles preventing blacks from "making it" economically in the great urban centers of the North.[21] *Fortune* editor Charles Silberman was breaking relatively new ground for the intellectual community when he observed in 1962: "Speeding the Negro's integration into American life—helping the *big-city* Negroes move up into the great American middle class—is the largest and most urgent piece of

public business facing the United States today." [22] The counsel of
Silberman and other prophets would go unheeded as long as the
ghettos remained quiet.

II

The course Lyndon B. Johnson would chart between the doom-
sayers and the complacent was unclear when he succeeded to the
Presidency in November 1963. John Kennedy had occupied the
middle ground, utilizing the rhetoric of crisis, but not redirecting
significant national resources to urban areas. Whether Johnson
would even employ the rhetoric appeared doubtful since the Texan
seemed to be the cultural-intellectual antithesis of the man from
Massachusetts. "If Kennedy gave the White House the best flavors
of Boston, from its Irish vigor to its Harvard polish," a journalist has
noted, "Lyndon Johnson [brought] to the White House the manner
and style of rural America." [23] A product of the hill country of the
Lone Star State, a region that was only a century removed from
being the preserve of roving Indians, Johnson had been raised in a
community of less than 1000 people. Its rutted dirt streets were lined
with low rickety buildings. Although a series of government positions kept Johnson in Washington for most of the thirty years before
he entered the White House, he still did not feel at ease in the
Northeastern megalopolis of which the capital was a part.[24] Johnson's rural background made him uncomfortable in cities, but it also
sensitized him to an outstanding urban problem: poverty. The hill
country is poor country, and Johnson, his own family not far above
penury during his youth, developed a deep compassion for those at
the lower rungs of the economic ladder. As a freshman congressman
in the late 1930s, Johnson worked hard to get the nation's first public
housing project under the 1937 act for the biggest city in his district,
Austin.[25] Two decades later, as Senate majority leader, he used his
legislative wizardry to assist the poor by gaining congressional
approval for public housing appropriations most liberals thought
impossible to pass. But Northern liberals also found Johnson's

penchant for accommodation and compromise infuriating. For instance, in 1959, as the majority leader, he had supported amendments cutting $250 million from the omnibus housing bill in a vain attempt to avoid an Eisenhower veto condemning the Democrats as excessive spenders.[26] Because of his failure to challenge the Republicans aggressively on the domestic front, and because of his Southern image, few urban liberals backed Johnson in his campaign for the Democratic Presidential nomination in 1960. Commenting upon a Johnson visit to New York that winter, a columnist for a local paper wrote: "Lyndon Johnson in Brooklyn is almost as pathetic a spectacle as a Brooklyn congressman in Washington. Neither has the slightest thing to do with the reality of the environment." [27]

When fate placed Lyndon Johnson in the White House three years later, the Texan still felt his estrangement from metropolitan America and he turned to the intellectual community for advice. Among the first to receive the Presidential summons was Princeton historian Eric F. Goldman. In the course of a rambling conversation with Johnson in December 1963, Goldman observed that "our cities, now heading for such disarray, appeared certain to be a prime problem in the years ahead." His mind clearly on something else, Johnson nevertheless murmured: "The cities, yes. They are something I am going to have to learn a lot about." To educate himself on this and other matters, the President enlisted Goldman to serve as his link to the "best minds" in the country.[28]

Goldman's "domestic brains trust" proved to be of limited value. Although its members included some of the brightest luminaries in the academic universe, most were not the type of idea men the President could understand. Johnson desired proposals that could be transformed immediately into legislation; what they gave him were grand concepts more appropriate to philosophy than to statute books. The functioning of the Goldman group was further hampered by the President's obsession with secrecy. By the summer of 1964, the brains trust had been phased out.[29]

Some of the group's bold designs, however, found expression in the commencement address, written by White House aide Richard

Goodwin, the President delivered at the University of Michigan in May 1964. Two months before, at a dinner celebrating the St. Louis Bicentennial, Johnson had declared that "our cities are in crisis." At Michigan, the President put this crisis in the perspective of American history and his vision of the future—The Great Society:

For a century we labored to settle and subdue a continent. For half a century we called upon unbounded invention and untiring industry to create an order of plenty for all of our people. . . . The challenge of the next half century is whether we have the wisdom to use that wealth to enrich and elevate our national life, and to advance the quality of our American civilization.

Johnson proposed to begin constructing this Great Society "in our cities, in our countryside, and in our classrooms." As to the first, the President noted that over the remainder of the twentieth century urban populations would double and the nation would have "to build homes, highways, and facilities equal to all those built since the country was settled." But it was not simply a matter of "rebuilding the entire urban United States"; rather, it was the task of the new generation "to make the American city a place where [people] will come, not only to live, but to live the good life." Few were finding the good life in the cities in 1964; "the catalog of ills" was long. "Our society will never be great," Johnson told the graduates, "until our cities are great. Today the frontier of imagination and innovation is inside those cities and not beyond their borders." [30]

The Johnson administration now had its guiding theme, but it still lacked definite proposals to realize the Great Society. To supply these ideas, Johnson announced plans for the creation of "working groups." Unlike the abandoned brains trust, these new panels would be under the direction of the President's chief political aide, Bill Moyers, and influential speech writer, Goodwin. Nor would there be a total reliance on academics; the President wanted the groups to "think big" but in a practical sort of way. Launched in the summer of 1964, this study project was supposed to furnish Johnson with material for his election campaign, the 1965 legislative agenda, and the years beyond.[31] For his 1964 legislative program, however, the President had been obliged to look elsewhere.

III

"Let us continue," Johnson advised Congress and the nation five days after Kennedy's assassination, and the President's 1964 housing proposals adhered to this dictum. The program that the Housing and Home Finance Agency had prepared for Kennedy now merely carried the Johnson imprint. The President's message on housing, transmitted to Congress in late January, attracted somewhat more attention than usual because it was the new President's first communication to the legislature on a single subject, but aside from this pace-setting role, the Chief Executive's requests generally followed familiar lines. Johnson recommended extension of public housing for another four years so as to add 240,000 units to the stock of decent low-rent dwellings. Not all this money would be earmarked for new construction, however; on the basis of its demonstration program, HHFA wanted local authorities to be able to purchase or lease existing private housing as a way of cutting costs and speeding up the accommodation of poor families. For urban renewal, the administration urged another $1.4 billion over two years, plus additional aid for displaced small businesses and families, including the provision of rent subsidies for up to two years for citizens of low and moderate income. Johnson also endorsed Kennedy's previous appeal for mass transit assistance and the establishment of an urban affairs cabinet department, renamed for the moment, Housing and Community Development.

The one big surprise in the proposed legislation was the President's espousal of a federal program to encourage the building of "totally new and complete communities." Urbanization, Johnson explained, had been going on in "a sprawling, space-consuming, unplanned and uneconomical way"; to insure that "our communities become desirable places in which to live, future growth must take place in a more orderly fashion." He proposed extending grants and loans to states and localities for the planning and provision of necessary public facilities and extending Federal Housing Administration loan guarantees for private developers. This program, HHFA Administrator Robert Weaver claimed, represents "the first time we've come to grips with a land policy." [32]

But Congress proved to be in no mood to consider seriously the new towns idea or reforms in public housing. The men on Capitol Hill had election-year fever and were anxious to get home and onto the campaign trail. They were not prepared to let the Public Housing Administration operate in the private housing market until they had more time to examine the implications of this step for business and city neighborhoods. Nor were the legislators ready to explore thoroughly, much less pass, a new towns proposal that enjoyed little organized backing. Except for HHFA, no group, in or out of government, expressed much interest in the scheme. An architectural critic had called the contemplated enterprise perhaps "the most significant, in terms of planned growth, that this country has ever seen," [33] but it was for that very reason that most housing industry spokesmen opposed the program. Fearing restrictions on their freedom to build, they denounced the proposal as another "federal boondoggle" that would lead to "windfall profits for those developers who happen to be in the good graces of the administration." [34] Citing the "complex and far-reaching nature" of the new towns measure, the housing subcommittees in both chambers kept it bottled up.

Intensive, old-fashioned lobbying, however, did free a long standing administration request—federal aid for mass transit—for floor action and passage. In 1962 Kennedy had asked for $500 million in grants to help finance mass transportation improvements in metropolitan areas. Neither house made any move on the bill that year, so Kennedy revived his suggestion when the 88th Congress met the following January. After slashing the grant authorization to $350 million, the Senate passed the measure on a party line vote in April, but over on the House side the Democratic leadership doubted it could count upon the loyalty of the rural, conservative rank-and-file. The proposal was allowed to sit in the Rules Committee for a year, practically forgotten by the White House and its lieutenants on Capitol Hill. However, the transit companies and the mayors refused to concede defeat. They organized the Urban Passenger Transportation Association and hired an experienced Washington lobbyist to press their case. With the help of some urban and suburban Republicans, the association was able to convince the Speaker in May 1964 that the necessary votes were in hand. And they were: on the all important motion to recommit, thirty-three Republicans supplied the margin of victory in the 215–190 tally.[35] Eight years after the Interstate Highway System was approved, other modes of urban transportation had gained access, although in a much more limited way, to the federal Treasury.

The closeness of the mass transit triumph and the critical role played by G.O.P. congressmen on that occasion seemed to vindicate the White House's decision not to push the departmental issue in 1964. Although the word "urban" had been dropped to disassociate it from the needs of the big cities and the term "affairs" replaced by the more specific and functionally descriptive "development," [36] the President's legislative strategists still did not feel that memories of the Kennedy versus Republican-Southern Democrats clash of 1962 had been sufficiently dissipated. Unlike the mass transit measure, the departmental bill did not have an aggressive lobby behind it. White House aides reasoned that it would be better to take their chances with the Congress to be elected in the fall.[37]

One fight the administration could not avoid in 1964 involved urban renewal. This controversy had been brewing for years, as both liberals and conservatives became increasingly disturbed by the program's operations. Liberals were upset by Title I's poor record in helping those it displaced, especially minority groups. Too often, went the frequently repeated charge, urban renewal had meant "negro removal." [38] For their part, the conservatives argued that urban renewal had turned into a great pork barrel, with favored developers receiving government subsidies and thereby putting private investors in non-renewal areas at a severe disadvantage. Pointing to the large amounts of cleared renewal land still lying vacant, these foes of the program contended that "far from halting the spread of blight, urban renewal actually has encouraged it." From the conservative perspective, the "most striking achievement" of Title I was the "wholesale bulldozing of human and property rights." Urban renewal was nothing more than "eminent domain— and bureaucratic arrogance—run wild." [39]

The administration's reform proposals were designed to end the complaints of the liberals. Since 1956 the Federal Government had been making relocation payments to all uprooted families to cover at least part of the costs of moving; the HHFA amendments would go beyond that, helping those in the low-income category to find decent accommodations by offering extra subsidies to local public housing authorities who took them in, or by paying for a portion of their rent in private dwellings. With the relocation expense system well-established, Congress accepted the rehousing scheme, after reducing its scope, without much debate.

The Republicans, however, sought more far-reaching changes. Conservative business groups disliked urban renewal's emphasis upon the central business district because they felt that localities could redevelop these areas profitably without using the taxpayers' money. Their main fire was directed at the statutory exemption to the "predominantly residential" requirement, first set at 10 per cent of federal grants by the Republican Congress in 1954 and then raised to 30 per cent in 1961 at the request of the Kennedy administration. These exemptions had been instigated by the mayors and powerful downtown commercial and office interests who linked the economic health of the cities to the revival of the central business district. Mobilizing their allies in Congress, this formidable coalition turned back the Republican challenge.

Another G.O.P. complaint met a more favorable response. Although the 1954 Housing Act had laid special stress on rehabilitation as a less expensive means of reversing urban decay, most municipalities continued to use the clearance and rebuilding procedures set forth by the 1949 act. To fiscal conservatives, this latter method seemed unduly expensive and disruptive of neighborhood patterns, especially as it affected the patronage of local merchants. With the assistance of social welfare organizations, which hoped that greater reliance on rehabilitation would ease the rehousing dilemma, the Republicans were able to insert a prohibition against the demolition of additional buildings unless municipalities could demonstrate that the objectives of the plan could not be achieved through rehabilitation of the project area. A new program of low-interest loans to slum homeowners to fix up their properties was also started at the Republicans' suggestion.[40]

As passed, the Housing Act of 1964 was essentially a stopgap measure. Neither the White House nor the Congress was eager for a full-scale urban debate; the President, because he did not have a program he truly could call his own yet, the legislature, because it was uncertain of which way the political winds were blowing. The agreement between the White House and Capitol Hill provided for a one-year extension of the present programs: another $725 million for urban renewal and 37,500 units of new public housing. Hardbitten conservatives indicated that they had no intention of letting up their fight against Title I, but the general reaction to the finished product in urban circles was favorable. A significant dissent, however, came from the editorial board at the *New York Times*. "Traditionally," the paper noted, "housing bills have been an uneasy compromise between the demands of the private real estate industry and the moral claims of the slum-dwellers, the elderly and the minority groups, with Congress usually more responsive to the former than to the latter." The 1964 act, according to the *Times*, followed this formula, thereby raising serious questions about the Great Society:[41]

If the big city is to remain a place for ordinary people to live as well as work, and if the suburbs are to become more than an ugly sprawl and a commuter's nightmare, the President is going to have to lift the next housing bill out of the ruts of compromise and put it on a new intellectual level. The public interest demands major changes in housing policy and urban planning.

Whether the Great Society could meet that challenge depended first of all, of course, on whether Lyndon Johnson maintained his hold on the White House in November.

IV

In the immediate aftermath of its heartbreaking 1960 defeat, the Republican party showed signs of interest in making the cities the main political battleground in 1964. A study prepared by the Republican National Committee's Research Division in early 1961 concluded that the greatest fall-off in G.O.P. strength the previous November had occurred in metropolitan areas; the study seemed to suggest that Vice-President Nixon had lost the election in the urban North. The Research Division also pointed out that in 1964 eleven states, seven of them with large concentrations of metropolitan voters, would cast 268 electoral votes, just two less than the number needed to win.[42] Afraid that this "Big City Gap" threatened to doom the G.O.P.'s chances of ever recapturing the White House, the National Committee, in January 1961, established a group, headed by Ray Bliss of Ohio, to determine "what steps have to be taken everywhere to erode the monolithic Democratic big city vote." [43]

The designation of Bliss and the restricted range of his group's work reflected the deep strains within the Republican party. The Ohioan was a political technician who left the definition of policies to the candidates; organization was Bliss's specialty and it was the mechanics of campaigning in the cities that occupied the attention of the Committee on Big City Politics. This avoidance of issues was the product, in part, of the G.O.P.'s belief that diligent activity at the grass roots would yield results: "What the hell," National Committee Chairman William Miller explained when asked what positions his party was developing to meet the political realities of megalopolis, "we need muscle and money, not a new image." [44] That the Republicans were short on bodies was undeniable—in Philadelphia, for example, of the 1600 precincts in the city about 500 were

unmanned by Republicans on Election Day 1960—but the decision
to sidestep policy was dictated by a more pressing reason: the fear of
dividing a party already split between moderates like New York
Governor Nelson Rockefeller and conservatives gathered around
Arizona Senator Barry Goldwater.[45]

Hardly had the 1960 ballots been counted when Goldwater and
Rockefeller began charting sharply divergent strategies for their
party. The Arizonan emphasized the fallacy of trying to outpromise
liberal Democrats. He argued that Republicans should instead seek
to enlarge their base in the conservative heartland of America on a
platform of limited government and move aggressively to widen
their inroads in the South by championing states' rights.[46] Rockefeller, on the other hand, stressed that 75 per cent of the electorate lived
in urban areas and that the future of the party hinged on how well
the G.O.P. could demonstrate that "we can do the best job for
them." [47] Top Rockefeller aides attached special importance to a
campaign in which the G.O.P. identified itself more clearly with the
interests of minority groups. Condemning Goldwater for, in effect,
writing off the black vote, one adviser to the governor declared:
"The Senator from Arizona has, I fear, proposed a Republican
requiem in the cities when the challenge and the times require a
Republican reveille." [48]

The Goldwater approach prevailed. At the National Committee's
January 1962 meeting, Bliss outlined an ambitious program for
upgrading party machinery in cities—for example, candidate recruit-
ment, dealing with ethnic blocs and minorities, public relations, the
use of surveys—but the committee did not implement it. Neither of
the party's titular leaders, Eisenhower or Nixon, showed much
concern for making an extra effort to woo city voters, and Chairman
Miller, from a small upstate New York community, was ideologically much closer to Goldwater than to Rockefeller.[49] Rockefeller
himself had to trim his sails to adjust to his party's move toward the
right; he joined the G.O.P.'s conservative spokesmen on Capitol Hill
in denouncing Kennedy's proposal for a Department of Urban
Affairs and Housing in early 1962.[50] While the National Committee's

"operation Dixie" picked up Southern converts, the 102-page Bliss report gathered dust, forgotten and unmourned. It would remain on the shelf as the G.O.P. battled through the primaries and finally chose Goldwater as its candidate for 1964.

Goldwater had metropolitan roots, but he shared little of the intellectuals' apprehensiveness of the urban future. The metropolitan area of Phoenix, his home town, had experienced phenomenal growth in the post-war era: its population jumped about two-and-one-half times between 1950 and 1964, going from 332,000 to 820,000. But this booming metropolis was not yet as plagued as the crowded cities of the East with noise, congestion, and friction. Expansion was the key note and the propelling force was unbridled private enterprise. Almost alone of the nation's larger communities, Phoenix had no urban renewal plan and no housing code. Believing that more freedom for individual initiative and greater local autonomy was what the older cities needed too, Goldwater had voted against every omnibus housing bill during his twelve-year senatorial career.[51]

The Republican platform approved at the San Francisco convention reflected these views. "The administration has moved," the G.O.P. charged in a section on "weakening responsibility," [52]

through such undertakings as its so-called war on poverty, accelerated public works, and the New Communities Program in the 1964 Housing proposal, to establishing new Federal offices duplicating existing agencies, bypassing the state capitals, thrusting aside local government, and siphoning off to Washington the administration of private citizen and community affairs.

Disregarding the warning of the Republican mayor of Louisville, who appeared in behalf of the USCM-AMA, that "the urban revolution cannot be satisfied with outdated and old-fogey resentment against city and federal cooperation," [53] the G.O.P. pledged to transfer federal taxes and programs to the states to meet "pressing urban and suburban problems." The party also promised revitalization of municipal and county governments throughout America by encouraging them, and private citizens as well, to develop new solutions of their major concerns through a streamlining and modernizing of state and local processes of government, and by a renewed consciousness of their ability to reach these solutions, not through federal action, but through their own capabilities.

For good measure, the Republicans endorsed a Constitutional amendment to override the Supreme Court and allow states to take other factors besides population into consideration when apportioning one house of a bicameral legislature.[54]

The Democrats who assembled across the continent in Atlantic City a month later adopted a radically different, but at the same time familiar, platform. Unlike the Republican document, the Democrats' declaration of policy contained a section on "The City." Repeating the projection of a doubling of the urban population by the year 2000 made by the President in his Michigan speech, the platform proclaimed: "The vitality of our cities is essential to the healthy growth of American civilization." From there it went on to pledge fulfillment of the 1949 Housing Act's goal of "a decent home for every American family," and continuing aid, as outlined in the 1960 platform, for urban renewal, mass transit, open spaces, "and other programs for our metropolitan areas." Last, but not least, the Democrats expressed the belief that "because our cities and suburbs are so important to the welfare of all our people, a department devoted to urban affairs should be added to the President's cabinet." [55]

Urban issues did not play a significant role in the campaign that followed. After the early controversy created by his apparent call for the end of social security, Goldwater tended to speak in generalities on the dangers of big government. Even these remarks were overshadowed by the furor surrounding the Republican's attitude toward the employment of nuclear weapons; Goldwater spent much of his time trying to erase the impression that he would have a heavy finger on the atomic button. In his travels, the G.O.P. standard-bearer stumped mainly in states south and west of the Ohio River; only once did he venture to that Babylon on the Hudson, New York City. There, before a wildly enthusiastic throng that packed the old Madison Square Garden, Goldwater denounced what he called "political Daddyism": "Lyndon Johnson and his curious crew seem to believe that progress in this country is best served simply and directly through the ever-expanding gift power of the everlastingly growing Federal Government." [56] Despite his limited campaigning, the President made two visits to New York and his remarks in the Garden struck a theme quite different from Goldwater's. Describing the Great Society as "the concern for the quality of the life of each person in America," Johnson declared that "nowhere is that concern more urgent than in the American city. . . . The work of the American city is a challenge that is worthy of the finest traditions of American liberalism." Winning that test, the President said, would require the development of "a new set of relationships between the Federal Government and the American city." [57] He did not, however, elaborate any further and over the last ten days before the election Johnson spoke about little besides war and peace.

Residents of metropolitan areas helped swell the Johnson landslide. Well over half of the President's 8.5 million national plurality was rolled up in these urban regions. Of the country's sixty-one largest cities, Goldwater carried just five, all but one of them in the South; he took Phoenix by less than 600 votes. In 1960 Nixon had taken the suburbs by a net vote of 757,000; four years later Goldwater ran 2.68 million ballots behind Johnson.[58] Swept into office along with the President were two more Democratic senators and thirty-seven new Democratic representatives, giving Johnson 2 to 1 majorities in both chambers. With this added strength on Capitol Hill, Johnson now had the opportunity to realize his dream of the Great Society—just what shape it would take, however, remained to be determined.

V

Specific proposals for accomplishing the Great Society were nearing completion by election day. A month after the President's Michigan address in May, White House aides had assembled thirteen task forces on domestic topics, ranging from the preservation of natural beauty to the development of an anti-recession policy. Since the very aim of the task force concept was to break away from the models of the past, members were recruited from outside the federal establishment; bypassing agency heads, many of whom Johnson had inherited from Kennedy, would also make it easier to put the Johnson brand on whatever programs emerged.[59] Although there was a conscious effort to avoid loading down the task forces with academics, the eleven-man Task Force on Metropolitan and Urban Problems did have a distinctly intellectual coloration. Six of the participants, including the chairman, Robert Wood of M.I.T., were on university faculties; another headed a psychiatric research hospital; and still another directed the Ford Foundation's urban affairs program. Only one practicing politician was included, along with a prominent newspaper editor, and a financial analyst for the National Association of Mutual Savings Banks.[60] Their recommendations were ready for Presidential consideration by early December.

The 1964 Task Force on Metropolitan and Urban Problems produced the first high-level federal examination of cities not set in the context of housing.[61] Unlike the earlier congressional and Executive efforts, which had come up with the public housing and urban renewal programs, and unlike its Kennedy-created predecessor, the Johnson task force was not interested so much in juggling interest rates to spur housing construction or in keeping the building industry active as it was in making America's metropolitan centers fit places to live:

The provision of choices in social, economic and political life is the prime function of a great urban community. Now that the United States is a nation of cities of all sorts and sizes, the maintenance of free choices for its citizens is an increasingly complex affair. But the need to ensure options in choice of residence, place of work, meaningful leisure time activities, and effective civic participation was never greater.

To "preserve and extend these options in an era of population growth and city building unmatched in our history," the task force sought to offer "new approaches in national public policy responsive to the dramatically new kinds of urban communities that are now evolving." [62]

While many of the task force's recommendations necessarily dealt with the physical structure of urban areas, the group placed special emphasis upon improving the social environment. More and better housing and attractive downtowns were very important goals, but they were not enough; cities were conglomerations of people and neighborhoods, and the needs of urban residents went beyond decent homes and fancy stores. Safe streets, a good education, adequate recreational facilities, and the opportunity to live wherever one chose had to be guaranteed before the urban Great Society could be achieved. In order to meet these objectives, the task force urged extension of the Executive order barring discrimination in housing, a new program to construct community centers especially designed for social purposes, the inauguration of block grants to municipalities to allow localities to determine their own priorities in social services, and a federal assistance program to upgrade the training of law enforcement personnel. These aids would be conditioned upon local preparation of a Social Renewal Plan (SRP). Complementing the Title I Workable Program, which required cities to mobilize their resources to reverse the deterioration of the urban physical plant, the SRP would focus municipal attention on human renewal.[63]

The task force also warned that existing federal developmental programs should be reviewed with an eye on their social dimension. Criticizing urban renewal for concentrating on the central business district and for operating almost wholly divorced from welfare programs, the panel called for a "much broader strategy: long-term, city-wide, in some respects region-wide, and above all more directly geared to social goals." Restating Title I's primary objective as a "good home in good neighborhoods for all families," the task force declared that urban renewal had to be viewed as "an on-going process concerned as much with providing essential public facilities, assistance to individual families and altering the social aspects of neighborhoods as with the execution of specific physical plans." The public housing program, to which the group paid a backhanded compliment by labelling it "the only positive tool since its enactment in 1937 for the rehousing of slum dwellers," also required an overhaul. The panel suggested modifications to bring the program closer to the mechanisms of the private housing market; among its many proposals was a system of rent supplements, whereby the Federal Government would help low- and moderate-income families cover the costs of suitable accommodations in private housing. Despite Congress's lack of interest in the administration's new towns scheme in 1964, the task force advocated that another try be made. As in other areas, it also recommended that any assistance furnished under this program be contingent upon the drafting of a general regional plan including both physical and social components.[64]

This stress upon the human element in urban revival served as the basis for Johnson's March 1965 special message to Congress on "The Nation's Cities"—the first by any President on that subject. While striking the familiar theme used in previous housing messages that the convergence of "two giant and dangerous forces, growth and decay," in urban areas had created "one of the most critical domestic problems of the United States," Johnson departed from the usual script when he delineated the nature of the crisis and his objectives:

Let us be clear about the core of this problem. The problem is people and the quality of the lives they lead. We want to build not just housing units, but neighborhoods; not just to construct schools, but to educate children; not just to raise income but to create beauty and end the poisoning of our environment. We must extend the range of choices available to all our people so that all, and just not the fortunate, can have access to decent homes and schools, to recreation and to culture. We must work to overcome the forces which divide our people and erode the vitality which comes from the partnership of those with diverse incomes and interests and backgrounds.

In terms never before used by a resident of the White House, Johnson expressed his hopes for what the future would bring:

The American city should be a collection of communities where every member has a right to belong. It should be a place where every man feels safe on his streets and in the house of his friends. It should be a place where each individual's dignity and self-respect is strengthened by the respect and affection of his neighbors. It should be a place where each of us can find the satisfaction and warmth which comes only from being a member of the community of man. This is what man sought at the dawn of civilization. It is what we seek today.

Admitting that the roads toward fulfillment of this vision would be long and difficult, Johnson presented Congress with proposals on how to begin the journey. They ranged from the establishment of a temporary national commission to study building codes and zoning laws to new incentives to metropolitan cooperation. Many of the suggestions were simply revisions of already operating programs; the open spaces endeavor started in 1961, for example, would be broadened to permit the acquisition of land for small inner city parks and squares, malls, playgrounds, and gardens. Public housing was to be extended, but with greater reliance upon the purchase or lease of existing private units. Bigger sums would be spent on urban renewal and although the central business district would continue to receive assistance, more and more attention would be shown to "the development of residential areas so that all our tools—from the poverty program to education and construction—can be used together to create meaningful and liveable communities within the city." [65] Johnson also endorsed the task force's suggestions for neighborhood facilities grants and for requiring metropolitan regions to draw up master plans for long-range growth. The President once again asked for aid to new towns, but he placed his greatest faith in rent supplements. An extremely flexible device that would promote integration across income levels and harness the energies of private enterprise, rent supplements were, Johnson declared, "the most crucial new instrument in our effort to improve the American city."

Even with the administration's lopsided majorities in Congress, some features of Johnson's "far-sighted and far-reaching" [66] program encountered trouble on Capitol Hill. In large measure this was because the administration had broken with past practice in drafting the bill. Previously, omnibus housing legislation had been put together after an informal consensus among the various segments of the private and public housing community had been achieved. None of these groups, however, was invited to the meetings where the 1965 bill was written; only White House staff members, Bureau of the Budget officials, task force representatives, and top HHFA people attended these sessions. The results were programs that either threatened the status quo or failed to live up to the monetary expectations of certain pressure groups. Not having been consulted in the preparatory stages, these organizations felt free to attack the administration's proposals. [67]

The sharpest row occurred over rent supplements. As outlined by the administration, rent supplements were intended to help families in the moderate income category, those earning just enough to make them ineligible for public housing, but not enough to afford decent private accommodations. Under the administration program, the Federal Government, through the Federal Housing Administration, would pay non-profit project owners the difference between 20 per cent of the occupant's income and the full economic rent for the dwelling unit. [68] The 1961 Housing Act had instituted a new program to aid this group, Section 221(d)(3) Below Market Interest Rate (BMIR), in which the Federal National Mortgage Association subsidized mortgages through its purchases on the secondary market. This section, however, was having only a marginal impact because of the general rise in the cost of borrowing money. Financial advisers to the President were afraid that any attempt to modify the BMIR approach to make it more effective would necessarily impose heavy drains on the federal budget. Rent supplements seemed to be a less expensive method and potentially a much more productive one. Since 1961, 221(d)(3) BMIR had underwritten the construction of less than 50,000 units; administration spokesmen estimated that 500,000 new units would be built in the first five years of rent supplements. Some observers believed, although no one from the Executive Branch broached the subject in public, that if this rate of construction could be maintained, it might in time end the need for additional public housing. Through the filtering-down process decent housing would become available to the low-income group in whose behalf less than 600,000 units had been built in the fifteen years since the Housing Act of 1949.[69] A variant of the rent supplement plan had been advocated by a number of housing and banking organizations in the 1940s as a substitute for public housing; many of these groups, along with the mayors, social welfare organizations, and the AFL-CIO, supported the rent supplement idea in principle in 1965.

Attacks on the administration's plans for rent supplements came from three sides. Professionals in the public housing field contended that the public housing financial formula—federal payment of principal and interest on long-term bonds—would be a cheaper way of meeting the needs of the moderate income group. Instead of rent supplements, they recommended combined private-public sponsorship of projects whereby local housing authorities would purchase an interest in privately financed developments for the use of eligible families. To many people, including such a long-time champion of public housing as Senator Paul Douglas (D.-Ill.), the public housers' objections to rent supplements seemed to be the typical bureaucratic response to any new scheme that would end an agency's monopoly of programs.[70] But Douglas, the mayors, and other liberal groups did agree with the professionals on one point: if rent supplements were instituted, they should not be restricted to families of moderate means but made available to poor people as well. It was unconscionable, the liberals believed, to launch another endeavor to help families above the poverty line while the needs of those below it continued unmet. In addition, by reaching further down on the income scale, rent supplements might be able to demolish some of the walls concentrating poor families in central cities.[71] It was rent supplements' potentiality as a tool for "social engineering" that most disturbed conservatives. While raising the traditional cries that government subsidies would kill individual incentive and threaten the homeownership ideal, the conservatives emphasized the danger of "across-the-board economic integration." [72] The rent supplements provision, warned a Republican congressman from New York City, would give the HHFA administrator "far-reaching control that could extend into every nook and cranny of American residential patterns" and allow the Federal Government "to experiment in *reweaving* the national social fabric." Together, the liberals and conservatives succeeded in reversing completely the administration's proposed eligibility standards for rent supplements: that is, instead of specifically excluding families qualified for public housing, the rules passed by Congress limited rent supplements to those families who were entitled to public housing; then, the conservatives alone came within six votes in the House and seven votes in the Senate of defeating the program outright.[73] Johnson's "crucial new instrument to improve the American city" had gotten off to a very shaky start.

The new communities program did not get off to a start at all; in fact, it never even came to a vote. Despite the controversy that swirled around rent supplements, that program at least had some important friends; new towns had none. Since the administration had placed such great stock in rent supplements, Johnson was forced, in order to preserve his prestige, to mobilize his resources to see it through Congress. There was no such commitment on new towns. As far as the White House was concerned, new towns was HHFA's creation; if the agency could not round up support for it, new towns would be offered up as a sacrifice for the rest of the legislative package. But after a year of searching, HHFA had lined up only a small group of "architects, planners and a few idealistic builders with no political muscle." [74] Private interests feared the effects of governmental supervision and the mayors wanted no part of a program that might further spur decentralization. Detroit's Jerome Cavanaugh candidly explained the mayors' position:[75]

My job principally as the Mayor of Detroit is to try and make that city a more attractive place in which to live and retain what industry we have. . . . [T]here is a reluctance on my part—and I admit that I might not be taking the broad view—to encourage the construction of more new suburbia next to my city to be able to compete with me for industry or for housing or anything else.

Citing the necessity for more study, the housing subcommittees in both chambers once again prevented the proposal from reaching the floor.

One beneficiary of the furor over rent supplements was urban renewal. What strength conservatives could muster in the 89th Congress had been expected to be directed against Title I, but with the announcement of the rent supplements plan, conservative energies were diverted to that dispute. Consequently, urban renewal, as had happened in 1949 when the decisive battle raged over public housing, passed through the legislature almost unnoticed.[76] But having prepared themselves for a struggle, the coalition of groups backing Title I—bankers, downtown merchants, mayors—did not let their efforts go to waste. With the blessing of the administration, which had made government-private enterprise cooperation a prime goal, they succeeded in having the exemption from the "predominantly residential" requirement raised to 35 per cent. Instead of reversing the stress on the central business district, the 1965 Housing Act actually added to it.

As passed, the Housing and Urban Development Act of 1965 was placed high on the list of administration triumphs in Congress, alongside Medicare and aid to education. The President had received most of what he had requested: authorizations for rent supplements; 240,000 units of public housing; $2.9 billion for urban renewal; and new programs for neighborhood facilities and urban beautification. It was an extremely happy Lyndon Johnson who predicted to the guests, gathered in the White House Rose Garden to witness the signing of the bill, that "this Act will become known as the single most valuable housing legislation in our history." But as the difficult fight over rent supplements demonstrated, the job of "making the American city a better and more stimulating place to live" would not be an easy one. Even with its unusually large Democratic majorities, the administration had been able to enact only part of its ambitious program. There were still appropriations battles to be won and agreements to be reached with local governments on how the programs that had survived were to be operated. The urban Great Society had cleared its first hurdle in July 1965, but many others remained in the path to its fuller realization.

VI

In sharp contrast to the bruising housing battle, the administration's request for a department of housing and urban development encountered little serious opposition. The Johnson landslide in 1964 had materially weakened the conservative Republican-Southern Democratic coalition in the House that had defeated Kennedy's cabinet proposal in 1961–62. Not one to take unnecessary chances when dealing with Congress, Johnson also made some cosmetic alterations in the Kennedy bill to give it more appeal. The most noticeable concerned the name: instead of Urban Affairs and Housing, Johnson substituted Housing and Urban Development (HUD). By placing housing first, the administration hoped to ease the anxiety of those in the construction industry, especially the home-builders and bankers, who feared that their interests would be submerged in an urban department. Wide misunderstanding about the term "urban affairs" led to the use of the phrase "urban development." Critics of the Kennedy bill had charged that the department would be set up on a geographical rather than a functional basis and that it would eventually include all programs relating to urban problems. Having no such intention in mind, the administration chose the term "development" to indicate that HUD's primary mission extended only to the quality of the physical environment of urban areas.[77] The call for a department of housing and urban development, "to give greater force and effectiveness to our efforts in the cities," topped the list of Presidential recommendations in Johnson's message to Congress on "The Nation's Cities" in March.

For the most part the congressional hearings on the administration measure (S. 1599) proved perfunctory. The usual urban groups—the mayors, public housers, labor unions, and planners—expressed support for the department; more qualified endorsements came from the bankers and home-builders who wanted FHA to be kept intact in the new department. An amendment drawn up by the National Association of Home Builders assigning responsibility for private mortgage operations to one of the assistant secretaries was subsequently adopted, with some changes in language, in both houses. Adamant opposition to S. 1599 was voiced by the realtors, the National Association of Manufacturers, the Chamber of Commerce, and the American Farm Bureau Federation, but a sense of futility ran through their remarks. The administration had the votes and everyone knew it.

With the fate of HUD not really in doubt, Senator Abraham Ribicoff (D.-Conn.), the chairman of the Senate Subcommittee on Executive Reorganization, and the man charged with shepherding S. 1599 through the upper chamber, wanted to be sure that the department was created on an adequate foundation. Questioning Kermit Gordon, the director of the Bureau of the Budget and the administration's chief spokesman for the bill, Ribicoff asked if thought had been given to transferring other, non-HHFA, programs, to HUD:[78]

This Federal Government of ours [noted Ribicoff] is way behind the times. We have a conglomeration; we have functions in one department that belong in another. We are operating basically with a type of governmental structure that goes back to 1933. If we are going to reorganize and do a job in urban affairs, should we not try and do it right?

Gordon, while contending that there were good managerial reasons for not moving such urban-oriented programs as air pollution control and highway construction to HUD, also indicated that the architects of the Great Society were not prepared to push their legislative majorities too far:[79]

I frankly confess that the proposal [S. 1599] was kept as simple as possible. We regard it as a very important objective to establish HUD, and it was our conclusion, which might have been an incorrect one, that the most attractive form in which this could be effected would be a single piece of legislation which would do essentially the job of transforming HHFA to a cabinet-level department.

Ribicoff's interest in "scoring a breakthrough against second generation bureaucracy in the Federal Government" found little favor with the mayors. When the Connecticut senator observed that "if we are going to tackle the problems of cities we should do it right and have a real Department of Urban Affairs and not just a narrowly based department that takes care of housing only," Boston's John Collins responded that the mayors were willing to take HUD as it was as the price for gaining a seat at the cabinet table: "We do not want the hour of decision deferred for eight or ten more years while we study collecting every single federal program that has any direct or indirect effect on cities under one tent." [80] Although Ribicoff remained disturbed at the limited scope of HUD's operations, his committee reported the measure, as the House committee had done earlier, without substantial change.

The debate on the House floor highlighted the contrasts between 1962 and 1965. At issue was not so much whether cities deserved recognition at the loftiest levels of the Federal Government as what form this representation should take. Intransigent conservatives, mainly Republicans, persisted in calling HUD "the first step of a long-range strategy apparently designed to bring the solutions of the day-to-day problems of community life under the direction of centralized government," [81] but the more moderate members of the G.O.P., undoubtedly impressed by the party's dismal showing in urban districts in November 1964, attacked HUD's alleged administrative shortcomings rather than its intended goals. Arguing that HUD's "almost total lack of jurisdiction over urban programs would seem to doom it to becoming merely another bureaucratic maze which would merely confuse the public, employ the faithful, and further waste taxpayer dollars," the Republicans urged instead the creation of an office of urban affairs and community development in the Executive Office of the President. If better coordination was the objective, the Republicans maintained, then a Presidential aide working with a small staff was better equipped to handle the job than a departmental secretary whose agency did not encompass sixty programs operating in urban areas. A White House office, not a circumscribed HUD, would provide the "one stop" service the mayors wanted; policy ideas for urban regions would also be more likely to command Presidential and congressional attention if formulated at 1600 Pennsylvania Avenue rather than at a department downtown.[82] Democrats were prepared to parry this kind of thrust. Since coordination and operations were closely related in urban programs, insisted backers of the administration, it was unwise to separate these functions between line and staff agencies. It would be better to strengthen the authority of the operating agency in the field, HHFA-HUD, and make it the focal point for the consideration and conduct of federal efforts in urban affairs and housing. Managerial experts might disagree on who had won the debate, but the White House had decided that a cabinet department would have more symbolic impact and when it came time to vote, party affiliation was the key determinant: the G.O.P. motion to recommit the HUD bill and replace it with the Republican substitute lost, 259–141.[83]

Action and inaction by the Johnson administration helped move the departmental proposal through the House. Two years of heavy dosages of Presidential rhetoric about federal responsibility to make cities more liveable, plus Johnson's smashing victory in 1964, created the feeling in Washington, if not in the country at large, that the federal role in urban affairs was here to stay and destined to grow bigger. The conservative challenge had been repulsed and repudiated decisively; building of the Great Society, which Johnson had clearly given an urban cast, could now begin. In addition, by remaining silent on his choice for secretary of HUD, Johnson was able to avoid the bitter controversy engendered by Kennedy's designation of Weaver in 1962. Given the passage of the Civil Rights Act of 1964 and the Voting Rights Act of 1965, it is questionable whether any strife would have developed, but Johnson, by making it plain that the field of possible appointees was wide open, prevented the interjection of the racial issue. On the crucial recommittal vote, 73 Southern Democrats, more than five times the number in 1962, lined up behind the administration.[84]

Over on the other side of the Capitol, the Senate ran quickly through the motions of deliberating the measure. Attendance was sparse and debate lackadaisical during the two days when S. 1599 was the Senate's main order of business. The only moment of drama came when G.O.P. Minority Leader Everett Dirksen (Ill.) offered to bet Ribicoff that the establishment of HUD would lead to a proliferation of new federal urban programs. Turning down the wager, Ribicoff readily conceded what three years earlier would have been a damaging and, perhaps, fatal point: HUD was only a beginning; its function was to serve as the center for a growing federal effort to improve the nation's cities. With this issue clarified, the Senate then approved the bill, 57–33.[85] On September 9, 1965, President Johnson signed the act creating the Department of Housing and Urban Development.

11

The Federal Government
and Urban America: 1933–65

The Congress hereby declares that the general welfare and security of the Nation and the health and living standards of our people require, as a matter of national purpose, sound development of the nation's urban communities and metropolitan areas. . . .

Department of Housing and Urban
Development Act (1965)

In 1965, nearly a half-century after the Bureau of the Census reported that the United States had become an urban nation, the Federal Government established a cabinet department "to provide for full and appropriate consideration, at the national level, of the needs and interests of the Nation's communities and of the people who live and work in them." The creation of the Department of Housing and Urban Development articulated a national commitment to the improvement of the urban environment, the environment in which more than two-thirds of the country's people resided, and confirmed the revolution in American federalism that had begun thirty years earlier. Neither the commitment nor the revolution had come easily, however, since each had run counter to the prevailing trends of American ideology and political styles.

I

The lure of greater economic opportunity and wider cultural diversion had drawn Americans into urban centers since the start of colonial settlement. Emotionally, however, Americans remained tied to the farm and small town. Indeed, the more the United States became urbanized, the more appealing was its rural creed. The American city in the first part of the twentieth century presented serious challenges to familiar concepts of liberty and individualism, and the ascendancy of urban political machines raised troubling questions about the future of democratic processes. Explaining the poignant opposition Alfred E. Smith's candidacy for the Presidency in the 1920s aroused across the hinterland, Walter Lippmann observed: "It is inspired by the feeling that the clamorous life of the city should not be acknowledged as the American ideal." As a Minnesota newspaper noted after the Tammany Hall scion's bid for the White House had been rejected by the voters in 1928: "America is not yet dominated by its great cities. Control of its destinies still remains in the smaller communities and rural regions, with their traditional conservative and solid virtues. . . . Main Street is still the principal thoroughfare of the nation." [1]

American migratory habits insured that Al Smith's East Broadway would not replace Main Street in the decades ahead. Thanks in part to the inventive genius of that Michigan farm boy Henry Ford, who declared, "We shall solve the problem of cities by leaving the city," and to national programs of home-mortgage insurance and highway construction, millions of people were able to enjoy the advantages of the big-city while living beyond its physical boundaries. Between 1890 and 1920 the percentage of the nation's population residing in communities of more than 500,000 people more than doubled, jumping from 7.1 per cent to 15.5 per cent; forty years later in 1960 the figure stood at 16 per cent. By contrast, municipalities in the 10–50,000 population group increased their share of the national total from 11.5 per cent to 18.1 per cent during the 1920–60 period. Most of these medium-sized communities were located in suburbia, and, indeed, the suburb had become metropolitan American's surrogate for the small town.[2] Although urbanized, the suburban communities stoutly resisted becoming citified, and suburban political unity, insofar as it existed, was based almost entirely on a common fear of and dislike for the city.

Traditional beliefs about the nature of the federal system, many of them rural in origin, also inhabited a national response to the challenges of urbanization. The Sage of Monticello, Thomas Jefferson, summed up these ideas when he wrote: "Were we directed from Washington when to sow, and when to reap, we should soon want bread." The grass roots philosophy of democracy, that the government closest to the people is the most representative government and that the least government is the best government, held a strong attraction for Americans in 1787 and was still strong in the twentieth century. Despite a more sympathetic popular attitude toward national action after 1933, the burden of proof was always on those advocating an expanded federal role. Defenders of the status quo enjoyed the advantages not only of political inertia, but also of an ingrained public distaste for centralization. It would be "simply absurd," proclaimed the *Wall Street Journal* in a 1960 editorial denouncing proposals for an urban Executive department,[3]

to add another leaf into the long cabinet table to accommodate a fellow who will keep the President up to date on how each troubled city is fairing. Creation of a Secretary of Urban Affairs . . . can only cast a long shadow over home rule, can only substitute bureaucratic edict for community judgement, can only broaden and tighten Washington's grip on our whole society. Fight City Hall? The day may not be too far distant when, for all the nation, there's only one City Hall to fight.

In a capital city where between the decline of the New Deal and the rise of the Great Society rural congressmen from the South and agrarian and suburban representatives from the North and West controlled the legislature, this kind of sentiment often determined the course of decision-making on urban areas.

The very choice of Washington as the seat of government has, as

Daniel P. Moynihan notes, influenced the state of national-city relations. Before the agreement to remove it to a swamp on the banks of the Potomac, the capital had been located in New York, which soon became the first city of the land, the cosmopolitan center of finance, culture, and publishing. But unlike London or Paris, New York was not to be the political capital of the nation.[4] Both symbolically and substantively, Washington remained the bastion of a more provincial America, an America of open spaces and white marble and sandstone palaces.

When the politicians who populated Washington began to contend with urban needs in the 1930s, their background and outlook dictated an approach that was essentially indirect. The leaders at either end of Pennsylvania Avenue lacked a vision of the good city, had little comprehension of the mechanics of urban areas, and represented constituencies with parochial interests. Following their instincts, national officials ducked issues until they had been narrowly defined and their solution had become acute. Through the 1950s, federal urban aid programs came partially disguised under the rubric of another national purpose. Federal assistance was also sent in piecemeal fashion, with each separate program directed to a specific problem and oblivious of its impact on another problem area.[5] Covert tactics and specialization precluded consideration of broader urban developmental questions; nevertheless, the reconstruction of American politics inaugurated by the New Deal would usher in a new era in federal-city relations.

II

Contemporary observers and historians have long debated whether the New Deal marked a continuation or a break with prior reform movements, particularly Progressivism. Insofar as cities were concerned, at both the national and municipal levels, the years of the Roosevelt Presidency departed sharply from the patterns of the first two decades of the century. Theodore Roosevelt and Woodrow Wilson had each reinvigorated the Federal Government to make it an influential, but still neutral arbiter; Franklin Roosevelt, however, transformed the Federal Government into a "powerful promoter of society's welfare." [6] When the Progressives launched national aid programs, most of the benefits flowed to rural districts. A Presidential Commission on Country Life was appointed in 1908, and in 1914 Congress set up a matching fund system with the states for an extension service to educate farmers in the latest techniques in agriculture and home economics. Credit facilities for farmers were improved and a new program of federal aid for rural roads was started. The New Deal, while greatly expanding the federal presence in the countryside, significantly also brought the national government into urban areas truly for the first time. In the interest of domestic tranquility, economic recovery, and political gain, as well as because of its compassion for people, the New Deal embarked upon ambitious programs of relief and public works. Accompanying the money from the national treasury were teams of data collectors and social scientists. The century-old wall of federal indifference to urban conditions had been breached and direct contacts with municipal governments established.

The New Deal probably would not have shattered the battlements of tradition if there had not been a corresponding dramatic shift in municipal attitudes about federal action in city affairs. Those advocating the Progressive standard of good government had been adamant in resisting state and national entanglements with local administration. Decrying the disposition of the states to mix in local affairs, a "goo goo" wrote in 1909:[7]

Were Congress constantly intermeddling with the local policy and internal administration of Boston and San Francisco, Chicago and New Orleans, Philadelphia and St. Louis, New York and Omaha and the other cities of the country large and small, the absurdity and inequity of such a course would be plain to everyone. It violates the most cherished principle of free government. The very idea of it is repulsive.

Not until the Great Depression demonstrated the insufficiency of available municipal resources and the incapacity of the states to extend to cities the necessary assistance did big-city mayors cast aside their old ideas and begin lobbying for federal-municipal ties. They were led by such men as Frank Murphy, Daniel Hoan, and Fiorello La Guardia, heirs of the social welfare brand of reform. Rebuffed by an ideologically rigid Hoover regime, the municipal chief executives found more sympathetic listeners among the New Dealers, and together the mayors and flexible federal officials refashioned American federalism into a tripartite arrangement with the cities—which had not even been mentioned in the Constitution —as cooperating members.

Other urban groups soon broadened the links forged by the mayors and the New Dealers. The first permanent federal-city cooperative endeavor was the handiwork of social workers. Disturbed by the inability of private builders to supply enough decent low-cost accommodations, these reformers, along with their trade union allies, lobbied for and in 1937 pushed through a federal public housing program. Although many of public housing's supporters were themselves recent converts to the idea of positive government intervention, perhaps the most significant change of heart about the virtues of laissez-faire and municipal self-sufficiency occurred among influential big-city businessmen. The great economic contraction of the 1930s exposed the areas of urban blight and decay that previously had been hidden by urban expansion. Fearing for the safety of their investments in an unsubsidized urban land marketplace and disliking what the social workers had wrought, realtors and other city business leaders dropped their hitherto blanket opposition to federal grants-in-aid and drafted expensive programs of their own. Urban redevelopment was enacted under the aegis of a liberal administration, but the program had its origins in conservative business circles and would continue to enjoy the benevolent protection of private entrepreneurs.

Though the New Deal had widened the municipal political universe, it could not eliminate the divisions within the urban polity. As the bitter disputes over public housing and Title I illustrated, conflicting interests within the urban community were as much responsible for the crippling or delaying of urban programs as were the rural enemies of urban interests in the national capital. Some of the important advances of the 1960s were possible simply because the Executive Branch kept its plans under wraps and rushed them in and out of Congress before well-organized opposition—rural and urban—could emerge.

On the other hand, when powerful segments of the city population were able to combine in support of a federal program, conservatives in Washington found themselves on the defensive. Dwight Eisenhower came to the White House with the intention of eliminating, or at least reducing, federal-municipal ties, but at the end of his eight years the national commitment to urban renewal and urban highways was firmer. Nonetheless, by the use of the veto and other obstructive tactics, Eisenhower held off those city leaders seeking still more federal aid for such projects as mass transit and pollution control. The resulting stalemate was an indication of the potential power of an urban coalition and of the need for a sympathetic Chief Executive. The cities would be back.

It was the unwillingness of the states to come to the cities' assistance, Eisenhower realized, that brought urban lobbyists to Washington. "Like nature," he told the 1957 gathering of the Governors' Conference, "people and their governments are intolerant of vacuums. Every state failure to meet a pressing public need has created the opportunity, developed the excuse and fed the temptation for the national government to poach on the states' preserves." But aside from exhortations, Eisenhower offered the states no incentives to become more responsible members of the federal system, and Presidential warnings were hardly enough to reverse century-old political patterns of anti-urban behavior in rural-dominated state capitals. As John Kennedy observed in 1958, Congress, for all of its faults, was, because of its greater diversity, far more receptive than the state legislatures to city appeals.

III

The election of Kennedy in 1960 consolidated many of the trends in the federal-municipal relationship that had developed since 1933 and indicated the direction they would take for most of the decade. Franklin Roosevelt had made the Democratic party the home of urban voters through his economic programs and his dispensing of patronage to ethnic blocs. A quarter of a century later, Kennedy utilized these old approaches and employed the new one of promising to lead metropolitan residents across the urban frontier to the good life. In post-war affluent America, pleasant neighborhoods, quality schools, reliable transportation, and clean air were beginning to assume the same importance as jobs and hyphenated loyalties. Kennedy also made a determined and generally profitable effort to break the Republican encirclement of the big cities by establishing a Democratic foothold in the suburbs. Helping to formulate the candidate's strategy were academicians, the people disturbed most keenly by the deterioration of the core cities and the isolation of suburbia. The America of the intellectuals and of Kennedy was not Al Smith's America. Aside from their religious and party affiliation, the two candidates had little in common. If Smith represented the immigrant Lower East Side, then Kennedy symbolized the urbane sophistication of the Northeast. The electorate turned down the New Yorker in 1928, but in 1960 it chose the man who read the *New Yorker*.

Kennedy's margin of victory was razor thin, however, and instead of guiding the nation to its urban destiny, the most the new President could do was point out the route. He attracted to Washington men and women who looked at cities and saw not homes and highways, but people, communities, and regions. Programs were reoriented to meet peculiarly urban requirements rather than general economic objectives, coordination of programs was improved and central city-suburban cooperation encouraged. None of these endeavors held top priority with Kennedy and none produced immediate or dramatic changes in the urban landscape, but along with the

President's call for a cabinet department for cities, they signalled the beginning of a new approach to urban policymaking.

What Kennedy had begun, Lyndon Johnson brought to fruition. Working in a more hospitable economic and political environment than his predecessor had, the Texan conceived the goal of the Great Society and placed special urgency on improving its urban components. Johnson, whose roots and attitudes were far removed from metropolis, adopted this urban framework after a crash educational course conducted by scholars. The initiatives of 1965 were not the product of a breakdown in urban life or a widely felt sense of crisis; they resulted from the new President's determination to accelerate the pace of domestic reform and his reliance upon intellectuals for ideas. As never before, a vision of the good urban life suffused official rhetoric regarding the cities, and for the first time the Federal Government explicitly acknowledged and accepted the challenge of building great cities.

IV

Acceptance of the challenge, of course, carried no guarantee that great cities would actually be built. "A complicated system," Robert Wood has observed, "undertaking to resolve a complicated problem does not immediately calibrate—and has difficulty in matching—the challenge and the response." [8] Good intentions could not insure good results when some of the basic facts about urban dynamics were as yet poorly understood, when governmental responsibility was divided, and when there was little popular agreement on what a desirable result would be. The establishment of the Department of Housing and Urban Development in 1965 and the later passage of the Model Cities Act of 1966 and the Housing Act of 1968 (a "Magna Carta for the cities," Johnson called it) all represented sincere, but so far futile, efforts to fulfill the Aristotelian description of the city Kennedy and Johnson were so fond of quoting. It was a sad, yet generally held, conclusion that as the Great Society ended, the United States seemed closer to a "nightmare urban society" [9] than it had been before 1933.

But even to admit this harsh fact (and for all the gloomy talk the historical verdict is not yet in) is not to argue that the more than three decades of federal involvement in urban affairs and the seven or eight years of intensive attention to urban problems have been to no avail. Indeed, despite the dysfunctional features of some national programs, the cities probably would have been worse off without the federal intervention. Rather, the cities' plight was due, in part, to the Federal Government's inability to come to their aid in a suitable and adequate fashion. A federal-city partnership had been forged between 1933 and 1965 in the face of the agrarian ideal, states' rights, and a political system that responded most readily to crisis. This partnership could not function effectively, however, under these same constraints.

A more productive partnership is necessary if the cities are to become good places in which to live. For in the years after 1933 the cities have become increasingly dependent upon the Federal Government. Whereas before the New Deal municipal governments and urban residents went about their business without concern for what Washington was doing, by the mid-1960s, federal decisions about interest rates, taxes, military procurement, and scores of other economic matters had a direct and substantial impact upon nearly all facets of urban life, and federal grants-in-aid had become perhaps the "single most important determinant" [10] of municipal policies. Between 1933 and 1965 a revolution occurred in federal-city relations; making best use of that revolution will be in the hands of later generations.

Notes

CHAPTER 1

1. So much has been written about the negative view of urban life that the important pro-urban literature of the eighteenth and nineteenth centuries has been almost completely forgotten. For good counterweights to the usual descriptions of anti-urban arguments, see Frank Freidel, "Boosters, Intellectuals, and the American City," in *The Historian and the City*, eds. Oscar Handlin and John Burchard (Cambridge, Mass., 1963), pp. 115–20; Daniel J. Boorstin, *The Americans: The National Experience* (New York, 1965), pp. 113–68; and the balanced account in Charles N. Glaab and A. Theodore Brown, *A History of Urban America* (New York, 1967), pp. 53–81.
2. The term is Sam Bass Warner's. He uses it to refer to the American tradition of emphasis upon the individual and the individual's pursuit of wealth. It is this tradition, he contends, that has "determined the shape and quality of America's big cities." Warner, *The Private City* (Philadelphia, 1968), pp. 3–4, x.
3. Glaab and Brown, *History of Urban America*, p. 168. In practice, the charters were granted by the provincial governments; Carl Bridenbaugh, *Cities in the Wilderness* (New York, 1955), pp. 6–8.
4. Edward C. Banfield and James Q. Wilson, *City Politics* (Cambridge, Mass., 1966), p. 63.
5. *City of Clinton v. The Cedar Rapids and Missouri River Railroad Co.*, 24 Iowa 455 (1868). For earlier developments, see Jon Teaford, "City Versus State: The Struggle for Legal Ascendancy," *The American Journal of Legal History*, XVII (Jan. 1973), 51–65.
6. *Hunter v. Pittsburgh*, 207 U.S. 161, 178, 179 (1907).
7. *Trenton v. New Jersey*, 262 U.S. 182 (1923); Charles S. Rhyne, *Municipal Law* (Washington, D.C., 1957), pp. 66–68. For a softening of the Supreme Court's

attitude in recent years, see *City of Tacoma v. Taxpayers of Tacoma*, 357 U.S. 320 (1958).

8. John A. Fairlie, "Municipal Development in the United States," in National Municipal League, *A Municipal Program* (New York, 1900), p. 10.

9. Thomas H. Reed, *Municipal Government in the United States* (New York, 1934), pp. 65–66.

10. William Bennett Munro, *The Government of American Cities* (New York, 1915), pp. 14–15, 61; Fairlie, "Municipal Development," pp. 21–22; Glaab and Brown, *History of Urban America*, p. 173.

11. Quoted in Frank J. Goodnow, *City Government in the United States* (New York, 1904), pp. 85–86.

12. *Ibid.,* p. 77.

13. Robert Luce, *Legislative Principles* (Boston, 1930), pp. 364–65; Robert G. Dixon, Jr., *Democratic Representation* (New York, 1968), p. 71.

14. *Report of the Proceedings and Debates of the New York State Constitutional Convention of 1821* (Albany, 1821), pp. 221, 220.

15. *Revised Record of the New York State Constitutional Convention of 1894* (5 vols.; Albany, 1900), III, 1075.

16. *Ibid.,* IV, 10–11; III, 1083–96.

17. *Ibid.,* III, 1226.

18. Quoted in Gus Tyler and David I. Wells, "New York: 'Constitutionally Republican,'" in *The Politics of Reapportionment*, ed. Malcolm E. Jewell (New York, 1962), p. 221.

19. Daniel J. Elazar, "Urban Problems and the Federal Government: A Historical Inquiry," *Political Science Quarterly*, LXXXII (Dec. 1967), 513–14.

20. A. Theodore Brown, *Frontier Community—Kansas City to 1870* (Columbia, Mo., 1963), p. 148; Richard C. Wade, *The Urban Frontier: The Rise of Western Cities, 1790–1830* (Cambridge, Mass., 1959), pp. 66–68.

21. Samuel Eliot Morison, *The Maritime History of Massachusetts, 1783–1860* (Sentry Edition; Boston, 1961), p. 191; Rollin G. Osterweis, *Three Centuries of New Haven, 1638–1938* (New Haven, 1953), pp. 201–2; Wade, *Urban Frontier*, pp. 40, 60, 61, 161–62.

22. Daniel J. Elazar, *The American Partnership* (Chicago, 1962), pp. 265–69, 276–77, 299–300; Bureau of the Census, *Historical Statistics of the United States: Colonial Times to 1957* (Washington, 1960), Series Q 245.

23. Carter Goodrich, *Government Promotion of American Canals and Railroads, 1800–1860* (New York, 1960), pp. 169–204.

24. Many municipalities did, however, buy large amounts of railroad company stocks and bonds until the Panic of 1873 threw most of the nation's roads into receivership. As part of the consequent revulsion against public aid, a number of states passed laws or constitutional amendments forbidding local promotion of internal improvements; *ibid.,* pp. 230–62.

25. Paul Gates observes: "The urban development of Illinois during the 'fifties and 'sixties was, to a considerable extent, the work of the [federally subsidized] Illinois Central." Gates, *The Illinois Central Railroad and Its Colonization Work* (Cam-

bridge, Mass., 1934), p. 147. While often quickly overtaken by the railroads, canals too were a great shot in the arm to local economies. Real estate values in Cincinnati, for instance, jumped 20 to 25 per cent in the three years after the opening of the federally aided Miami Canal in 1828; Harry N. Scheiber, *Ohio Canal Era* (Athens, Ohio, 1969), p. 205.

26. In 1864, for example, Kansas City elected its mayor to Congress so he could devote his full time to presenting the town's case for a connection to the transcontinental railroad; Brown, *Frontier Community*, pp. 203, 210–11.

27. Wyatt W. Belcher, *The Economic Rivalry Between St. Louis and Chicago, 1850–1880* (New York, 1947).

28. George Rogers Taylor, *The Transportation Revolution, 1815–1860* (New York, 1951), p. 98.

29. Douglas's motives for introducing the bill have been a matter of debate among historians, but that the interests of Chicago in the railroad were involved has not seriously been questioned. For a summary view of Douglas's attitude, see Allan Nevins, *Ordeal of the Union* (New York, 1947), II, 102–6.

30. John A. Garraty, *The American Nation* (New York, 1971), I, 453. Richard Wade has suggested that Chicago's victory over St. Louis bound the West to the North and ensured the Union's triumph over the Confederacy in the Civil War; Wade, "The City in History—Some American Perspectives," in *Urban Life and Form*, ed. Werner Z. Hirsch (New York, 1963), p. 65.

31. Glaab and Brown, *History of Urban America*, pp. 133–66.

32. Wade, "City in History," p. 68.

33. Andrew D. White, "The Government of American Cities," *Forum*, X (Dec. 1890), 357, 368.

34. *Report of the Commission to Devise a Plan for the Government of Cities in the State of New York* (New York, 1877), p. 13.

35. Charles A. Beard, "Politics and City Government," *National Municipal Review*, VI (March 1917), 202.

36. Goodnow, *City Government*, p. 69.

37. The 1904 observation was not entirely in accord with reality when written or in 1920. While there were no formal ties between Washington and localities such as cooperative grants-in-aid programs (such programs then in existence worked only with the states; the Corps of Engineers, rather than cities, actually received the rivers and harbors appropriations), there were contacts between federal and local officials. Professionals employed by the federal and local governments in fields such as education and public health freely exchanged information useful to the other. Similarly, the Corps of Engineers consulted with municipal technicians in drawing up their blueprints for local port facilities. But these relations were on the lowest level and were not officially acknowledged by either the Federal Government or municipalities. Wylie Kilpatrick, "Federal Relations to Urban Government," in *Urban Government*, Volume I of the Supplementary Report of the Urbanism Committee to the National Resources Committee (Washington, D.C., 1939), pp. 57–65; see also, Austin F. MacDonald, *Federal Aid* (New York, 1928). Census Bureau reports on the financial statistics of cities before the 1930s had no information on federal contributions to municipal budgets.

38. Fred L. Israel, ed., *State of the Union Messages of the Presidents of the United States* (4 vols.: New York, 1966), IV, 2669–70.
39. Paul V. Betters, "The Federal Government and the Cities," *Municipal Yearbook 1934* (Chicago, 1934), p. 33.

CHAPTER 2

1. C. A. Dykstra, "The Challenge of Urbanism," *Public Management*, XVI (Nov. 1934), 338.
2. The fullest treatment of his gubernatorial years, Bernard Bellush, *Franklin D. Roosevelt as Governor of New York* (New York, 1955), mentions New York City's slum situation in but one sentence. Frank Freidel, *The Triumph* (Boston, 1956), refers to New York City only in the context of the Mayor Walker case.
3. Roosevelt was opposed by many of the urban machine leaders in his quest for the Democratic nomination. Jersey City's Frank Hague, for example, called him "the weakest candidate before the people." William E. Leuchtenburg, "The Election of 1936," in *The History of American Presidential Elections, 1789–1968*, ed. Arthur M. Schlesinger, Jr. (New York, 1971), III, 2830.
4. Raymond Moley, *The First New Deal* (New York, 1966), p. 9. In 1931 Roosevelt wrote a South Dakota newspaper editor: "By the way I am not, as you say, an 'urban leader' for I was born and brought up and have always made my home on a farm in Dutchess County." Quoted in Bellush, *Roosevelt as Governor*, p. 76.
5. Roosevelt's passion for planning also spurred his interest in the idea. But while FDR saw regional planning and subsistence homesteads as completely complementary, the regional planners clustered around Lewis Mumford rejected the homesteads proposal as leading to a lowering of living standards. For a discussion of Mumford's view of the city, see *infra*, pp. 131–32.
6. *The Public Papers of Governor Franklin D. Roosevelt* (4 vols.; Albany, 1930–39), *1931*, 752–59.
7. William E. Leuchtenburg, *Franklin D. Roosevelt and the New Deal* (New York, 1963), p. 35; *Public Papers of Governor Roosevelt, 1932*, 33–34.
8. Catherine Bauer, *Modern Housing* (Boston, 1934), p. 249.
9. Daniel B. Creamer, *Is Industry Decentralizing?* (Philadelphia, 1935). The Greenbelt communities of the Resettlement Administration, which more accurately understood this trend, are discussed *infra*, pp. 133–34.
10. Harold W. Dodds, "The Future of Municipal Government," *National Municipal Review*, XXIII (Dec. 1934), 647.
11. Murray Seasongood, "The Local Government Muddle," *Annals*, CLXXXI (Sept. 1935), 161–62.
12. Paul V. Betters, "The Federal Government and the Cities," *Municipal Yearbook 1934* (Chicago, 1934), p. 33.
13. The background of the AMA is best told in Harold D. Smith, "Associations of Cities and of Municipal Officials," in *Urban Government*, Volume I of the Supplementary Report of the Urbanism Committee to the National Resources Committee (Washington, D.C., 1939), pp. 185–207. Also see Harold D. Smith,

"Work Program for the American Municipal Association," in American Municipal Association, *Proceedings 1931–1935* (Chicago, 1936), pp. 59–65; and Louis Brownlow, "The Role of the Association," in *ibid.*, pp. 156–58.

14. A decade later the AMA changed its policies to allow direct membership by large municipalities and to lobby on the cities' behalf in Washington; see *infra*, p. 166.

15. For a somewhat jaded look at the Motor City on the eve of the Depression, see Matthew Josephson, "Detroit: City of Tomorrow?" *Outlook*, CLI (Feb. 13, 1929), 243–46, 275, 278.

16. Helen Hall, "When Detroit's Out of Gear," *Survey*, LXIV (April 1930), 9, 10; William J. Norton, "The Relief Crisis in Detroit," *Social Service Review*, VII (March 1933), 129–36.

17. For Murphy's background and the campaign, see J. Woodford Howard, Jr., *Mr. Justice Murphy* (Princeton, 1968) and Richard D. Lunt, *The High Ministry of Government: The Political Career of Frank Murphy* (Detroit, 1965).

18. Detroit *News*, Sept. 16, 1930, p. 1.

19. *American City*, XLIV (Feb. 1931), 5; Bureau of the Census, *Financial Statistics of the Cities, 1930, 1931* (Washington, D.C., 1934, 1935); Ralph G. Hurlen and Anne E. Geddes, "Public and Private Relief During the Current Unemployment Emergency," National Conference of Social Work, *Proceedings 1931* (Chicago, 1931), p. 439.

20. "Two Mayors Who Care About the Unemployed," *The Unemployed*, n. 3 (Spring 1931), pp. 19, 29–30. A draft of this statement in Murphy's mayoralty papers is dated March 4, 1931; Mayor's Unemployment Committee (1), Box 6, Mayors' Records 1931, Burton Historical Collection, Detroit Public Library [hereafter cited as BHC].

21. For the New York experience, see Irving Bernstein, *The Lean Years* (Boston, 1960), pp. 291–96; for Philadelphia, Bonnie R. Fox, "Unemployment Relief in Philadelphia, 1930–1932: A Study of the Depression's Impact on Voluntarism," *Pennsylvania Magazine of History and Biography*, XCIII (Jan. 1969), 86–108. In Chicago, private agencies actually increased their share of the load from 1928 to 1931. Also, the responsibility for relief lay with the county, not the city; thus it was not an issue in the municipal elections in the Spring of 1931, and Mayor Anton Cermak did not make an appeal for federal aid until May 1932. Clorinne M. Brandenburg, "Chicago Relief Statistics, 1928–1931," *Social Service Review*, VI (June 1932), 270–79; Alex Gottfried, *Boss Cermak of Chicago* (Seattle, 1962), pp. 218–21, 257, 278.

22. Frederick L. Bird, *The Municipal Debt Load in 1935* (New York, 1935), p. 7; "Real Property Assessed Valuation Changes in American Cities, 1929–1933," AMA Report #37 (mimeographed, July 1933); Egbert S. Wengert, *Financial Problems of the City of Detroit in the Depression* (Detroit, 1942), p. 16.

23. Detroit *News*, June 23, 1931, p. 2. See also, Murphy to Benjamin C. Marsh, Sept. 26, 1931, United States, Box 9, Mayors' Records 1931, BHC.

24. Roy Chapin to Mrs. C. P. White, April 10, 1933, Box 99, Roy Chapin MSS., Michigan Historical Collections, University of Michigan Library. The margin of

victory was nearly 2 to 1. Writing to congratulate Murphy on his triumph, Newton D. Baker remarked: "The modern American city, particularly an industrial city, is a complex and apparently a refractory problem, but it is immensely encouraging and stimulating to find how overwhelmingly it responds to genuine leadership, and takes to its heart a candid and thoughtful just man." Baker to Murphy, Nov. 11, 1931, Box 10, Frank Murphy MSS., Michigan Historical Collections, University of Michigan Library.

25. Detroit *News*, May 18, 1932, p. 1; Detroit *Free Press*, May 19, 1932, pp. 1, 3. Copy of mayors' petition, May 23, 1932, in Mayors' Conference, Box 7, Mayors' Records 1932, BHC.

26. See Hoan to Robert M. LaFollette, Jr., Dec. 16, 1930, File 135, Box 35, Daniel W. Hoan MSS., Milwaukee County Historical Society.

27. Hoan to Mayors, July 29, 1931, *ibid.*

28. See, for example, Hilary E. Howse (Nashville) to Hoan, Aug. 11, 1931; Charles O. Schonert (Hammond, Ind.) to Hoan, Aug. 6, 1931; James M. Curley (Boston) to Hoan, Aug. 4, 1931, *ibid.* There are 16 generally favorable replies in the Hoan papers; only 3 came from Republican mayors.

29. Frederick W. Donnelly (Trenton) to Hoan, Aug. 4, 1931; Walter E. Batterson (Hartford) to Hoan, July 31, 1931; Charles E. Roesch (Buffalo) to Hoan, Aug. 6, 1931, *ibid.* Mayor Thomas A. Tully's (New Haven) negative reply is not in the Hoan collection but was reported in the press; *New York Times* [hereafter *NYT*], Aug. 4, 1931, p. 32. All but Donnelly were Republicans.

30. Hoan statement, n.d., File 135, Box 35, Hoan MSS.; Hoan to Benjamin C. Marsh (copy), Sept. 14, 1931, Box 9, Mayors' Records 1931, BHC. Hoan counted seventeen favorable replies and five negative answers; thus, only about 20 per cent of those queried bothered to respond. In November 1931 Senator Robert M. LaFollette, Jr. of Wisconsin sent out a questionnaire to municipal officials all over the nation asking them if they felt federal aid was necessary to deal with unemployment. Of the 729 replies, 271 supported federal aid, 372 opposed it or did not want it to take the form of a dole, and 86 took a neutral position. Most of these replies, however, came from small cities. *Congressional Record*, 72nd Cong. 1st Sess., pp. 3068–260.

31. James J. Walker to Murphy, May 20, 1932, Mayors' Conference, Box 7, Mayors' Records 1932, BHC; Detroit *News*, June 1, 1932, p. 1. Mayor Cermak of Chicago did not attend, but he sent his controller. Among those present was Jacob S. Coxey, the mayor of Massillon, Ohio, who had led his famous "Army" on a march to Washington in 1894 to demand federal public works to combat the depression.

32. Transcript of the Conference of Mayors, Detroit, June 1, 1932, mimeographed, pp. 12–21, U.S. Conference of Mayors files, Washington, D.C.

33. Louis Brownlow, "Looking Ahead at City Government," *Municipal Yearbook 1934*, p. 4.

34. Some quarters in Washington credited the mayors with a large role in the bill's passage; *NYT*, June 8, 1932, pp. 1, 11. For the legislative background of the Emergency Relief and Construction Act, see Jordan A. Schwarz, *The Interregnum of Despair* (Urbana, Ill., 1970), pp. 146–73.

35. Detroit received $3.892 million from the RFC for the second half of 1932. This represented about one-third of the city's rate of relief expenditures during the first six months of 1931.

36. Paul V. Betters to Lent D. Upson (copy), Jan. 21, 1933, U.S. Reconstruction Finance Corporation, Box 8, Mayors' Records 1933, BHC; Detroit *News,* Feb. 12, 1933, pp. 1, 3; Transcript of the Conference of Mayors, Washington, Feb. 17, 1933, mimeographed, pp. 4–9, 78–79, U.S. Conference of Mayors files.

37. Betters memo re: National Conference of Mayors, n.d. [probably summer 1932], 1932 Conference of Mayors folder, U.S. Conference of Mayors files; Betters to Murphy, Sept. 23, 1932, Mayors' Conference, Box 7, Mayors' Records 1932, BHC; Betters memo, "What a United States Mayors' Group Can Do," n.d. [probably Nov. 1932], *ibid.*; Betters to Hoan, Nov. 23, 1932, File 136, Box 36, Hoan MSS.

38. Betters's hopes for intimate federal-city personal contacts were more than realized after Fiorello H. La Guardia became New York's mayor in 1934. On very close terms with Roosevelt and able to commute at least twice weekly to Washington, "the Little Flower" personified the new federal-city relationship. He held the USCM presidency from 1936 until his retirement from City Hall in 1945.

39. By 1940, 176 cities, 84 per cent of those eligible, were members of the USCM.

40. C. A. Dykstra, "Municipal Costs and Unemployment Relief," in *City Manager Yearbook 1932* (Chicago, 1932), p. 31.

41. Senate Committee on Manufactures, 72nd Cong. 2nd Sess., *Hearings on S. 5125: Federal Aid for Relief* (Washington, D.C., 1933), pp. 204–8. Detroit had a very difficult time with Michigan's governors—both Republican and Democratic; neither wished to antagonize rural elements in the legislature. Detroit *News,* Sept. 22, 1932, p. 1; March 26, 1933, p. 1; March 28, 1933, p. 4; Michigan Municipal League, *Proceedings 1932* (Ann Arbor, n.d.), pp. 82–83. For another mayor's problems, see Burnet R. Maybank to Murphy, July 26, 1932, Box 9, Mayors' Records 1932, BHC.

42. Washington *Post,* June 22, 1932, p. 2; Chicago *Tribune,* June 22, 1932, pp. 1, 2; *NYT,* June 22, 1932, p. 2.

43. Arthur E. Burns, "The Federal Emergency Relief Administration," in *Municipal Yearbook 1937* (Chicago, 1937), pp. 412–13; Anita Wells, "The Allocation of Relief Funds by the States Among their Political Subdivisions," *FERA Monthly Report, June 1–June 30, 1936* (Washington, 1937), pp. 65–87.

44. Burns, "Federal Emergency Relief Administration," p. 412.

45. Neville Miller, "The American City in Relation to the WPA and Direct Relief," *Social Service Review,* X (Sept. 1936), 416.

46. Josephine Brown, *Public Relief 1929–1939* (New York, 1940), pp. 202–4; James T. Patterson, *The New Deal and the States* (Princeton, 1969), pp. 56–57.

47. C. A. Dykstra, "Relief from the Municipal Viewpoint," in *City Problems of 1934* (Chicago, 1934), pp. 61–64.

48. The ninety-three largest cities with 29.6 per cent of the total population had, in the period 1933–36, from 42.5 per cent to 54.6 per cent of the nation's relief population; they received about half of FERA's expenditures. Burns, "Federal Emergency Relief Administration," pp. 393, 410.

49. A. E. Geddes, *Trends in Relief Expenditures 1910–1935* (Works Progress Administration Research Monograph No. X; Washington, D.C., 1937), pp. 43–45; Arthur E. Burns and Edward A. Williams, *Federal Work, Security and Relief Programs* (WPA Research Monograph No. XXIV; Washington, D.C., 1941), pp. 131–32.

50. Rural-directed programs also aided cities, but usually only in an indirect way. Here a program created in response to a basically urban problem—when legislators discussed relief they usually referred to city unemployment—was directly aiding rural areas. As will be noted *infra,* pp. 63–65 the same thing happened to the public housing effort.

51. The ninety-three largest cities received 39 per cent of the CWA's funds; even more significantly, the CWA set up wage differentials based on regional and size-of-city factors. The WPA continued this policy. Corrington Gill, "The Civil Works Administration," in *Municipal Yearbook 1934*, p. 429.

52. Hopkins memo for Roosevelt, Feb. 15, 1934, OF 444; Roosevelt to Herbert H. Lehman, March 9, 1934, OF 444-B, Franklin D. Roosevelt MSS., Franklin D. Roosevelt Library; La Guardia to T. Semmes Walmsley, March 12, 1934, Louisiana folder, Box 2688, Fiorello H. La Guardia MSS., Municipal Archives and Records Center, New York City.

53. The USCM was successful in moderating the periodic cuts in WPA employment rolls that the President ordered; see John Morton Blum, *From the Morgenthau Diaries: Years of Crisis* (Boston, 1959), p. 277. A new federal program of public assistance to unemployables also left much to be desired from the mayors' standpoint. Not only was it administered by the states, but a requirement that states or localities both match the federal funds placed another heavy drain on municipal treasuries.

54. Miller, "American City in Relation to WPA," pp. 420–22.

55. Betters to La Guardia, March 6, 1935, Folder #502, Box 2594, La Guardia MSS.; Hoan to F. Macmillan, April 15, 1935, File 87, Box 23, Hoan MSS.; Donald Howard, *The WPA and Federal Relief Policy* (New York, 1943), pp. 596–603.

56. L. Laszlo Ecker-R., "Financing Relief and Recovery," in *Municipal Yearbook 1937*, p. 372. New York City alone accounted for 14 per cent of WPA spending through December 1936; six industrial states plus New York City absorbed 55 per cent. Emerson Ross, "The Works Progress Administration," in *ibid.,* pp. 437–41.

57. Roosevelt, Press Conference, Jan. 17, 1939. Although Roosevelt opposed a rigid statutory requirement on local contributions, he had instructed Hopkins to raise the sponsor's share to as close to 40 per cent as possible; Roosevelt memo for Hopkins, July 27, 1937, OF 444-C, Roosevelt MSS.

58. The percentage of WPA employment in big cities showed a steady decline after 1937, while that in cities under 25,000 population increased. WPA efforts to appease rural sentiment probably accounts for this trend. In one field, WPA showed a distinct rural bias: of the twenty-six monographs prepared by its Research Division, fourteen dealt with rural themes; only five concerned urban-related topics.

59. These figures are based upon the biographical and district information in the *Congressional Directory*. While five of the eight big-city Republicans still in the

House after the 1936 elections opposed WPA on most key votes, the other Republicans voted against it in even more overwhelming numbers: 9 to 1 vs. 5 to 3. Only eleven of the seventy Democratic votes against WPA on three roll calls (1937–38) came from big-city congressmen. Of the twenty-four Democratic representatives James T. Patterson (*Congressional Conservatism and the New Deal* [Lexington, Ky., 1967]) classified as urban conservatives, only three cast more than one vote against WPA.

60. Betters testimony, Senate Committee on Banking and Currency, 72nd Cong. 2nd Sess., *Hearings on S. 5336: Further Unemployment Relief Through the RFC* (Washington, D.C., 1933), pp. 69–73. RFC loaned $398 million to 176 political units under this provision. Of this amount, $310 million went to the Metropolitan Water District of Southern California and the San Francisco-Oakland Bay Bridge. Secretary of the Treasury, *Final Report on Reconstruction Finance Corporation* (Washington, D.C., 1959), pp. 99–101.

61. *City Problems of 1933* (Chicago, 1933), pp. 99, 102–6; Harold L. Ickes, *The Secret Diary of Harold L. Ickes* (3 vols.; New York, 1954), I, 96, 100.

62. *City Problems of 1935* (Washington, D.C., 1935), pp. 3, 10. PWA's slow pace was not completely Ickes's fault. Some mayors, such as the Republican chief executive of Philadelphia, disliked the New Deal and tried to stymie its recovery efforts. In other cities, such as Boston, conflicts between state and local politicians delayed PWA, as well as CWA and WPA, projects. John F. Bauman, "The City, the Depression, and Relief: The Philadelphia Experience, 1929–1939" (unpublished Ph.D. dissertation, Rutgers University, 1969), pp. 229–58; Charles H. Trout, "Boston During the Great Depression" (unpublished Ph.D. dissertation, Columbia University, 1972), pp. 297–324.

63. Betters memo for Roosevelt, Feb. 16, 1935, OF 1892, Roosevelt MSS. Milwaukee's Daniel Hoan was the USCM's president at the time and its logical choice as delegate, but he probably felt he could not spare the time to go to Washington at least twice a month.

64. The role of ACA is discussed in Arthur W. MacMahon, *et al.*, *The Administration of Federal Work Relief* (Chicago, 1941), pp. 105–13.

65. *City Problems of 1935*, p. 14; *NYT*, May 26, 1935, p. 26.

66. Bird, *Municipal Debt Load*, pp. 6–7; Frederick L. Bird, *The Trend of Tax Delinquency* (New York, 1941), p. 14. In 1929, the combined budgets of the thirteen cities over 500,000 population totalled $1.8 billion; interest costs came to $213 million. In 1933, the figures were $1.6 billion and $238 million. *Financial Statistics of Cities, 1929, 1933,* Table 3.

67. Detroit *News*, Feb. 12, 1933, pp. 1, 3; Murphy to Cermak, Feb. 8, 1933, Mayors' Conference, Box 5, Mayors' Records 1933, BHC.

68. Detroit *News*, March 2, 1933, p. 1.

69. *Ibid.*, March 19, 1933, pp. 1, 2.

70. *Ibid.*, March 18, 1933, pp. 1, 4; April 3, 1933, pp. 1, 2; Murphy to Rep. John C. Lehr, March 28, 1933, Mayors' Conference, Box 5, Mayors' Records 1933, BHC; Murphy to mayors, April 28, 1933, File 136, Box 36, Hoan MSS.

71. House of Representatives, Committee on Ways and Means, 76th Cong. 1st Sess.,

Hearings on Proposed Legislation Relating to Tax-Exempt Securities (Washington, D.C., 1939), p. 479.

72. "Detroit's New Deal," *Business Week*, July 22, 1933, p. 13.

73. William C. Beyer, "Financial Dictators Replace Political Boss," *National Municipal Review*, XXII (April 1933), 162–67; Frederick L. Bird, "Current Trends in Municipal Finance," Governmental Research Association, *Proceedings 1937* (mimeographed), p. 38.

74. *City Problems of 1936* (Washington, D.C., 1936), pp. 12, 166. A major reason for better tax collections was that the Home Owners' Loan Corporation assumed responsibility for back taxes on houses it financed; this was a great boon for the cities.

75. *Ashton v. Cameron County Water Improvement District*, 298 U.S. 513 (1936).

76. Paul V. Betters, *Municipal Financial Problems and Proposals for Federal Legislation* (Chicago, 1933); Hoan to Frederick Macmillan, July 9, 1932, File 86, Box 23, Hoan MSS.

77. Murphy to Mrs. Edward Andrews, Dec. 13, 1932, Box 11, Murphy MSS.

78. Murphy to Dudley Field Malone, Jan. 12, 1932, Box 10, *ibid.* Murphy was also probably influenced by the fact that he faced difficult negotiations with his city's creditors on his request for additional loans; he probably did not want to antagonize them by endorsing a bill with very dim prospects of being enacted.

79. Murphy to Theodore Roosevelt, Jr., Nov. 22, 1932, Box 11, *ibid.*

80. William S. Myers and Walter H. Newton, *The Hoover Administration* (New York, 1936), pp. 227–28.

81. Transcript of Conference of Mayors, Feb. 17, 1933, pp. 77–78; Detroit *News*, Feb. 19, 1933, pp. 1, 3; *United States Daily*, Feb. 20, 1933, pp. 1, 3. The idea of loans got as far as it did in July 1932 only because it was part of an omnibus measure intended to embarrass Hoover. It did not have any strong support in Congress by itself.

82. Roosevelt memo for the attorney general, March 31, 1933; Roosevelt to Morris S. Tremaine, Sept. 8, 1933; Roosevelt to George Morris, Dec. 28, 1933, OF 260, Roosevelt MSS.; Roosevelt, Press Conference, May 31, 1933; Louis Brownlow Diary, Dec. 7, 1933, Brownlow MSS., University of Chicago Library.

83. Roosevelt memo for the attorney general, March 31, 1933, OF 260, Roosevelt MSS.; Roosevelt, Press Conference, May 5, 1933.

84. This is the account of his meeting with the mayors that the President gave reporters at his Press Conference of May 31, 1933. Roosevelt's hesitancy about passing judgment on the conduct of local government helped the cities when Senator Byrnes wanted to require a minimum local contribution on WPA projects. See Roosevelt to Byrnes, June 11, 1937, OF 444-C, Roosevelt MSS., and his Press Conference of June 15, 1937.

85. Simeon Leland, "Memo on Public Credit," USCM Report #48 (mimeographed, Dec. 20, 1933); Leland memo for Stanley Reed, Feb. 24, 1934, General Correspondence Files, Department of the Treasury, Box 43, Records of the Reconstruction Finance Corporation, Record Group 234, National Archives.

86. "Memorandum on the Public Credit Situation," in Brownlow Diary, Jan. 16,

1934, Brownlow MSS. Assisting Hopkins with the memo were Jerome Frank, the AAA's General Counsel; Adolf Berle, soon to be La Guardia's city chamberlain; and a lawyer from the Justice Department. Frank had been asked by Brownlow to draft a bill for this purpose; Diary, Dec. 24, 1933.

87. Morgenthau never made a public statement on this issue; his diaries at Hyde Park contain no material about it. His general attitudes are covered in Blum, *Years of Crisis*, pp. 232, 386. Morgenthau's negative role was discussed by Simeon E. Leland in an interview, Evanston, Ill., Feb. 19, 1970.

88. *NYT*, Jan. 30, 1934, p. 29; House of Representatives, Committee on Banking and Currency, 73rd Cong. 2nd Sess., *Hearings on H.R. 3082: To Provide Loans Through the Reconstruction Finance Corporation* (Washington, D.C., 1934), pp. 10–13; Leland interview. A short time later the RFC began buying some of the municipal bonds held by the PWA in order to increase the PWA's lending capacity; despite Jones's fears, he actually disposed of these bonds at a profit.

89. Jesse Jones to Senator Carter Glass, May 14, 1934, reprinted in *Congressional Record*, 73rd Cong. 2nd Sess., p. 8736.

90. Leland to Jones, April 4, 1934, reproduced in Brownlow Diary, April 8, 1934, Brownlow MSS.; *NYT*, May 4, 1934, p. 15. There is a typescript copy of Leland's final report, "The Short-Term Borrowings of Local Government in 1933 and 1934," which confirmed his earlier findings, in the Department of the Treasury Library.

91. Practically every annual meeting of the USCM heard a plea for an alternative to the real estate tax.

92. In 1941, at Roosevelt's suggestion, Morgenthau appointed a three-member committee to investigate intergovernmental fiscal relations. Its report, issued in 1943, urged among other things: metropolitan area cooperation, more state sharing of revenues with localities, and municipal "collaboration with the Federal Government on broader and more generous programs of federal aids." *Federal, State, and Local Fiscal Relations*, 78th Cong. 1st Sess., Sen. Doc. 69 (Washington, D.C., 1943), p. 45.

93. Edith Elmer Wood, "A Century of the Housing Problem," *Law and Contemporary Problems*, I (March 1934), 137–47; Fiorello H. La Guardia to Edith Elmer Wood, July 14, 1932, Folder A, Box 3, Edith Elmer Wood MSS., Avery Library, Columbia University.

94. In defense of the slow pace of the PWA's housing effort, it should be noted that PWA had very little on which to base its projects. As one housing expert observed in 1936: "Nothing really meriting the name [of slum clearance] has ever taken place in any American city previous to the activities of the PWA Housing Division. . . . All previous municipal attempts were complete fiascoes." Edith Elmer Wood memo for the Chief of Branch VI, Jan. 4, 1936, PWA Box 1, Wood MSS.

95. Roosevelt, Press Conferences, Jan. 3, 1934, Oct. 17, 1934, Feb. 14, 1936.

96. Ickes, *Secret Diary*, I, 443; Ickes, letter to the editor, *Forum*, XCII (Nov. 1934), x. In his written statement to the Senate Education Committee in 1937, Ickes declared that "the elimination of slums and the providing of decent housing were

regarded as a means to relieve unemployment rather than a distinct objective for which careful planning and research were necessary." Senate Committee on Education and Labor, 75th Cong. 1st Sess., *Hearings on S. 1685: To Create a United States Housing Authority* (Washington, D.C., 1937), p. 49.

97. Catherine Bauer, "Now, At Last Housing," *New Republic*, XCII (Sept. 8, 1937), 119; Lyle J. Woodyatt, "The Origins and Evolution of the New Deal Public Housing Program" (unpublished Ph.D. dissertation, Washington University, 1968), pp. 102, 105. Also stimulating national discussion of the slum situation was the Real Property Survey made under the auspices of the works program; for the first time the country had detailed facts on the size and scope of the housing shortage. See Peyton Stapp, *Urban Housing: A Survey of Real Property Inventories Conducted as Works Projects 1934–1936* (Washington, D.C., 1938).

98. Timothy L. McDonnell, *The Wagner Housing Act* (Chicago, 1957), pp. 186–90, 212–15, 271–72, 342–45; J. Joseph Huthmacher, *Senator Robert F. Wagner and the Rise of Urban Liberalism* (New York, 1968), pp. 205–16, 224–26.

99. McDonnell, *Wagner Housing Act*, pp. 324–39, 360–88. The House and Senate imposed different limits on construction costs. When the bill emerged from conference, it set one limit for cities over 500,000 population and another, lower one, for cities under that figure, on the premise that bigger cities had higher expenses. This was "the first piece of legislation to set up two classifications of cities," and thus was a victory of sorts for the big cities; Paul V. Betters, "The Federal Government and the Cities: A Problem in Adjustment," *Annals*, CXCIX (Sept. 1938), 192.

100. Ickes, *Secret Diary*, II, 231.

101. Rural congressmen may have supplied the decisive votes that killed the bill, but it would be inaccurate to explain the balloting solely on the basis of urban-rural animosities. Urban Republicans were practically solid against the measure, as were rural Republicans. Almost all the urban Democrats voted for the bill; rural Democrats backed it 2 to 1. The reversal in USHA's fortunes from 1937 to 1939 can be attributed, in large part, to the big Republican gains in the 1938 elections. Many administration Democrats from rural districts, who had supported public housing out of loyalty to Roosevelt, were swept out of office on the conservative, G.O.P. tide; their replacements were ideologically opposed to the program. Partisanship, more than place of residence, seems to have been the determining factor in USHA's defeat.

102. Despite this rebuff, Straus went ahead and used some of his previously authorized funds to start a farm housing program. United States Housing Authority, *Annual Report for 1941* (Washington, D.C., 1942), pp. 47–49.

103. Daniel J. Elazar, "Urban Problems and the Federal Government: A Historical Inquiry," *Political Science Quarterly*, LXXXIII (Dec. 1967), 505–25, minimizes the precedent-setting features of the 1930s in regard to federal-municipal relations. He feels that 1913, not 1933, saw the beginning of specialized urban demands on the national government; but he ignores the substantive changes after 1933 in the nature of the relationship between the federal and municipal governments and in the nature of the requested federal aid. Nor does he treat the

rise of urban lobbying groups and the passage of urban-oriented legislation beginning in 1933. Interestingly, neither Jane Perry Clark in her contemporary account of federalism in the 1930s, *The Rise of a New Federalism* (New York, 1938), nor James T. Patterson's more recent *The New Deal and the States* discusses these developments.

104. Brownlow, in AMA, *Proceedings 1931–1935*, p. 298.

105. C. A. Dykstra, "City, State, and Nation," *Municipal Yearbook 1937*, p. 12; Cornelius D. Scully, address to Kentucky Municipal League, reprinted in *U.S. Municipal News*, Oct. 15, 1939, p. 115. La Guardia rarely had a good word for the states. When one Michigan city manager wrote him to complain about the unfair treatment the government at Lansing afforded cities, La Guardia replied: "I guess all states are alike. What the country needs is for a few mayors to run for President, then we will hold them in line." George W. Welsh to La Guardia, Feb. 15, 1944; La Guardia to Welsh, Feb. 17, 1944, Michigan folder, Box 2688, La Guardia MSS.

106. Leonard D. White, "Municipal Government, 1933," *Municipal Finance*, VI (Feb. 1934), 1.

107. *NYT*, Oct. 20, 1936, p. 24.

108. After the results were in, a Republican congressman from Kansas wrote that Roosevelt and his group "have become the party of the great cities and the industrial labor groups of the country. I, personally, cannot see what Agriculture stands to gain anything by tying up with that alignment, so it seems to me a logical division would be that of the South and West against the cities and industrial centers of the East." Clifford R. Hope to R. J. Laubengayer, Nov. 13, 1936, quoted in Patterson, *Congressional Conservatism*, p. 84.

109. Raymond S. Short, "Municipalities and the Federal Government," *Annals*, CCVII (Jan. 1940), 44–53; Richard E. Saunders, "Under the Dome in Washington," *Municipal Finance*, VII (Feb. 1935), 5–7.

110. For this aspect of the 1930s, see *infra*, pp. 82–96.

111. Dykstra, "Municipal Costs and Unemployment Relief," p. 30; Dykstra, "Your City and You in National Life," *Vital Speeches*, III (April 1, 1937), 366. But if the Federal Government was not prepared to cope with local problems, municipalities were acting to formalize their ties to the national government; in 1936, Cleveland was the first city to create an Office of Federal Relations.

CHAPTER 3

1. J. D. B. De Bow, *Statistical View of the United States: Compendium of the Seventh Census* (Washington, D.C., 1854), p. 192.

2. Carroll D. Wright, *The History and Growth of the United States Census* (Washington, D.C., 1900), pp. 58–69.

3. Bureau of the Census, *Compendium of the Tenth Census: 1880* (Washington, D.C., 1883), p. xxx.

4. Bureau of the Census, *Tenth Census: Population of the United States* (Washington, D.C., 1883), pp. xxviii–xxx.

5. G. W. Hanger, "Present Condition of Municipal Statistics in the United States," in *Proceedings of the 7th Annual Meeting of the National Municipal League* (Philadelphia, 1901), pp. 264–77.

6. Bureau of the Census, *Tenth Census: Social Statistics of Cities* (2 vols.; Washington, D.C., 1886), I, 531–32.

7. Bureau of the Census, *Thirteenth Census: Population* (Washington, D.C., 1913), pp. 73–77. The 1910 Census also saw the adoption of a new population definition of urban communities: 2500 people.

8. Bureau of the Census, *Census Tract Manual* (5th ed.; Washington, D.C., 1966), pp. 1–2. The census tract also offers great benefits to business; Bureau publications have tended to emphasize this fact.

9. Bureau of the Census, *Annual Report: 1912* (Washington, D.C., 1913), p. 9.

10. Walter F. Willcox, "Census of Cities," *National Municipal Review*, III (Jan. 1914), 159; National Resources Committee, Research Committee on Urbanism, "Interim Report" (mimeographed, 1936), pp. 18–19, Table III.

11. *Third National Conference on City Planning* (Boston, 1911), pp. 250–58; Philip Kates, "A National Department of Municipalities," *American City*, VI (Jan. 1912), 405–7.

12. *Eighth National Conference on City Planning* (New York, 1916), pp. 267–72. Cf. *Third National Conference*, pp. 285–92.

13. A. W. Crawford, "A Proposed Federal Agency to Deal with Housing, Town Planning and Other Municipal Affairs," *American City*, XX (Feb. 1919), 179; Harlean James, "Service—The Keynote of a New Cabinet Department," *American Review of Reviews*, LIX (Feb. 1919), 187–90.

14. Paul V. Betters, *Federal Services to Municipal Governments* (New York, 1931), p. 5.

15. Seymour I. Toll, *Zoned American* (New York, 1969), pp. 35–187, 201–3. This federal intervention was not "an unmixed blessing." The model act fostered overall zoning unsupported by a thoughtfully prepared general plan for the future development of the city; a later revision tended to perpetuate the rather narrow scope of city plans and to encourage city planning commissions to develop piecemeal plans rather than a thoroughly integrated, comprehensive plan. Nor did the model acts provide any safeguards against the use of zoning in behalf of racial or economic segregation. Mel Scott, *American City Planning Since 1890* (Berkeley, 1969), pp. 194–95, 243.

16. *American City*, XXXVII (Nov. 1927), 576; Louis Brownlow, *A Passion for Anonymity* (Chicago, 1958), pp. 278–79. For similar ideas in the 1910s and 1920s, see Frank M. Stewart, *A Half Century of Municipal Reform* (Berkeley, 1950), pp. 89–90, 92; and William Anderson, "The Federal Government and the Cities," *National Municipal Review*, XIII (May 1924), 288–93.

17. Quoted in James F. Short, Jr., ed., *The Social Fabric of the Metropolis: Contributions of the Chicago School of Urban Sociology* (Chicago, 1971), p. xix.

18. President's Research Committee on Social Trends, *Recent Social Trends in the United States* (New York, 1933), pp. xxi–xxiii. The committee's "Review of Findings" was written mainly by its chairman, Wesley G. Mitchell, the Columbia University economist.

19. David Cushman Coyle, "Frederic A. Delano: Catalyst," *Survey Graphic*, XXXV (July 1946), 252–54; Horace W. Peaselee, "Make No Little Planners," *Journal of the American Institute of Architects*, XX (Sept. 1953), 136–39; Charles W. Eliot, 2nd, "Frederic A. Delano: A Biographical Minute," *Landscape Architecture*, XLIII (April 1953), 130–31.

20. "The Merriam Political Legacy," *National Municipal Review*, XLII (Feb. 1953), 64.

21. Merriam's campaign manager in 1911 was Harold L. Ickes. In 1934, Ickes tried to drum up support for another Merriam candidacy for City Hall. Harold L. Ickes, *The Secret Diary of Harold L. Ickes* (3 vols.; New York, 1954), I, 246. A short autobiographical sketch of Merriam, "The Education of Charles Merriam," can be found in Leonard D. White, ed., *The Future of Government in the United States* (Chicago, 1942), pp. 1–24.

22. Albert Lepawsky to author, July 14, 1970.

23. Charles E. Merriam, *et al., The Government of the Metropolitan Region of Chicago* (Chicago, 1933); Merriam, "Breaking the Clinch," *State Government*, IV (Dec. 1931), 8–9. Merriam was not the first to make this proposal; see, for example, "Shall Our Great Cities be Made States," *American City*, X (Feb. 1914), 142–44.

24. In 1942, one board staff member, referring to Merriam, Delano, and Eliot, wrote: "Two members of the NRPB and its executive director have had a life-long interest in urban problems and are eager to see real advances made." Charles S. Ascher to Sherman S. Sheppard, Feb. 6, 1942, Box 823, Central Office Correspondence [hereafter COC], Records of the National Resources Planning Board [hereafter NRPB Records], Record Group 187, National Archives. The third member of the original NPB, Wesley C. Mitchell, concerned himself mainly with economic matters. After 1935, Merriam was clearly the dominant figure on the board.

25. Merriam appears to have begun thinking about the project in the fall of 1934 and probably discussed it with his colleagues at the University of Chicago. See, for example, Louis Wirth to Merriam, Dec. 15, 1934, Folder 2, Box CCVII, Charles E. Merriam MSS., University of Chicago Library. Albert Lepawsky to author, July 14, 1970. It is first mentioned in the NRB Advisory Committee minutes of Jan. 6, 1935, Folder 7, Box CLXXIX, Merriam MSS.

26. Merriam statement on "Urbanism," June 11, 1935, Vol. I, File 106–29, COC, NRPB Records. In May 1935, the Joint Conference on Planning, an amalgam of the National Conference on City Planning, the American City Planning Institute, the American Civic Association, and the American Society of Planning Officials also supported the project. *Planning for the Future of American Cities* (Chicago, n.d.), pp. 186–87. NRB Advisory Committee, Minutes, Jan. 20–21, 1935, Folder 7, Box CLXXIX, Merriam MSS.

27. Merriam to William Anderson, Feb. 18, 1935, Folder 2, Box CCVII, Merriam MSS.

28. Merriam, "The Role of the Urban Community in the National Economy," May 21, 1935, Box 836, COC, NRPB Records.

29. Goodrich did not remain on the committee very long due to the press of other obligations. No one was appointed to replace him.

30. In practice, however, Wilson contributed little to the committee. He was supposed to work with Wirth on the section comparing the urban and rural ways of life, but only when the final report was virtually completed did he submit a statement on "Rural-Industrial Pattern of Life: An Alternative." Research Committee on Urbanism, Minutes, Sept. 25, 1936, Box 840; Wilson to Wirth, Jan. 15, 1937, Box 849, *ibid.*

31. National Resources Committee, Research Committee on Urbanism, *Our Cities: Their Role in the National Economy* (Washington, D.C., 1937), p. 71. It was originally planned to publish these monographs in five supplementary volumes, but budget stringencies and unfavorable comments by reviewers on some of the pieces cut this down to two: *Urban Government* (Washington, D.C., 1939) and *Urban Planning and Land Policies* (Washington, D.C., 1939).

32. Stuart A. Rice to Eliot, April 7, 1936; W. L. Austin to Eliot, April 7, 1936, Box 838, COC, NRPB Records; Wirth to Merriam, Jan. 16, 1936; Eliot to Merriam, Feb. 27, 1936, Folder 2, Box CCVII, Merriam MSS.

33. Merriam was not officially a member of the Urbanism Committee, but he sat in on most of its sessions and kept in close contact with its staff; Ladislas Segoe to author, July 15, 1970; Roscoe C. Martin to author, July 31, 1970. Merriam later wrote that the committee "functioned only under very great pressure from me." Merriam to Walter Blucher, April 30, 1941, Folder 10, Box XLV, Merriam MSS.

34. "Interim Report," draft of May 20, 1936, typewritten copy, p. 48, Box 839, COC, NRPB Records.

35. Albert Lepawsky to L. Segoe, May 22, 1936, Box 869, *ibid.* The President's Committee on Administrative Management had already been created; Merriam and Brownlow were members.

36. L. Segoe to members of the Research Committee, May 27, 1936; Eliot to Delano, June 17, 1936, Box 832, *ibid.;* Research Committee on Urbanism, "Interim Report" (mimeographed edition), pp. iii–iv, 45–49.

37. Segoe to members of the Research Committee, Feb. 15, 1937, Box 832; Lloyd George, Editorial Comment, n.d. [probably Winter/Spring 1937], Box 843, COC, NRPB Records; "Our Cities," draft of Feb. 13, 1937, typescript, Box 5, Ladislas Segoe MSS., Collection of Regional History and University Archives, Cornell University Library.

38. Research Committee on Urbanism, *Our Cities*, p. 4.

39. Henry S. Dennison memo for Eliot, n.d. [July 1937], Box 860; Lloyd George, Editorial Comment, Box 843, COC, NRPB Records.

40. "Bureau of Urban Research Inaugurated by Princeton University," *American City*, LVI (Sept. 1941), 87. Due to inadequate financial support, however, the bureau never accomplished very much.

41. L. Segoe, "City Planning and the Urbanism Study," *Planning for the Future of American Cities*, p. 9.

42. The fact that the Urbanism Committee was a mere subgroup of the NRC, and not a presidentially appointed body, meant that its report received far less attention from Roosevelt, Congress, and the mass media.

43. "Our Cities," *Public Management*, XIX (Oct. 1937), 290; John Blanchard, "The

National Government Surveys Urban Life," *National Municipal Review*, XXVI (Oct. 1937), 479–83.

44. *Wall Street Journal*, Sept. 20, 1937; Philadelphia *Inquirer*, Sept. 20, 1937, clippings in Box 845, COC, NRPB Records. This collection of clippings, gathered from newspapers all over the country, contained fewer than thirty articles and editorials on the report.

45. Among the papers that ran feature articles were the *Christian Science Monitor*, the St. Louis *Post-Dispatch*, and the Milwaukee *Journal*. Only two national magazines, *Business Week* and the *Nation*, mentioned the report. *Business Week* carried a summary of the report's findings on the urban industrial structure: "Urges City Industrial Planning," *Business Week*, Sept. 25, 1937, pp. 42, 44. The *Nation* printed a review which criticized the committee's recommendations for staying "well within the safety zone of more and more facts, more and more education, more and more cooperation with agencies, public and private, hopelessly prevented from taking any drastic, long-range action." Howard Ward, "Cities that Consume Men," *Nation*, CXLVI (Jan. 22, 1938), 91–93.

46. Washington *Post*, Sept. 20, 1937, p. 6; New York *Herald Tribune*, Sept. 20, 1937, p. 22; Jacksonville *Tribune*, Oct. 8, 1937; Cincinnati *Enquirer*, Sept. 22, 1937; Cleveland *Plain Dealer*, Sept. 20, 1937, clippings in Box 845, COC, NRPB Records.

47. Merriam was alert to the deteriorating situation on Capitol Hill and tried to shield the report from this rebellion in Congress. The changes in phraseology and the recommendations have already been mentioned. In addition, Merriam decided against the publication of a committee staff study on "Urbanism and National Politics." He felt its comments on legislative malapportionment and rural control of congressional committee chairmanships would "rub a number of people 'on the Hill' the wrong way and invite unnecessary animosity." Segoe to Eliot, Oct. 2, 1937, Box 832, COC, NRPB Records.

48. Eliot memo for NRPB, March 19, 1941, Box 883, *ibid.* For the role of NAREB, FHA, and NRPB in spurring urban redevelopment, see *infra*, pp. 112–18, 122–26.

49. Delano to Louis Brownlow, March 21, 1941, Box 791, COC, NRPB Records. similar letters were sent to the AMA, USCM, ICMA, the city planner Alfred Bettman, Dykstra, and the real estate developer J. C. Nichols.

50. Replies are in Vol. 2, File 106.29, *ibid.* Merriam to Wirth, April 21, 1941; Wirth to Merriam, April 23, 1941, Folder 20, Box LVIII, Merriam MSS.

51. Louis Wirth, "Functions of the Urban Section," Sept. 16, 1942, Box 853, COC, NRPB Records.

52. National Resources Planning Board, *National Resources Development Report for 1942* (Washington, D.C., 1942), pp. 106–8.

53. Brownlow memo for Samuel I. Rosenman, Oct. 30, 1941; Ascher, Comments on Woodbury's memo for Judge Rosenman on Housing Reorganization, Oct. 19, 1941, Box 64, Division of Administrative Management, Records of the Bureau of the Budget, Record Group 51, National Archives. In March 1942, Merriam urged that consideration be given to the establishment of a national "bureau or department of urbanism, in view of the proportion of our people who dwell in

cities and the importance generally of cities in our political and economic system." *The Problems of the Cities and Towns* (Cambridge, Mass., 1942), p. 39.

54. Ascher memo for John B. Blandford, Jr., Feb. 25, 1942, Box 138, OA 1942–1946, Records of the Department of Housing and Urban Development, Record Group 207, National Archives.

55. Albert Lepawsky, "Washington Gathers Municipal Data," *Public Opinion Quarterly*, I (July 1937), 101.

CHAPTER 4

1. Jacob Riis, *How the Other Half Lives* (New York, 1890), pp. 22, 32–33.

2. National Resources Committee, Research Committee on Urbanism, *Our Cities* (Washington, D.C., 1937), p. 75.

3. Mabel L. Walker, *Urban Blight and Slums* (Cambridge, Mass., 1938), pp. 4–35.

4. Testimony of John B. Blandford, Jr., and accompanying charts and tables, in Senate Special Committee on Post-War Economic Policy and Planning, 79th Cong. 1st Sess., *Hearings Pursuant to S. Res. 102: Housing and Urban Redevelopment* [hereafter cited as *Hearings on Housing and Urban Redevelopment*] (Washington, D.C., 1945), pp. 1228–37. This data had been collected in the 1930s.

5. Edith Elmer Wood, *Slums and Blighted Areas in the United States* (Washington, D.C., 1935), p. 19.

6. David E. Lilienthal, *Journals: The TVA Years* (New York, 1964), p. 41. The aide was Louis Howe.

7. Land values in cities over 30,000 population rose from $25 billion in 1920 to $50 billion in 1926. By contrast, the total value of farm properties dropped from $55 billion to $37 billion over the same period. Urban assessment valuations fell an average of 17.8 per cent between 1929 and 1933. Charles N. Glaab and A. Theodore Brown, *A History of Urban America* (New York, 1967), p. 279; Frederick L. Bird, *The Municipal Debt Load in 1935* (New York, 1935), pp. 6–7.

8. Annual expenditures for home repairs decreased from $50 million in 1928 to $0.5 million in 1933. Glaab and Brown, *History of Urban America*, p. 299.

9. Nelson quoted in House of Representatives, Select Committee on Lobbying Activities, 81st Cong. 2nd Sess., *Hearings Pursuant to H. Res. 298: Housing Lobby* (Washington, D.C., 1950), p. 25.

10. Arthur Holden, "Facing Realities in Slum Clearance," *Architectural Record*, LXXI (Feb. 1932), 75–82; "Gabriel Over Block 326-A," *Architectural Forum*, LXI (Jan. 1935), 104–7; "Group Action," *Land Usage*, III (April/May 1936).

11. "NAREB Suggests Plan for Reclaiming Blighted Areas," *National Real Estate Journal*, XXXVI (Oct. 1935), 33–34.

12. *Planners Journal*, III (Sept./Oct. 1937), 135; Ira S. Robbins, "Proposed Rehabilitation Procedures," in Walker, *Urban Blight and Slums*, pp. 227–31; Robert B. Mitchell, "Prospects for Neighborhood Rehabilitation," in *Housing Yearbook 1938* (Chicago, 1938), pp. 144–45; "For the Replanning of Cities by Neighborhood Areas," *American City*, LII (Feb. 1938), 56.

13. Arthur Binns, "Making Rehabilitation Pay," *Freehold*, IV (April 15, 1939),

268–73; "NAREB Studies Slum Clearance," *National Real Estate Journal*, XL (May 1939), 41; "Rebuilding American Cities: A Task to be Faced," *ibid.*, XLI (Feb. 1940), 14–17; "The Philadelphia Convention," *Freehold*, VII (Dec. 1, 1940), 370–71.

14. "Memorandum on the Program of the Committee on Housing and Blighted Areas," *Freehold*, VII (Aug. 1941), 14, 15–16.

15. The term "urban redevelopment" was not actually mentioned in the NAREB report, but it was coming into common usage at about this time. It is not known when the expression was used for the first time; a New York State law passed in 1941 contained the phrase in its title and "urban redevelopment" immediately became very popular as a shorthand way of describing the goal of salvaging blighted areas. One of the authors of the New York act defined urban redevelopment as "a method not for rehousing *slum dwellers* so much as for rehabilitating slums" [Thomas C. Desmond, "Blighted Areas Get a New Chance," *National Municipal Review*, XXX (Nov. 1941), 629], but as will be indicated below, the term came to have different meanings for different people. On certain points, however, there was general agreement: 1) private capital would be utilized as much as possible, in contrast to public housing; 2) rebuilding would not be restricted *solely* to low-rent dwellings, again in contrast to public housing; 3) the city's economy, in some vague way, was to be helped. As used in this chapter, urban redevelopment will simply connote a program of tearing down decaying urban structures and replacing them with new ones that will aid city residents and, therefore, the city.

16. Frederic A. Delano to Charles S. Ascher, July 5, 1941, Box 14, Urban Section Files, Records of the National Resources Planning Board, Record Group 187, National Archives; Ladislas Segoe to Delano, July 19, 1941, Box 7, Ladislas Segoe MSS., Collection of Regional History and University Archives, Cornell University Library; Dorothy Rosenman, "Comment," in *National Conference on Planning 1941* (Chicago, 1941), p. 163.

17. Guy Greer and Alvin H. Hansen, *Urban Redevelopment and Housing—A Plan for Post-War* (Washington, 1941), pp. 10–12, 23–24; Alvin H. Hansen, "Four Methods of Financing Redevelopment Costs," in *Proceedings of the National Conference on Housing* (n.p., 1944), pp. 36–42.

18. Frederic A. Delano, "To Meet the Housing Needs of the Lower Income Groups," *American City*, LII (Jan. 1937), 45–48. Background material on the memorandum can be found in Central Housing Committee Files, Box 118, Records of the Department of Housing and Urban Development, Record Group 207, National Archives. Coming across the memorandum seven years later, one housing official found it "a rather remarkable document; it embodies most of the ideas that we have considered for an urban redevelopment bill." Warren J. Vinton memo for Philip M. Klutznick, Sept. 14, 1944, Box 28, Warren J. Vinton MSS., Collection of Regional History and University Archives, Cornell University Library.

19. Albert Mayer, Henry Wright, and Lewis Mumford, "A Concrete Program," *New Republic*, LXXVIII (March 7, 1934), 91.

20. United States Housing Authority, *Annual Report (Non-Defense Activities): 1941*

(Washington, D.C., 1942), pp. 43–44; Housing and Home Finance Agency, *Housing Statistics Yearbook* (Washington, D.C., 1948), p. 59.

21. Federal Home Loan Bank Board, *Seventh Annual Report: Fiscal Year 1939* (Washington, D.C., 1939), pp. 37–38; FHLBB, *Waverly: A Study in Neighborhood Conservation* (Washington, D.C., 1940).

22. Rehabilitation received greater attention in the 1950s when the Eisenhower administration looked for ways to cut the costs of urban redevelopment; see *infra*, pp. 171–76.

23. Harland Bartholomew, "Present and Ultimate Effects of Decentralization Upon American Cities," *Mortgage Bankers Association of America Yearbook 1940* (Chicago, 1940), pp. 63–64; "Rebuilding the Cities," *Business Week*, July 6, 1940, pp. 38–39; *Freehold*, VII (Dec. 1, 1940), 370.

24. None of the voluminous statistics on the characteristics of FHA-insured mortgages deals directly with the central city versus suburb issue. A 1942 FHA publication, *FHA Homes in Metropolitan Districts*, touched upon the question only to say that since suburban areas grew faster than central cities between 1930 and 1940, "the major portion of home financing under the FHA has been in these areas" [p. 6]. During the late 1930s, FHA annual reports included data on the distribution of FHA mortgages within metropolitan areas by city size. These figures tend to support the contention that big cities (500,000 people and up) received less than their proportionate share of FHA assistance; this material does not, however, draw a clear distinction between core city and suburbs. FHA's post-war annual reports gave geographical breakdowns by states only.

25. Jacob Crane, "Location Factors in Housing Programs," in National Resources Committee, *Housing: The Continuing Problem* (Washington, D.C., 1940), pp. 125–26.

26. *Freehold*, VI (Feb. 15, 1940), 111–12; Federal Housing Administration, *Seventh Annual Report: 1940* (Washington, D.C., 1941), pp. 19, 23.

27. The Resources Board's Land Committee did, however, issue a report in April 1941 entitled *Urban Lands*. The committee called for greater public control over land use and more extensive acquisition of land by municipalities. But on the question of federal aid to local government to finance these purchases, the report was noncommittal. National Resources Planning Board, Land Committee, *Urban Lands* (Washington, D.C., 1941), pp. 15–17, 30–31.

28. Charles E. Merriam to Louis Wirth, April 21, 1941, Folder 20, Box LVIII, Charles E. Merriam MSS., University of Chicago Library.

29. Merriam to Walter Blucher, April 30, 1941, Folder 10, Box XLV, *ibid.;* Eliot memo for NRPB, March 19, 1941, Box 883, Central Office Correspondence [hereafter cited as COC]; Delano to Louis Brownlow, March 21, 1941, Box 791, COC; Delano to Charles S. Ascher, June 12, 1941, Box 14, Urban Section Files, NRPB Records.

30. Ascher to Ernest J. Bohn, Jan. 8, 1942; Ascher to L. Deming Tilton, Jan. 8, 1942, Box 823, COC, NRPB Records.

31. Ascher memo for Eliot, April 3, 1942, Folder 5, Box CCLII, Merriam MSS.; Ascher memo for NRPB, Nov. 26, 1941, Box 823, COC; Earle S. Draper to

Delano, April 21, 1942, Box 853, COC; "Proposed Program for Urban Conservation and Development, 1942–1943," n.d.; "A Program of Planning for Urban Conservation and Development, Fiscal Year 1943," Box 14, Urban Section Files, NRPB Records.

32. "Memorandum . . . Program . . . Committee . . . Housing and Blighted Areas," p. 14; Greer and Hansen, *Urban Redevelopment*, p. 7; Charles S. Ascher, "Urban Conservation and Development," in National Resources Planning Board, *National Resources Development Report for 1942* (Washington, D.C., 1942), p. 102.

33. Jacob Crane, "Notes on Consideration of Uncle Sam's Post-War Role in Housing," Jan. 15, 1943, OA 1942–1946, Box 142; NHA, Program Council, "Meetings on Land Assembly," Box 42, HUD Records.

34. Bettman's brief in *Village of Euclid v. Amber Realty Co.*, 272 U.S. 365 (1926), is usually credited with playing a big part in the Supreme Court's decision upholding the constitutionality of zoning legislation. See Seymour I. Toll, *Zoned American* (New York, 1969), pp. 236–42. At the time he aided Hansen and Greer, Bettman was chairman of the Legislative Committee of the American Institute of Planners, and chairman of the American Bar Association's Committee on Planning Law Legislation.

35. Thomas, a liberal Democrat, was probably asked to submit the measure because the most obvious sponsor of this piece of urban legislation, Robert F. Wagner, was too closely identified with public housing, a subject Bettman wished to steer clear of. The senator from Utah played no conspicuous role in advancing urban redevelopment after he introduced the bill.

36. The ULI wanted Wagner's name on the bill to allay liberal fears that the program would be a federal giveaway to vested interests. But Wagner, in his remarks to the Senate, made it clear that he was presenting the bill only at ULI's request and was not prepared to endorse its specific provisions. *Congressional Record*, 78th Cong. 1st Sess., p. 5357.

37. The Bettman bill provided for federal "advances" which amounted to grants; the ULI called for 99-year, low-interest loans. By 1944, NAREB's Nelson was urging that the federal aid come in the form of tax exemptions for investors who bought redevelopment bonds. In this way, absolutely no federal supervision would be required, and the only cost to the government would be a loss of revenue. Herbert U. Nelson, "Interest-Free Bonds for Slum Clearance," *Urban Land*, III (May 1944), 2–3.

38. Nathan Straus, *The Seven Myths of Housing* (New York, 1944), pp. 69–73.

39. Henry Reed, "These Men Have Plans," *Task*, no. 3 (Oct. 1942), pp. 13–20; Walter Blucher to Catherine Bauer Wurster, June 2, 1943, "B" folder, Catherine Bauer Wurster MSS., College of Environmental Design Library, University of California, Berkeley; Charles Abrams, "Real Estate Radicals," *Public Housing*, X (April 1944), 6–7.

40. Catherine Bauer, "Urban Redevelopment," *Public Housing Progress*, IX (Jan. 1943), 2.

41. Leon H. Keyserling to Sergei N. Grimm, Jan. 24, 1945, Box 2; Catherine Bauer memo to National Public Housing Conference, *et al.*, April 18, 1943, Box 4, Vinton MSS.

42. Edwin S. Burdell, "Rehousing Needs of the Families on the Stuyvesant Town Site," *Journal of the American Institute of Planners*, XI (Oct./Dec. 1945), 16–19. In 1940, New York Governor Herbert Lehman had vetoed an urban redevelopment bill because it made no provision for rehousing; the 1941 act he signed contained a section requiring redevelopers to find equivalent housing for displaced families. But after two years of non-action, the state acceded to Metropolitan Life's demand to eliminate this rule; plans for Stuyvesant Town were announced shortly thereafter. Before it was all over, however, Metropolitan had spent $200,000 to relocate 3,000 families from the site. Stuyvesant Town also raised the racial issue; for the problems of race in urban redevelopment, see *infra,* pp. 212–13.

43. Roger S. Nelson, "Federal Aid for Urban Land Acquisition," *Journal of Land and Public Utility Economics*, XXI (May 1945), 126–30; Herbert Emmerich memo for John Blandford, June 14, 1943, Urban Redevelopment Folder, Legislative Files, Office of the General Counsel, Department of Housing and Urban Development, Washington, D.C.; Keyserling memo for Blandford, June 22, 1943, OA 1942–1946, Box 126, HUD Records.

44. Bauer memo, April 18, 1943, Box 4, Vinton MSS.; Jacob Crane memo for Coleman Woodbury, May 28, 1943; Keyserling memo for Blandford, June 1, 1943; Blandford to F. J. Bailey, June 9, 1943, Box 126; NHA, Program Council, "Meetings on Land Assembly," Box 42, OA 1942–1946, HUD Records.

45. Walter Blucher memo for Charles Merriam, Aug. 1, 1941, Box 14, Urban Section Files; Bettman to Eliot, March 20, 1943, Box 854, COC, NRPB Records; Bettman memo for Hansen, April 8, 1943, Reel 27, Alfred Bettman MSS., Collection of Regional History and University Archives, Cornell University Library; Ascher to Coleman Woodbury, Jan. 27, 1944, OA 1942–1946, Box 131, HUD Records; *Hearings on Housing and Urban Redevelopment*, pp. 1605–6.

46. Henry Wright, "Sinking Slums," *Survey Graphic*, XXII (Aug. 1933), 419.

47. Lewis Mumford, "Memorandum on Proposed Federal Program for Urban Development and Housing," Oct. 31, 1941, Box 20, Urban Section Files, NRPB Records. Mumford continued: "In terms of the future, an FSA overnight camp in California is closer to the pattern of a new community than a 12-story USHA slum replacement project. . . . Unconsciously, everyone today assumes that metropolitan standards will again become universal ones. I would challenge that belief. In terms of the post-war world, it is much safer to assume that no country will have the means to continue at a metropolitan level."

48. Lewis Mumford, "How Can Our Cities Survive?" *New Republic*, CVIII (Feb. 8, 1943), 187.

49. Henry S. Churchill, "America's Town Planning Begins," *New Republic*, LXXXVI (June 3, 1936), 98; Tracy Augur, "New Towns in the National Economy," *Planners Journal*, III (March/April 1937), 40–41. Also see Clarence S. Stein, "New Towns for the Needs of a New Age," *NYT Magazine*, Oct. 8, 1933, pp. 6–7; Jacob Crane, "Garden Cities," *American City*, L (Feb. 1937), 65.

50. Quoted in Arthur M. Schlesinger, *The Coming of the New Deal* (Boston, 1958), pp. 370–71; Rexford G. Tugwell, "The Meaning of the Greenbelt Towns," *New Republic*, XC (Feb. 17, 1937), 43.

51. Fiorello H. La Guardia, "The Federal Work Program and the Cities," in *City Problems of 1935* (Washington, D.C., 1935), pp. 13–14; *American City*, LI (Feb. 1936), 43 (comments of Edith Elmer Wood); Harland Bartholomew, "The Case for Downtown Locations," *Planners Journal*, IV (March/June 1939), 32–33.

52. Tugwell, "Meaning of the Greenbelt Towns," 43. As chairman of the New York City Planning Commission from 1936 to 1941, Tugwell took a different position. He hoped to create "a city without suburbs as we know them—because the city itself is a good place to live." He searched in vain for a redevelopment scheme that would reverse the "centrifugal forces" posing a serious financial threat to the city. S. J. Woolf, "Planning the City of Tomorrow," *NYT Magazine*, June 18, 1939, p. 15; Tugwell memo for Fiorello La Guardia, July 23, 1940, City Planning Commission folder, Box 2614, Fiorello H. La Guardia MSS., Municipal Archives and Records Center, New York City; Tugwell, "San Francisco as Seen from New York," in *National Conference on Planning 1940* (Chicago, 1940), pp. 186–88.

53. During the 1930s, central-city population increased 6.1 per cent, suburban areas grew 16.9 per cent, and the nation as a whole gained 7.2 per cent. In the 1930s, unlike the 1920s, the suburbs actually gained more people than the central cities. In the 1940s, the suburbs continued to outstrip the central cities; the respective growth figures were 13.9 per cent, 36.5 per cent, and 14.5 per cent.

54. Delano, "Must Urban Redevelopment Wait on Bombing?" *American City*, LVI (May 1941), 35.

55. On Radburn, see Roy Lubove, *City Planning in the 1920s* (Pittsburgh, 1963), pp. 62–67.

56. Bauer memo, April 18, 1943, Box 4, Vinton MSS.; she claimed that the "main objective of the bold ULI proposals was the confusion of the liberals and professionals in the planning and housing fields in which they succeeded, temporarily, at least." Bauer, "Is Urban Redevelopment Possible Under Existing Legislation?" in *Planning 1946* (Chicago, 1946), p. 67.

57. "Housing's White Knight," *Architectural Forum*, LXXXIV (March 1946), 119; NHA, Post-War Council, "Meeting with Catherine Bauer Wurster," July 7, 1943, Box 42, OA 1942–1946, HUD Records; Bauer, "Cities in Flux," *American Scholar*, I (Jan. 1944), 78; Bauer, "Is Redevelopment Possible?" 69, 70.

58. "Housing's White Knight," 119. Miss Bauer's views were apparently shared by the man in the White House. Discussing housing matters with his budget director in the fall of 1941, Roosevelt said he thought the reformers "might be making a mistake in trying to rehabilitate slums as against using land farther out and with that bringing about a further decentralization of industry, or providing some cheaper means of transportation." Conversations with the President, 1941 [Oct. 14, 1941], Harold D. Smith MSS., Franklin D. Roosevelt Library. FDR had, of course, always been interested in breaking up the big urban centers, but he might have ended up supporting urban redevelopment just as he did public housing for political reasons. As it was, the war kept him removed from such domestic issues, and he never expressed a definite opinion on the subject before his death.

59. Boyden Sparkes, "Can the Cities Come Back?" *Saturday Evening Post*, CCXVII (Nov. 4, 1944), 43.

60. "The Broadening Concept of the City Problem Over Two Decades," *Federal Home Loan Bank Review*, X (Oct. 1944), 177.

61. Ruth G. Weintraub and Rosalind Tough, "Redevelopment Without Plan," *National Municipal Review*, XXXVI (July 1948), 364–70; "The Status of Urban Redevelopment," *Urban Land*, IX (Oct. 1948), 1, 3–7. The two exceptions were Illinois, which appropriated $10 million for slum clearance, and Indiana, which allowed Indianapolis to levy a special tax for redevelopment.

62. *Hearings on Housing and Urban Redevelopment*, pp. 1305–6. Only one other NHA official, Philip Klutznick, commissioner of the Federal Public Housing Administration [successor to the USHA], discussed urban redevelopment; he underscored Blandford's remarks on rehousing, *ibid.,* p. 1557. In 1944, the NHA had objected to a proposed urban redevelopment bill for the District of Columbia because it made no provision for the relocation of displaced families; Blandford to F. J. Bailey, May 12, 1944, Box 126, OA 1942–1946, HUD Records.

63. *Hearings on Housing and Urban Redevelopment*, pp. 1738–39.

64. Arthur Binns, "Is the Wagner Bill for Rebuilding Our Cities Desirable?" *National Real Estate Journal*, XLIV (Oct. 1943), 16–20.

65. *Hearings on Housing and Urban Redevelopment*, pp. 1606–12. Bettman died shortly after his appearance.

66. Arthur M. Schlesinger, Jr., "His Eyes Have Seen the Glory," *Colliers*, CXIX (Feb. 22, 1947), 13, 34; Richard O. Davies, " 'Mr. Republican' Turns 'Socialist': Robert Taft and Public Housing," *Ohio History*, LXXIII (Summer 1964), 135–43; Charles Abrams, *The City Is the Frontier* (New York, 1965), pp. 81–82.

67. *Hearings on Housing and Urban Redevelopment*, pp. 1614–18, 1699, 1909.

68. In a 1942 memorandum prepared for Ascher at the NRPB, political scientist V. O. Key had observed that "if a thoroughgoing program of redevelopment is prosecuted—having serious repercussions on the real estate market both within and without the central cities—the need for a metropolitan agency will be urgent. But if the program is to have little effect outside slum and blighted areas—if the program were merely to rehouse the same people in about the same areas—the need for a metropolitan agency would not be so pressing." V. O. Key, "Local Governmental Structures and Federal Financing of Urban Redevelopment" (mimeographed, June 22, 1942), Folder 6, Box CCLIII, Merriam MSS. Since almost all the testimony the Taft Subcommittee heard dealt with blighted areas, and since Taft was only interested in slum districts, the report he issued did not mention metropolitan planning.

69. Senate, 79th Cong. 1st Sess., Report to the Special Committee on Post-War Economic Policy and Planning by the Subcommittee on Housing and Urban Redevelopment, *Post-War Housing* (Washington, D.C., 1945), pp. 17, 23.

70. See Truman's "Special Message to the Congress: 21-Point Program for the Reconversion Period," Sept. 16, 1945, in *The Public Papers of the Presidents: Harry S Truman 1945* (Washington, D.C., 1961), pp. 291–92. He endorsed urban redevelopment as part of a comprehensive housing program.

71. The only witness from the business world in four years of congressional hearings to endorse the urban redevelopment title of the W-E-T bill without reservation

was a representative from the brokerage house of Shields & Co., which dealt heavily in municipal bonds. Senate Committee on Banking and Currency, 79th Cong. 1st Sess., *Hearings on S. 1592: General Housing Act of 1945* (Washington, D.C., 1946), pp. 473–74.

72. *Ibid.,* pp. 386, 438, 444–45, 481, 837–38; House of Representatives Committee on Banking and Currency, 80th Cong. 2nd Sess., *Hearings on S. 866: General Housing* (Washington, D.C., 1948), pp. 901, 1114; Senate Committee on Banking and Currency, 81st Cong. 1st Sess., *Hearings on S. 138: General Housing Legislation* (Washington, D.C., 1949), pp. 413–14, 571, 727, 744–45; *Headlines,* XII (Nov. 5, 1945); XIII (Feb. 1946), Part II; XIV (July 7, 1947); "Taft's New Housing Bill," *Urban Land,* VI (March 1947), 2–3; *Savings and Loan Annual 1947* (Chicago, 1948), pp. 307–8.

73. Senate Committee on Banking and Currency, 80th Cong. 2nd Sess., *Hearings on Perfecting Amendments to S. 866: Housing* (Washington, D.C., 1948), p. 169. From the start NHA officials had known that the annual contributions formula would be controversial, but they backed it as the least costly method. Leon H. Keyserling to Sergei N. Grimm, Dec. 12, 1944, Box 65, OA 1942–1946, HUD Records.

74. The mayors, whose lobbying organization—the U.S. Conference of Mayors—was almost inactive during the war years because of personnel losses, did not figure significantly in the formulation of the W-E-T bill. Once the measure was introduced, however, they backed it, particularly the public housing provisions. Toward the late 1940s, the mayors began showing greater interest in the urban redevelopment title, seeing it as the answer to their decentralization troubles. *City Problems of 1943–44* (Washington, D.C., 1944), p. 215; cf. La Guardia's testimony, Senate, *Hearings on S. 1592,* p. 147, with that of George W. Welsh (Grand Rapids), Senate Committee on Banking and Currency, 80th Cong. 1st Sess., *Hearings on S. 866: Housing* (Washington, D.C., 1947), pp. 230–32.

75. Blandford testimony, Senate, *Hearings on S. 1592,* p. 74.

76. Catherine Bauer, "Freedom of Choice," *Nation,* CLXVI (May 15, 1948), 536; AIP, Report of the Committee on Urban Land Policies, *Journal of the American Institute of Planners,* XII (Spring 1946), 36–43; AIP, Report of the Subcommittee on Principles for Federal Urban Redevelopment Legislation, *ibid.,* XIV (Fall 1948), 48–49.

77. See, for example, Alfred Caldwell, "Atomic Bombs and City Planning," *Journal of the American Institute of Architects,* IV (Dec. 1945), 298–99; Tracy B. Augur, "Planning Cities for the Atomic Age," *American City,* LXI (Aug. 1946), 75–76.

78. Paul Windels, "At the Crossroads," *Regional Plan Bulletin,* no. 70 (June 1948), pp. 6–7; "New Towns," *Journal of the American Institute of Planners,* XIV (Summer 1948), entire issue; "New Towns," *Planning 1948* (Chicago, 1948), pp. 9–26.

79. Robert Moses, "Mr. Moses Dissects the 'Long-Haired Planners,'" *NYT Magazine,* June 26, 1944, pp. 16–17; Moses, "Slums and City Planning," *Atlantic,* CLXXV (Jan. 1945), 63–68.

80. In 1947, the NHA, under the provisions of Reorganization Plan No. 3 of that year, became the Housing and Home Finance Agency. For the background to this change, see *infra,* pp. 246–48.

81. Philip B. Fleming, "Federal Services for Urban Public Works," in *American Planning and Civic Annual 1947* (Washington, D.C., 1947), pp. 109–10; Federal Works Agency, *Eighth Annual Report 1947* (Washington, D.C., 1947), p. 6; FWA, *Ninth Annual Report 1948* (Washington, D.C., 1948), pp. 1, 41–46.

82. Philip B. Fleming to Truman, Jan. 19, 1949; FWA, "Draft of Proposed Urban Redevelopment Legislation," Jan. 12, 1949, R2-3/48.4, Records of the Bureau of the Budget, Record Group 51, National Archives.

83. R. E. Neustadt/J. E. Reeve memo for the Director, March 3, 1949, *ibid.*; Truman to Fleming, April 20, 1949, OF 63, Harry S. Truman MSS., Harry S. Truman Library. Significantly, the redevelopment section of the bill finally passed did not include the word "urban" in its title; it was called "Slum Clearance and Community Development and Redevelopment."

84. See, for example, the statement of Congressman Vursell (R.-Ill.): "The $1,500,000 provided for in this bill for slum clearance [the $1.5 billion figure he used was the total of $500 million in grants and $1.0 billion in loans which had to be repaid in full] will go, most of it, for the purchase of land in the heart of big cities like Chicago, New York and several other big cities. . . . [C]ity administrations and city politicians through the years have brought about the slum conditions because of neglect of their duty, and big waste and extravagance of public funds. The taxpayers in my district of southern Illinois, who have worked and saved to build their own homes, are called upon after they have paid their own taxes and kept their own homes in livable condition to contribute money in taxes and rentals." *Congressional Record*, 81st Cong. 1st Sess., p. 7387.

85. Catherine Bauer, "Redevelopment: A Misfit in the Fifties," in *The Future of Cities and Urban Redevelopment*, ed. Coleman Woodbury (Chicago, 1953), p. 9.

CHAPTER 5

1. Bureau of the Census, *Census of Population: 1950* (Washington, D.C., 1951), Vol. I, Table 27.

2. Bureau of the Census, *Home Construction Statistics, 1889–1964* (Washington, D.C., 1966), Tables, B-5, B-6; Bureau of the Census, *Census of Housing: 1950* (Washington, D.C., 1953), Vol. I, p. xxvii.

3. Bureau of the Census, *Census of Business, Retail Trade 1939* (Washington, D.C., 1943), Tables 17A, 17C; U.S. Bureau of the Census, *Census of Business, Retail Trade 1948* (Washington, D.C., 1952), Vol. I, Table 1H; Bureau of the Census, *Census of Business, Retail Trade 1954* (Washington, D.C., 1957), Vol. I, Table 1N.

4. "Tax Rates of American Cities," *National Municipal Review*, XL (Jan. 1951), 17–37.

5. Seymour Freedgood, "New Strength in City Hall," in The Editors of *Fortune, The Exploding Metropolis* (Garden City, N.Y., 1957), p. 63.

6. For Tucker, see "Death of the Blues," *Time*, LXIX (April 15, 1957), 35, and "The Man Who Saved St. Louis," *Look*, XXI (Dec. 10, 1957), 60–65; on Morrison, "A New Face," *Time*, LXVI (Sept. 12, 1955), 28, and "A Mayor and His City," *Newsweek*, LI (Feb. 17, 1958), 29–30; on Cobo, *Current Biography 1951* (New

York, 1952), pp. 113–15. The activities of Clark and Dilworth are discussed *infra*, pp. 233–34, 256–58.

7. Hal Burton, *The City Fights Back* (New York, 1954), p. 207. See the three-part *Saturday Evening Post* series entitled "Downtown Isn't Doomed," CCXXVI (June 5, June 12, June 19, 1954).

8. Sam Bass Warner, *The Private City* (Philadelphia, 1968), pp. 85–86, 214; Jeanne R. Lowe, *Cities in a Race With Time* (New York, 1967), pp. 119–21.

9. Lowe, *Cities in a Race With Time*, pp. 124–48; Roy Lubove, *Twentieth Century Pittsburgh* (New York, 1969), pp. 106–41.

10. Lowe, *Cities in a Race With Time*, pp. 405–36; Allan R. Talbot, *The Mayor's Game* (New York, 1967), pp. 9–26, 59–86; Robert Dahl, *Who Governs?* (New Haven, 1961), pp. 61–62, 115–40.

11. For the reasons for this tardiness, see *infra*, pp. 205–07.

12. Bureau of the Census, *Large City Finances in 1949* (Washington, 1950), Table 1; Dell H. Stevens, "Municipal Credit Today is Not Over-Extended," *Barrons*, XXX (May 15, 1950), 15; "Inflation Spills Red Ink on City Budgets," *Business Week*, Jan. 5, 1952, pp. 80, 82.

13. Suzanne Farkas, *Urban Lobbying* (New York, 1971), pp. 138–39, 62–64, 298; interview with Joseph S. Clark, Philadelphia, June 23, 1971.

14. Roy H. Owsley, "The American Municipal Association Reorganizes," *American City*, LXIII (Jan. 1948), 110; Farkas, *Urban Lobbying*, pp. 63–65.

15. House of Representatives Committee on Government Operations, 85th Cong. 1st Sess., *H. Report 575: Replies from State and Local Governments to Questionnaires on Intergovernmental Relations* (Washington, D.C., 1957), pp. 14–16. It is significant that Senator Joseph Clark's bill to create a Department of Urban Affairs (1957) would have combined HHFA and the Federal Civil Defense Administration. For the cabinet department proposal, see *infra*, pp. 260–62.

16. "The Fox in Charge," *New Republic*, CXXVIII (March 9, 1953), 7; "Administrative Strangle," *ibid.*, CXXVIII (April 6, 1953), 9.

17. The president of the National Association of Home Builders, an anti-public housing group, quoted Eisenhower during the 1952 campaign as saying he "wanted none of it [public housing]," but the candidate's aides disclaimed the statement. The consensus at the time was that Ike abhorred the program, but did not know how to get rid of it. *House and Home*, II (Oct. 1952), 36; "The Washington Scene," *Journal of Housing*, IX (Dec. 1952), 42; National Housing Conference, *Membership Newsletter*, V (Nov. 25, 1952), 1.

18. *NYT*, Nov. 2, 1952, VIII, 1; Albert Cole memo for Sherman Adams, July 17, 1953, OF 120, White House Central Files, Dwight D. Eisenhower Library; *House and Home*, VI (June 1954), 126.

19. Robert J. Donovan, *Eisenhower: The Inside Story* (New York, 1956), p. 224; *House and Home*, VI (Aug. 1954), 126; Catherine Bauer, "The Dreary Deadlock of Public Housing," *Architectural Forum*, CVI (May 1957), 140–42; National Housing Conference, *Membership Newsletter*, XI (Aug. 1958), 1.

20. *House and Home*, III (Feb. 1953), 104–5; III (March 1953), 37. The HHFA post's lack of prestige also made Eisenhower's search more difficult; see *infra*, p. 260.

21. Charles Abrams, *The City Is the Frontier* (New York, 1965), p. 86.

22. "Committed" meant that HHFA had reserved a specified amount for an applicant city pending final acceptance of the locality's projected scheme. There was no guarantee that the plans would eventually go through. For the data, see testimony of James Follin, Senate Committee on Banking and Currency, 83rd Cong. 2nd Sess., *Hearings on S. 2889: Housing Act of 1954* (Washington, D.C., 1954), pp. 232–33.

23. Catherine Bauer, "Redevelopment: A Misfit in the Fifties," in *The Future of Cities and Urban Redevelopment*, ed. Coleman Woodbury (Chicago, 1953), pp. 7–26.

24. Miles L. Colean, *Renewing Our Cities* (New York, 1953), pp. 40–41.

25. The chairman of the group's Subcommittee on Urban Redevelopment, Rehabilitation, and Conservation was James W. Rouse. A Baltimore builder, Rouse was one of the leading advocates of federal aid for urban renewal and remained so through the 1950s and 1960s. His firm was responsible for Columbia, the "new town" constructed between Washington and Baltimore.

26. Chalmers M. Roberts memo for Gabriel Hauge, June 8, 1953, OF 120-C; Albert Cole memo for Sherman Adams, Oct. 21, 1953, OF 120, White House Central Files, Eisenhower Library.

27. Cabinet Paper 56–53, "Federal-State-Local Relations," June 29, 1956, Box 4, Records of Meyer Kestnbaum, Eisenhower Library.

28. Robert H. Connery and Richard H. Leach, *The Federal Government and Metropolitan Areas* (Cambridge, Mass., 1960), pp. 135–36.

29. See *infra*, pp. 191–92.

30. Howard Pyle, "The Federal Role in Intergovernmental Relations," *Proceedings, Ninth Annual Legislative Conference 1956* (mimeographed), p. 42.

31. Connery and Leach, *Federal Government and Metropolitan Areas*, pp. 135–36.

32. Testimony of Mayor Ben West of Nashville, House of Representatives Committee on Government Operations, 85th Cong. 1st Sess., *Hearings on Federal-State-Local Relations: State and Local Officials* (Washington, D.C., 1958), p. 598. Also see testimony by John E. Bebout, assistant director, National Municipal League, *ibid.*, p. 127.

33. Commission on Intergovernmental Relations, Advisory Committee on Local Government, *Report* (Washington, D.C., 1955), pp. 24–25; Commission on Intergovernmental Relations, *Report* (Washington, D.C., 1955), pp. 52–53.

34. Howard Pyle to Agency Chiefs, Oct. 10, 1957; Minutes of the First Meeting of the *Ad Hoc* Interagency Committee on Metropolitan Area Problems, Oct. 30, 1957, Box 2, Records of Robert E. Merriam, Eisenhower Library. Those attending were on the assistant secretary level or lower.

35. Merriam's campaign attracted nationwide attention: Joseph N. Bell, "Merriam of Chicago," *Harpers*, CCIX (Nov. 1954), 52–58; "Convert to the Fray," *Newsweek*, XLIV (Nov. 29, 1954), 29–30; "Twenty-four Years After Big Bill," *Time*, LXV (Jan. 3, 1955), 16; James V. Cunningham, "Political Battle in Chicago," *Commonweal*, LXI (Feb. 11, 1955), 497–501; Richard Lewis, "Chicago Puzzle: Who Got the Morality?" *New Republic*, CXXXII (March 7, 1955), 5–6. The stakes were higher than just who would capture City Hall. Political analysts felt a defeat for the Democratic organization would hurt Stevenson's bid for the White House in 1956. As it was, even with Daley's victory, Chicago went for Ike in 1956.

36. Connery and Leach, *Federal Government and Metropolitan Areas*, p. 137.

37. Merriam memo for Pyle, July 9, 1956, Box 4, Kestnbaum Records; Merriam memo for Pyle, Nov. 2, 1956, Box 2, Merriam Records; Merriam, "Partners or Rivals?" *National Municipal Review*, XLV (Dec. 1956), 532–36.

38. Minutes of these meetings are in Box 7, Merriam Records. The primary topic under discussion was an urban cabinet department; see *infra*, p. 269.

39. Bureau of the Budget Staff Paper, "Coordination of Federal Metropolitan Development Activities," Dec. 19, 1960; Merriam memo for David Bell and Frederic Dutton, Jan. 17, 1961, Box 2, Merriam Records. Kennedy, already committed to a cabinet department for cities, rejected the substance of Merriam's recommendations; he also abolished the *Ad Hoc* Committee.

40. Merriam, "Significant Trends in Municipal Politics," *Vital Speeches*, XXII (March 1, 1956), 316–20; Merriam, "Partners or Rivals?" 532.

41. "Increasing Attention to Intergovernmental Relations," *Public Administration Review*, XVIII (Spring 1958), 148. Merriam's campaign for mayor in 1955 was a throwback to the first two decades of the century; he ran on a platform that "there is no Republican or Democratic way to collect garbage." Daley, on the other hand, clothed himself in the New Deal-Fair Deal reform tradition. See Cunningham, "Political Battle," 501; Lewis, "Chicago Puzzle," 5–6; Elmer Gertz, "Chicago's Hectic Race," *Nation*, CLXXX (April 2, 1955), 281–83. See also, Merriam, "Federal Fiscal Policy: Its Impact on Local Government Finance," *Municipal Finance*, XXXII (Aug. 1959), 10–16.

42. Merriam memo for Gerald Morgan, and accompanying papers, Dec. 26, 1956, Box 7, Merriam Records. James L. Sundquist notes that in Eisenhower's 1957 State of the Union Message "the usual 'human concerns' section had shriveled" to practically nothing. Sundquist, *Politics and Policy: The Eisenhower, Kennedy, and Johnson Years* (Washington, D.C., 1968), p. 425.

43. For the problems of public housing, see *infra*, pp. 199–204.

44. Eisenhower captured 25 of the 36 largest cities, compared with 17 of 35 in 1952; in no sense were "urban problems" an issue. Charles A. H. Thomson and Frances M. Shattuck, *The 1956 Presidential Campaign* (Washington, D.C., 1960), p. 350.

45. The 1957 budget debacle is best described in Richard Neustadt, *Presidential Power* (New York, 1960), pp. 64–76.

46. Percival Brundage memo for the President, March 1, 1957, R 2–3/57.3, Files of the Bureau of the Budget, Executive Office of the President, Washington, D.C. Both the Federal Reserve Board and the Council of Economic Advisors supported the cuts.

47. *House and Home*, IX (Feb. 1956), 53.

48. *New York Times*, March 15, 1957, p. 1; March 26, 1957, p. 21; April 9, 1957, p. 36; Senate Committee on Banking and Currency, 85th Cong. 1st Sess., *Hearings on Housing Amendments of 1957* (Washington, D.C., 1957), pp. 580–81, 609; Pyle to Sherman Adams, April 1, 1957; Adams to Norris Poulson, April 24, 1957, OF 120-C, White House Central Files, Eisenhower Library.

49. Senate Committee on Banking and Currency, *Hearings on Housing Amendments of 1957*, p. 146; Jeanne R. Lowe, "Rebuilding Cities—and Politics," *Nation*,

CLXXXVI (Feb. 8, 1958), 118–21; "Rebuilding Our Cities," *Atlantic*, CXCV (June 1955), 7–8; House of Representatives, 85th Cong. 1st Sess., *H. Report 313* (Washington, D.C., 1957), p. 15; Senate, 85th Cong. 1st Sess., *S. Report 368* (Washington, D.C., 1957), p. 16. Floor debate was minimal; administration supporters were ready to accept the $250 million figure.

50. A resolution calling for establishment of a department of urban affairs was approved by the AMA in Nov. 1956 by only a slim margin; in Nov. 1957, a similar resolution asking for a federal urban policy council passed with ease. See *infra*, pp. 252, 255–56.

51. Cf. the AMA's statements of National Municipal Policy issued annually through the decade. Though often repetitious, they show a growing desire for greater and different kinds of federal aid as the 1950s progressed.

52. The mayors' campaign was bipartisan. Democrats predominated, but Republicans helped out. Mayor Norris Poulson of Los Angeles, although elected in a non-partisan contest, was a registered Republican; his attack on the President's policy was just as sharp as his Democratic colleagues. House of Representatives Committee on Banking and Currency, 85th Cong. 2nd Sess., *Hearings on Slum Clearance and Related Housing Problems* (Washington, D.C., 1958), pp. 262–63.

53. *NYT*, Dec. 5, 1957, p. 24.

54. "Should States Relieve U.S. of Some Programs?" *Congressional Quarterly Weekly Report*, XVI (Jan. 3, 1958), 21–23. For an examination of the committee's failure, see Morton Grodzins, *The American System*, ed. Daniel J. Elazar (Chicago, 1966), pp. 307–26.

55. See *supra*, p. 146, and Ashley A. Foard and Hilbert Fefferman, "Federal Urban Renewal Legislation," *Law and Contemporary Problems*, XXV (Autumn 1960), 672–84.

56. The suggestion for reducing the federal share probably came from Budget Director Percival Brundage who, while recognizing that the change might impose hardship on localities and slow the program, felt that the federal budget outlook was even more bleak. Percival Brundage memo for Sherman Adams. Dec. 16, 1957; Cole memo for Adams, Dec. 16, 1957, OF 120-C, White House Central Files, Eisenhower Library.

57. Cole memo for Sherman Adams, Sept. 19, 1957; Cole, "Cabinet Presentation," Nov. 15, 1957, HHFA Administrators' Files, Box 16, Records of the Department of Housing and Urban Development, Record Group 207, National Archives; Cole memo for Adams, Dec. 16, 1957, OF 120-C, White House Central Files, Eisenhower Library. Cole's vigorous defense of urban renewal made him unpopular at the White House; he resigned in Jan. 1959 to take a well-paying job in the private renewal sector; *House and Home*, XV (Feb. 1959), 38–39.

58. Pyle memo for Sherman Adams, Dec. 16, 1957, Box 28, Records of Howard Pyle, Dwight D. Eisenhower Library.

59. The *NYT* noted that the budget amounted to "the first federal retrenchment in the jointly financed 'welfare state' programs since the Roosevelt Administration set most of them in motion"; Jan. 14, 1958, p. 1.

60. As in 1957, Democratic mayors led the fight, but Republicans were also critical of

the President; Charles P. Taft to Meyer Kestnbaum, July 1, 1957, Aug. 12, 1957, Box 1, Kestnbaum Records; George Christopher to Gerald D. Morgan, Sept. 22, 1958, GF 146-B, White House Central Files, Eisenhower Library.

61. Eisenhower's decision to use the veto came against the advice of the Republicans' chief spokesman on housing in Congress, Senator Homer Capehart of Indiana. Capehart, whose conservative credentials were impeccable, warned that a veto might have "bad political effects" and argued that since the housing bill dealt only with authorizations that would not require any spending for years to come, its effect on the President's budget would be negligible. But Eisenhower, convinced that a great principle was at stake, ignored Capehart's practical view of the situation. Merriam memo for General Persons, June 30, 1959, OF 120, White House Central Files, Eisenhower Library.

62. *NYT*, July 7, 1960, p. 22; Secretary of the Treasury Robert Anderson in testimony to House of Representatives Committee on Government Operations, 85th Cong. 2nd Sess., *Hearings on Federal-State-Local Relations: Joint Federal-State Action Committee* (Washington, D.C., 1958), p. 5. Cf. Walter Williams memo for Sherman Adams, Oct. 14, 1953, with Pyle memo for Tom Stephens, June 27, 1958, Box 29, Pyle Records, for the White House's declining opinion of the AMA.

63. Merriam did address the AMA in Dec. 1960 when it was known that the Republicans were on their way out.

64. Bureau of the Census, *Census of Population: 1960* (Washington, D.C., 1961), Vol. I, p. xxv.

65. Bureau of the Census, *Census of Business, Retail Trade 1958* (Washington, D.C., 1961), Table J, Table 8; John F. Kain, "The Distribution and Movement of Jobs and Industry," in *The Metropolitan Enigma*, ed. James Q. Wilson (Washington, D.C., 1967), pp. 10–19.

66. Bureau of the Census, *Compendium of City Government Finances in 1952* (Washington, D.C., 1953), Tables 4, 14, 15, 24; Bureau of the Census, *Compendium of City Government Finances in 1960* (Washington, D.C., 1961), Tables 3, 4, 7, 14.

67. See tables and discussion in National Advisory Commission on Civil Disorders, *Report* (New York, 1968), pp. 239–47.

68. Philip M. Hauser, "The Challenge of Metropolitan Growth," *Urban Land*, XVII (Dec. 1958), 5.

CHAPTER 6

1. Welfare programs were not a major issue in federal-municipal politics after 1940 and prior to the 1960s, because the relief rolls stayed fairly stable and manageable in the post-war era thanks to the generally good economic picture and the tractability of the poor. Also, in many instances, relief was a county, not a city responsibility. In either case, states, not the Federal Government, were the instrumentality localities had to deal with in this program.

2. Leonard Freedman, *Public Housing: The Politics of Poverty* (New York, 1969), pp. 15–57.

3. Catherine Bauer, "The Dreary Deadlock of Public Housing," *Architectural Forum*, CVI (May 1957), 141–42.

4. National Federation of Settlements and Neighborhood Centers, *A New Look at Public Housing* (New York, 1958), p. 4.

5. Elizabeth Wood, "Public Housing and Mrs. McGee," *Journal of Housing*, XIII (Dec. 1956), 427–28.

6. Robert M. Fisher, *Twenty Years of Public Housing* (New York, 1959), pp. 164–70.

7. William G. Grigsby, *Housing Markets and Public Policy* (Philadelphia, 1963), pp. 282–83; H. Warren Dunham and Nathan D. Grundstein, "The Impact of a Confusion of Social Objectives in Public Housing: A Preliminary Analysis," *Marriage and Family Living*, XVII (May 1955), 110–12.

8. For examples of Ickes's insistence upon fairness, see Ickes memo for Roosevelt, July 3, 1935; A. R. Clas memo for Ickes, Dec. 12, 1935, OF 63, Franklin D. Roosevelt MSS., Franklin D. Roosevelt Library; Robert C. Weaver, "Racial Policy in Public Housing," *Phylon*, I (Second Quarter 1940), 149–61.

9. Davis McEntire, *Residence and Race* (Berkeley,. 1960), p. 329; Commission on Civil Rights, *Report* (Washington, D.C., 1959), p. 475.

10. The classic study of the issues involved in site selection is Martin Meyerson and Edward C. Banfield, *Politics and Planning, and the Public Interest: The Case of Public Housing in Chicago* (New York, 1955). Also see Elizabeth Wood, "Public Housing," *Planning 1958* (Chicago, 1958), p. 198.

11. For a good discussion of "the implications of the new Federal system," see Charles Abrams, *The City Is the Frontier* (New York, 1965), pp. 238–49. Civil rights groups filed a suit in federal court in 1971 contesting the constitutionality of the local control provisions of the 1937 Housing Act.

12. John P. Dean, "The Myths of Housing Reform," *American Sociological Review*, XIV (April 1949), 281–88.

13. Public housing is defended in Roger Starr, *The Urban Choices* (Baltimore, 1967), pp. 83–92; and National Commission on Urban Problems, *Building the American City* (Washington, D.C., 1969), pp. 118–19, 131.

14. National Housing Conference, *Membership Newsletter*, XI (Feb./March, 1958), 5–6; *Journal of Housing*, XIV (Dec. 1957), 423.

15. Daniel Seligman, "The Enduring Slums," in The Editors of *Fortune*, *The Exploding Metropolis* (Garden City, N.Y., 1958), p. 103.

16. Housing and Home Finance Agency, *14th Annual Report: 1960* (Washington, D.C., 1961), p. 287; "The Halting Progress of Urban Renewal," *Architectural Forum*, CVII (Oct. 1957), 240.

17. Richard H. Leach, "The Federal Urban Renewal Program: A Ten-Year Critique," *Law and Contemporary Problems*, XV (Autumn 1960), 779–80; Commission on Urban Problems, *Building the American City*, pp. 165–69; Frederick O'R. Hayes to Roscoe C. Martin, Sept. 27, 1960, R 4–23/57.1, Bureau of the Budget Files, Executive Office of the President, Washington, D.C. One member of HHFA's legal staff called Title I "the most complicated grant-in-aid program in the Federal Government." Quoted in "Our Confused Housing Program," *Architectural Forum*, CVI (April 1957), 236.

18. Cited in Jeanne R. Lowe, *Cities in a Race With Time* (New York, 1967), p. 172.

19. Lyman Brownfield, "The Disposition Problem in Urban Renewal," *Law and Contemporary Problems*, XXV (Autumn 1960), 740.

20. Raymond Foley to Elmer Staats, Jan. 27, 1949; R. E. Neustadt/J. E. Reeve memo for the director, March 3, 1949, R 2–3/48.4, Records of the Bureau of the Budget, Record Group 51, National Archives; B. T. Fitzpatrick memo for Foley, Sept. 28, 1950, HHFA Administrators' Files, Box 2, Records of the Department of Housing and Urban Development, Record Group 207, National Archives.

21. See *supra*, pp. 171–75.

22. Grigsby, *Housing Markets and Public Policy*, pp. 323–25; Raymond Vernon, *The Myth and Reality of Our Urban Problems* (Cambridge, Mass., multilithed, 1962), pp. 69–71; Scott Greer, *Urban Renewal and American Cities* (Indianapolis, 1965), pp. 82–84, 91–97. The National Commission on Urban Problems found that most municipalities conceived of urban renewal "as a federally financed gimmick to provide relatively cheap land for a miscellany of profitable, prestigious enterprises"; *Building the American City*, p. 153.

23. Herbert J. Gans, "The Human Implications of Current Redevelopment and Relocation Policy," *Journal of the American Institute of Planners*, XXV (Feb. 1959), 16–18; Abrams, *City Is the Frontier*, pp. 116–23.

24. HHFA, *14th Annual Report: 1960*, p. 287; National Commission on Urban Problems, *Building the American City*, p. 125; Greer, *Urban Renewal*, p. 3; John H. Staples, "Urban Renewal: A Comparative Study of Twenty-Two Cities, 1950–1960," *Western Political Quarterly*, XXIII (June 1970), 294–304.

25. Public housing could be built on renewal sites, but the cities would have to pay more of the costs than if it was built in other areas. Besides having to pick up the normal local share of public housing subsidies, municipalities also had to contribute one-third of the write-down expense for renewal land. Rather than contract for this "double-subsidy," most cities put their low-rent housing elsewhere or, as sometimes happened, built none at all. Thus Title I, which public housers had hoped would solve many of the land price problems of their program, only made public housing construction more difficult.

26. "My present theme song," Catherine Bauer declared in 1949, "is that 25 years from now someone will write a book proving that the thing that finally ruined our cities was passing a big clearance program in the middle of a chronic housing shortage." Bauer to Warren J. Vinton, Oct. 30, 1949, Box 4, Warren J. Vinton MSS., Collection of Regional History and University Archives, Cornell University Library. Cf. Merlin Smelker memo for R. E. Neustadt, Jan. 14, 1949, R 2–3/48.4, Bureau of the Budget Records.

27. Guy Greer, "City Planning: Battle of the Approach," *Fortune*, XXVIII (Nov. 1943), 164–65.

28. Stephen G. Thompson, "The Future of Title I," *Architectural Forum*, CXI (Sept. 1959), 69.

29. Quoted in Lowe, *Cities in a Race With Time*, p. 77.

30. The best account of Moses and urban renewal is *ibid.*, pp. 45–98.

31. Greer, *Urban Renewal*, pp. 119–23; James Q. Wilson, "Planning and Politics:

Citizen Participation in Urban Renewal," *Journal of the American Institute of Planners*, XXIX (Nov. 1963), 242–49. For a case study of Chicago, see Peter H. Rossi and Robert Dentler, *The Politics of Urban Renewal* (New York, 1961).

32. Robert A. Dahl, *Who Governs?* (New Haven, 1961), pp. 122–37.

33. Martin Millspaugh, "Problems and Opportunities of Relocation," *Law and Contemporary Problems*, XXVI (Winter 1961), 8–11; Paul L. Niebanck, *Relocation in Urban Planning* (Philadelphia, 1968), pp. 7–27.

34. Bauer, in *Planning 1943* (Chicago, 1943), pp. 103–4; Nathaniel S. Keith, "Relocation Problems in Urban Redevelopment," in *Planning 1952* (Chicago, 1952), p. 169.

35. As Charles Abrams points out, the 1949 act's relocation requirements were in direct opposition to the act's finding of a "serious housing shortage." Abrams, *City Is the Frontier*, p. 136.

36. Quoted in Lowe, *Cities in a Race With Time*, p. 207. Robert Moses, whose belief that the only way slums could be fought was to blast the whole neighborhood off the map created terrific relocation problems in New York, brushed off his critics with the retort: "Look, in ten years you will have forgotten all about these people, and you'll thank me for the project." Quoted in *House and Home*, XVII (April 1960), 69.

37. Chester Hartman, "The Housing of Relocated Families," *Journal of the American Institute of Planners*, XXX (Nov. 1964), 266–86; Gans, "Human Implications," 19–22; Marc Fried, "Grieving for a Lost Home," in *The Urban Condition*, ed. Leonard J. Duhl (New York, 1963), Chapter 12.

38. Robert C. Weaver, "Racial Minorities and Public Housing," *Proceedings, National Conference of Social Work 1940* (New York, 1940), p. 290.

39. Robert C. Weaver, *The Negro Ghetto* (New York, 1948), p. 324; George B. Nesbitt, "Relocating Negroes from Urban Slum Clearance Sites," *Journal of Land Economics*, XXV (Aug. 1949), 275–88; Joseph B. Robison, "The Story of Stuyvesant Town," *Nation*, CLXXII (June 2, 1951), 514–16.

40. The fact that the Bricker-Cain amendment barring segregation applied only to public housing and not to urban redevelopment is confirmation both of its authors' lack of sincerity and Title I's wide popularity even among conservatives. See Charles Abrams, "Human Rights in Slum Clearance," *Survey*, LXXXVI (Jan. 1950), 28.

41. Memo comparing Federal Works Agency proposal and Title I of S. 138, undated [early 1949], R 2–3/48.4, Budget Bureau Records. The HHFA's race relations advisor wrote that the urban redevelopment program "will be made or broken largely by the caliber of the appreciation of governmental representatives to the minority group considerations involved." Frank S. Horne memo for Raymond Foley, Sept. 12, 1949, HHFA Administrators' Files, Box 2, HUD Records.

42. The 1959 study of the Commission on Civil Rights noted that the Urban Renewal Administration required local agencies to submit detailed data on their plans to rehouse minorities, but that URA never checked to see that these promises were carried out. Unlike PHA, URA had no racial relations service of its own; Commission on Civil Rights, *Report*, pp. 483–88.

43. *Ibid.,* p. 459. For a case study, see Theodore J. Lowi, *The End of Liberalism* (New York, 1969), pp. 251–63.

44. Nathaniel S. Keith, "Urban Redevelopment: A Challenge to Cities," in *Planning 1949* (Chicago, 1949), pp. 41–42.

45. When the Workable Program was first proposed, one Budget Bureau staff member wrote that in order for it to be effective, "Mr. Cole will have to be as firm in dealing with the cities as Mr. Dulles has been in enlisting the cooperation of the French." But such close supervision of local communities ran counter to the Republican desire to eliminate federal interference in most sectors of the nation's economic and social life. In no time at all, HHFA was characterizing its lax administration as a virtue. No one, declared a HHFA official, could accuse his agency of "playing God" to every locality in the country; "I think we did a surprising thing by resisting temptation." Cole believed development of the Workable Program idea was one of the chief accomplishments of his tenure but saw absolutely nothing wrong in the fact that he never rejected any plan "however weak." J. E. Reeve memo for Alan L. Dean, Dec. 21, 1953, R 4–12/53.1, Budget Bureau Files; William A. Ulman, "Proposal for Analysis of Housing and Its Relationship to the Political Campaign of 1956," Box 11, Records of Bryce Harlow, Dwight D. Eisenhower Library; *Journal of Housing,* XV (Dec. 1958), 408; *House and Home,* XV (Feb. 1959), 38–39; "Mr. Mason's Opportunity," Architectural Forum, CX (March 1959), 91; National Commission on Urban Problems, *Building the American City,* p. 294.

46. Hayes to Martin, Sept. 27, 1960, Budget Bureau Files.

47. Lowe, *Cities in a Race With Time,* pp. 405–551; Allan R. Talbot, *The Mayor's Game* (New York, 1967).

48. Catherine Bauer, "First Job: Control New City Sprawl," *Architectural Forum,* CV (Sept. 1956), 105–12; Leach, "Urban Renewal: Ten-Year Critique," 779–92; Lloyd Rodwin, *Nations and Cities* (Boston, 1970), pp. 238, 260; Peter Marris, "A Report on Urban Renewal in the U.S.," in *The Urban Condition,* pp. 130–34.

49. Charles Abrams, *The Future of Housing* (New York, 1946), p. 237.

50. The best discussion of the National Housing Act of 1934 is William L. C. Wheaton, "The Evolution of Federal Housing Programs" (unpublished Ph.D. dissertation, University of Chicago, 1953), pp. 46–67. Wheaton points out that an early draft of the measure instructed FHA to refuse to insure "socially undesirable or purely speculative building." The act as passed, however, contained only the requirement that mortgages be "economically sound." By commonly accepted standards of legislative intent, this was almost an order to FHA, which FHA officials were quick to cite, not to interest itself in the "social" aspects of home-building. *Ibid.,* p. 67.

51. Earle S. Draper, "FHA-Insured Mortgage Financing in the Reconversion Period," in *Mortgage Bankers Association of America Yearbook 1944* (Chicago, 1944), pp. 154–55; Congress, Joint Committee on Housing, 80th Cong. 1st Sess., *Hearings on the Study and Investigation of Housing* (Washington, D.C., 1948), pp. 2755–56; "FHA Policies Said to Hinder Urban Rebuilding," *American City,* LXIII (March 1948), 120; National Commission on Urban Problems, *Building the*

American City, pp. 100–101; Miles L. Colean, "Impotency of FHA Policies in Apartment Finance," *Architectural Forum*, CII (June 1955), 110–11, 162; "Our Confused Housing Program," 128–29; Charles M. Haar, *Federal Credit and Private Housing* (New York, 1960), pp. 192–201; Louis Winnick, *Rental Housing: Opportunities for Private Investment* (New York, 1958), pp. 20–21, 171–211.

52. Richard Goode, *The Individual Income Tax* (Washington, D.C., 1964), pp. 122–29. One welfare expert has estimated that in 1962 the Federal Government subsidized home ownership to the amount of $2.0 billion in income tax deductions. Federal appropriations for publicly assisted housing for the poor, by contrast, came to only $820 million. Alvin Schorr, "National Community and Housing Policy," *Social Service Review*, XXXIX (Dec. 1965), 434.

53. House of Representatives Committee on Banking and Currency, 84th Cong. 1st Sess., *Hearings on the Investigation of Housing* (Washington, D.C., 1955), p. 18.

54. John T. Howard, "The Role of the Federal Government in Urban Land Use Planning," *Fordham Law Review*, XXIX (April 1961), 665.

55. "Our Confused Housing Program," 244; "FHA in Suburbia," *Architectural Forum*, CVII (Sept. 1957), 160–61.

56. Norman P. Mason, quoted in *House and Home*, XIX (Jan. 1961), 45.

57. David Carlson, "FHA in the City," *Architectural Forum*, CVII (July 1957), 151–52; Haar, *Federal Credit*, pp. 204–9. In the period 1954–60, FHA insured 22,500 units under Section 220; in 1960 alone, it guaranteed mortgages on 150,000 units under the regular 203 program. HHFA, *14th Annual Report: 1960*, p. 66.

58. Quoted in Charles Abrams, *Forbidden Neighbors* (New York, 1955), p. 156.

59. Charles Abrams, "Slums, Ghettos, and the G.O.P.'s Remedy," *Reporter*, X (May 11, 1954), 28–29.

60. Abrams, *Forbidden Neighbors*, pp. 150–68, 229–37; Gunnar Myrdal, *An American Dilemma* (New York, 1944), pp. 349–50.

61. *Corrigan v. Buckley*, 271 U.S. 323 (1926); *Shelley v. Kramer*, 334 U.S. 1 (1948). For the background on these cases, see Clement E. Vose, *Caucasians Only* (Berkeley, 1959).

62. Vose, *Caucasians Only*, pp. 168–74, 191–93; Frank S. Horne memo for Raymond Foley, Feb. 9, 1949; B. T. Fitzpatrick memo for Foley, April 12, 1949; Foley memo for Fitzpatrick, May 11, 1949, HHFA Administrators' Files, Box 2, HUD Records; David K. Niles memo for the President, Oct. 31, 1949, Box 6, Philleo Nash MSS., Harry S. Truman Library. It is significant that the announcement of the new FHA rules did not come from FHA itself, but in a speech by the solicitor general to a New York civil rights group. *NYT*, Dec. 3, 1949, p. 1.

63. Eunice and George Grier, *Privately Developed Interracial Housing* (Berkeley, 1960), pp. 122–24, 130–55; Commission on Civil Rights, *Report*, pp. 465–68.

64. It is, of course, one thing to move from a policy of positive support for segregation to one of neutrality and quite another to move from neutrality to positive support of integration. Negro leaders pleaded with Truman to bar FHA aid to any segregated housing, but he refused. Walter White to Truman, Sept. 25, 1951; Philleo Nash memo for Truman, June 23, 1952, Box 6, Nash MSS.

65. These demands came from the usual Negro groups, the two dozen national

organizations joined together in the National Committee Against Discrimination in Housing, the Fund for the Republic-financed Commission on Race and Housing, and the U.S. Commission in Civil Rights (in 1959). The fight for an Executive order barring segregation is discussed in Irving Berg, "Racial Discrimination in Housing: A Study of the Quest for Government Access by Minority Interest Groups, 1945–1962" (unpublished Ph.D. dissertation, University of Florida, 1967), pp. 239–76.

66. Maxwell Rabb to Paul Cooke, June 8, 1956, OF 120, White House Central Files, Dwight D. Eisenhower Library.

67. Norman P. Mason, quoted in Commission on Civil Rights, *Report*, p. 461.

68. Charles Abrams, "Segregation, Housing, and the Horne Case," *Reporter*, XIII (Oct. 6, 1955), 30–33.

69. Charles L. Dearing, *American Highway Policy* (Washington, D.C., 1941), pp. 47, 219–65. The 1916 act was among the first modern federal programs of grants-in-aid to the states.

70. The report was actually issued in the name of the Presidentially appointed National Interregional Highway Committee, but the chairman of the committee was the chief of the BPR, and the bureau supplied all of the staff assistance.

71. National Interregional Highway Committee, *Interregional Highways* (Washington, D.C., 1944), pp. 3, 61.

72. Philip H. Burch, Jr., *Highway Revenue and Expenditure Policy in the United States* (New Brunswick, N.J., 1962), pp. 165, 223–24.

73. *Ibid.,* pp. 111–35, 225; Wilfred Owen, *The Metropolitan Transportation Problem* (Washington, D.C., 1956), pp. 61–62.

74. One political scientist has called the highway lobby "the most unique and massive coalition of single-minded pressures ever to hit the American scene." From the big automobile manufacturers, oil firms, and construction companies down to the neighborhood service stations and the car owner himself, there was a loud and insistent demand for more and better roads. It was perhaps inevitable that consideration of the side effects of road-building would get lost in the headlong drive to cater to this popular desire. See Paul Ylvisaker, "The Deserted City," *Journal of the American Institute of Planners*, XXV (Feb. 1959), 5.

75. National Interregional Highway Committee, *Interregional Highways*, pp. 53–56, 63–64, 70–71.

76. Testimony of Philip B. Fleming and Thomas H. McDonald, in Senate, Special Committee on Post-War Economic Policy and Planning, 79th Cong. 1st Sess., *Hearings Pursuant to S. 102: Housing and Urban Redevelopment* (Washington, D.C., 1945), pp. 1526–32; Thomas H. McDonald, "The Case for Urban Expressways," *American City*, LXII (June 1947), 92–93; Philip B. Fleming, "Highways and Urban Redevelopment," *Public Construction*, n. 68 (March 1949), pp. 1–3.

77. Cf. the mayors' testimony, pp. 197–215, with that of the chief of BPR, pp. 672–73, in Senate Committee on Public Works, 84th Cong. 1st Sess., *Hearings on National Highway Program* (Washington, D.C., 1955).

78. Edward Chase, "The Hundred Billion Dollar Question," *Architectural Forum*, CVII (July 1957), 135.

79. Daniel P. Moynihan, "New Roads and Urban Chaos," *Reporter*, XXII (April 14, 1960), 19.

80. Quoted in *Architectural Forum*, CVII (Nov. 1957), 206.

81. The state highway departments' change in attitude toward urban roads was due to the unique financing arrangements of the Interstate System. The regular highway program was paid for out of general revenues, but the Interstate System's expenses were covered by a special Highway Trust Fund which received most gasoline, tire, and other automobile excise taxes. To maximize receipts, it was thus necessary to build highways where they would be most used.

82. Helen Leavitt, *Superhighway-Superhoax* (Garden City, N.Y., 1970), p. 38; George M. Smerk, *Urban Transportation: The Federal Role* (Bloomington, Ind., 1965), p. 74. A 1960 Department of Commerce study concluded: "Merely adding highways which will attract more automobiles which will in turn require more highways is no solution to the problem of urban development." Department of Commerce, *Rationale of Federal Transportation Policy* (Washington, D.C., 1960), p. 52.

83. "Arresting the Highwaymen," *Architectural Forum*, CX (April 1959), 93.

84. John T. Howard, "Impact of the Federal Highway Program," in *Planning 1957* (Chicago, 1957), pp. 38–39; "41,000 Miles to Tomorrow," *American Planning and Civic Annual 1957* (Washington, D.C., 1957), pp. 63–95. Cf. "Who Should Design Our Urban Highways?" *Roads and Streets*, C (Nov. 1957), 55.

85. Wilfred Owen, *Cities in the Motor Age* (New York, 1959), summarizes the conference.

86. "Highways Must Become Factors in Renewal Plans," *Journal of Housing*, XIV (Oct. 1957), 338. Cf. McDonald, "Urban Expressways," p. 4: "The redevelopment of our urban areas is a whole book within itself, and highway planning is one of the most important chapters." One small, but concrete step toward linking the HHFA and BPR programs was an agreement reached in Nov. 1960 to pool the two agencies' planning funds. HHFA/Department of Commerce, "Joint Policy and Procedural Statement on Improved Coordination of Highway and General Urban Planning," Nov. 23, 1960, Box 14, Records of John S. Bragdon, Dwight D. Eisenhower Library.

87. Memo for the Record, July 13, 1959, Box 7, Records of Robert E. Merriam, Dwight D. Eisenhower Library; Bragdon memo for Eisenhower, June 17, 1959, Box 41; Bragdon memo for Frederick Mueller and Maurice Stans, Sept. 18, 1959, Box 38; "Federal Highway Program—Interim Report," March 1960, Box 41; Memo for the Record, April 8, 1960, Box 4, Bragdon Records; *NYT*, Sept. 22, 1959, p. 1; Oct. 18, 1959, p. 84.

88. Eisenhower memo for the secretary of Commerce, April 11, 1960, Box 5, Merriam Records; Richard J. Daley and A. E. Johnson, "Better Transportation for Your City," *Proceedings, American Municipal Congress 1959* (Washington, D.C., n.d.), pp. 8–10, 14; "Washington Newsletter," *Roads and Streets*, CIII (Feb. 1960), 19; House of Representatives Committee on Public Works, 86th Cong. 2nd Sess., *Hearings on H.R. 10495: Federal Highway Act of 1960* (Washington, D.C., 1960), pp. 157–58.

89. Owen, *Metropolitan Transportation Problem*, pp. 32–42, 70–75, 93–98; "Municipal

Transit," *Time*, LXV (April 18, 1955), 96; "The Crisis in Local Transit," *Business Week*, July 23, 1955, p. 120; "No Transit," *Fortune*, LII (Sept. 1955), 57–58.

90. Walter Blucher, "Your City is What You Make It," *Public Management*, XXX (Aug. 1948), 223; Blucher, "Moving People," *Virginia Law Review*, XXXVI (Nov. 1950), 849; John Bauer, "The Crisis in Urban Transit," *Public Management*, XXXIV (Aug. 1952), 176; Owen, *Metropolitan Transportation Problem*, pp. 253–54.

91. "Crisis in City Transit," *Architectural Forum*, CVI (June 1957), 109.

92. Cf. recommendations of the Urban Land Institute's Central Business District Council in *Urban Land*, V (Jan. 1946), 1; VI (May 1947), 1, 4; VI (Dec. 1947), 1, 3; with "Can Public Transit Come Back?" *ibid.*, XIII (March 1954), 2; Boyd T. Barnard, "A Businessman Looks at Transit," *ibid.*, XIV (Nov. 1955), 3–6. Also see, "Traffic Troubles," *Architectural Forum*, C (March 1954), 37–38.

93. "No One—But No One—Loves a Commuter," *Business Week*, Feb. 9, 1952, pp. 96–101; "Privately-Owned Transit Sees a Bleak Road Ahead," *ibid.*, March 1, 1952, pp. 86–90; House of Representatives Committee on Public Works, 84th Cong. 1st Sess., *Hearings on H.R. 4260: National Highway Program* (Washington, D.C., 1955), pp. 1284–86; Smerk, *Urban Transportation*, pp. 127–29. It should be noted that some cities were far more dependent on mass transit than others. In Los Angeles, for example, less than one-third of the people who entered downtown daily came by public transportation; in New York the figure was 83 per cent. This disparity hindered any united drive for federal aid.

94. Owen, *Metropolitan Transportation Problem*, pp. 99–104; Michael Danielson, *Federal-Metropolitan Politics and the Commuter Crisis* (New York, 1965), pp. 10–20, 28–52.

95. Lowe, *Cities in a Race With Time*, pp. 382–91; Danielson, *Commuter Crisis*, pp. 95–99; *NYT*, Nov. 26, 1956, p. 29; Nov. 28, 1956, p. 70; May 28, 1957, p. 25.

96. Danielson, *Commuter Crisis*, pp. 101–6; *NYT*, Dec. 1, 1959, pp. 1, 24. The Eastern railroads tried to get the endorsement of the Association of American Railroads, but the Western and Southern carriers were adamantly opposed to federal subsidies; *NYT*, Jan. 30, 1960, p. 9. The AMA's commitment to mass transit was something less than total; at the same time it supported Dilworth's proposals, it also asked for a brand new program of federal aid to urban roads; "Better Urban Transportation," *Proceedings, American Municipal Congress 1959*, pp. 29–53.

97. Danielson, *Commuter Crisis*, pp. 109–13, 129–46; Royce Hanson, "Congress Copes With Mass Transit, 1960–1964," in *Congress and Urban Problems* (Washington, D.C., 1969), pp. 314–21.

CHAPTER 7

1. Harold D. Seidman, *Politics, Position, and Power* (New York, 1970), p. 14; Richard Neustadt, *Presidential Power* (New York, 1960), p. 47.

2. Seidman, *Politics, Position, and Power*, pp. 210–11.

3. Richard F. Fenno, Jr., *The President's Cabinet* (Cambridge, Mass., 1959), p. 21.

4. *Ibid.*, p. 22; Lloyd M. Short, *The Development of National Administrative Organization in the United States* (Baltimore, 1923), pp. 205–13.

5. Leonard D. White, *The Jacksonians* (New York, 1954), pp. 502–8.

6. Leonard D. White, *The Republican Era, 1869–1901* (New York, 1958), p. 234; William L. Wanlass, *The United States Department of Agriculture* (Baltimore, 1920), pp. 9–24.

7. Fenno, *President's Cabinet*, p. 27.

8. Short, *Development of National Administrative Organization*, pp. 449, 468–69. The only important exception to this was the Budget and Accounting Act of 1921, which brought business methods to the handling of federal finances.

9. President's Committee on Administrative Management, *Report* (Washington, D.C., 1937), passim. Perhaps recognizing this oversight, the study of the Urbanism Committee, which Brownlow and Merriam had a hand in writing, released later in 1937, urged that "a prompt and thorough study be undertaken by a division of administrative research in the Bureau of the Budget of the best methods and administrative techniques for bringing about the closer coordination of federal activities in urban communities and for improving and facilitating collaboration between cities and the Federal Government." No investigation of this sort occurred until the 1950s. National Resources Committee, Research Committee on Urbanism, *Our Cities* (Washington, D.C., 1937), p. 80.

10. Senate, 75th Cong. 1st Sess., *S. Report 1275: Investigation of Executive Agencies of the Government* (Washington, D.C., 1937), pp. 33, 210, 306, 1070–71.

11. Richard Polenberg, *Reorganizing Roosevelt's Government* (Cambridge, Mass., 1966), pp. 34, 49, 133, 167.

12. Guy Greer memo for Charles S. Ascher, Oct. 4, 1941, Urban Section Files, Box 3, Records of the National Resources Planning Board (NRPB), Record Group 187, National Archives; Thomas G. Blaisdell, Jr. memo for Charles W. Eliot, 2nd, March 3, 1940, Central Office Correspondence (COC), Box 791, *ibid.*

13. Louis Wirth memo for Charles E. Merriam, Aug. 26, 1941, Folder 4, Box VIII, Louis Wirth MSS., University of Chicago Library.

14. George S. Duggar memo for Charles S. Ascher, Dec. 16, 1941, COC, Box 823, NRPB Records.

15. Jesse C. Bourneuf, "The Executive Order Setting Up the National Housing Agency: A Case Study," typescript, March 4, 1944, Bureau of the Budget Study #229, Records of the Bureau of the Budget (BOB), Record Group 51, National Archives. Also see, material in Box 41, Samuel I. Rosenman MSS., Franklin D. Roosevelt Library.

16. William L. C. Wheaton, "The Evolution of Federal Housing Programs" (unpublished Ph.D. dissertation, University of Chicago, 1953), pp. 103–4, 139–60; Herbert U. Nelson to Samuel I. Rosenman, Feb. 26, 1941, Box 5, Rosenman MSS.

17. Bourneuf, "Executive Order Setting Up NHA," p. 22; Charles S. Ascher memo for John B. Blandford, Jr., Feb. 25, 1942, OA 1942–1946, Box 138, Records of the Department of Housing and Urban Development (HUD), Record Group 207, National Archives.

18. National Housing Agency, General Order #21-5, Nov. 24, 1942, OA 1942–1946, Box 71, HUD Records.

19. See *supra*, pp. 149–51.

20. V. O. Key memo for Ascher, April 15, 1942, Urban Section Files, Box 1, NRPB Records; Catherine Bauer to Alfred Bettman, June 8, 1943, Reel 27, Alfred Bettman MSS., Collection of Regional History and University Archives, Cornell University Library; Producers' Council, *Towards A Post-War Housing Program* (Washington, D.C., 1944), p. 8.

21. Senate Special Committee on Post-War Economic Policy and Planning, 79th Cong. 1st Sess., *Hearings Pursuant to S. Res. 102: Housing and Urban Redevelopment* (Washington, D.C., 1945), pp. 1685, 1690; Senate Committee on Banking and Currency, 79th Cong. 1st Sess., *Hearings on S. 1592: General Housing Act of 1945* (Washington, D.C., 1945), p. 540.

22. *Headlines*, XI (June 26, 1944); Senate Special Committee, *Hearings on Housing and Urban Redevelopment*, p. 2018.

23. Senate Special Committee on Post-War Economic Policy and Planning, 79th Cong. 1st Sess., *Post-War Housing* (Washington, D.C., 1945), pp. 8–10, 11–13; Senate, 79th Cong. 2nd Sess., *S. Report 1131* (Washington, D.C., 1946), pp. 14–15; Wheaton, "Evolution of Federal Housing Programs," pp. 246–48.

24. Robert C. Weaver, "Urban Renewal and Housing," in *City Problems of 1961* (Washington, D.C., 1961), p. 108. Cf. William L. C. Wheaton to Catherine Bauer Wurster, Dec. 19, 1946, Wheaton folder, Catherine Bauer Wurster MSS., College of Environmental Design Library, University of California, Berkeley.

25. "An Open Letter to General Eisenhower," *House and Home*, III (Jan. 1953), 121; "G.O.P. hits snags finding a new HHFA chief," *ibid.*, III (Feb. 1953), 104.

26. *Congressional Record*, 83rd Cong. 2nd Sess., p. 11768; J. Arthur Younger, "We Need a Department of Urbiculture," *This Week*, Aug. 5, 1956, p. 8. Younger exaggerated the nation's urban population; according to the 1950 Census, the figure was 64 per cent of the national total, in 1960, 69.9 per cent.

27. Younger, "We Need a Department of Urbiculture," p. 17.

28. San Mateo County was, by Bureau of the Census definition, largely urban, though its largest city had only 41,500 people.

29. House of Representatives, Committee on Government Operations, 87th Cong. 1st Sess., *Hearings on H.R. 6433: Department of Urban Affairs and Housing* (Washington, D.C., 1961), pp. 9–10.

30. Lee F. Johnson to Neal J. Hardy, Nov. 7, 1953, copy in files of Citizens Planning and Housing Council of New York.

31. *Journal of Housing*, XI (Nov. 1954), 380.

32. "Redevelopment Restated," *Urban Land*, XII (March 1953), 1; "A Department of Urbiculture," *ibid.*, XIII (Sept. 1954), 2.

33. *Architectural Forum*, CI (Dec. 1954), 39.

34. The *NYT* ran a front-page article on the hearings under the heading: "Word (?) 'Urbiculture' is Born in Congress, Which Doesn't Care." Written by Russell Baker, the story began: "This Federal District—language butcher of the English-speaking world—offered 'urbiculture' to the mother tongue today. Judging from 'urbiculture's' reception this morning when it was loosed full-blown in a congressional hearing room, the offer will not be accepted." *NYT*, July 27, 1955, p. 1.

35. S. 3159, 84th Congress. The eight co-sponsors, all Democrats, were Humphrey (Minn.), Morse (Ore.), Neuberger (Ore.), Magnuson (Wash.), Murray (Mont.), Hennings (Mo.), McNamara (Mich.) and Douglas (Ill.). With the exception of Murray, each came from a state with at least one big urban center.

36. *House and Home*, XI (May 1957), 37.

37. *New York Times*, Nov. 28, 1956, p. 70; American Municipal Association, *National Municipal Policy: November, 1956* (Washington, D.C., n.d.), p. 6.

38. *Current Biography 1952* (New York, 1952), pp. 107–9; Stewart Alsop, "The Paradox of Gentleman Joe," *Saturday Evening Post*, CCXXIX (April 27, 1957), 40–41, 143–44; Jeanne R. Lowe, *Cities in a Race With Time* (New York, 1967), pp. 328–32.

39. John Senning, "Senator Joe Clark: new champion of government in housing," *House and Home*, XV (April 1959), 43. Coincidentally, Clark inherited Lehman's suite of Senate offices.

40. Quoted in *ibid.*, p. 47.

41. The co-sponsors this time were Humphrey, Magnuson, Morse, Neuberger, and Murray, plus Long (D.-La.) and two Republicans, Javits (N.Y.) and Case (N.J.).

42. Joseph S. Clark, "A Voice for the Cities," *Nation*, CLXXXVIII (March 7, 1959), 199, 201; Clark, "The Future of the City," *Journal of the American Institute of Architects*, XXVII (June 1957), 138.

43. Interview with Joseph S. Clark, Philadelphia, June 23, 1971.

44. Seidman, *Politics, Position, and Power*, p. 91.

45. Commission on Organization of the Executive Branch of Government, *General Management of the Executive Branch* (Washington, D.C., 1949), p. 34.

46. PACGO memo for the President, March 24, 1953, R 4-21/53.1; Arnold Miles memo for William F. Finan, Oct. 22, 1953, R 4-21/53.2, Bureau of the Budget Files, Executive Office of the President, Washington, D.C. Cf. President's Advisory Committee on Government Housing Policies and Programs, *Report* (Washington, D.C., 1953), pp. 368–72.

47. Nelson Rockefeller memo for the President, Jan. 30, 1954, OF 25, White House Central Files, Dwight D. Eisenhower Library; Guy T. Hollyday to Sherman Adams, Feb. 19, 1954; Feb. 26, 1954, Box 10, Sherman Adams MSS., Dartmouth College Library; William L. C. Wheaton to Catherine Bauer Wurster, n.d. [1954], Wheaton folder, Wurster MSS.; "Reorganization Plan No. 3 of 1954," draft copy, May 27, 1954; William F. Finan memo for the files, June 4, 1954, R 4-21/53.2, BOB Files.

48. Albert Cole memo for Arthur S. Flemming, Feb. 21, 1955, R 4-21/53.1, BOB Files. BOB staff members believed that separation of the FHLBB would have been much more difficult if HHFA had been "an executive department with a direct voice in the Cabinet." Staff memorandum, "Departmental Status for Housing and Community Development Functions," Oct. 15, 1956, Box 13, Records of the President's Advisory Committee on Government Organization (PACGO), Dwight D. Eisenhower Library.

49. Alan Dean memo for B. T. Fitzpatrick, May 17, 1954, HHFA Administrators' Files, Box 20, HUD Records; "Reorganization Plan No. 3 of 1954," draft copy, May 27, 1954, R 4-21/53.2, BOB Files.

50. Arthur A. Kimball and Jerry Kieffer memo for PACGO, Nov. 9, 1956, Box 13, PACGO Records. This briefing paper was based upon the BOB staff memorandum cited in footnote 48.

51. Arthur A. Kimball memo for William Finan and Arnold Miles, Nov. 15, 1956; "Status of Pending Issues," Feb. 12, 1957, Box 5, PACGO Records; Nelson Rockefeller memo for the President, Dec. 18, 1956, R 4-20/55.1, BOB Files.

52. PACGO memorandum for the President, draft, July 2, 1957, Box 13, PACGO Records. The memo reflected the views of Rockefeller and Flemming; Milton Eisenhower was ill at the time of its preparation and was not ready to make any recommendation before he had a chance to discuss the issue with the agencies involved. Kimball to Rockefeller, June 19, 1957, *ibid.*

53. Kimball memo for Percival Brundage, July 5, 1957, *ibid.*

54. Kimball memo for PACGO, Sept. 6, 1957, *ibid.*; PACGO memo for Sherman Adams, Sept. 26, 1957, R 4-20/55.1, BOB Files.

55. Leo A. Hoegh to Hubert Humphrey, Aug. 5, 1957, R 4-2/65.1; William Finan memo for the budget director, Sept. 6, 1957, R 4-20/55.1, *ibid.* In early 1958, Eisenhower, on PACGO's recommendation, submitted a Reorganization Plan merging FCDA and the Office of Defense Mobilization into the Office of Defense and Civilian Mobilization; the consolidation took effect that summer. Roger W. Jones to Dwight Waldo, July 28, 1958, *ibid.*

56. "Minutes of Meetings with the President," Oct. 10, 1957, Box 3; "Data Sheet on Department of Housing and Community Development Proposal," Dec. 15, 1958, Box 6, PACGO Records.

57. *NYT*, Sept. 24, 1957, p. 28. An early draft of the speech, dated July 31, 1957, lauded the idea of a cabinet post for urban affairs; R 4-20/55.1, BOB Files.

58. S. 2159, 85th Congress (Clark bill).

59. Nathaniel Keith, "Blueprint for Full Community Development, 1957–1975," mimeographed, n.d. [1957], copy in files of the Citizens Planning and Housing Council of New York.

60. National Association of Housing and Redevelopment Officials testimony, in Senate Committee on Banking and Currency, 86th Cong. 2nd Sess:, *Hearings on Housing Legislation of 1960* (Washington, D.C., 1960), pp. 252–53.

61. Albert Rains, "Congressman Cites Need—Cabinet Post for Urban Affairs," *Alabama Municipal Review*, XVII (May 1960), 14–15. Cf. Patrick J. Healy, "A Federal Department of Urban Affairs," in *Planning 1958* (Chicago, 1958), p. 172.

62. Robert H. Connery and Richard H. Leach, *The Federal Government and Metropolitan Areas* (Cambridge, Mass., 1960), pp. 187–88. Cf. Blandford's testimony, in Senate Special Committee, *Hearings on Housing and Urban Redevelopment*, p. 1314.

63. Alan Dean, draft of letter to Rep. Dawson, March 30, 1956, R 4-20/55.1, BOB Files.

64. William L. C. Wheaton testimony, in House of Representatives Committee on Government Operations, 86th Cong. 1st Sess., *Hearings on Metropolitan Problems and Urban Development* (Washington, D.C., 1959), p. 147. Cf. Robert W. Hartley memo for Charles S. Ascher, May 21, 1942, COC, Box 853, NRPB Records.

65. William L. C. Wheaton, "A New Cabinet Post," *National Civic Review*, XLVIII (Dec. 1959), 577.

66. William L. C. Wheaton, Review of *The Federal Government and Metropolitan Areas*, by Connery and Leach, in *Journal of the American Institute of Planners*, XXVI (Nov. 1960), 333.

67. See *supra*, pp. 179–80, 181. One Budget Bureau staff member wrote that the *Ad Hoc* Committee "was intended primarily as a political lightning rod rather than as a means of formulating or coordinating federal policies on metropolitan areas." Frederick O'R. Hayes to Norman Beckman, Oct. 20, 1960, R 4-23/57.1, BOB Files.

68. Robert E. Merriam, in *Proceedings, American Municipal Congress 1960* (Washington, D.C., n.d.), pp. 127–29.

69. Connery and Leach, *Federal Government and Metropolitan Areas*, pp. 186, 153–63. For expressions of similar views, see *NYT*, June 22, 1958, p. 61; Norman Beckman, Interviews with Joseph Intermaggio, Sept. 13, 1960, and Harvey Perloff, Sept. 14, 1960, R 4-23/57.1, BOB Files; Charles P. Taft testimony, in Senate Committee on Banking and Currency, 86th Cong. 1st Sess., *Hearings on Housing Act of 1959* (Washington, D.C., 1959), p. 605.

70. Robert C. Wood, "The Federal Role in the Urban Environment," *Public Administration Review*, XXVIII (July/Aug. 1968), 342–43.

71. Joseph S. Clark, "Towards National Federalism," in *The Federal Government and the Cities* (Washington, D.C., 1961), p. 48; Wheaton, "A New Cabinet Post," 578. Winning a seat at the cabinet seemed especially important during the late 1950s since Eisenhower appeared to rely so heavily upon the cabinet in making major policy decisions. See John V. Lindsay, "The Crisis of Our Cities," *Progressive Architecture*, XLI (Sept. 1960), 167.

72. For the administration's views on H.R. 781, H.R. 984, and S. 2397, see Philip S. Hughes to William L. Dawson, June 4, 1959, and Hughes to John L. McClellan, Aug. 20, 1959, R 4-20/59.1, BOB Files.

73. Brownlow came out against a department of urban affairs at the 1957 meeting of the American Political Science Association. The switch from his 1941 position— when he told Rosenman that there should be "a department of urbanism to do for city dwellers what the Department of Agriculture has done for rural dwellers" (see *supra*, p. 102.)—was due to his feeling that it was now impossible to combine the many federal programs having implications for local government in a single department. Brownlow favored the re-establishment of the National Resources Planning Board as the best organizational approach to federal-city relations. Douglas E. Chaffin memo for Annabelle Heath, Dec. 9, 1957, HHFA Administrators' Files, Box 11, HUD Records. Gulick supported a Council of Urban Advisors at a 1957 conference on the Interstate Highway System; Wilfred Owen, *Cities in the Motor Age* (New York, 1959), pp. 124–25. Also see Gulick's *The Metropolitan Problem and American Ideas* (New York, 1962), pp. 133–34. The Connery-Leach study was part of a larger project under Gulick's direction.

74. *Congressional Record*, 86th Cong. 1st Sess., p. 13551; S. 1431.

75. H.R. 5565, 85th Cong. Ostertag's district included some of the suburbs of

Rochester. His bill was prompted by a suggestion from the National Planning Association that the President call a White House Conference on Metropolitan Area Problems; see *infra*, pp. 279–80.

76. Percival Brundage to William L. Dawson, July 27, 1957, R 2-16/57.1, BOB Files.

77. Norman Beckman memo for William F. Finan, May 20, 1959, *ibid.; Ad Hoc* Interagency Committee on Metropolitan Area Problems, Minutes of May 25, 1959 meeting, Box 7, Records of Robert E. Merriam, Dwight D. Eisenhower Library; Philip S. Hughes to John L. McClellan, Aug. 3, 1959, reprinted in Senate Committee on Government Operations, 86th Cong. 1st Sess., *Hearings on S. 1431: Create a Commission on Metropolitan Problems* (Washington, D.C., 1959), p. 18.

78. Especially damaging to the Metropolitan Commission bill in the House was the passage in August of a measure creating an Advisory Commission on Intergovernmental Relations (ACIR). This body was to serve as "a forum for the discussion of the administration and coordination of federal grants requiring intergovernmental cooperation." Thus, the Republicans on the House Government Operations Committee claimed that establishment of ACIR made the Metropolitan Commission unnecessary; Clark and other liberals disagreed, arguing that ACIR's scope of operations was so broad that a detailed examination of urban problems would not be possible. ACIR did identify metropolitan ills as one of the first matters for its attention, but in June 1960 a member of the Public Works Planning Unit in the White House complained to his chief that ACIR "has shown little vigor in attacking the problem." ACIR, Minutes of Second Meeting, Feb. 10, 1960, Box 1, Merriam Records; Henry Brooks memo for John S. Bragdon, June 16, 1960, Box 14, Records of John S. Bragdon, Dwight D. Eisenhower Library.

79. Seidman, *Politics, Position, and Power*, p. 210.

80. Cole to Dawson, July 20, 1956, R 4-20/55.1, BOB Files.

81. HHFA, Major Legislative Proposals, Aug. 1956, Files of the Office of General Counsel, Department of Housing and Urban Development, Washington, D.C.

82. *House and Home*, XIV (Aug. 1958), 131; Charles M. Haar, *Federal Credit and Private Housing* (New York, 1960), pp. 331–32.

83. Martin L. Baitling, quoted in National Housing Conference, *Membership Newsletter*, XIII (March 1960), 3. NAHB itself was sharply divided on the issue of a cabinet department; the small builders were not so dependent upon federal programs as the giant firms and feared that a new department would lead to greater federal control of their operations. Many NAHB members—big and small—were also afraid that housing would be relegated to a secondary position in a broad-based department of urban affairs.

84. Frederick O'R. Hayes memo for Sam R. Broadbent, May 6, 1959, R 4-23/57.1, BOB Files; M. Carter McFarland memo for Annabelle Heath, Oct. 1, 1958, HHFA Administrators' Files, Box 18, HUD Records. Cole had created the Office of Program Policy shortly before leaving HHFA to analyze "the manifold problems accompanying the rapid urbanization of the United States and problems resulting from the changing patterns of urban life." *House and Home*, XIV (Oct. 1958), 65.

85. Norman P. Mason to Robert E. Merriam, April 17, 1959, Box 8, Records of

Douglas Price and John Stambaugh, Dwight D. Eisenhower Library; Hayes memo for Broadbent, May 6, 1959, R 4-23/57.1, BOB Files.

86. Materials in HHFA Administrators' Files, Boxes 23, 25, and 35, HUD Records.
87. Ed Strait memo for Fred Levi, Jan. 14, 1960; HHFA, "Reorganization Plan No. 1 of 1960," draft of Feb. 5, 1960; HHFA, "Analysis of Proposal to Transfer HHFA Functions to a New Department," Feb. 23, 1960, R 4-20/59.1, BOB Files.
88. BOB staff memo for PACGO, April 7, 1960; Fred E. Levi memo for the Budget Director, April 26, 1960, *ibid.*
89. Maurice Stans to Norman P. Mason, June 20, 1960, *ibid.*
90. Clark interview, June 23, 1971.
91. Philip S. Hughes to A. Willis Robertson, May 9, 1960, reprinted in Senate Banking and Currency, *Hearings on Housing Legislation of 1960*, p. 72.
92. *Ibid.*, p. 70.
93. See *infra*, p. 297.
94. Four of the bills were sponsored by Republicans: Younger and three congressmen from New York, Keating, Lindsay, and Halpern.

CHAPTER 8

1. A good summary of the 1960 Census's implications for cities is Philip Hauser, "Dynamic Forces Shaping the City," in *Proceedings, American Municipal Congress 1961* (Washington, D.C., n.d.), pp. 8–15.
2. John C. Bollens, *et al., The States and the Metropolitan Problem* (Chicago, 1956), pp. 132–47; *State Government*, XXIX (Dec. 1956), 242; XXX (Jan. 1957), 14–17.
3. "Six States and Their Metropolitan Problems," *State Government*, XXX (Nov. 1957), 234–37; *NYT*, Sept. 22, 1957, pp. 1, 42; Sept. 24, 1957, pp. 1, 29. The conference provided some of the impetus for the establishment of the *Ad Hoc* Interagency Committee on Metropolitan Area Problems by Presidential aide Howard Pyle in Oct. 1957. Robert E. Merriam memo for Robert Anderson, Oct. 2, 1957, Box 7, Records of Robert E. Merriam, Dwight D. Eisenhower Library.
4. *NYT*, Sept. 9, 1958, p. 30.
5. Charlton F. Chute, "Today's Urban Regions, II," *National Municipal Review*, XLIV (July 1956), 336.
6. "A Ten-Year Program for Metropolitan Areas," *Looking Ahead*, V (Feb. 1957), 1–3. The plan merited first-page coverage by the *NYT*, Feb. 4, 1957, pp. 1, 10.
7. John S. Bragdon memo for Gabriel Hauge, Dec. 12, 1956; Bragdon memo for the Record, April 4, 1957, Box 19, Records of John S. Bragdon, Dwight D. Eisenhower Library.
8. For the conference's coverage and conclusions on this point, see Meyer Kestnbaum, "Federal Responsibility," and the Conference's "General Report," in *Proceedings, National Conference on Metropolitan Problems 1956* (New York, 1957), pp. 70–73, 11.
9. Bragdon memo for the Record, April 1, 1957, Box 19, Bragdon Records.
10. *Public Papers of the Presidents: Dwight D. Eisenhower, 1957* (Washington, D.C., 1958), pp. 473–74, 491–92; Albert Cole memo for Gabriel Hauge, June 27, 1957; Bragdon memo for the Record, July 2, 1957, Box 19, Bragdon Records.

11. Albert Cole memo for Gabriel Hauge, Feb. 14, 1954; Cole memo for Hauge, Oct. 13, 1955, OF 147-B-1, White House Central Files, Dwight D. Eisenhower Library; *Public Papers of the Presidents: Dwight D. Eisenhower, 1954* (Washington, D.C., 1960), pp. 1051-52.

12. "ACTION's Rousing Mr. Rouse," *Architectural Forum*, CX (May 1959), 128-29; *NYT*, May 5, 1959, p. 35; May 6, 1959, p. 41.

13. Robert T. Daland, "Political Science and the Study of Urbanism," *American Political Science Review*, LI (June 1957), 491-506.

14. "Exploding Cities," *Economist*, CLXXXVI (Jan. 4, 1958), 35.

15. Robert H. Connery and Richard H. Leach, *The Federal Government and Metropolitan Areas* (Cambridge, Mass., 1960), pp. 109-15. The committee's report, submitted in Jan. 1959, urged a limited federation of Washington-area local governments, but the 86th Congress took no action on the proposals, except for those in the field of transportation.

16. "A Country of Crowded Clusters," *Newsweek*, LIV (Dec. 14, 1959), 44-46. Cf. "By the Year 2000—10 'Supercities,' " *U.S. News and World Report*, XLVII (Nov. 9, 1959), 82-83.

17. Gordon E. Baker, *Rural Versus Urban Political Power* (Garden City, N.Y., 1955), pp. 15-18.

18. Ben West, "The Effect of Reapportionment on State Actions," in *Proceedings, American Municipal Congress 1962* (Washington, D.C., n.d.), pp. 48-53.

19. Richard C. Cortner, *The Apportionment Cases* (Knoxville, Tenn., 1970), pp. 53-57, 63-69, 74-75, 88. The 1946 case was *Colegrove v. Green*, 328 U.S. 549.

20. The Connery and Leach monograph, *The Federal Government and Metropolitan Areas*, was part of a series sponsored by the Stern Family Fund. The quote is from the Foreword by Luther Gulick.

21. For the Ford Foundation's activities, see its *Annual Reports* for the period 1955 to 1960; *Metropolis* (New York, 1959); *Urban Extension* (New York, 1966); Paul N. Ylvisaker, "New Ideas for Cities as Learned from Foundation Grants," in *Proceedings, American Municipal Congress 1963* (Washington, D.C., n.d.), pp. 24-31; Ylvisaker, "A Foundation Approach to City Problems," in *American Community Development* (New York, 1963), pp. 5-9.

22. Catherine Bauer Wurster, "Framework for an Urban Society," in *Goals for Americans* (Englewood Cliffs, N.J., 1960), pp. 225-47.

23. Angus Campbell, *et al., The Voter Decides* (Evanston, Ill., 1954), pp. 65-67, 175-77; Angus Campbell, *et al., The American Voter* (New York, 1960), pp. 54-57; Carl N. Degler, "American Political Parties and the Rise of the Cities: An Interpretation," *Journal of American History*, LI (June 1964), 58. Contemporary conventional wisdom held that the suburbs were the most important element in Eisenhower's victory. Robert Taft gloated that "the Democratic party will never win another national election until it solves the problem of the suburbs." Stevenson aide Jacob Arvey concurred: "the suburbs beat us," he explained. This analysis, however, does not hold up under closer scrutiny. Democratic defections in the cities, not Republican gains in the suburbs, were primarily responsible for the G.O.P. triumph; central cities in the fifteen largest metropolitan areas showed

greater shifts to the Republicans than did the suburbs. Robert C. Wood, "The Impotent Suburban Vote," *Nation*, CXC (March 26, 1960), 272–73.

24. *House and Home*, X (July 1956), 77.

25. Kirk H. Porter and Donald Bruce Johnson, *National Party Platforms, 1840–1964* (Urbana, Ill., 1966), pp. 534–35.

26. *Ibid.*, p. 550.

27. Oakley Hunter memo for Bryce Harlow, Sept. 28, 1956, Box 11, Records of Bryce Harlow, Dwight D. Eisenhower Library; *Public Papers of the Presidents: Dwight D. Eisenhower, 1956* (Washington, D.C., 1959), pp. 486, 503, 507.

28. Clifford Case memo for Sherman Adams, Oct. 23, 1956; Adams to Case, Oct. 31, 1956, OF 147-B, White House Central Files, Eisenhower Library.

29. "Cities Ask for More," *Economist*, CXCIV (Jan. 1, 1960), 36; "Cry Subsidy," *Time*, LXXIV (Dec. 14, 1959), 18.

30. For the DAC, see Cornelius P. Cotter and Bernard C. Hennessy, *Politics Without Power* (New York, 1964), pp. 211–24.

31. *Architectural Forum*, CXI (Oct. 1959), 14, 16; *Democratic Digest*, VI (Sept. 1959), 11.

32. *Democratic Digest*, VII (Dec. 1959/Jan. 1960), 7; *NYT*, Dec. 7, 1959, p. 39.

33. Theodore H. White, *The Making of the President 1960* (New York, 1961), pp. 34, 112–14.

34. See *supra*, pp. 234, 268–70. For Johnson's strategy, see White, *Making of the President 1960*, pp. 43, 46, 131–35.

35. John F. Kennedy, "The Shame of the States," *NYT Magazine*, May 18, 1958, pp. 12, 37–38, 40.

36. *NYT*, Dec. 1, 1959, p. 27; "Cry Subsidy," 18.

37. Kennedy, "The Great Unspoken Issue," in *Proceedings, American Municipal Congress 1959* (Washington, D.C., n.d.), pp. 23–28. Cf. William O'Hallaren, "A Fair Share for the Cities," *Reporter*, XXI (Nov. 12, 1959), 22–24.

38. White, *Making of the President 1960*, pp. 55, 85, 95, 139–41, 159, 166. Two of the key figures in Kennedy's victory were Chicago's Richard Daley and Pittsburgh's (now Pennsylvania Governor) David Lawrence.

39. *U.S. Municipal News*, XXVII (July 20, 1960), 49; *NYT*, July 7, 1960, p. 22; Suzanne Farkas, *Urban Lobbying* (New York, 1971), p. 186; James L. Sundquist, Oral History Interview, John F. Kennedy Library, pp. 3–4.

40. Porter and Johnson, *National Party Platforms*, pp. 592–93. On the unprecedented urban characteristics of the platform, see Francis E. Rourke, "Urbanism and the National Party Organizations," *Western Political Quarterly*, XVIII (March 1964), 155.

41. White, *Making of the President 1960*, p. 247; Theodore Sorensen, "The Election of 1960," in *The History of American Presidential Elections*, ed. Arthur M. Schlesinger, Jr. (New York, 1971), p. 3462. Kennedy was, of course, also relying upon his running mate, Lyndon Johnson, to carry the South.

42. John S. Bragdon memo for Robert Anderson, Oct. 15, 1957, Box 13; Henry Brooks memo for Bragdon, June 16, 1960, Box 14, Bragdon Records.

43. Cotter and Hennessy, *Politics Without Power*, pp. 195–204.

44. The other members were the Undersecretary of HEW, a professor, the president of a North Carolina county Republican women's club, a New York attorney, and the governor of West Virginia.
45. Republican Committee on Program and Progress, *Decisions for a Better America* (Garden City, N.Y., 1960), pp. 40–42.
46. Porter and Johnson, *National Party Platforms*, p. 617.
47. *NYT*, Aug. 7, 1960, p. 53. See Nixon's remarks in *The Urban County Congress* (Washington, D.C., n.d.), pp. 6–7. Nixon's only serious challenger for the Republican nomination, New York Governor Nelson Rockefeller, had proven himself an able vote-getter in urban centers, but none of the changes that Rockefeller forced upon Nixon in the Republican platform dealt with city issues.
48. Nixon is quoted in White, *Making of the President 1960*, p. 206. White concludes that Nixon really had no strategy at all; pp. 267, 352.
49. For examples, see *The Speeches of John F. Kennedy*, Senate Report 994, Part I, 87th Cong. 1st Sess. (Washington, D.C., 1961), pp. 69, 75, 90, 116, 193, 229, 246, 344, 364.
50. *NYT*, Sept. 29, 1960, p. 1.
51. *The Speeches of Richard M. Nixon*, Senate Report 994, Part II, 87th Cong. 1st Sess. (Washington, D.C., 1961), pp. 325–28.
52. *NYT*, Sept. 29, 1960, p. 21; *Wall Street Journal*, Sept. 29, 1960, p. 9.
53. *NYT*, Oct. 11, 1960, p. 50; Oct. 8, 1960, p. 12; Nov. 4, 1960, p. 32.
54. Marjorie Hein memo for Bryce Harlow, Sept. 30, 1960; draft of speech, "Our Urban Areas," Sept. 29, 1960, Box 2, Merriam Records.
55. *Speeches of Richard M. Nixon*, pp. 688–89.
56. White, *Making of the President 1960*, p. 304.
57. "The Urban Issue in the 1960 Presidential Campaign," Memorandum, n.d.; and other materials in Box 20, Alphabetical Secretary's File, Adam Yarmolinsky MSS., John F. Kennedy Library.
58. *Speeches of John F. Kennedy*, pp. 193–94; *NYT*, Sept. 21, 1960, p. 29; Oct. 11, 1960, pp. 1, 50.
59. *Speeches of John F. Kennedy*, pp. 551–52.
60. Kennedy had his facts slightly wrong. The Department of Agriculture was, indeed, created in 1862, but it did not become an Executive department until 1889.
61. *Speeches of John F. Kennedy*, pp. 552–54.
62. Only the *NYT*, of six major big-city papers examined, gave front-page coverage to either candidate's statement. The Washington *Post* totally ignored Nixon's and gave one sentence to Kennedy's. The St. Louis *Post-Dispatch* allotted one paragraph to Nixon and several to Kennedy. Nixon's remarks were completely overlooked by the Milwaukee *Journal* and Denver *Post*, and mentioned in passing by the New York *Herald-Tribune*; the *Journal* and *Herald-Tribune* carried wire service stories on Kennedy, the *Post* nothing at all. Washington *Post*, Sept. 29, 1960, p. A2; Oct. 11, 1960, p. A2; St. Louis *Post-Dispatch*, Sept. 28, 1960, p. 20; Oct. 11, 1960, p. 8; New York *Herald-Tribune*, Sept. 29, 1960, p. 6; Oct. 11, 1960, p. 11; Milwaukee *Journal*, Sept. 29, 1960, p. 18; Oct. 11, 1960, p. 15; Denver *Post*, Sept. 29, 1960, p. 19; Oct. 11, 1960, p. 1.

63. *The Joint Appearances of John F. Kennedy and Richard M. Nixon*, Senate Report 994, Part III, 87th Cong. 1st Sess. (Washington, D.C., 1961), pp. 268–69.

64. White, *Making of the President 1960*, pp. 321, 353–54. Sorensen writes: "The suburbs surrounding the nation's great cities became a hotly contested key to the outcome for the first time." "Election of 1960," p. 3449.

65. Of course, Kennedy's victory was in large measure due to Johnson's ability to carry much of the South—particularly Texas—for the Democratic ticket. White, *Making of the President 1960*, p. 353.

66. *Ibid.*, pp. 353–54; Theodore Sorensen, *Kennedy* (New York, 1965), p. 222; Joseph K. Zikmund II, "Suburban Voting in Presidential Elections: 1948–1964," *Midwest Journal of Political Science*, XII (May 1968), 248. Kennedy's success in reducing Republican pluralities in the suburbs was instrumental in his winning the electoral votes of Illinois, Michigan, New York, and Maryland. Baltimore, for example, gave Kennedy an 88,000-vote lead (Eisenhower had taken the city by 37,000 votes in 1956), but J.F.K. won Maryland only because the Republican margin in the rest of the state dropped from the 1956 total of 149,500 to 11,800. Of the 12 states having the largest percentage of their population in Standard Metropolitan Statistical Areas, Kennedy carried all but California, and he lost that by a narrow margin. For the G.O.P. reaction to this Democratic sweep in urban-suburban areas, see *infra*, pp. 362–65.

67. Quoted in *House and Home*, XIX (Jan. 1961), 43.

CHAPTER 9

1. *NYT*, Dec. 9, 1960, pp. 1, 25; *House and Home*, XVIII (Dec. 1960), 39.

2. Unlike previous Presidential appointments of HHFA administrators, Kennedy's designation of Weaver merited front-page coverage in the *NYT* and Washington *Post*. The strong possibility of HHFA's elevation to cabinet rank, and the special qualities that Weaver brought to the post, as noted below, explain this unprecedented interest. *NYT*, Dec. 31, 1960, pp. 1, 6; Washington *Post*, Dec. 31, 1960, pp. 1, 2.

3. For summaries of Weaver's career, see *Current Biography 1961* (New York, 1962), pp. 474–76; and A. H. Raskin, "Washington Gets 'The Weaver Treatment,'" *NYT Magazine*, May 4, 1961, pp. 16, 30.

4. *NYT*, Dec. 31, 1960, pp. 1, 6.

5. Robert C. Weaver, Oral History Interview, John F. Kennedy Library, pp. 19–21; Interview with Adam Yarmolinsky, Boston, Jan. 29, 1975.

6. Robert C. Weaver, "The Negro in a Program of Public Housing," *Opportunity*, XVI (July 1938), 200–201; Weaver, "Racial Policy in Public Housing," *Phylon*, I (Second Quarter 1940), 149–61.

7. Robert C. Weaver, *The Negro Ghetto* (New York, 1948), pp. 333–34; Weaver, "Integration in Public and Private Housing," Annals, CCCIV (March 1956), 86; Weaver, "Non-White Population Movements and Urban Ghettos," *Phylon*, XX (Fall 1959), 235–41; Weaver, "Class, Race and Urban Renewal," *Land Economics*, XXXVI (Aug. 1960), 235–51.

8. *NYT*, Jan. 6, 1961, pp. 1, 19. Ironically, Weaver had served as McMurray's deputy when the latter was New York State housing commissioner in the mid-1950s.

9. *Ibid.*, Jan. 7, 1961, pp. 1, 8; Dec. 31, 1960, pp. 1, 6.

10. Senate Committee on Banking and Currency, 87th Cong. 1st Sess., *Hearings on the Nomination of Robert C. Weaver* (Washington, D.C., 1961), pp. 16–22, 30–40; Weaver to Ralph Dungan, Jan. 11, 1961, Box 11, Harris Wofford MSS., John F. Kennedy Library. Weaver credits Vice-President Johnson with suggesting this softening of his position without any sacrifice of principles; Weaver, Oral History, p. 57.

11. "Three Big Changes in Housing Policy That Will Affect Us All," *House and Home*, XIX (Feb. 1961), 83–87; *ibid.*, XXI (June 1962), 50, 71. The sociologist was Nathan Glazer.

12. Robert C. Weaver, *The Urban Complex* (Garden City, N.Y., 1964), pp. 36–37.

13. Quoted in *NYT*, Feb. 15, 1961, p. 28.

14. "Three Big Changes," 83.

15. Weaver, *Urban Complex*, p. 37.

16. Weaver, Oral History, pp. 36–39; William L. Slayton, Oral History Interview, John F. Kennedy Library, pp. 4–5; *NYT*, Feb. 18, 1961, p. 8; March 26, 1961, p. 56.

17. "An Immediate Program in Urban Development and Housing," a report submitted to the President-elect by the Pittsburgh Conference, Nov. 22, 1960, mimeographed, Box 12-W (A), Joseph S. Clark MSS., Historical Society of Pennsylvania; American Municipal Association, *National Municipal Policy 1961* (Washington, D.C., 1960), pp. 26–30; *NYT*, Dec. 18, 1960, VIII, 1.

18. Laurin L. Henry, "The Transition: Transfer of Presidential Responsibility," in *The Presidential Election and Transition 1960–1961*, ed. Paul T. David (Washington, D.C., 1961), pp. 215–18; "Pre-Inaugural Task Forces Unprecedented in History," *Congressional Quarterly Weekly Report*, XIX (April 7, 1961), 620–23.

19. *NYT*, Jan. 8, 1961, pp. 32, 33. Some of the reports were reprinted in full in *New Frontiers of the Kennedy Administration* (Washington, D.C., 1961), but only a two-page abstract of the urban affairs panel's findings was published. *House and Home*, however, did provide a fairly detailed analysis; "The New Frontier for Housing," *House and Home*, XIX (Feb. 1961), 132–39.

20. Robert C. Wood, Oral History Interview, John F. Kennedy Library, p. 11.

21. Task Force on Housing and Urban Affairs, Report to the President-elect, Dec. 30, 1960, mimeographed, President's Office Files, John F. Kennedy Library. The report also discussed the Federal National Mortgage Association, housing for the elderly, college housing, community facilities, and an urban cabinet department.

22. Wood, Oral History, p. 11.

23. Harold Wolman, *Politics of Federal Housing* (New York, 1971), pp. 83–84; Robert C. Wood, *The Necessary Majority: Middle America and the Urban Crisis* (New York, 1972), pp. 39–40. Weaver does not mention the task force report in his Oral History discussion of the drafting of the 1961 housing bill; pp. 80–82.

24. Senate Committee on Banking and Currency, 87th Cong. 1st Sess., *Hearings on Housing Legislation of 1961* (Washington, D.C., 1961), p. 245.

25. In 1949 the 81st Congress authorized sufficient funds to cover the construction of 810,000 units. Due to increased costs, however, when the 87th Congress finally appropriated the last of this sum in 1961, there was enough money for a total of only 525,000 units.

26. Special Message to Congress on Housing and Community Development, March 9, 1961, *Public Papers of the Presidents: John F. Kennedy, 1961* (Washington, D.C., 1962), pp. 165–66.

27. *Ibid.*, p. 167.

28. Part of the reason for Weaver's and the White House's hesitancy about moving ahead quickly on mass transit was the unresolved question of which agency would administer the program; both HHFA and the Department of Commerce had good claims. It was hoped that a year's delay would clear up this dispute. In addition, Weaver feared that in the absence of comprehensive metropolitan planning any federal aid would be a waste of money, and that transit subsidies might gobble up funds earmarked for housing. Michael N. Danielson, *Federal-Metropolitan Politics and the Commuter Crisis* (New York, 1965), p. 158.

29. "For Housing—The Same, But More," *Business Week*, March 18, 1961, pp. 32–33; Wolman, *Politics of Federal Housing*, pp. 83–84.

30. *House and Home*, XIX (June 1961), 44.

31. *NYT*, April 5, 1961, p. 20; April 6, 1961, p. 17; May 14, 1961, VIII, 1, 6; June 9, 1961, pp. 1, 20.

32. *Congressional Record*, 87th Cong. 1st Sess., pp. 9891, 9895; *House and Home*, XX (July 1961), 48–49; Weaver, Oral History, p. 95.

33. The congressional commitment to mass transit was less than wholehearted, however; the grant money came out of the urban renewal authorization. For the details on the maneuvering between Williams and the White House, see Danielson, *Federal-Metropolitan Politics*, pp. 169–74; and Royce Hanson, "Congress Copes with Mass Transit, 1960–1964," in *Congress and Urban Problems* (Washington, D.C., 1969), pp. 321–28.

34. *House and Home*, XIX (April 1961), 71.

35. As in previous years, the voting on the 1961 omnibus housing bill was primarily along party lines, with some deviation for urban-rural constituencies. House Democrats split 210–38 in favor of the measure, with most of the dissenters from the South; House Republicans opposed it, 140–25. In the Senate, the Democrats divided 52–8 in support, while the Republicans, a number of whom came from industrial states, voted against the bill by a narrow 17–12 margin.

36. Hanson, "Congress Copes with Mass Transit," pp. 328–42.

37. *Congressional Quarterly Weekly Report*, XX (Feb. 2, 1962), 153–69; Harold Wolman, "Who Said America is an Urban Nation?" *Commonweal*, LXXXIX (Oct. 25, 1968), 104–5; Andrew Hacker, "Voice of Ninety Million Americans," *NYT Magazine*, March 4, 1962, pp. 11, 80. Malapportionment also reduced "urban" representation; one study estimated that rural areas had nearly 20 per cent more seats than they were entitled to on a strict population basis, and that suburban regions were underrepresented by approximately the same amount. Central cities had about the right number of seats. Andrew Hacker, *Congressional*

Districting (rev. ed.; Washington, D.C., 1964), pp. 88–95. The Senate, of course, is even more malapportioned than the House, but since World War II the upper chamber has traditionally been more liberal than the House. Political scientists have explained this phenomenon by noting that senators are usually obliged to appeal to much larger constituencies where urban voters are often significant in both their numbers and independence; see Lewis A. Froman, *Congressmen and Their Constituencies* (Chicago, 1963), pp. 80–83.

38. A former managerial specialist at the Bureau of the Budget has observed that, unlike Eisenhower, Kennedy showed little interest in organizational structure and administration; his orientation was almost always towards individuals and programs. Harold D. Seidman, *Politics, Position, and Power* (New York, 1970), pp. 92–93.

39. Kennedy, *Public Papers*, 1961, p. 169.

40. The Democrats controlled the Senate, 65–35, and the House, 260–172.

41. When Kennedy offered the HHFA job to Weaver, the President-elect told Weaver that he would be the logical candidate for secretary of the urban department, but nothing was said for public release; Weaver, Oral History, p. 15. Nearly all the newspaper speculation about a possible nominee, however, focused on Weaver.

42. What thought Kennedy and his advisers, at the time of Weaver's selection as HHFA chief, gave to the impact of this appointment on the departmental issue is not known. They undoubtedly realized that the choice of Weaver could not help the bill, but it is possible that they believed that Weaver's service at HHFA would soften the opposition to his later nomination to the cabinet.

43. Weaver, Oral History, p. 111; Jack T. Conway memo for Lawrence O'Brien, May 10, 1961, Reel 2, HHFA Records, John F. Kennedy Library.

44. Richard E. Neustadt memo for Theodore Sorensen and Myer Feldman, Jan. 25, 1961, R 4-20/Vol. I, Bureau of the Budget Files, Executive Office of the President, Washington, D.C.; James L. Sundquist, draft of memo, Nov. 7, 1960, Box 12-W (D), Clark MSS.

45. Judith Heimlich Parris, "Congress Rejects the President's Urban Department, 1961–1962," in *Congress and Urban Problems*, p. 187. The chairman of the House Committee on Government Operations, William L. Dawson (D.-Ill.), had traditionally abstained from sponsoring important legislation and guiding bills through floor debate. In this instance the White House was glad to respect Dawson's wishes, since he was a Negro, and by playing a prominent role would only serve to highlight the Weaver issue. Responsibility for the departmental bill was assumed by Dante Fascell (Fla.) of Miami, the next ranking Democrat on the reorganization subcommittee. Although Fascell was not an influential man in the House, the administration hoped his Southern background would prove useful in debate.

46. Neustadt memo for Sorensen and Feldman, Jan. 25, 1961, BOB Files; Milton P. Semer memo for Weaver. April 28, 1961; Weaver to William L. Dawson, May 18, 1961, HHFA Administrators' Files, Box 58, Records of the Department of Housing and Urban Development, Record Group 207, National Archives.

47. Neustadt memo for Sorensen and Feldman.

48. *Ibid.;* "A Cabinet Seat for the Cities," *Business Week*, Nov. 26, 1960, pp. 71–73; William L. C. Wheaton memo for Hugh Mields, Jr., Nov. 11, 1960, R 4-20/60.1, BOB Files; *NYT*, May 20, 1961, p. 47; National Housing Conference, *Membership Newsletter*, XIV (Feb. 1961), 2.

49. Neustadt memo for Sorensen and Feldman; Myer Feldman memo for Kenneth O'Donnell, Feb. 2, 1961, Box 1550, Myer Feldman MSS., John F. Kennedy Library.

50. House of Representatives, Committee on Government Operations, 87th Cong. 1st Sess., *Hearings on H.R. 6433: Department of Urban Affairs and Housing* (Washington, D.C., 1961), pp. 111–12.

51. *Ibid.,* pp. 138–42; Senate Committee on Government Operations, 87th Cong. 1st Sess., *Hearings on S. 1633: Establish a Department of Urban Affairs and Housing* (Washington, D.C., 1961), pp. 152–60.

52. House, *Hearings on H.R. 6433*, pp. 108–10. For similar comments from the National Association of Manufacturers and the Chamber of Commerce of the United States, see *ibid.,* pp. 170–77, 206–9.

53. Senate, *Hearings on S. 1633*, pp. 103–4.

54. *Ibid.,* p. 112. Significantly, none of the governors came from the South. Only one Republican chief executive, John Volpe, from highly urbanized Massachusetts, publicly endorsed the proposal; *Congressional Record*, 87th Cong. 1st Sess., p. 18407.

55. Senate, *Hearings on S. 1633*, p. 17.

56. *Ibid.,* pp. 68–70.

57. House, *Hearings on H.R. 6433*, pp. 70–72. The American Farm Bureau Federation sent a written statement denouncing the DUAH bill; Senate, *Hearings on S. 1633*, pp. 64–65.

58. Neustadt memo for Sorensen and Feldman, Jan. 25, 1961, BOB Files.

59. Senate, *Hearings on S. 1633*, pp. 17, 34–38.

60. Patrick H. McLaughlin to Myer Feldman, June 9, 1961; Norman Beckman memo for the Records, July 17, 1961, R 4-20/Vol. I, BOB Files; Milton P. Semer to Lee C. White, July 25, 1961, Reel 5, HHFA Records, Kennedy Library. The two subcommittees reported out identical bills.

61. Senate, 87th Cong. 1st Sess., *S. Report 879: Minority Views* (Washington, D.C., 1961), pp. 24–30.

62. Lee White memo for Kennedy, Aug. 21, 1961, Box 18, Lee White MSS., John F. Kennedy Library; "Federal Legislation Matters Affecting HHFA," memo, Jan. 15, 1962, Joint Chronological File/87th Congress, Files of the General Counsel, Department of Housing and Urban Development, Washington, D.C.; *House and Home*, XX (Oct. 1961), 50–51.

63. *NYT*, Jan. 17, 1962, pp. 1, 18; Jan. 22, 1962, p. 1.

64. The key defectors were Carl Elliott (Ala.) and James Trimble (Ark.). Smith (Va.) and Colmer (Miss.) had consistently opposed the administration, but Elliott and Trimble were moderates who normally followed the administration in the absence of racial questions. The strong possibility of Weaver's nomination, however, had injected race into the vote and neither Elliott—who had to run for re-election at

large against fellow Democratic congressmen because of the legislature's failure to draw new districts—nor Trimble was willing to go against Southern opinion. The only Southerner to line up with the administration was Homer Thornberry of Texas. Less than a week after the Rules Committee action, he was appointed to a federal judgeship. *NYT*, Jan. 25, 1962, pp. 1, 13; Jan. 29, 1962, p. 12.

65. Theodore Sorensen, *Kennedy* (New York, 1965), p. 481.

66. Walter Lippmann, "Much Ado," Washington *Post*, Feb. 1, 1962, p. A23. Columnist William S. White gave Kennedy high grades in "political gamesmanship" for his "twisting the tail of the G.O.P. elephant." Reprinted in *Congressional Record*, 87th Cong. 2nd Sess., p. 1053. Also see, James Reston in *NYT*, Jan. 25, 1962, p. 13.

67. Quoted in "Mousetrapped," *Newsweek*, LIX (Feb. 5, 1962), 22.

68. A special target of Kennedy's was New York Governor Nelson Rockefeller, who seemed to have a good chance of capturing the G.O.P. nomination in 1964. Because of his liberal positions on many public issues, Rockefeller was unpopular with large segments of the Republican party; to overcome this hostility, the New Yorker had moved much closer to the center after 1960 and was often critical of the New Frontier for its "centralizing" and "big government" tendencies. He attacked the DUAH bill as a possible "subterfuge to bypass the Constitutional sovereignty of the states and to gain direct political control over the nation's cities." Replying to these charges at a news conference, Kennedy observed that Rockefeller, as chairman of Eisenhower's Advisory Committee on Government Organization in 1956 and 1957, had "recommended the exact proposal that we recommend" except for the inclusion of civil defense. Kennedy greatly amused the reporters with his comment that while broadcaster Fulton Lewis had said that "no one could get to the right of Barry Goldwater, I [Kennedy] am now not so sure." *NYT*, June 30, 1961, p. 12; Aug. 29, 1961, p. 29; Feb. 2, 1962, p. 16; Feb. 4, 1962, pp. 1, 39; Robert D. Novak, *The Agony of the G.O.P. 1964* (New York, 1965), pp. 67–69; *Public Papers of the Presidents: John F. Kennedy 1962* (Washington, D.C., 1963), p. 123.

69. *NYT*, Jan. 30, 1962, p. 13.

70. David Bell memo for Theodore Sorensen, Feb. 5, 1962, Box 18, White MSS.

71. Washington *Daily News*, Jan. 31, 1962, reprinted in *Congressional Record*, 87th Cong. 2nd Sess., p. 1433.

72. Bell memo for Sorensen; *NYT*, Feb. 17, 1962, p. 20.

73. The fact that all 100 senators were present and voting, for the first time since 1936, was a sign of how emotional the issue had become. Only four Republicans sided with the administration: Javits and Keating of New York, Case (N.J.), and Scott (Pa.). More than offsetting these gains was the loss of eighteen Southern Democrats and eight Northern, Borderstate, and Western Democrats. The non-Southern defectors represented overwhelmingly rural states and/or belonged to the conservative wing of the party. In addition, four of the eight were committee chairmen. For analyses of the voting, see *Congressional Quarterly Almanac 1962* (Washington, D.C., 1963), p. 383; and Parris, "Congress Rejects the Urban Department," pp. 210–19.

74. Excluding Kentucky, Oklahoma, and Tennessee, only three Southern Democrats

supported Kennedy: Fascell (Fla.), Gonzalez, and Thomas (both Texas). Thomas's vote is the most interesting, since in the 1950s he was public housing's "enemy number one." But his Houston district had grown rapidly and become more cosmopolitan over the years, and Thomas had to make an adjustment. Furthermore, through Vice-President Johnson, Thomas had close ties to the White House and undoubtedly felt the pangs of loyalty. Fascell, from Miami, had sponsored the 1961 administration bill, and Gonzalez was a very liberal congressman from San Antonio. Republicans from urban and suburban districts split 56–7 against DUAH, a reflection of the extreme partisanship that had developed over the issue and the divisions within the broad category of "urban."

75. "Debacle," *Newsweek*, LIX (March 5, 1962), 24.
76. Quoted in Tom Wicker, *Kennedy Without Tears* (New York, 1964), p. 55.
77. Milton P. Semer to Lee White, Jan. 8, 1963, HHFA Administrators' Files, Box 108, HUD Records. Weaver later called DUAH's inclusion in the 1963 legislative program simply "a gesture"; Oral History, p. 125.
78. Hugh Mields, Jr., memo for Weaver, Sept. 19, 1961, Box 59; Morton J. Schussheim memo for Lee White, Box 97; Weaver memo for Victor Fischer, Nov. 9, 1962, Box 113, HHFA Administrators' Files, HUD Records; Weaver, *Urban Complex*, pp. 147–48, 153–54. HHFA attempted to work more closely with the Federal Highway Administration and was assisted in these efforts by the Highway Act of 1962 which required, as of Jan. 1965, the preparation of metropolitan transportation plans.
79. Marie McGuire, Oral History Interview, John F. Kennedy Library; Public Housing Administration, "Low Income Housing Demonstration Program," Reel 1; PHA/HEW, Memorandum of Agreement, Oct. 24, 1963, Reel 2, HHFA Records, Kennedy Library; Weaver, *Urban Complex*, pp. 277–84; *NYT*, April 8, 1962, p. 65; Gilbert Y. Steiner, *The State of Welfare* (Washington, D.C., 1971), pp. 148–53.
80. Steiner, *State of Welfare*, pp. 155–58; Elizabeth Brenner Drew, "The Long Trial of Public Housing," *Reporter*, XXXII (June 17, 1965), 15.
81. "Rebuilders of Cities—or a New Pork Barrel?" *Business Week*, Dec. 7, 1963, pp. 64–70; "Glitter of Real Estate Lures Industry Dollars," *ibid.*, March 2, 1963, pp. 32, 34; Hubert Kay, "The Third Force in Urban Renewal," *Fortune*, LXX (Oct. 1964), 130–33.
82. "Cities: The Renaissance," *Time*, LXXIX (March 23, 1962), 19.
83. On Banks, see Jeanne R. Lowe, *Cities in a Race With Time* (New York, 1967), pp. 210–31; James Banks, Oral History Interview, John F. Kennedy Library. Also see Housing and Home Finance Agency, "The Housing of Relocated Families," offset, March 1965.
84. Weaver, *Urban Complex*, pp. 95–125.
85. David B. Carlson, "Urban Renewal: Running Hard, Sitting Still," *Architectural Forum*, CXVI (April 1962), 99–101; Paul Douglas, *In the Fullness of Time* (New York, 1972), pp. 410–12; Chester W. Hartman, "Relocation: Illusory Promises and No Relief," *Virginia Law Review*, LVII (1971), 745–817.
86. See, for example, John C. Sparks, "The Fallacy of Urban Renewal," *Reader's Digest*, LXXXI (Oct. 1962), 114–16.

87. Weaver, *Urban Complex*, pp. 197–99.
88. Senate Committee on Banking and Currency, 90th Cong. 1st Sess., *Progress Report on Federal Housing Programs* (Washington, D.C., 1967), Table E-4.
89. Philip Klutznick to Theodore Sorensen, April 17, 1961; Lee White to Weaver, May 2, 1961, Box 358, White House Central Files, John F. Kennedy Library. Also see material in HHFA Administrators' Files, Box 58, HUD Records.
90. Milton P. Semer memo for Weaver, May 15, 1961, Joint Chronological File/87th Congress, General Counsel Files, HUD; Weaver to White, May 23, 1961, Box 358, White House Central Files, Kennedy Library.
91. John J. Gunther memo for Theodore Sorensen, Jan. 23, 1963, Box 500, White House Central Files, Kennedy Library; William K. Brussat memo for Harold Seidman, May 14, 1963, R 4–20/1, BOB Files.
92. Substitution of the word "community" for "urban" reflected the administration's desire not to antagonize rural and small town groups; Brussat memo for Seidman.
93. *NYT*, July 14, 1963, p. 28; Wayne Philips memo for Lee White, July 30, 1963, HHFA Administrators' Files, Box 120, HUD Records.
94. For an indication of Weaver's doubts about the wisdom of the conference, see Weaver memo for White, Jan. 21, 1963, *ibid.* Also Weaver to author, Nov. 16, 1972.
95. The National Housing Conference, for example, was very critical of the administration in early 1963 for its failure to make "any comprehensive analysis of needs or of the adequacy of present programs" and looked to the conference as the starting point for a bigger (and costlier) housing bill in 1964. *House and Home*, XXIII (April 1963), 21; NHC, *Membership Newsletter*, Sept. 1963, p. 3.
96. *The Speeches of John F. Kennedy*, S. Report 994, Part I, 87th Cong. 1st Sess. (Washington, D.C., 1961), pp. 576, 971.
97. Sorensen, *Kennedy*, pp. 480–81. Interestingly, Sorensen discusses nearly all of the administration's housing and urban activities within the context of explaining the White House's policy on open occupancy.
98. Lee White memo for the President, Nov. 13, 1961, Box 22, White MSS.; *NYT*, Nov. 27, 1961, pp. 1, 22; J. Anthony Lukas, "Integrated Housing: A Matter of Timing," *Reporter*, XXVI (Feb. 15, 1962), 30–33.
99. Sorensen, *Kennedy*, p. 482; Lawrence O'Brien to Lee White, Sept. 11, 1962, Box 21, White MSS. Home builders and others involved in the construction industry also insisted that housing starts would decline by one-third if the order was issued, thus hindering economic expansion. HHFA sharply disagreed. White memo for the President, July 17, 1962, *ibid.*
100. Executive Order 11063, Nov. 20, 1962.
101. Charles Abrams, "The Housing Order Its Limits," *Commentary*, XXXV (Jan. 1963), 10–14; American Friends Service Committee, *A Report to the President on Equal Opportunity in Housing* (Philadelphia, 1967).
102. Sorensen, *Kennedy*, pp. 488–501.
103. For the background, see *supra*, p. 282.
104. Richard C. Cortner, *The Apportionment Cases* (Knoxville, Tenn., 1970), pp. 76–77, 83–84, 88–90.

105. President Kennedy, as noted *supra*, pp. 293–94, had written an article in 1958 attacking state discrimination against urban areas; the attorney general's decision to intervene in *Baker v. Carr* was not, therefore, unexpected. It was necessary, however, to overcome the objections of Solicitor General Archibald Cox, a disciple of Justice Frankfurter, who had wanted the courts to keep out of this "political thicket." The political benefits accruing to the Democrats for breaking rural rule were, of course, not ignored by the administration. Malapportionment became a special interest of Robert Kennedy; the only case he personally argued before the Supreme Court as attorney general was *Gray v. Sanders*, which contested the Georgia county unit voting system. Victor Navasky, *Kennedy Justice* (New York, 1971), pp. 299–306.

106. Navasky, *Kennedy Justice*, pp. 298–99; Robert G. Dixon, Jr., *Democratic Representation* (New York, 1968), p. 177.

107. Quoted in Cortner, *Apportionment Cases*, p. 195; Navasky, *Kennedy Justice*, pp. 306–22.

108. *Reynolds v. Sims*, 377 U.S. 533, 562, 567 (1964); Dixon, *Democratic Representation*, pp. 250–60.

109. Wolf von Eckardt, "New Towns in America," *New Republic*, CXLIV (Oct. 26, 1963), 16. The cruise was a reference to the symposium being conducted at sea by the Greek city planner, Constantinos Doxiadis.

110. Weaver, Oral History, pp. 98–99.

111. Arthur M. Schlesinger, Jr., *A Thousand Days* (Boston, 1965), p. 660.

112. Wood, *Necessary Majority*, p. 10; Richardson Dilworth, Oral History Interview, John F. Kennedy Library, pp. 24–25; also see *infra*, pp. 349–54.

113. Weaver, Oral History, pp. 146–47.

114. Schlesinger, *Thousand Days*, pp. 1011–12; James L. Sundquist, *Politics and Policy: The Eisenhower, Kennedy, and Johnson Years* (Washington, D.C., 1968), pp. 114–37; Daniel P. Moynihan, *Maximum Feasible Misunderstanding* (New York, 1969), pp. 61–80.

115. Richard Leach, "A Fitting Memorial," *America*, CX (Feb. 8, 1964), 186–88.

CHAPTER 10

1. Paul Ylvisaker, "The Miraculous City," *National Civic Review*, L (Dec. 1961), 587.

2. Robinson O. Everett and Richard H. Leach, "Urban Problems and Prospects—A Foreword," *Law and Contemporary Problems*, XXX (Winter 1965), 1.

3. Raymond Vernon, *The Myth and Reality of Our Urban Problems* (Cambridge, Mass., multilithed, 1962), p. 1.

4. Jean Gottmann, *Megalopolis* (New York, 1961), p. 15; Robert C. Wood memo for Eric F. Goldman, April 29, 1964, Box 1574, James Gaither MSS., Lyndon B. Johnson Library.

5. Staughton Lynd, "New Order of the Ages?" *New Republic*, CXLVI (April 23, 1962), 27.

6. *Ibid.*, Morton and Lucia White, *The Intellectuals Versus The City* (Cambridge, Mass., 1962), p. 1.

7. Allan Temko, "How Civilized Can Urban Man Be?" *NYT Book Review*, April 16, 1961, p. 1.

8. John Keats, "Who's to Live Here Anyway, People or Automobiles?" [review of *Sick Cities* by Mitchell Gordon] *ibid.*, June 2, 1963, p. 3; also see Jane Jacobs, *The Death and Life of Great American Cities* (New York, 1961); Edward J. Logue and Edward T. Chase, "American Cities: Dead or Alive?—Two Views," *Architectural Forum*, CXVI (Feb. 1962), 89–91; C. W. Griffin, Jr., "Specialists Diagnose the Stricken American City," *Saturday Review*, XLVI (Aug. 3, 1963), 22–24.

9. Victor Gruen, "Who is to Save Our Cities?" *Harvard Business Review*, XLI (May/June 1963), 107; also see Leland Hazard, "Are We Committing Urban Suicide?" *ibid.*, XLII (July/Aug. 1964), 152–60; Mitchell Gordon, "Doomed Cities?" *Wall Street Journal*, Oct. 16, 1962, p. 12; Richard J. Whalen, "A City Destroying Itself," *Fortune*, LXX (Sept. 1964), 115–22.

10. Robert C. Wood, *The Necessary Majority: Middle America and the Urban Crisis* (New York, 1972), pp. 44–45. For a sample of public opinion, see *Gallup Poll Index*, Report No. 5, July 1965, p. 5.

11. See Vernon, *Myth and Reality*, p. 31. Cf. the amusing yet revealing comments by Robert C. Wood in his *Suburbia: Its People and Their Politics* (Boston, 1958), pp. vii–viii. Also see Edward C. Banfield, *The Unheavenly City* (Boston, 1970).

12. "For U.S. Cities A Surge of New Life," *Business Week*, July 4, 1964, p. 12.

13. David B. Carlson, "Downtown's Dramatic Comeback," *Architectural Forum*, CXX (Feb. 1964), 99; "Under the Knife, or All for Their Own Good," *Time*, LXXXIV (Nov. 6, 1964), 60–75; "Big Cities Try for a Comeback," *U.S. News and World Report*, LVII (Dec. 28, 1964), 34–38.

14. "America's Cities," *Economist*, CCXIV (Feb. 6, 1965), 541. Cf. "1963—The Brightening Morning of the Golden Urban Age," *American City*, LXXVIII (Jan. 1963), 7.

15. "Cities Feel the Squeeze," *Business Week*, March 9, 1963, pp. 26–28; "In States, Cities: A Cry for Services, A Revolt on Taxes," *U.S. News and World Report*, LV (Oct. 28, 1963), 102–4; "As Cities and Counties Get Frantic for Cash," *ibid.*, LVII (Sept. 14, 1964), 79–80; Reuben A. Zubrow, "Recent Trends and Developments in Municipal Finance," *Public Management*, XLV (Nov. 1963), 247–54; Roger A. Freeman, "Urban Financing—Difficult but not Desperate," *American City*, LXXIX (March 1964), 7, 23; "Why Big-City Financing is in a Mess," *Business Week*, April 23, 1966, pp. 36–38.

16. "The Decentralization of Jobs," *Monthly Labor Review*, XC (May 1967), 7–13; *NYT*, Oct. 15, 1972, pp. 1, 58. But cf. Alexander Ganz and Thomas O'Brien, "The City: Sandbox, Reservation, or Dynamo?" *Public Policy*, XXI (Winter 1973), 107–23.

17. Bureau of the Census, *Census of Population: 1960, Standard Metropolitan Statistical Areas* (Washington, D.C., 1963), Table 8.

18. Advisory Commission on Intergovernmental Relations, *Fiscal Balance in the American Federal System: Volume II, Metropolitan Fiscal Disparities* (Washington, D.C., 1967), pp. 6, 27–31, 50, 53, 62, 71, 76; Alan K. Campbell and Seymour

Sacks, *Metropolitan America: Fiscal Patterns and Governmental Systems* (New York, 1967), pp. 98–126.

19. National Advisory Commission on Civil Disorders, *Report* (Washington, D.C., 1968), pp. 116–21.

20. Frances Fox Piven and Richard A. Cloward, *Regulating the Poor* (New York, 1971), Table 2; Bureau of the Census, *Compendium of City Finances 1960* (Washington, D.C., 1961), Table 7; Bureau of the Census, *City Government Finances in 1965–1966* (Washington, D.C., 1967), Table 7.

21. George Reedy memo for Lyndon B. Johnson, April 23, 1963, Box 73, Theodore Sorensen MSS., John F. Kennedy Library; Theodore H. White, *The Making of the President 1964* (New York, 1965), p. 225.

22. Charles E. Silberman, "The City and the Negro," *Fortune*, LXV (March 1962), 89 (emphasis added). Robert Wood memo for Goldman, April 29, 1964, Box 1574, Gaither MSS.; Robert C. Wood to author, Dec. 20, 1972.

23. White, *Making of the President 1964*, p. 36.

24. Hugh Sidey, *A Very Personal Presidency* (New York, 1968), p. 99.

25. Warren Jay Vinton, "The President and Public Housing," *Journal of Housing*, XXI (No. 1, 1964), 15–16.

26. Rowland Evans and Robert Novak, *Lyndon B. Johnson: The Exercise of Power* (New York, 1966), pp. 150–51, 206–8.

27. Murray Kempton, in the New York *Post*, Jan. 22, 1960, quoted in *ibid.*, p. 243.

28. Eric F. Goldman, *The Tragedy of Lyndon B. Johnson* (New York, 1969), pp. 8–9; Goldman memo for Johnson, Dec. 21, 1963, Box 12, SP 2–4, Civil Rights Papers, Lyndon B. Johnson Library.

29. Goldman, *Tragedy of Johnson*, pp. 129–42, 159–63; "What the Future Holds for America as the President's 'Idea Men' See It," *U.S. News and World Report*, LVI (June 22, 1964), 40–67; Wood memo for Goldman, April 29, 1964, Box 1574, Gaither MSS.; Paul Ylvisaker memo for Richard Goodwin, n.d. [1964], Task Force Folder, Richard Goodwin MSS., Lyndon B. Johnson Library.

30. For background on the Great Society speech, see Goldman, *Tragedy of Johnson*, pp. 163–67; and Sidey, *Personal Presidency*, pp. 49–66. Also, Bill Moyers memo for George Reedy, May 21, 1964, Box 36, SP 3–28, Johnson Library.

31. William E. Leuchtenburg, "The Genesis of the Great Society," *Reporter*, XXXIV (April 21, 1966), 36–39; Goldman, *Tragedy of Johnson*, pp. 166–67. Also see, Norman C. Thomas and Harold L. Wolman, "Policy Formulation in the Institutionalized Presidency: The Johnson Task Forces," in *The Presidential Advisory System*, eds. Thomas C. Cronin and Sanford D. Greenberg (New York, 1969), pp. 124–43.

32. "Face-Lifting," *Newsweek*, LXIII (Feb. 10, 1964), 68; Wolf von Eckardt, "The President's Plan for Urban America," *New Republic*, CL (Feb. 8, 1964), 9.

33. *NYT*, Feb. 17, 1964, p. 28.

34. "Face-Lifting," 68.

35. Royce Hanson, "Congress Copes with Mass Transit," in *Congress and Urban Problems* (Washington, D.C., 1969), pp. 328–47. Hanson's analysis of the House vote indicates that party affiliation was the prime determinant of voting, but that

without the defection of twenty Republicans from urban-suburban districts, the recommittal motion would have carried. On the other hand, twenty-nine metropolitan Republicans stayed with their party.

36. These changes had been planned during the last year of the Kennedy administration; Kermit Gordon to Kennedy, Feb. 27, 1963, R 4–27, Bureau of the Budget Files, Executive Office of the President, Washington, D.C.

37. Lawrence O'Brien to Henry S. Reuss, March 6, 1964, Box 1, FG 170, White House Central Files, Lyndon B. Johnson Library.

38. See *supra,* pp. 212–13.

39. "Rebuilder of Cities—or a New Pork Barrel?" *Business Week,* Dec. 7, 1963, pp. 64–70; "Arrogant Domain," *Barrons,* July 27, 1964, p. 1; John Dowdy, "The Mounting Scandal of Urban Renewal," *Reader's Digest,* LXXXIV (March 1964), 51–57; Chamber of Commerce of the United States, *The Impact of Federal Urban Renewal and Public Housing Subsidies* (Washington, D.C., 1964).

40. Harold Wolman, *The Politics of Federal Housing* (New York, 1971), p. 80.

41. *NYT,* Sept. 18, 1964, p. 34.

42. Republican National Committee, Research Division, "The 1960 Elections," April 1960, mimeographed, pp. 16–20, 44.

43. *NYT,* Jan. 8, 1961, p. 41.

44. Quoted in George F. Gilder and Bruce K. Chapman, *The Party that Lost Its Head* (New York, 1966), p. 56.

45. Robert D. Novak, *The Agony of the G.O.P. 1964* (New York, 1965), pp. 53–55.

46. *NYT,* Jan. 16, 1961, p. 1.

47. *Ibid.,* April 18, 1962, p. 27.

48. *NYT,* March 17, 1961, p. 60. For the differing perspectives of moderate and conservative Republicans, cf. Jacob K. Javits, *Order of Battle: A Republican's Call to Reason* (New York, 1964), pp. 165–84; and Raymond Moley, *The Republican Opportunity in 1964* (New York, 1964), pp. xi, 7–8, 134.

49. Republican National Committee, Committee on Big City Politics, *Report* (n.p., n.d.); *NYT,* Jan. 13, 1962, p. 10; Gilder and Chapman, *Party that Lost Its Head,* pp. 57–58; John F. Bibby, *The Republicans and the Metropolis: The Role of National Party Leadership* (Chicago, 1967), p. 16.

50. *NYT,* Feb. 2, 1962, p. 16.

51. White, *Making of the President 1964,* p. 212; *NYT,* Oct. 15, 1964, p. 38; *Congressional Quarterly Weekly Report,* XXII (July 3, 1964), 1361.

52. Kirk H. Porter and Donald Bruce Johnson, eds., *National Party Platforms 1840–1964* (Urbana, Ill., 1966), pp. 680, 682.

53. *NYT,* July 8, 1964, p. 21; "AMA Goes to the Conventions—With Mixed Success," *Nation's Cities,* II (Oct. 1964), 19–20.

54. Porter and Johnson, *National Party Platforms,* p. 686.

55. *Ibid.,* p. 648.

56. *NYT,* Oct. 27, 1964, pp. 1, 30.

57. *Public Papers of the Presidents: Lyndon B. Johnson, 1963–1964* (Washington, D.C., 1965), pp. 1349–51.

58. Republican National Committee, Research Division, "The 1964 Elections," Oct. 1965, mimeographed, pp. 38–40.

59. Leuchtenburg, "Genesis of the Great Society," 38–39; Wolman, *Federal Housing*, p. 84; Harry McPherson, *A Political Education* (Boston, 1972), pp. 297–98.

60. Besides Wood, the academicians were: Martin Meyerson (dean of the College of Environmental Design, University of California, Berkeley); Catherine Bauer Wurster (professor of regional and city planning, College of Environmental Design, Berkeley); Nathan Glazer (professor of sociology, Berkeley); W. Norman Kennedy (professor of transportation engineering, Berkeley); and Raymond Vernon (professor of economics, Harvard). The other members were: Dr. Karl Menninger, Paul Ylvisaker, Mayor Jerome Cavanaugh (Detroit), Ralph McGill (Atlanta *Constitution*), and Saul Klaman (Savings Banks).

61. See the background Issue Paper, "Metropolitan and Urban Problems," June 17, 1964, prepared by the Bureau of the Budget for the task force's use; HHFA Administrators' Files, Box 133, Records of the Department of Housing and Urban Development, Record Group 207, National Archives; and "Notes for Meeting with Task Force on Metropolitan and Urban Problems," Sept. 9, 1964, Box 3, HS 3, White House Central Files, Johnson Library. *Our Cities*, of course, also had a broad scope, but it had been prepared by a subcommittee of an inter-agency committee with limited access to the White House.

62. Task Force on Metropolitan and Urban Problems, *Report*, Nov. 30, 1964, processed, p. 1, in FG 600, White House Central Files, Johnson Library.

63. *Ibid.*, pp. 4–12; Robert C. Wood, Oral History Interview, Lyndon B. Johnson Library, pp. 8–12.

64. Task Force, *Report*, pp. 13–17 (urban renewal); 22–27 (housing); 17–20 (new towns).

65. Despite Johnson's reference to these programs, there was no mention of the Social Renewal Plan the task force had urged. The President was following the old practice of dividing up federal activities in the cities along physical and social lines. Near the end, Johnson declared that "this message can only deal with a *fragment* [emphasis added] of the effort increasingly directed toward improving the quality of life in the American city." Action against poverty, aid for education and health, programs for natural beauty, pollution control and law enforcement were dealt with separately in other Presidential Messages, thereby obscuring their urban dimensions.

66. Ada Louise Huxtable, in the *NYT*, March 22, 1965, p. 32. But cf. *NYT* editorial: "The Johnson administration needs a housing and city development program worthy of its rhetoric. The President's message set forth the scope and complexity of urban problems in vivid language. . . . But the stirring strains of this John Philip Sousa prose serve only to introduce a penny-whistle program." March 3, 1965, p. 40.

67. "Housing Bill: Complex and Controversial," *Nation's Cities*, III (April 1965), 12–14; testimony of Ira S. Robbins, National Association of Housing and Redevelopment Officials, in Senate Committee on Banking and Currency, 89th Cong. 1st Sess., *Hearings on S. 1354: Housing Legislation of 1965* (Washington, D.C., 1965), p. 302; Robert Wood to author, Dec. 20, 1972.

68. For details, see HHFA Administrator Weaver's testimony, in House of Repre-

sentatives Committee on Banking and Currency, 89th Cong. 1st Sess., *Hearings on H.R. 5840: Housing and Urban Development Act of 1965* (Washington, D.C., 1965), pp. 167–69.

69. Elizabeth Brenner Drew, "The Long Trial of Public Housing," *Reporter*, XXXII (June 17, 1965), 15–18; National Commission on Urban Problems, *Building the American City* (Washington, D.C., 1969), p. 148.

70. See Douglas's comments, in Senate, *Hearings on S. 1354*, p. 525.

71. *Ibid.*, pp. 18–19, 521, 698. Unlike public housing, rent supplements—as proposed by the administration—did not require participation by the local government; the Federal Government would contract directly with private sponsors of the housing. Thus, aside from zoning laws, there was no obvious local legal impediment to rent supplements projects. However, after the rent supplements authorization was approved by Congress, an amendment was added to the appropriations bill which required the permission of local governments, or the existence of a Workable Program (which most suburbs did not have), before rent supplements could be used in the community.

72. House of Representatives, 89th Cong. 1st Sess., *H. Report 365: Minority Views* (Washington, D.C., 1965), p. 179.

73. The House balloting was 208–202 on the motion to recommit. Fifty-one Southern Democrats and twenty-one Northern Democrats deserted the administration; four Republicans saved the White House's plan by voting with the majority of Democrats. Rent supplements survived by the narrowest margin of any important Presidential proposal since Johnson took office and required the President's most determined personal effort of the year. *NYT*, July 2, 1965, p. 1; "Aborted Revolt," *Newsweek*, LXVI (July 12, 1965), 16.

74. *NYT*, May 5, 1965, p. 46.

75. House, *Hearings on H.R. 5840*, pp. 550–51 (NAHB); 671–72 (MBAA); 699 (ABA); 878–79 (NAREB); 523–24 (Cavanaugh). Also see, "New Towns—More Facts Needed," *Nation's Cities*, III (July 1965), 6; Wolf von Eckardt, "The Case for Building 350 New Towns," *Harpers*, CCXXXI (Dec. 1965), 85–86.

76. Arlen J. Large, "Renewal's Renewal," *Wall Street Journal*, July 16, 1965, p. 8. Publication by the Joint Harvard-M.I.T. Center for Urban Studies of Martin Anderson's *The Federal Bulldozer* (Cambridge, Mass., 1964) in late 1964 had added considerable fuel to the urban renewal controversy. Anderson's sharp attack on the program is criticized in Robert P. Groberg, "Urban Renewal Realistically Reappraised," *Law and Contemporary Problems*, XXX (Winter 1965), 212–29.

77. Kermit Gordon, Director of the Bureau of the Budget, testimony in Senate Committee on Government Operations, 89th Cong. 1st Sess., *Hearings on S. 497 et al.: Establish a Department of Housing and Urban Development* (Washington, D.C., 1965), p. 113. With his comfortable majorities in both chambers, Johnson probably felt secure enough to revert to the use of "urban" in place of the term "community" which had been used in the 1964 bill. But the Johnson measure did not have the elaborate Declaration of Policy which had created trouble for Kennedy in 1961–62.

78. *Ibid.*, pp. 108–9.

79. *Ibid.*, p. 110.
80. *Ibid.*, pp. 11, 149.
81. House of Representatives, 89th Cong. 1st. Sess., *H. Report 337: Minority Views* (Washington, D.C., 1965), p. 44.
82. *H. Report 337: Supplementary Views of Florence Dwyer, Robert Griffin, Frank Horton and Donald Rumsfeld*, pp. 45–49; *Congressional Record*, 89th Cong. 1st Sess., p. 13376.
83. The balloting saw 122 Republicans joined by 19 Democrats (all from the South) voting for recommittal, while 254 Democrats and 5 Republicans opposed the motion. Voting with the majority of the G.O.P. members against HUD was J. Arthur Younger, the author of the first urban department bill back in 1954.
84. These figures are based upon *Congressional Quarterly*'s definition of Southern Democrats.
85. *Congressional Record*, 89th Cong. 1st Sess., pp. 20014–15.

CHAPTER 11

1. Walter Lippmann, *Men of Destiny* (New York, 1927), pp. 8–9; St. Paul *Pioneer-Press*, quoted in Roy V. Peel and Thomas C. Donnelly, *The 1928 Campaign: An Analysis* (New York, 1931), p. 121.
2. Daniel J. Elazar, "Are We a Nation of Cities?" *The Public Interest*, n. 4 (Summer 1966), pp. 48–49.
3. *Wall Street Journal*, May 23, 1960, p. 12.
4. Daniel P. Moynihan, "The City in Chassis," in *Towards a National Urban Policy*, ed. Daniel P. Moynihan (New York, 1970), pp. 324–25.
5. Robert C. Wood, "City Building in the Great Society," Aug. 17, 1965, Box 1, Local Government, White House Central Files, Lyndon Baines Johnson Library.
6. William E. Leuchtenburg, *Franklin D. Roosevelt and the New Deal* (New York, 1963), p. 331.
7. Horace E. Deming, *The Government of American Cities* (New York, 1909), pp. 31–32.
8. Robert C. Wood, *The Necessary Majority: Middle America and the Urban Crisis* (New York, 1972), p. 9.
9. Johnson used the expression in his remarks at the HUD bill signing ceremony; see *supra*, pp. 348–49.
10. Remarks of New York City Deputy Mayor Edward K. Hamilton, quoted in *NYT*, Dec. 31, 1973, p. 1.

A Note on Sources

[The following is a highly selective summary of materials consulted in preparing this study. Should further documentation be desired, my dissertation on deposit at the Columbia University Library may be consulted.]

Primary

Urban affairs is a relatively new subject for federal attention, and the archival resources of the national government reflect Washington's growing appreciation of the issue. The development of its acquaintance can be traced most clearly in the holdings and arrangements of the Presidential Libraries. Materials concerning cities at the Franklin D. Roosevelt Library are sparse and widely scattered throughout the Official Files, with the most significant located in Housing (OF 63) and Relief (OF 444). Aside from the folders in the Samuel I. Rosenman MSS. relating to the establishment of the National Housing Agency, none of the other collections at Hyde Park were of much help. At the Harry S.Truman Library, only Housing (OF 63) of the White House Central Files, along with the correspondence on racial matters in federally assisted housing found in the Philleo Nash MSS., proved useful. In line with the increasing importance of the

White House staff, most of the relevant papers at the Dwight D. Eisenhower Library are located in the files of Presidential assistants, particularly those of Robert E. Merriam and John S. Bragdon. Merriam has also done an oral history interview in which he touches upon his urban activities. Also pertinent were the records of the President's Advisory Committee on Governmental Organization (PACGO). The John F. Kennedy Library has opened all of the White House Central Files for 1961–63, and under the new classification system Housing (HS) and Local Government (LG) covered the administration's activities in the urban field. Since the cities did not command top priority at the Executive Mansion, the holdings are limited, as are the files of Theodore Sorensen and Lee White and the microfilmed selection of records from the Housing and Home Finance Agency. A folder in the Adam Yarmolinsky files yielded some materials on the 1960 campaign. There are good oral histories by Robert C. Weaver, Robert C. Wood, and some of the important HHFA personnel. Urban affairs attained national prominence during the administration of Lyndon B. Johnson, and at the President's direction the L.B.J. Library gave precedence to the processing of materials on cities, along with those on education and civil rights. The work of the 1964 Task Force is laid out in the Richard Goodwin MSS. and the James Gaither MSS.; other materials are in the White House Central Files under HS and LG. Weaver and Wood also have illuminating oral histories of their experiences in the Great Society.

The National Archives has only within the past four years accessioned the records of the Housing and Home Finance Agency (now the Department of Housing and Urban Development/Record Group 207). For the most part they consist of the Administrators' Files, which for all of their bulk shed disappointingly little light on important policy decisions. The papers of the National Resources Planning Board (Record Group 187) relating to the Urbanism Committee are more substantial, although they should be supplemented by the Charles E. Merriam MSS. at the University of Chicago. Most of the relevant files of the Bureau of the Budget concerning an urban cabinet department were consulted at the Records Division of the Office of Management and Budget in Washington.

In addition to the Presidential Libraries and the National Archives, another important depository of primary materials is the Collection of Regional History and University Archives at the Cornell University Library. Cornell has attempted to gather the papers of leading city planners and planning organizations; among those examined for this study were the Alfred Bettman MSS. (actually a microfilm reproduction of the collection at the University of Cincinnati), Ladislas Segoe MSS., and Warren Jay Vinton MSS. The papers of Charles Abrams were still being processed when research for this project was completed. Columbia University's Avery Library has the Edith Elmer Wood MSS., which illuminates the early public housing movement. The Catherine Bauer Wurster MSS. at the College of Environmental Design Library, University of California, Berkeley, shows the range of that remarkable woman's interests from about 1940 to her death in 1964.

A major loss was the destruction of the U.S. Conference of Mayors' records. During a change of quarters in the 1960s, the USCM discarded almost all of its files from the previous three decades. Typed proceedings of the conference's 1932 and 1933 meetings, a few memos, and mimeographed copies of notices sent to member cities are the only remaining documents of the USCM's early years. This material was examined at the USCM's offices in Washington. The Mayors' Records at the Burton Historical Collection of the Detroit Public Library, the Frank Murphy MSS. at the University of Michigan Library, the Daniel Hoan MSS. at the Milwaukee County Historical Society, and the Fiorello H. La Guardia MSS. at New York City's Municipal Archives and Records Center helped fill some of the gaps for the Depression decade. Particularly useful for this period were the diaries kept by Louis Brownlow; one set is at the University of Chicago Library and another is part of the Louis Brownlow MSS. at the Kennedy Library.

Both the USCM and the American Municipal Association (since

1965, the National League of Cities) have published the proceedings of many of their annual meetings. The USCM volumes, entitled *City Problems of . . . ,* appeared annually between 1933 and 1940 and were resumed on a regular basis in the mid-1950s when the organization's fortunes improved. Similarly, the AMA proceedings are available for 1931–35, 1943–44, and from 1955 on. After 1933, the International City Managers Association stopped putting out proceedings of its meetings and began publishing the authoritative *Municipal Yearbook,* a helpful compendium of statistics and informed comment on city issues. The American Society of Planning Officials assumed responsibility in 1935 for printing the reports of the National Conference on Planning, which since 1943 have gone under the title of *Planning.* Between 1935 and 1944, the *Housing Yearbook* was sponsored by the National Association of Housing Officials; a magazine with the same name was started by the National Housing Conference in the mid-1950s.

The USCM's newsletter, *U.S. Municipal News,* covers developments in the nation's capital and the cities from the 1930s to the present. In the mid-1950s, the AMA resurrected the *Washington Newsletter* it had published in the late 1930s and early 1940s. With words of greeting from President Kennedy, the AMA launched a glossy-paged magazine, *Nation's Cities,* in 1962. The oldest journals on urban affairs are the *National Municipal Review* (now *National Civic Review*), the organ of the good government National Municipal League, and *American City,* started by Harold Buttenheim during the Progressive era and still published by his family's company. Unfortunately, except for occasional articles on planning or intergovernmental relations, *American City* ignores the political side of urban life in order to concentrate upon the latest improvements in sewage treatment. Nearly every professional or trade group mentioned in this study issued its own periodical: *Freehold* and *Headlines* (National Association of Real Estate Boards); *Journal of the American Institute of Planners; Journal of Housing* (National Association of Housing and Redevelopment Officials); National Housing Conference, *Membership Newsletter; Public Management* (International City Managers Association); and *Urban Land* (Urban Land Institute). Beginning in the 1950s, the best magazine coverage of urban developments was in *Architectural Forum* and *House and Home.*

The number of publications touching upon urban affairs churned out by the Government Printing Office is truly staggering. Congressional hearings, agency annual reports and special studies, *ad hoc* commissions' findings, etc., could by themselves fill up a good-sized library. Most, however, deal with the city in a tangential way, and cutting through the verbiage to uncover the relevant material is the difficult part of the job. Two outstanding exceptions to this general rule are the National Resources Committee's *Our Cities* (1937) and the National Commission on Urban Problems' *Building the American City* (1969). The contrast between them is particularly revealing.

Secondary

The urban revolution in American federalism has naturally, given the revolution's recent date and the novelty of urban history's popularity, attracted more attention from political scientists than historians. Writing in 1965, Charles N. Glaab noted that "urban history is a relatively new and unestablished division of American history," and none of the works cited in his bibliographic survey of "The Historian and the American City," in Philip Hauser and Leo F. Schnore, *The Study of Urbanization* (New York, 1965), dealt with federal-local ties. Most scholarly city biographies stop before 1933, and even those that go beyond that year, such as Roy Lubove's *Twentieth Century Pittsburgh: Government, Business and Environmental Change* (New York, 1969), tend to concentrate on internal developments. None of the urban textbooks that have appeared to fill the gap in history courses handle the federal-city partnership very successfully. Charles N. Glaab and A. Theodore Brown's pioneering *A History of Urban America* (New York, 1967) barely makes it through the New Deal, while Zane L. Miller's brief *The Urbanization of Modern America* (New York, 1973) is prone to oversimplified statements about the Federal Government's "urban policy." *The Urban Wilderness* (New York, 1972), Sam Bass Warner's ambitious endeavor to update Lewis Mumford's *The Culture of Cities* (1938) treats the rise of federal-city ties only in passing, although his interpretive framework helps place national politics in perspective. The "federal-metropolitan convergence" is a key element in Blake McKelvey's encyclopedic *The Emergence of Metropolitan America, 1915–1966* (New Brunswick, N.J., 1968), but it is often obscured by the abundant detail on such matters as the introduction of parking meters and the multiplication of symphony orchestras.

Practically all of the historical monographs which cover urban programs at the national level since 1933 concern the New Deal or housing, and usually both. Timothy McDonnell's conventional *The Wagner Housing Act* (Chicago, 1957) might be supplemented with Lyle J. Woodyatt, "The Origins and Evolution of the New Deal Housing Program" (unpublished doctoral dissertation, Washington University, 1968). The story through the Fair Deal is recounted in Richard O. Davies, *Housing Reform During the Truman Administration* (Columbia, Mo., 1966). The New Deal's predilection for a return to the land is expertly handled in Paul Conkin, *Tomorrow a New World* (Ithaca, N.Y., 1957). Joseph L. Arnold, *The New Deal in the Suburbs* (Columbus, Ohio, 1971), is a full-scale study of the Greenbelt Towns. The conventional wisdom about the Roosevelt Revolution's effect on urban politics is undermined in Bruce Stave, *The New Deal and the Last Hurrah: Pittsburgh Machine Politics* (Pittsburgh, 1970). James T. Patterson's *Congressional Conservatism and the New Deal* (Lexington, Ky., 1967) explores the rural-urban tension in the New Deal coalition, but the same author's *The New Deal and the States: Federalism in Transition* (Princeton, 1969) slights the cities' role in the revamped federal system. For an analysis of the federal-city relationship which is different than that offered in the present study, see Kenneth Paul Fox, "The Census Bureau and the Cities: National Development of Urban Government in the Industrial Age: 1870–1930" (unpublished doctoral dissertation, University of Pennsylvania, 1972).

There is no adequate examination of the cities' legal position in American federalism. Most of what is available was done during the Progressive era. Anwar Hussain Syed, *The Political Theory of American Local Government* (New York, 1966), is a good introduction, but much remains to be done. A wide-ranging survey is W. Brooke Graves, *American Intergovernmental Relations* (New York, 1964). Political scientist Morton Grodzins presents his "marble cake" analysis of federalism in *The American System* (Chicago, 1966). His historical framework was provided by Daniel J. Elazar, *The American Partnership* (Chicago, 1962). The Grodzins/Elazar thesis on cooperative federalism is challenged by Harry N. Scheiber, *The Condition of American Federalism: An Historian's View* (Washington, D.C., 1966). For the argument that 1913 was the real watershed in federal-city relations, see Daniel J. Elazar, "Urban Problems and the Federal Government: An Historical Inquiry," *Political Science Quarterly*, LXXXII (Dec. 1967), 505–25. Also see, Elazar, "Are We A Nation of Cities?" *The Public Interest*, n. 4 (Summer 1966), pp. 42–58. Roscoe C. Martin, *The Cities and the Federal System* (New York, 1965) utilizes the airport construction grant-in-aid program to illustrate the "operational aspects of American federalism," but the study lacks an historical dimension. Richard C. Cortner, *The Apportionment Cases* (Knoxville, Tenn., 1970), documents the legal attack upon rural domination of state politics. A more philosophical approach is taken by Robert G. Dixon, Jr., *Democratic Representation* (New York, 1968).

There are detailed case studies of federal legislation for cities in Frederic N. Cleaveland and Associates, *Congress and Urban Problems* (Washington, D.C., 1969). Aside from examinations of Kennedy's abortive effort to create an urban department and the drive for mass transportation aid, the subjects covered (airport construction, air and water pollution control, food stamps, and juvenile delinquency) fall outside the mainstream of federal-city relations. Suzanne Farkas, *Urban Lobbying* (New York, 1971) explores the operation of the "federal urban policy subsystem" in the late 1960s. Robert C. Weaver gives his views in *The Urban Complex* (Garden

City, N.Y., 1964) and *The Dilemmas of Urban America* (Cambridge, Mass., 1966). Reminiscences are combined with prescriptions in Robert C. Wood, *The Necessary Majority: Middle America and the Urban Crisis* (New York, 1972).

A planner-political scientist, William L. C. Wheaton, has done a study which benefits from his participation in the federal bureaucracy, "The Evolution of Federal Housing Programs" (unpublished doctoral dissertation, University of Chicago, 1953). Harold L. Wolman, *The Politics of Federal Housing* (New York, 1971), based upon extensive interviewing, focuses on the 1960s, particularly on the period after HUD's creation. The volumes in the ACTION Series on Government and Housing, published in the late 1950s and early 1960s, are useful, as are William G. Grigsby, *Housing Markets and Public Policy* (Philadelphia, 1963), and Robert M. Fisher, *Twenty Years of Public Housing* (New York, 1959). The planner Lloyd Rodwin discerns a federal "quest to save the central city" in his *Nations and Cities* (Boston, 1970). Mel Scott, *American City Planning Since 1890* (Berkeley, 1969) is required reading for anyone interested in the subject.

Urban renewal has generated a large number of studies. Coleman Woodburg edited a two-volume collection of articles for the Urban Redevelopment Study, the first volume of which, *The Future of Cities and Urban Redevelopment* (Chicago, 1953), contains an important article by Catherine Bauer. Later in the decade, Herbert Gans published "The Human Implications of Current Redevelopment and Relocation Policy," *Journal of the American Institute of Planners,* XXV (Feb. 1959), 15–25. The 1960s saw a plethora of books by sociologists, political scientists, and economists detailing Title I's effects upon cities. Among the best is Scott Greer, *Urban Renewal and American Cities* (Indianapolis, 1965). The program's defects are highlighted in Jane Jacobs, *The Death and Life of Great American Cities* (New York, 1961), Martin Anderson, *The Federal Bulldozer* (Cambridge, Mass., 1964), and Theodore J. Lowi, *The End of Liberalism* (New York, 1969), while its attributes are given their due in Jeanne R. Lowe, *Cities in a Race With Time* (New York, 1967).

Lawrence M. Friedman, *Government and Slum Housing* (Chicago, 1968) provides a comprehensive summary. James Q. Wilson, ed., *Urban Renewal: The Record and the Controversy* (Cambridge, Mass., 1967), and Jewel Bellush and Murray Hausknecht, eds., *Urban Renewal: People, Politics, and Planning* (Garden City, N.Y., 1967) are useful collections.

The problems of mass transit are discussed in Michael N. Danielson, *Federal-Metropolitan Politics and the Commuter Crisis* (New York, 1965), and George M. Smerk, *Urban Transportation: The Federal Role* (Bloomington, Ind., 1965), as well as the study in the Cleaveland volume noted above. Unfortunately, there is no examination of federal highway policy, particularly the Interstate Highway System, nor is there a good monograph on the Federal Housing Administration.

The work of Charles Abrams stands in a class by itself. Active on the housing scene from the 1930s until his death in 1970, Abrams produced a large number of books and articles full of informed insights that were usually years ahead of their public acceptance. His *The Future of Housing* (New York, 1946) has stood the rigors of time, while *Forbidden Neighbors* (New York, 1955) dealt with the problem of housing discrimination long before it became a political issue. *The City Is the Frontier* (New York, 1965) remains the standard work on the urban condition in the 1960s. For a biographical sketch of Abrams, see Bernard Taper, "A Lover of Cities," *New Yorker*, XLII (Feb. 4, 1967), 39–81, (Feb. 11, 1967), 45–115.

Index

List of
Frequently Used Abbreviations

ACA	Advisory Committee on Allotments
ACTION	American Council to Improve Our Neighborhoods
AMA	American Municipal Association
BOB	Bureau of the Budget
BPR	Bureau of Public Roads
CWA	Civil Works Administration
DAC	Democratic Advisory Council
DUAH	Department of Urban Affairs and Housing (proposed)
FCDA	Federal Civil Defense Administration
FERA	Federal Emergency Relief Administration
FHA	Federal Housing Administration
FHLBB	Federal Home Loan Bank Board
FLA	Federal Loan Agency
FSA	Federal Security Agency
FWA	Federal Works Agency
HHFA	Housing and Home Finance Agency
HUD	Department of Housing and Urban Development (proposed)
ICMA	International City Managers Association
LHA	Local Housing Authorities
NAHB	National Association of Home Builders

NAHRO	National Association of Housing and Redevelopment Officials
NAREB	National Association of Real Estate Boards
NHA	National Housing Agency
NHC	National Housing Conference
NPA	National Planning Association
NRB	National Resources Board
NRPB	National Resources Planning Board
PACGO	President's Advisory Committee on Government Organization
PBA	Public Buildings Administration
PHA	Public Housing Administration
PWA	Public Works Administration
RA	Resettlement Administration
RFC	Reconstruction Finance Corporation
ULI	Urban Land Institute
URA	Urban Redevelopment Authority (proposed) *or* Urban Renewal Administration
USCM	United States Conference of Mayors
USHA	United States Housing Authority
WPA	Works Progress Administration